Premier Soccer

Michael Parker

Human Kinetics

Library of Congress Cataloging-in-Publication Data

Parker, Michael, 1946-
  Premier soccer / Michael Parker.
    p. cm.
  Includes index.
  ISBN-13: 978-0-7360-6824-6 (soft cover)
  ISBN-10: 0-7360-6824-4 (soft cover)
  1. Soccer. I. Title.
  GV943.P347 2008
  796.334--dc22

                          2007052148

ISBN-10: 0-7360-6824-4
ISBN-13: 978-0-7360-6824-6

Acquisitions Editor: Tom Heine; **Developmental Editor:** Amanda Eastin-Allen; **Assistant Editor:** Laura Koritz; **Copyeditor:** Tom Tiller; **Proofreader:** Anne Meyer Byler; **Indexer:** Nan Badgett; **Graphic Designer:** Nancy Rasmus; **Graphic Artist:** Francine Hamerski; **Cover Designer:** Keith Blomberg; **Photographer (cover):** Michael Steele/Getty Images; **Photographer (interior):** Neil Bernstein, unless otherwise noted; **Photo Asset Manager:** Laura Fitch; **Photo Office Assistant:** Jason Allen; **Art Manager:** Kelly Hendren; **Associate Art Manager/Illustrator**: Alan L. Wilborn; **Printer:** Sheridan Books

We thank the University of North Carolina at Greensboro in Greensboro, North Carolina, for assistance in providing the location for the photo shoot for this book.

Human Kinetics books are available at special discounts for bulk purchase. Special editions or book excerpts can also be created to specification. For details, contact the Special Sales Manager at Human Kinetics.

Printed in the United States of America   10   9   8   7   6   5   4   3   2   1

Human Kinetics
Web site: www.HumanKinetics.com

United States: Human Kinetics
P.O. Box 5076, Champaign, IL 61825-5076
800-747-4457
e-mail: humank@hkusa.com

Canada: Human Kinetics
475 Devonshire Road Unit 100
Windsor, ON N8Y 2L5
800-465-7301 (in Canada only)
e-mail: info@hkcanada.com

Europe: Human Kinetics
107 Bradford Road, Stanningley
Leeds LS28 6AT, United Kingdom
+44 (0) 113 255 5665
e-mail: hk@hkeurope.com

Australia: Human Kinetics
57A Price Avenue
Lower Mitcham, South Australia 5062
08 8372 0999
e-mail: info@hkaustralia.com

New Zealand: Human Kinetics
Division of Sports Distributors NZ Ltd.
P.O. Box 300 226 Albany
North Shore City, Auckland
0064 9 448 1207
e-mail: info@humankinetics.co.nz

This book is dedicated to my wife, Ginger, my sons, John and Patrick, and my dog, Guinness, for their sacrifices and support over the years, which have allowed me to put my energies into the game of soccer. Thanks a bunch, guys.

CONTENTS

PREFACE

I started coaching in the United States a little over 30 years ago, and the changes in the game since then have been unimaginable. In my own state of North Carolina, the quality of the club programs and their players have improved tenfold in the last few years alone. I believe this acceleration of the game's development is due not only to increased interest among and opportunities for young players, but also to huge improvement in coaching quality. When I first arrived in the States, good coaching was very difficult to find. Now it is everywhere.

This book draws from my experiences as a head coach at many levels, ranging from U8 youth soccer (under 8 years old) to Olympic development, on to college, and finally the professional ranks. Most of my experience has come in the college game, including all NCAA levels, with national championships in Division III and Division II and a number one ranking in Division I at the University of North Carolina at Greensboro. I also have two boys who have come through the youth ranks, so I am very aware of the challenges found at that level.

It is my hope that this book will provide information for older youth players—middle school through small college—and for coaches working with those age groups. Soccer involves huge complexities in areas such as strategy, set plays, sport psychology, physical fitness, nutrition, and game preparation. Yet I have always said that, at its core, it is a simple game and must be played that way. Thus this book is an attempt to simplify even the complexities and cover the topics most needed for everyday players and coaches.

When I first started coaching at the more basic levels of youth soccer, I quickly realized that much of what I had done with elite college scholarship athletes and Olympic development players did not immediately apply. There is obviously a need to develop a base of technical ability before one can go further, but with a careful and systematic approach, and with the natural increase of age and maturity, it is surprising how far one can take a team at any level. Players *will* learn—things just have to be done in the correct sequence, and in the right way. It is my hope that this book will help coaches and players do just that. Repetition with variety is crucial. This may sound odd, but players must have key coaching points reinforced over and over again, without making practice mundane and boring. The challenge is always to find new and enjoyable ways to make the same point. Players themselves must be prepared to practice, practice, and practice some more.

As a young coach just beginning my professional career in the States, I was greatly influenced by my roots as a typical Englishman. I leaned heavily on the coaching certifications I had received in the UK, and in particular the English FA (Football Association). At that time, the director of coaching for the English FA was Charles Hughes, and I initially gravitated toward his philosophy; even today, I feel his influence, though I would also like to believe that I have branched out into my own philosophy over the years. The game has changed enormously, both physically and tactically, but the fundamentals stay the same. Players must be sound with the fundamentals before they will experience success. If you are a player, attend to the fundamentals in this book and work hard to make yourself better. There is no easy solution and no quick way to success, but your hard work will pay off in the end.

In our young adult soccer programs, we seem to be continually struggling with the issue of developing players versus winning games. At what point and age does winning become the main priority for the club coach? When should player development stop and winning begin? Should everybody get equal playing time, regardless of ability? What about playing different positions? For classic or select soccer, winning games should become a priority at about age 14 or 15 (possibly later in recreational soccer). However, a winning attitude for the individual player should always be there. I believe it is healthy to play to win, and I get annoyed with my college players if they do not know the score of the game in a practice session, especially during small-sided game play. What does that say about their attitude toward practice?

I have coached many years now but still like to believe that I will get better each year. There is so much to learn as a coach. Since 2003, I have kept a log of all my practice sessions during the regular season.

I have always made a point of preparing every training session by putting pen to paper—no matter how long one has been coaching, there are no shortcuts to that process—but for years I did not keep those records of past sessions over the weeks and months of the season. Now I am shocked at how much I have forgotten. Things that I used to do are often gone from the memory banks. It took me a lot of years to make myself begin keeping these records, and in fact I now bind them at the end of season and file them as a permanent record. If only I had done that from the beginning . . . One of the best pieces of advice I can give is to keep a record of what you do as you read this book. It will help you in the future.

To those young players who are still learning the game (though I guess we all are always learning the game): Please have a *passion* for the sport. Read and watch all you can. There is no substitute for just watching the game being played at the highest level. You need to have idols you want to emulate; you should play pickup games when you can. (I fear that young players in this generation spend too much time in organized coaching sessions, thus missing out on the fun, challenge, and learning that comes from self-organized games.) Much of the game can be learned without coaching, especially in the early days. It is also extremely important that you go to each and every practice session with the right mental attitude. It is important that in each session you always give your best. It is easy to just go through the motions, especially when you are well into the season and practices are no longer as fresh, but you must try to put any and all personal issues aside and always give your best. It is my hope that this book will help you become a better player. Read the book, and go out and play this great game.

ACKNOWLEDGMENTS

Professional success does not come easy. It takes a lot of hard work, luck, and help from other people. I have been very fortunate in being surrounded by good people throughout my career, which not only have helped enormously in forming my style, character and philosophy, but also in my success as a coach.

Thanks to my wife, Ginger, for her love, support, and understanding in what can be a very difficult profession. To my sons, John and Patrick, who most definitely provided the insight into youth soccer that I would not have otherwise had. To my mother and father, Eileen and Tom, who gave me the support, love, and guidance growing up in postwar Britain. I do not think my father ever missed a game in my young career.

To all my assistants over the years: Barry Gorman, Mike Corney, Angelo Zalalas, Alan Dawson, Peter Broadley, Pat Barrett, Steve Harrison, Russell Scarborough, Darren Powel, and especially to the current ones, Scott Brittsan and Justin Maullin. Justin gets the privilege of working harder than any of them as the old man begins to slow down. To James Shipp, head athletic trainer at UNCG, for his help with the Nutrition and Physical Conditioning section. I could not have managed without any of them. Thanks, guys. You all made me look good.

I want to acknowledge the two universities I have worked at, Lock Haven and UNC Greensboro, for giving me the opportunity to be a head coach. And last but not least, to all the athletes who have played under me. It has been a privilege to work with you all.

KEY TO DIAGRAMS

X = defender

O = attacker

S = support

———⟶ = player movement

– – –⟶ = ball movement

numbers on arrows indicate sequence of movement

CHAPTER 1

Winning Attitude

Some soccer players look great in the easy games but do not show up and put out the effort when it counts. Others are so driven to win that they lose all perspective on what the game is about. Most successful soccer players are driven to win, but some bring an attitude that sets them above the rest. When the going gets tough, these players bring their A-game with hard work and a positive attitude. Good play, in fact, starts with a winning attitude, so it's important that players and teams cultivate one from the start.

This chapter covers creating and contributing to a winning attitude. It addresses the essentials both for individual success (positive mental attitude, practicing with variety, and learning through both success and failure) and for team success (developing chemistry through leadership, practicing with enthusiasm, and communicating) and puts winning into the greater context of the game of soccer. The chapter discusses how to set both individual and team goals and explains why goals are essential to developing strong players. It also covers the traits required for becoming a big-time player, including how to handle pressure, prepare for games, and focus on performance. Everyone can get better—much better. This chapter will help both players and coaches work toward the attitude needed to achieve success. Let's get to it!

Create a Winning Atmosphere

A winning atmosphere, from practice sessions to games and everything in between, is essential for individual and team success. A winning atmosphere creates an infectious enjoyment and motivates players to get better so they can have even more success, and that self-reinforcing process benefits the entire team. This section covers the individual and team factors that contribute to a positive atmosphere in which everybody gains and succeeds.

Individual Success

Players need to realize that if they put in enough effort, success will follow. They hold the key to success in their own hands, and their mental attitude plays a major part in their development. If players work to improve every day; if they look, listen, and learn; and if they experience even the smallest measure of success, then wins, losses, promotion, and relegation become secondary. As a player gets better, so will the team, and a better team will begin to win more games, become more successful, and become more confident. Here are four elements essential to player effort and success.

Have a positive attitude   First and foremost, a player must be enthusiastic, interested, and keen to play the game. People who are enthusiastic want to do more, and enthusiasm helps get better performances from the team because it is infectious. Everybody has been involved in practices that are quiet and "dead." It is difficult to get anything useful from these practices, as players drift into slow and uninspired activity. Enthusiasm improves players' focus, determination, and effort. It draws in other players who might not have been quite as prepared to practice and play. It creates a far better learning atmosphere, and the coach can get much more from his or her team. If a player does not like the training or playing atmosphere, he should not always leave it up to the coach to change. The player can do something about it herself. Individual players can make a difference.

Most successful players do have positive attitudes. They believe they are going to be successful and win. It is necessary to believe in oneself, one's teammates, and one's coach. Good players let each other know how they feel. They talk about good things, and it affects other players positively. I have yet to meet a successful player who thinks she's poor and is going to lose whenever she steps on the pitch. Invariably, good players bring positive attitudes and confidence.

It's important, however, to remain realistic with positivity. It can be detrimental to performance for a player to believe he is better than he really is. Players must set realistic goals for themselves and for the team (see the section on goal setting later in this chapter) then remain positive within those goals.

Players also like to listen to a coach with a positive attitude. A good coach can make players believe they are going to win, and if she has managed the right game preparation, both physically and tactically, and if the approach to the game has been positive, then the team might just win it!

So, for players and coaches, work hard and have fun while you are doing it. You cannot be serious all the time. Be organized and focused while maintaining a sense of humor. Fun creates better team chemistry and just makes the whole experience better. Enjoyment can make the difference between winning and losing. Keep winning and losing in perspective and focus on the positive in the face of adversity.

Practice with variety   When players are learning new skills, repetition is critical. Players need to perform skills over and over until they become second nature. Unfortunately, repetition can quickly become mundane, so players and coaches should be creative in trying fresh ways of doing the same things. Variety will help individual players maintain their interest in practice and will ensure that the practice is appropriate for players' current needs.

A coach can present technical skills in different and challenging ways. For example, a team might work on improving passing skills by playing a game of keep-away, in which one group makes as many passes in a row as they can without the other team intercepting the ball. Then the other group does the same. This skill can be practiced in many ways, each one catering to a player's changing abilities and needs. It is important that players have some success in repetition, so initially the drill needs to be set up in favor of success. One option is to give the team with the ball more players than the defending team; the activity might begin with an area measuring 40 by 30 yards (about 37 by 27 meters), in which a group of six attackers or passers works against only three defenders. (For good players, this would be too easy, but it makes a good starting point.) Attackers and defenders should rotate at regular intervals so that everybody gets equal time in passing the ball. Once success has been achieved, the ratio can be changed to, say, five attackers against four defenders, or the ratio could be kept the same while the playing area is decreased to, say, 30 by 20 yards (about 27 by 18 meters)—or both factors could be adjusted. These changes immediately inject variety into a practice, making it more challenging, more interesting, and certainly more difficult.

While much is done in organized, formal practice sessions, the more successful players usually practice by themselves as well. They become soccer "junkies" and cannot seem to get enough of the game. They work individually on skill and technique, and they play pickup games just for the enjoyment of it. Players should go out and play the game. They must put time in by themselves; it adds invaluable variety to their practice routine.

A player also needs to see examples of good play on a regular basis. There may be teammates he can look up to and respect, but he is more likely to home in on a professional player seen on television, or a local club player he can see in person. In any case, it is important that players have idols they can look up to and imitate in order to improve their tactical awareness. Players can learn an awful lot by just playing the game and watching it being played at a high level.

Many coaches prefer for players to work on weaknesses, but another source of variety is to work on strengths. In this modern era of soccer, coaches look for specialist players: Is he a good crosser of the ball? Can she win balls in the air? Is his tackling tenacious? What is her work rate? Can he score goals? Coaches who ask these important questions motivate players to bring something to the table that is better than what other players bring. Thus each player needs to find out what he does well and work on it, make it better than anybody else's, and make himself special.

Set goals   All successful athletes need to set goals, both individual and team oriented. A forward who scored 7 goals last year might aim for double figures this season, and a goalkeeper who had 4 shutouts might try for 6. Perhaps a player who has not worked as hard as possible will set a goal to improve his or her fitness. The section on goal setting later in this chapter explains what goals should include, why they are important to individual and group success, and how players can set goals for individual and team performance.

Learn through success (and failure)   Success motivates people and makes them want more. It's habit forming. The more a player sees himself progress, the more he feels encouraged to practice. Success is crucial to motivation; it keeps players coming back for more, and it makes the whole experience far more enjoyable. Success rarely comes straightaway, however, and often it takes a measure of failure to help players go forward in the right direction. In playing the game, a player rapidly finds techniques she can use, but only by experimenting to see if they help her improve specific skills. It is a trial-and-error process, and the player must filter out what does or does not work and change her game appropriately. Success and failure teach the fundamentals of the game, and every player should use each instance as a learning opportunity.

Team Success

Good chemistry is crucial to creating team success. Very rarely do teams win without it. When players enjoy being around each other, they tend to take criticism better, work harder for each other, enjoy themselves, and generally improve the quality of everything they do. Good chemistry leads to successful seasons. Practices are enjoyable, and teammates are fun to be around, even when the team is not winning. Thus plenty can be learned even in a loss, and players are able to improve and achieve better results.

Develop chemistry through leadership   A good starting point for developing team chemistry is to establish excellent leadership. The team should choose one or two captains. They do not have to be the best players, but they do need to have positive attitudes, be respected by the team, and be prepared to lead by example. A likable, positive approach by team captains can have an enormous effect on team performance. Remember, team chemistry is merely another way in which players mesh their personalities with each other. A captain with a negative personality can provoke dislike and unrest, but one with a great sense of humor and friendly demeanor can be invaluable, creating a relaxed and pleasant atmosphere, especially during difficult training sessions.

Every player must recognize that he has a role to play in team chemistry and in helping the leaders maintain positive energy, especially when a training session goes flat or a game is in the balance and needs a final renewed effort for victory. All players must step forward and take some responsibility. It takes players and coaches helping each other in any way they can to achieve true team success.

Coaches must be aware that many club teams include players who attend the same middle or high school, or live in the same neighborhood, and these players may form cliques. Before a coach knows it, there may be two or three different groups within the same team. I have seen this happen many times. At the college level, older players (juniors and seniors) often do not associate with first-years. Players do not necessarily have to be friends off the field, but division within a team can single-handedly destroy chemistry. Leaders can facilitate positive feelings between teammates, and team members should make a concerted effort to get on well with each other on the field.

Practice with enthusiasm   Players need to play and practice in a winning atmosphere, and everybody has to work to achieve this. The old adage "you play like you practice" may be overused, but it is also valid. Practice has to be important to each player. A good practice needs a good atmosphere—it needs character, and it needs personalities. Activities need to be interesting, challenging, and as varied as possible. A flat practice is quiet, without apparent enjoyment. It will happen at times, even with teams that enjoy great leadership and chemistry, so coaches and players alike need to be prepared to do something about it. Activities should be as gamelike as possible, and it should be important to players that they win. They should keep score and know at all times whether they are winning or losing.

Sometimes extra motivation is needed in the form of reward or punishment to help the player concentrate more on the task at hand. Many coaches often finish their sessions with some form of fitness activity. Care must be taken, but coaches can consider using this activity as part of a reward-or-punishment system. For example, players might play 30 minutes of small-sided games (five or six members per side), with the rule being "one goal and you're off": A goal wins the game, and the scoring side stays on the field to play the next team. Each team might be asked to do 12 shuttle runs at the end of practice, but every time a team wins a game its total number of runs is reduced by 1. Thus a team that wins 5 games will have only 7 runs to do at the end of practice. This always works so long as it's not overused. Coaches should not expect to do this every day—it should be reserved for sessions where a coach suspects performance and effort might be down a bit and a little extra encouragement is all it takes.

Physical climate can also play a big part in the quality of a practice session, and this problem can be rather acute in the United States. The higher the temperature, the more difficult it is for players to put maximum mental and physical effort into a training session. I always see much livelier sessions on cool, damp days than on hot, humid ones. Not much can be done about this, except for both players and coaches being aware that hot days call for extra motivation.

Communicate with teammates Though overlooked by many coaches and players, constant communication is essential to team success. It acts as a second pair of eyes for every player. When a player receives a ball, his head is normally down and his vision very limited, and it's an enormous help for him to be told what is happening around him. This is often a problem in the very early stages of a player's career, especially if the player is quiet by nature. Thus communication may need to be worked on intensively. Coaches need to demand that players communicate on the field of play. A player needs to get used to thinking like a coach, understanding the game well enough to verbalize what is happening—or, better still, verbalize it *before* it happens. With practice, this tactic becomes second nature. Many times I find myself shouting instructions to players, only to realize that the *players* should be the ones shouting.

Photo courtesy of Willis Glassgow/WG Sports Photos.

Chemistry, enthusiasm, and communication boost player morale and lead to team success both on and off the field.

Communication can be put into two different categories: informational (imparting information about the game to each other) and encouraging (boosting confidence by complimenting each other on a good performance). Informational communication is difficult for many players—perhaps because they lack confidence or do not understand the game well enough—so it's essential to address this type of verbal communication in practice sessions. For example, the passer of the ball might be required to *always* say something to the player who is receiving the pass. This might seem somewhat comical at first, but players will soon get the hang of it. Even just calling out the name of the pass recipient is a beginning. That exchange will soon develop into meaningful communication that helps the player receiving the ball make good decisions.

Communication that encourages can motivate. It should be easy to congratulate a teammate when he has done something well—made a good shot, a nice pass, or a great effort. Not only do these words boost morale, they also give more space to comment constructively on things not done so well. A player needs to know if he has just missed a wide-open teammate inside the penalty box, or if he is dribbling too much, and critical comments are much easier to accept if they are given in a context that is positive overall, especially if coming from the same person who made the positive remarks.

Putting Winning Into Context

What is the importance of winning to a team? Does being a successful program or player always require winning? Not necessarily! Not everybody has the same competitive drive, and winning games can mean more or less, depending on the individual. For some players, playing for a successful team that gets a lot of exposure is vital. To get a college scholarship, for example, one has to be not only good but also seen. Such a player needs to play for a team that not only wins but can get good tournament exposure and possibly advance toward a national championship. Teams that win are invited to the better tournaments, and the better tournaments are more likely to be attended by college coaches.

Conversely, many players are also playing in recreational leagues formed to allow players at all levels to just enjoy the game. Many of these players have needs and goals that are quite different from those of the "classic" or "select" player. For them, the game may be social, or played just for the love of it. These players are often not interested in college soccer scholarships, and winning is less important to them.

Everybody should want to win the game, and successful players need to be competitive and be placed in competitive environments. It usually brings out the best in them. But players also need also to understand that there is far more to playing soccer than just winning, and that not all players want to play in a winning-focused environment.

Thus players need to prioritize how important winning is to them. The team, the individual player, and the coach should consider how to measure success. What constitutes success? There are many issues to consider besides winning.

For players: Has a practice session been fun? Have they felt confident in all the situations the coach put them in? Do they understand what they are supposed to do every time they get the ball, and do they have the confidence to attempt to do it? Can they fail in a particular task and still keep their confidence high? Do they have the confidence to try different things without the fear of failure?

Success in such areas will increase a player's belief in himself, and with it his ability. The longer I have been involved in the game, the more I have begun to understand the major role that confidence plays. It's not uncommon for a striker who has regularly scored goals to suddenly have difficulty in finding the back of the net. This is known as a dry period, and it will likely be compounded by a drop in confidence. She is still the same player, with the same ability, yet now she cannot score goals. She must find her confidence again for her game to return to its previous high level.

Win or lose, players should behave with class and dignity. Winning should be important, but not at all costs. There is a fine line here that can easily be crossed, especially if a player is very competitive. I have seen far too many players who are poor losers. It may sound difficult, but a player should at least try to act the same way after a win as after a loss. He should try to avoid the emotional extremes of overcelebrating after winning a game, especially a big one, or falling prey to devastation after losing. He should try to say something positive to a losing opponent, and if he cannot then he should say nothing at all.

Set Appropriate Goals

It is vital to set both individual and team goals at the beginning of each year. Goals provide direction, keep players positive and motivated, and help measure progress and success. Being successful does not necessarily require winning all games, or even finishing in first place; in some cases, it may be a success just to win half the team's games. Regardless, goals are vital because they provide a destination, give direction, and elicit drive and motivation. They should be set both by individual players and by the coach. It may be helpful to use the SMART acronym: specific, measurable, attainable, realistic, and timely.

- *Specific.* A specific goal is clearly defined—for example, scoring 20 goals this season, versus a nonspecific goal such as "improving our goal-scoring opportunities."
- *Measurable.* A measurable goal can be assessed in terms of tangible indicators of progress—for example, "I'm going to practice five times a week for the rest of the season," versus a nonmeasurable goal such as, "I'm going to practice more often."
- *Attainable.* Goals should be achievable by the player or team. Sometimes this requires flexibility. If the player or team is failing to reach goals, the targets should be modified until they are within reach; otherwise, frus-

tration will set in. For example, a player might set the attainable goal of running 2 miles (3.2 kilometers) in 12 minutes for the Cooper fitness test, rather than the unreachable goal of 10 minutes.

- *Realistic.* It would be unrealistic for a 13-year-old to try running 2 miles in 12 minutes. Players (and their coaches) must understand what they are capable of and set goals that are challenging but achievable.
- *Timely.* Assign the goal a time frame—for example, one might aim to run 2 miles in 12 minutes by the start of August preseason camp, or to score 10 goals in 10 games.

If goals are to help players improve performance, they must be challenging and specific. More difficult goals—so long as they are not overly difficult—tend to improve performance more than easily attainable goals do. Similarly, a vague goal is not likely to enhance performance, but a specific goal will. At the beginning of each season, I sit down with my team and discuss general goals for the season—normally, my expectations for the team. These goals are always challenging but realistic. It may be appropriate to talk in terms of individual wins and losses, as well as the team's expectations. Should we win the league? If not, what target should we set? I also talk with individual players about their goals. How many goals should we expect our striker to score, and how many shutouts should our goalkeepers have? I may ask a key midfield player to make a certain number of assists. Another player may be asked to have a successful pass rate of 75 percent. We may ask our wingers to make 10 crosses into the opponent's penalty box per game. Coaches can use computer software to record and analyze each player's game or simply ask a coach or parent with a notepad on the sidelines to record the numbers. Setting measurable goals that players can use to track their progress will create opportunities for improved play and, in turn, higher chances of winning.

Short-term goals serve as stepping stones to long-term goals. Short-term goals provide immediate feedback as to whether a player or team is making progress, which is an important motivational factor. Returning to the example of the Cooper run, a coach might ask players to run 2 miles in less than 12 1/2 minutes. If this time is not immediately attainable, a series of short-term goals can be set to motivate and measure progress toward the long-term goal (e.g., 13 minutes, then 12 3/4 minutes). If a player can already run 2 miles within the coach's allotted time, she can set her own goal to challenge herself with a time she thinks is attainable. She might also set a series of short-term goals to help her track progress toward her new target time.

I often talk with high school soccer players whose ultimate goal is to play professionally. That is their long-term goal—sometimes very unrealistic, sometimes not. In many cases, they are unaware of the obstacles facing them, and certainly unaware of what will be required of them in pursuing their goal. Even if it is an acceptable long-term goal, achieving it will require the player to set many shorter-term goals along the way. It would be more appropriate to set the goal of receiving a soccer scholarship at a major Division I institution. This shorter-term goal might require a still-shorter-term one along the way (e.g., becoming the top player on the local club team in order to attract the attention of college coaches). Another example is a player wanting to play for the top local team in his area. It might be unreasonable to expect being selected and immediately playing for that team, so the player needs to set up an achievable strategy, such as playing for another local team that is not as strong but that provides a stage for increasing one's stock in the eyes of the top club.

It's important for each player to have individual goals, no matter how simple or complex. Individual goals tend to be skill oriented: goals scored, tackles made, or passes delivered. Each player needs to set her own goals, and, in keeping with the SMART method, they need to be clear and understandable so she knows what to do and what not to do. They need to be challenging enough that she will stay engaged and achievable so that she is unlikely to fail. It is also necessary to have a long-term goal in mind. What does he ultimately want to achieve as a player? At what level does he want to play the game next? What does he want from the game? Once he has decided on this, he can begin the task of setting short-term goals to get there–his ministeps. Many players, for example, would like to play in college. Each must identify his desired level of college play (i.e., her long-term goal), then forge a strategy for getting there. It might consist of the following steps:

1. Play for the very best local team I can join. Be involved in the Olympic Development Program or the newly formed academy teams to gain the best exposure to college coaches.

2. Play in top youth tournaments with my team to be seen by college coaches.

3. Select several schools I might be interested in. Research them to narrow the list to five or six.

4. Contact the schools' coaches no later than my junior year to express interest in their programs.

5. Visit the schools and coaches no later than spring of my junior year in order to personalize the recruiting process early on. (Spring break is a popular time to do this.)

6. Stay in regular contact throughout the process, updating the coaches on my progress.

Team goals are equally important. I stress regularly to players that individual success is often a by-product of team success. If a player's goal is to become an All-American, his chance of success is much higher if he plays on a successful team. Conversely, the player's individual success contributes to that of the team. The two go hand in hand (or, in this case, foot in foot!). At the same time, team goals differ from individual goals in that they can be much more focused on tactics. Such goals may change day by day, or game by game, especially the short-term ones. For example, in facing an opponent with a dangerous forward who does most of the scoring, a team might set its goal as stopping that player from doing well. More often than not, team goals are set by the coach, but that does not prevent players from setting their own team goals. A SMART team goal might be to win 75 percent of the games or to score 50 goals for the season. Team goals require cohesive play, enabled by the molding together of individuals. Key questions include: How can we play as a unit? What style of play shall we have? What formation can we play? This type of goal-oriented organization allows a team to come together and achieve overall success.

Become a Successful Player

Becoming the best player one can possibly be takes commitment and true passion for the game. This section discusses the kinds of discipline a player must have in order to be her best: developing a successful mode of daily living, taking a positive attitude, and handling pressure and preparing for games, especially the big ones. It also addresses the importance of consistency in one's play and looks at how a player must focus on the task at hand. This section is written directly to players.

Commit to the game   First and foremost, to be a successful player, you must commit yourself to a disciplined manner of daily living. Not everybody is going to be a professional player, but even good amateur players need to pay significant attention to the way they live, especially during the season. This discipline requires many sacrifices, and very often you cannot do the things your friends are doing. It may mean committing to stay behind when all your friends are going out. It certainly requires a training regime that is often painful, demanding, and time consuming. You must take care of your body, eat correctly, and get enough sleep. By living this way, however, you set yourself up to become a successful player.

Think and act positively   Big-time players normally focus on positive thoughts and keep the negative ones out of their minds. For example, when faced with injury, the player with a positive attitude is determined to get back to playing again as soon as possible and does not dwell on the injury. She does what it takes in the training room and works hard on the rehabilitation prescribed by the training staff. This athlete wants to be as ready as possible when opportunity comes again, and she uses this interim period to work on fitness areas she would normally not address. An athlete with a negative attitude, on the other hand, may get gloomy or even depressed. This athlete dwells on the injury and can't seem to focus beyond it. Without a doubt, the first athlete is going to be back on the field sooner.

The trick to a positive attitude is to learn how to recognize your negative thoughts and replace them with positive and productive ones. Realize, though, that positive thinking alone won't make you a successful player. A positive attitude must be combined with hard work in practice in order to achieve positive results.

Handle pressure If you want to be a successful player, you have to learn how to handle pressure—how to stay cool when it counts, especially in big games. There is an optimal level of excitement caused by adrenalin, but if it gets too high it can detract from athletic performance. Most people dislike the sensation of nervousness, and many do not know how to handle it, which leaves them vulnerable to performance anxiety. Some people respond by trying to avoid the stressful task, but the soccer player sitting in the dressing room before a big game must learn to deal with it. If he does not, he starts to make bad choices, the game begins to seem rushed, and he feels out of control. His confidence may drop, and he may begin "hiding" in order to avoid the ball, thus becoming unavailable for other players when they need him. (We have all been there and know what it feels like.) In this situation, you face a mental battle to get yourself back into the flow of the game. For the benefit of the team, you must try. For hugely important games, it's often best to downplay the moment and keep stress as low as possible. Do not overthink the task at hand; wait until an hour or two before kickoff to begin visualizing the game.

How do top soccer players learn to handle pressure? First, you must understand that it's okay to be nervous; it is, in fact, normal. I get concerned when my players are not nervous before big games, as it usually indicates a lack of pregame concentration and preparation. Normally, the more experienced a player is, the better she is able to handle nervousness, but even the most experienced players should feel anxiety before a big game. I have found that handling nervousness well can actually improve your performance, since it brings your adrenalin level to an optimal point.

Nervousness can be decreased by muscle relaxation and deep breathing. Some players find it helps to sit and visualize the task in front of them. Others like to listen to a certain type of music and shut themselves off from the world. Some prefer to talk a lot, and others prefer complete silence. In any case, routine definitely helps, because it provides familiarity and comfort. Maybe a player likes to walk on to the pitch upon arriving at the facility, or sit in the locker room cleaning his boots. Many players follow superstitions, such as which boot they put on first, or the order in which they leave the locker room. (I had an All-American last year who just had to be the last player out.) So, find a routine you are comfortable with and stick with it. It will help.

Prepare for big games Preparing for a big game requires far more than just pregame mental preparation. It begins days before, both on the practice field and at home. Training sessions need to be sharper, quicker, and more intense. I sometimes notice an irritability creeping into the team, a lack of patience with each other. This is normally a good sign, as heightened tension means focus and preparation are well under way and the team is getting ready to play. Players must recognize, however, when the tension becomes detrimentally high. In this case, you may need to step back, take a deep breath, and calm down. You also need to get a good night's sleep for 2 nights before the game; sleep is vital preparation. Meals and routines are also important. Keep distractions to a minimum and try to focus on the task at hand. (See chapter 7 for information on pregame meals and chapter 9 for in-depth coverage of how to prepare for a match.)

Focus on performance   This process is critical. It gets you thinking about your task and the importance of it, which in and of itself should get your adrenaline flowing. If you start this process too soon, it could have a negative effect, causing a type of fatigue and a possible decrease in performance. It's normal to think about a big game on the night before, but your *concerted* focus on the task at hand should begin an hour or two before game time. Sitting at breakfast worrying about the game that day will not help. Game focus can take many forms, depending on the individual player. It's a good idea to go through a mental checklist before the game. What is your role as designed by the coach for this game? It is vital that you recognize your role and responsibility to the team. Hopefully your coach has helped you with this one. What do you know about the opponent, and how do you plan to play? Think about your own strengths and weaknesses. What are you going to do today to enable a good performance? Believe in yourself, because confidence is essential, and do what you can to convince yourself that you are going to make a difference in this game. Focusing during the game tends to be less of a problem, especially for the higher-level player. Once play begins, most players naturally get immersed in the complexities of the game. The competitive spirit comes out, and the focus at this point is just on playing well and winning the game.

Achieve consistency   A key to all team and individual play is consistency. Most players, and especially coaches, would be very happy to see the same performance, effort, and intensity game after game. Unfortunately, many factors make this difficult. Early in the season, things tend to be fine, with most practices quite fresh, but as the year progresses the mundanity of practice tends to set in and players can become unmotivated and sluggish. Also, day-to-day living brings daily stresses (e.g., schoolwork, lack of sleep, relationship problems, even problems at home) that can result in subpar performances.

Nevertheless, with the right type of preparation, it's possible to be reasonably consistent in performance. Consistency has to do with mental strength, focus, and determination to be successful. The trick is to come to practice every day and, for 2 hours or so, put personal problems into the back of your mind. Concentrate on the task at hand and always try to play with a good attitude and a smile on your face. I have coached several players who have gone on to play in the MLS (Major League Soccer) even though their natural talent is not necessarily the best. They all have one thing in common: a natural drive to be successful and a determination to do well in every practice and every game. This is not to say that they do well every time, but they always try.

Consistency is improved by getting into a routine—including eating, sleeping, and getting up at regular times. It depends on coming to practice focused on the task at hand and *always* trying to do your best. This attitude eventually becomes a habit, and in the long run you will become a consistent player. It takes sacrifice, patience, and hard work, but it is worth it.

CHAPTER 2

Roles of Players and Coaches

Team sports challenge athletes to understand their team roles as well as their individual ones. A player's individual responsibilities are likely to be specific to the position he plays on the field, while the team is made up of individuals who each have unique responsibilities and attributes that must be molded together into a precise and well-organized effort. Each player must be on the same page as the rest of the team. This chapter covers the roles and responsibilities of specific positions on the field. It also discusses the coach's role in developing a strategy that combines these separate parts into a whole that works.

Positional Roles

Before addressing specific positions, it's important to note that a given player should not initially focus too much on one position. Players should give themselves the flexibility of trying various positions; it will help them greatly down the road. This generalist approach allows a player to see how his strengths and weaknesses fit into the different positions in the game. All positions require players to both defend and attack, so the general principles of attacking and defending (discussed later in the book) will always apply.

Good soccer teams are looked upon as a complete unit, meshing everybody's roles and responsibilities. However, the four distinct positions within that unit—goalkeeper, defender, midfielder, and forward—require varying talents, and each position involves further subdivisions with their own skill sets.

Goalkeeper This is the only player on the team who is legally allowed to use his hands, though only inside the specific area of the penalty box, or 18-yard area. He is the last line of defense and the first line of attack. He is expected to save the ball from entering the goal as the last defender, but can also begin the attack by catching the ball and feeding it out to one of his teammates. A number of years ago, the main skill of the goalkeeper was to save the ball with his hands. Today that is not so, since rule changes have required goalkeepers to use their feet with far greater frequency, especially as defenders need to pass back to the goalkeeper when under defensive pressure. The pressures on goalkeepers are enormous. A mistake in this position is far more amplified than in any other, often making her a hero or a goat. It takes a specific type of personality to play this position, and many goalkeepers are outgoing and self-confident. Size can also play a role: Small goalkeepers (under 6 feet [1.8 meters] tall at the adult level) are at a disadvantage. This does not mean that there are no good goalkeepers this size—there are—but it does mean they have to compensate and be very good at catching high balls.

Defender The primary responsibility of a defender is to stop the opposition from scoring goals. There are normally three or four defenders. They must be brave and use good tackling technique. There is a physical aspect to playing this position, since blocking shots from opposing forwards with one's body is not a great deal of fun, and it does require courage. Defenders can be put into two subgroups—wide defenders (fullbacks) and central defenders. The wide defenders (i.e., the right and left backs) need to be quick, agile, and capable of getting up and down the field with relative ease. They need to be able to react and change direction quickly. They must be good passers as well as good defenders, and they do not necessarily have to be big. Central defenders, on the other hand, usually do need size. They must play in the middle of the defense and often have to deal with high balls played down the middle or crossed from the flanks. They need to be good headers of the ball, as well as strong all-around defenders, since teams are more likely to attack down the middle.

Each position requires unique talents and traits. As the team's last line of defense, successful goalkeepers need to be agile, quick, and athletic.

Midfielder   Midfielders have distinct roles. They play in the middle of the field and normally are responsible for linking the defense with the attack. These roles vary greatly, depending on a team's tactics and formations. Often there are four midfielders, and they can have three different responsibilities. The two outside or wide midfielders need quickness and good dribbling skill. They are required to unlock defenses with good one-on-one play and to go "at" and "by" their marking defenders. They also need to be good crossers of the ball, because it's critical for them to deliver it from their wide positions to the forwards in the penalty box. The two central midfielders often play two different roles. One needs to be more defense oriented, while the other should be a better attacking player. The defensive one should operate mostly in front of the defensive group, whereas the attacking midfielder plays just behind the two forwards. All midfield players must have very good technical skills and be excellent passers. Size is not critical to any of these midfield positions.

Forward   Forwards are required to score goals. If they can do that on a regular basis, many other weaknesses can be forgiven. This skill is perhaps the most difficult to master, and it is one that many teams lack. Goals win games, and a team with a forward who can score goals is well on the way to victory. Forwards tend to be very confident individuals who are more selfish and less team oriented than their mates. Most forwards are asked to operate mainly in the attacking penalty or 18-yard box. It is a frequent mistake for young forwards to wander well away from the penalty box and be unable to get back into it when they are needed for a pass or cross. Size is useful in these positions but not essential. Mobility and quickness, however, are required, and good forwards have a knack for being in the right place at the right time. The most difficult aspect for young forwards to master is appropriate movement without the ball. Most young players can quickly be aware of what they are supposed to do when they have the ball, but struggle to understand playing "off" the ball—that is, when they do not have the ball. They need to understand that part of their responsibility is to make runs (without the ball) to pull defenders away from good defensive positions (defenders normally have to follow the run of the forward so that he does not break free), which gives teammates a chance to run into the resulting holes or spaces in the defense, thus possibly creating a scoring opportunity. They are also required to be good headers of the ball.

Several variables affect which position a team member will play: size, strength, and athleticism. Size is not critical in soccer, but it is helpful to goalkeepers, central defenders, and center forwards. Teams like size down the middle of the field. This preference notwithstanding, I did coach a college team that went to number one in the nation in Division I with *both* central defenders in the back four standing only 5 feet 8 inches (about 1.7 meters) tall. Quickness, intelligence, and bravery countered the height deficiency to the point that it was never really a problem.

An athletic player can play just about anywhere on the field. For those who are less athletic, lack of pace can be hidden in certain positions. A central defensive midfielder can compensate for lack of pace and athleticism by anticipating the play before it happens, enabling him to be in the right place at the right time. So can a forward, although if a team has one slow forward then it probably needs a quick one next to him in order to have sufficient ability to get behind the defense. It is important to make the opponent's defenders worry constantly about letting the play get behind them; otherwise, they will press from the back, shorten the field, and make life very difficult in the midfield. The wide players, wingers and defenders, normally will need pace. An attacking midfielder needs to be crafty with skills that can break down the opposition's defenses. A goalkeeper should be quick, agile, and, if possible, big.

A high school coach whose players bring limited ability should try to put the best talent in the middle positions, regardless of size. She should try to find at least one player who can score goals and is quick enough to get behind defenses, and use her as a forward. The team will thus be able to play balls over the top of the defense and let the dynamic forward chase them down. Speed is always a threat, especially if it is used correctly. For instance, a quick forward can be always "sitting on the shoulder" of the last defender—that is, as far upfield as the defense will allow without being offside. From this position, she will have a good chance of being first to the ball when it is played over the top of the defense.

Many players can be one-dimensional. They are either good at attacking or good at defending, but not both. Defenders must be encouraged to get forward, and forwards must get back. Failing to follow this principle can lead to problems in team shape: For example, a right back goes forward into the attack, and nobody fills in behind him. The ball is turned over, and now there is a big hole in the defense. Inexperienced players find it difficult to "sit" in the correct part of the field to maintain proper team shape, but this is crucial to team success. If one were to look at the field from above, there should be no huge spaces between positions and players. Forwards, midfielders, and defenders should all be connected. Another example: A young defender clears the ball forward, well into the attacking part of the field, but stays back to defend, creating a big gap between him and the midfielders and forwards. Team shape is now ineffective, and it can be corrected only by having the defenders follow the ball out, enabling them to stay connected with the rest of the team.

Regardless of the position played, the ideal player possesses the following tools and characteristics:

1. Diverse and sophisticated ball skills

2. Agile, deceptive, and efficient feints and body movements in order to beat an opponent

3. Very quick play-combinations based on superior speed of reaction and thought

4. A good mixture of short and long passes in order to penetrate the opposing defense

5. Multifunctional tactical capability to attack and defend with ease (including the goalkeeper)

6. Determination and goal orientation

7. Recognition of depth and width when in possession of the ball

8. A positive attitude toward all aspects of the game

Team Roles

An effective team needs players to serve in many roles, all complementing each other in a cohesive whole. Some roles—such as starter, substitute, and role player—are defined by a team member's playing time in a game, and a group of 11 starters will include many roles within its subgroup. Other roles, such as the vocal leader and the quiet leader, are defined by how a player interacts with the team, and anyone on the team can play these roles, regardless of how frequently they get game time. This section details some common roles.

Starter At the beginning of each year, most coaches and teams try to be open-minded about which players will be starters. Tryouts and preseason games will help determine the answers, which is a critical reason a player must come into each preseason physically and mentally ready to play. First impressions are always important. A coach will typically experiment during the early part of the season, trying players in various roles. It is vital that players do their best when given their chance during this time period; otherwise, the opportunity to start may pass them by. As the season moves on, coaches try to settle on a starting team in order to achieve consistency, and it's difficult at that point to break into the starting 11. It might, in fact, take an injury to a starting player. At the same time, if a starter becomes lethargic or takes the starting position for granted, someone may just take it from him. Players should go into every game as if it is their last, taking nothing for granted.

Substitute I would like to believe that no player is satisfied with being a substitute (thus often seeing little or no playing time). If that is a player's role on the team, he should be doing everything within his power to change it and become a starter. This begins in practice. Too many times have I seen bench players lose motivation and go through the motions, especially in practice. They may see very little opportunity to play, with those in front of them doing better. But this deflation only makes the situation worse, as the coach is then even less likely to play them in an upcoming game. Thus substitutes must practice hard and be ready to contribute when the opportunity presents itself. The picture can change quickly. A starter may get injured or red-carded. So, a word to subs: Be ready! Play your hardest (in practice and in games) and leave no question about whether you are giving your best.

Role player This is a must for every team. It can be fun to imagine a team of superstars, but it's very unlikely to happen, and even if it did there would be the stiff challenge of molding them together as a team. Almost all teams have role players; in fact, that is what most players are. So, what exactly is required of these players? Most of all, it takes consistency and reliability: someone who rarely misses practice, who arrives on time, who puts teammates ahead of himself, and who can be depended on to give a steady performance every time he plays. These players tend to know what is expected of them by both the coach and their teammates, and they often have very good attitudes. They are just as important to the team as the superstar.

Vocal leader One difficult skill to learn is to be a good communicator on the field of play. Coaches should insist that all players be capable of good, intelligent communication that helps teammates make better decisions during the game. This may be difficult for players who are by nature quieter than others or who have difficulty verbalizing the game as it is played, but it is important to team motivation and success. The vocal leader not only communicates good soccer advice to her teammates but also constantly encourages them. These players are invaluable, especially when the going gets tough and the game is on the line. They can fire up their teammates to give that little bit extra that might just be enough to win the game.

Quiet leader   This player leads by action and example and is every bit as important as the vocal leader. I believe there is nothing more inspiring than a teammate who goes the extra mile, especially when the game is at stake. This kind of player often intimidates the opposition and brings out the very best in his teammates. He is always in the mix of the action, running harder than the rest, tackling tougher than most. He is a gold mine on any team.

Coach's Role

Being a successful coach is about more than winning games, and it requires certain personal qualities in addition to performance of specific duties. A good coach is a mentor, an advisor, a psychologist, and a parental figure. She is a tactician and a motivator. She is an administrator and an organizer—and, above all, a leader through the example of her behavior.

Qualities

A coach must be proficient in the skills and techniques of coaching, and have an equally sound knowledge of all skills and techniques of playing the game itself. He will be capable of demonstrating, or arranging for the demonstration of, these skills and techniques at a high level.

The coach must be strong but not an overbearing disciplinarian. He must set high standards of behavior and appearance and instill in every player a respect and concern for the game and all those associated with it. His best assets are optimism, enthusiasm, patience, and a sense of humor. It is also important for the coach to be a good communicator—verbally, visually, and through the written word. He needs to be a good manager of people, and, like all good managers, he will be a diplomat, a psychologist, and at times a philosopher. Coaches need to be accessible to both players and parents and, rather than being aloof and separate, must try to be empathetic in responding to team and player problems whenever possible.

A good coach is also a motivator, able to inspire an individual player or the team as a whole. Possibly the most difficult task of all is to motivate the team. The coach must understand that, even though soccer is a team game, individual players' needs are important. While pregame motivational talks can be effective, they will not meet all individual needs. It can be quite effective to approach individual players and have a quiet word with them before a game. The coach can remind them what is expected of them and how he sees them making a difference in the game. Thus he can be a confidence booster for them. And while some players need to be stroked, others respond better to a tough approach. A coach has to be flexible, understanding when to be tough and when to be sympathetic, especially in the somewhat stressful environment of game day.

A good coach will be a sound administrator—sometimes an underrated aspect of her job. Recording information efficiently allows her to properly monitor a player's performance and progress. He will also be a capable technician, which is increasingly important in our technological age, where sophisticated video equipment has become an accepted part of the coach's inventory. (A team manager can help enormously with such responsibilities.)

Duties

The process normally begins with some sort of tryout where the coach evaluates players and decides who will be part of the squad for that year. In some cases, the coach must recruit players and thus needs the ability and personality to attract prospects.

Squad sizes vary in number, depending on the funds and other resources available to run the team, or even on the number of players who come out for the team. At the college level, 24 to 26 is a good size, as it allows periodic intersquad play of 11 versus 11, taking into account that there will often be one or two players injured or missing for various reasons. For many teams, however, these numbers are unrealistic due to facility size or lack of coaching assistants. In that case, 16 to 18 is a good target, since it allows realistic play during practice, gives a cushion in case of injury, and is manageable for one coach. Participation time for the individual also needs to be considered. The larger the squad, the less time each player is going to get, especially if the coach is trying to provide equal playing time for everybody on the squad. A typical club coach is often inundated by parents complaining that their child is not getting enough playing time. The player themselves often feel the same way. This is a difficult issue for a coach to manage, especially when trying to win a game. Which comes first? Player development, with equal playing time? Or winning games? There is no easy answer.

Once a coach has selected a team and is ready to begin practice, there are four areas of focus: technical, tactical, physical, and psychological. Each is a constant concern (in varying degrees) throughout the year. The age and level of the team will determine how much time should be spent on each aspect. Younger players should spend more time on technical training, as the fundamentals of the game need to be established as early as possible. For example, a player who cannot pass a ball correctly cannot be expected to perform the more advanced tactical task of keeping possession of the ball, especially in combination play. In contrast, an older, more experienced player's needs tend much more toward the tactical and physical. The psychological aspect applies at all levels, but it will be a more pressing concern with older players, where winning and its attendant pressures are more important (and player development less so). Managing these several broad needs can be a challenge for coaches as they plan training sessions. Very often, facilities are crowded and the training window for a specific team is tight, probably 90 minutes. Understanding that all facets of the game must be covered, the coach has to make sharp decisions about how much time to spend on technical, tactical, and physical aspects. The focus will likely shift as the season progresses, moving further toward tactical and away from physical as the season nears its completion.

Technical This area is sometimes overlooked during the regular season, when much time tends to be given to the other three areas, but neglecting it can exact a price. Players must be able to pass a ball, control it, dribble it, head it, and shoot it. Defenders must be able to tackle. If players are deficient in these skills, then time needs to be spent improving them. Coaches must avoid the temptation of neglecting them, and players must realize that although these practice sessions can be somewhat mundane, they are essential to gaining the technical ability to progress. The off-season, with its reduced demands and greater time available, provides a better opportunity to work on technical aspects of the game.

Tactical Every coach must ask: How is our team going to play? What formation are we going to use, and what is our style of play? This is a very complex area, but the more experienced the coach, the easier it can be. Individual players and the team as a whole must understand what is involved in trying to win a game. They need to understand the opposition's strengths and weaknesses and how to mitigate or take advantage of them. They also need to know their own weaknesses and how to hide or minimize them, but above all each team must understand how it is going to play to its own strengths. Should a team play from the back defenders through midfield and then to the forwards? The answer depends on the abilities of the midfield players; it may be necessary to bypass them and go directly to the forwards. Should the team attack down the flanks, or more directly down the middle? How is the team going to get the ball to the feet of its best player as often as possible? Does each player understand his or her role in the overall scheme of things? Tactical planning is complicated and time consuming, but it often makes the difference between winning and losing.

Physical This area includes physical fitness, mobility, flexibility, and strength training, and it needs to take the form of a program that continues year-round at varying intensities. This can be tricky for both players and coaches, especially understanding how much time to commit to it. If a player is committed to being as successful as possible, then she can adjust her lifestyle to encompass the physical aspect of being a player. She can work on fitness, flexibility, and strength in her own time. As a college coach, I am constantly disappointed by the lack of physical preparation apparent in first-year players as they arrive for the first time on campus. They are not close to being ready for the physical demands of the game at the next level. Players can and must do better in this area, and club coaches need to be more aware of how to prepare their players for this next level.

Psychological   This aspect can have a huge influence on the success of the player and the team. The psychological part of the game is one of those intangibles that cannot be measured, but it's every bit as important as the rest, if not more so. A coach who is strong in this area can take a team further than expected. It's important to understand that a team consists of individuals, each with different needs. By being positive and well prepared, a team can generate enormous confidence and belief in itself. The coach can encourage such an atmosphere through individual meetings with players to offer positive suggestions, as well as pregame and halftime talks in the locker room.

A successful coach should be always providing feedback to players to let them know just how they are progressing. Day-by-day communication is a must, and I can suggest a few practical ways of doing it. First, a coach should realize that his perception of a given player's roles and responsibilities is rarely the same as the player's own perception. In fact, they may be operating on quite different assumptions. How many times has a player believed she had a good game, only to find out that the coach disagrees? A coach and player can learn about each other's perceptions by each filling out a questionnaire (tailored to the position played) about the player's performance in a game. For example, a defender might be asked to rate his performance as a 1v1 defender or in terms of whether he helped keep proper team shape. The player and coach can independently rate the player's performance on a scale of 1 to 5, then discuss the results. Their perceptions and scores may or may not be the same, but in any case the resulting discussion will give the player food for thought and identify specific areas to improve on.

Another tool I have often used is to post the team roster in the locker room after a game with ratings (1 through 10) for each player in order to indicate how the coaching staff evaluated his or her performance in their last game. I encourage players to come and ask about their score if they do not like it. This method provides good feedback for players in a nonconfrontational environment, but I do not recommend using it with young players, since it requires that players be mature enough to handle its public nature.

A coach might also consider testing an individual player to evaluate his will to win, especially in relationship to the rest of the team. This can be done by arranging small-sided games in which the teams are randomly selected for every new game. For example, we may spend 15 minutes per practice session, two or three times a week, splitting our group into teams of perhaps four or five that play for 5 minutes a game. A player may play 3 games during practice twice a week for 4 weeks, totaling 24 games, each on a different team with different players. This variety means that a player's success or lack thereof cannot be attributed to playing on a strong or weak team, as every team is different. Every player must record the score of each game he plays, and points are awarded accordingly: 3 points for a win, 1 point for a tie, and none for a loss. The coach might also consider giving a bonus point if a team wins by more than 3 goals. At the end of the month, if the coach compares each player's point total, it will be evident who the more competitive players are. He will have a list from top to bottom, and the players will have ranked themselves.

So, coaches, how can you get the best out of your players day in and day out? Consistency in attitude and expectations is crucial. Try to be motivated and upbeat for every session, as players take their cue from you. Always demand—and accept—nothing but the best in training sessions. This can be difficult, but it is crucial in order to stay on top of the game.

Team Tryouts and Selection

One of the first jobs for a coach is selecting the team. College coaches have the major responsibility of recruiting players to fit their system and team needs. Middle school and high school coaches are far more likely to work with players who are from the area and have not been recruited; in short, they have to work with what is available in the area.

Players should prepare physically for weeks before the tryout, so that they can go into the session confident of performing their best. There is nothing worse for a player than being unable to show the coach his skills because his legs have gone and he can no longer run. Getting good sleep on the 2 nights just before the tryout will help a player feel well rested.

Players should get to the tryout early so that they do not feel rushed or pressured. The extra time can be spent getting physically and mentally prepared. It is imperative to stretch and warm up well during this time, as players may not get an appropriate chance to do so once the tryout begins. Players should dress in appropriate soccer clothing, with a clean pair of cleats, shin guards, long socks, and soccer shorts and shirt. I have known players who dressed distinctively (e.g., wearing different-colored socks or a bright top) in an effort to stand out. With luck, this might work, but if it is overdone it may look out of place and elicit a negative reaction from the coach.

Once the tryout has begun, players should act as confident as they can. They should be vocal, when appropriate, and seek the ball. If they are not getting it, they must go looking for it. It's best to keep the game simple, and do simple things quickly and efficiently. Players should work hard physically to show the coach they are individually fit *and* prepared to be good team players, not just individuals.

Once a coach has selected players, he must slot them into positions and determine their roles and responsibilities. It is important for the coach and players alike to understand that soccer is first and foremost a team game; each player's philosophy should be to play not as an individual but as part of a team. Each player must buy into the system and fully understand her role and responsibilities. Players will be asked to fulfill certain roles and perform in specific ways, and this approach may initially be somewhat foreign to some players. For example, a player might be used to dribbling the ball in a certain area of the field, and now the coach requires him to pass it rather than dribble from this area. How quickly can he adapt?

If a player is less successful than he had hoped in the early stages and is not selected for the starting 11, he should not give up. A lot can happen as the season progresses. Starting players get injured, go through periods of poor form and low confidence, and have to miss games as a result of getting carded. It is more than likely that a substitute will get her opportunity to play more, possibly even in the starting group. When the chance arrives, she must be ready to take advantage of it. Many coaches tell players to work on their weaknesses, but if you are a player I suggest to you the opposite: Work on your strengths. Try to find an area in the game where you might excel—such as heading the ball, tackling, or shooting. Then concentrate on getting better in that area so you can specialize. Coaches are always looking for players who can fulfill a specific role, and if you can do it better than someone else, you might just win yourself a position. You should still work on all areas, but being better than someone else at one specific job is going to help you win a place.

CHAPTER 3

Attacking Skills and Tactics

Teams that play attractive, attacking soccer are always a joy to watch, and players who possess flair and good attacking skills are in high demand. Good attacking skills pay high dividends, and, even for players who eventually end up playing as defenders, it is advantageous to spend considerable time working on attacking skills. These skills require sound technical ability, and, in combination with creativity and good physical and tactical sense, they create a very good attacking player.

It is always difficult to score goals, especially against good teams, and we have all had the experience of missing chance after chance and wondering when, if ever, we will score the goal that wins the game. This chapter begins with the fundamentals, then suggests ways to develop skills and incorporate them into a tactical approach to game play. The chapter also discusses how to use attacking soccer in order to not only create goal scoring opportunities but also *finish* them. Finally, it suggests both individual and team drills to improve attack capability.

Individual Attacking Skills

A well-coached team attacks on many fronts. It is fun to watch combination play, in which several players cooperate to create a goal-scoring opportunity. However, before a team can succeed at combination play, players must develop their individual attacking skills, and they need to be comfortable with the ball at their feet. This takes practice—lots of it—and much of it can be done in one's own backyard, without involving a coach. This section covers all of the essential individual attacking skills: dribbling, passing and support, ball control, and goal scoring.

Dribbling

To attack successfully, a team must be able to penetrate the opposition's defense, but it is not always possible to open up and penetrate a defense by means of combination play. It often requires the skill of an individual attacker dribbling in order to take on a defender in a 1v1 situation.

Dribbling is fun to watch and exciting to do. There is no single correct way to dribble, though there are some fundamentals. Almost anything can work, and it depends greatly on the confidence and skills of the individual player. Moves can be joined together in many ways, thus creating the dribbler's own unique style. Effective dribbling requires a confident player who is prepared to try new things without fear of failure. In turn, dribbling builds the player's confidence and makes him more comfortable with a ball at his feet. Even juggling practice—keeping the ball off the ground with different parts of the body—is good for building this comfort and confidence, as it helps a player develop "touch," a "feel" for the ball, and increases her confidence in handling the ball.

When dribbling, the player must maintain close control of the ball in relationship to his body and be able to use the various surfaces of both feet. Good body control is also required, since the dribbler must have the ability to stop quickly, change direction, and accelerate quickly. There are two basic types of dribble: In a crowded area, a dribbler needs to keep the ball close to her feet, but a player running in open space (especially down the wing) can and should get the ball well out in front of herself (speed is more important here than close technique). No matter what the technique or individual style, three basic principles always apply:

1. *Run directly at the defender.* This makes the defender commit to the tackle. Most good defenders do not want to engage in a tackle, knowing that if they are beaten the space conceded behind them is far more dangerous than the space in front. In fact, one defensive principle is for defenders to keep the play and the ball in front of them, and this principle is directly contradicted by being drawn into a tackle by good attacking dribbling (figure 3.1).

2. *Take the ball as close to the defender as possible.* The attacker can tempt a defender with the ball in order to prompt him to try to win it (figure 3.2 *a-c*). If the attacker "shows" the defender the ball

Figure 3.1   Dribbling at the defender.

by taking it close to him, he may be tempted to put his foot forward in an attempt to win the ball. If he fails, he is now off balance, with his weight forward, and he will be much slower in turning to try to retrieve the ball after it has gone by him.

3. *Knock the ball past the defender and accelerate.* The most basic attacking principle of all is to get the ball behind the defender. It doesn't take anything fancy or complicated—just good timing and enough speed at the correct time. The attacker plays the ball past the defender, then goes to get it. The closer she is to the defender, the easier it is. She *might* be able to knock the ball behind the defender from 3 yards (2.7 meters) away, but chances are slim that she will have enough

Figure 3.2   Dribbling with outside of foot using body swerve and acceleration: *(a)* attacking player runs at the defender; *(b)* attacking player drops his left shoulder and makes the defender commit; *(c)* after faking left, the attacker moves quickly to the right using the outside of his right foot.

speed to get to it before the defender does. She has a much better chance from about a yard (or meter) away.

The key to successful dribbling is to get the ball behind the defender and be quick or crafty enough to get to it first. Normally, the more touches the attacker has *in front* of the defender, the better it is for that defender, because he is successfully protecting his most vulnerable area—his back. A naturally quick player may not need sophisticated dribbling skills in order to attack successfully. With good technique, speed will enable her to just go at and by the defender. Slower players have to be craftier, deceiving the defender with quick feet and trickery, such as body feints and movements that get the defender off balance and allow the attacker to go by (figure 3.3).

Figure 3.3 Making a defender commit by getting him off balance

Passing and Support

Passing and support are probably one of the most important aspects of the game. Soccer is a game of possession, and games are often won by the team that keeps possession of the ball longer. When under pressure, the player who passes rather than dribbles generally has a better chance of succeeding. Indeed, without being able to pass, one cannot successfully play the game. Thus it is vital that all young players learn to be good passers of the ball, and it is especially important that they realize when and where to pass the ball. Good support play helps answer the "when and where" questions that can plague young players. It is very difficult to pass the ball if no one is there to receive the pass, and it is the teammates' responsibility to support the passer by being at the right angle and distance to make a good target.

The difficult part for coach and player is to know when to stop encouraging dribbling and start encouraging passing. Probably as soon as a player is comfortable with the ball at his feet, passing should be encouraged. There are numerous ways to pass the ball, which can be made to do different things depending on the kind of contact made with it. For example, a ball struck on its inside with the outside of the right foot will move from left to right in the air. If struck with the inside of the foot on the outside of the ball, it will move from right to left. If the ball is hit dead-center, with the instep imparting very little spin, it will "knuckle." Players need to practice such techniques over and over again, with both the left and the right foot.

Figure 3.4 First touch to side and out of feet: *(a)* player concentrates on the ball with her head down and contacts the ball with the outside of her foot; *(b)* touches away from her body at an angle; *(c)* lifts her head up and is now in a position to do anything she wants with the ball.

Quality of the first touch when receiving the ball is critical. Upon first touch, the ball should move about a yard (or meter) to the right or left of the receiving player's feet (figure 3.4*a-c*)—any closer and it will get caught underfoot (which will inhibit the ability to pass, dribble, or shoot), requiring a second touch to correct the matter, followed by a third touch to progress with the ball. If, on the other hand, the first touch is too far from the body, then a defender may step in and take the ball. It is vital to remember that soccer is always played better with speed and quickness: The more touches on the ball, the slower the team's play and the less effective the attack. Most teams include players who cannot play quickly enough because they take too many touches on the ball. These players must be encouraged to play one- and two-touch soccer, and the coach may have to put that limitation on them in practice.

Three factors contribute to a skillful pass:

1. *Accuracy.* A player must be able to strike the ball correctly and accurately, often with a teammate's feet as the target. The most accurate technique is to use the side of the foot, with the toe rotated outward (figure 3.5). This kind of pass should be used for shorter distances of 5 to 20 yards (about 4.5 to 18 meters). For longer passes, the instep of the foot should be used (figure 3.6 on page 32). This type of pass is more powerful but more difficult to do accurately.

Figure 3.5 Side of the foot pass.

Defenders try to read the pass so that they can quickly get into position to intercept it or quickly close down the player receiving the ball. Thus the attacker needs to disguise the pass as well as possible—for example, by running in one direction and passing in the other, by changing direction quickly, or by faking or delaying the pass.

2. *Timing.* The ball must be released at the right time. If it is released too soon, the receiving player may not have had time to get into good position to receive it; if it is released too late, players may have run offside or into positions where they can no longer receive it. A rule of thumb: If the pressuring defender is farther away than the player who is the target of the pass, then it is too soon to make the pass.

3. *Pace and power.* The speed of the pass makes a huge difference. During keep-away sessions

Figure 3.6 Instep pass.

in practice, it is critical to put good pace on the ball in order to create a better rhythm and make it harder for defenders to intercept the ball. In game play, however, good judgment is essential: If a pass is too slow, it will be intercepted. If it is too strong, the receiving player may have difficulty controlling it. Thus passing speed should be adjusted to the conditions of the field, the particulars of the game, and the ability of one's teammates. In general, the better the receiver, the faster the pass should be. Passers must work hard to put good pace on the ball, and the player receiving the ball must work even harder to control it. The passer knows he has done well when the receiver can do anything he wants with it on the first touch.

Before striking the ball, the passer should give special attention to the position of the defender marking the receiving player. The pass should arrive away from defensive pressure. If the defender is standing to the receiver's left, then the pass should be to his right, and vice versa (figure 3.7). The receiving player will then be able to protect the ball with his body, making it more difficult for the defender to get to it.

Players without the ball should move into good positions to receive it, trying always to create wider angles, away from

Figure 3.7 Receiving pass on the correct side.

defensive pressure. In figure 3.8, the player receiving the ball is moving *away* from the defender to improve the passing angle. The player who has just passed the ball now needs to move quickly into a different position, to create more passing options for the receiving player and thus more difficulty for the defensive team. Players should avoid passing and standing (i.e., watching the pass). They should pass and *move*.

Players also need to consider when to support a teammate who has the ball, and when not to. This can be a very difficult decision for many players to make. Most players who have progressed beyond the elementary levels of the game tend to go toward the ball

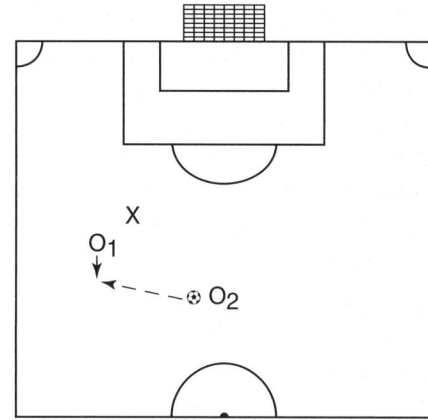

Figure 3.8 Player O1 improves the angle of the pass by moving away from X and toward the ball.

to support the player with the ball. If all players do this, however, the team will have too many players moving toward the ball and not enough making space away from it. The opposite problem can arise with beginning players, who tend to just run upfield, toward the opposition's goal and away from the ball. If nobody is coming short for the pass, the result will be a version of kickball rather than true soccer. Teams must achieve balance, with the appropriate number of players moving both toward the ball and away from it.

If a player is already in a support position when her teammate receives the ball—and if the receiving player is *not* under immediate pressure from the defender—then the support player should attack forward, beyond the ball and into the back of the defenders. Thus he should be moving away from the ball, because there is no need to provide support. In figure 3.9*a*, O3 can make a forward

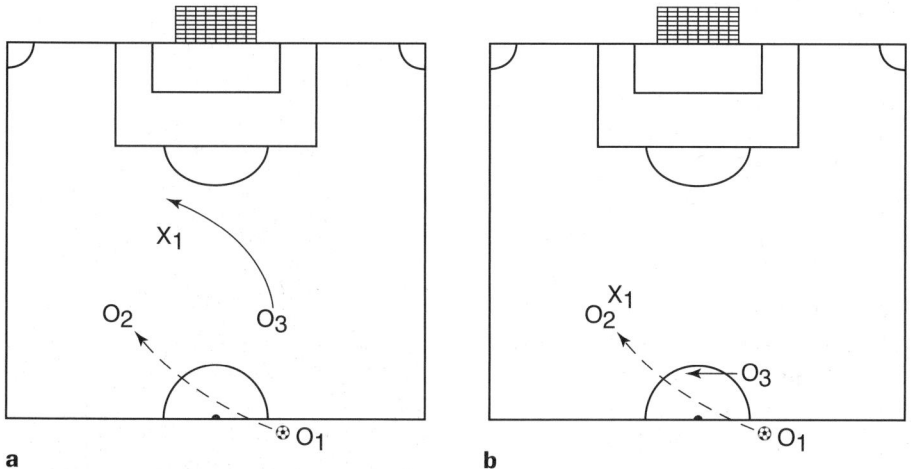

Figure 3.9 Supporting a teammate who has just received the ball: *(a)* player O3 makes a forward attacking run, since O2 is not under immediate pressure from X1; *(b)* player O3 remains in a support position as O2 is under pressure from X1.

run into the back of defender X1, since O2 does not need immediate support. In figure 3.9b, O3 holds to provide support since O2 has come under immediate pressure from X1.

When possible, it is usually better to play forward balls rather than backward or square balls (a square or flat pass goes straight across the field, parallel to the end line)—that is, it is better to use positive rather than negative passing. Players are always encouraged to switch the field of play from left to right, or right to left, and get the ball wide, because such movement can wrong-foot the defense and create more space and time for the attack. This should not, however, be done at the expense of neglecting a forward ball. If the angle is good and the target is available, the ball should be played forward to that target, rather than wide to the wingers.

Players should look as deep as they can and pass the ball to the deepest target available. This type of pass is more likely to draw defenders to the ball and therefore out of position. Ultimately, soccer is a game not of side-to-side movement but of forward penetration—a difficult skill requiring much practice. As the old adage says: "Look deep first. If you can't go deep, go wide." In figure 3.10, O1 has two options: the easier (more obvious) pass to O2 and the longer (more difficult) pass to O3. The play is more likely to produce decisive results if O1 chooses the longer option to O3. To do so, he needs to get his head up and look for the deepest target he can find, in this case O3.

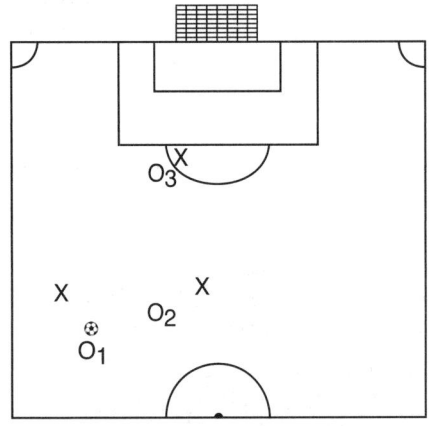

Figure 3.10 With two options available, O1 should play deep to X3 rather than short to O2.

Eventually, the various types of passes and movements have to be put into a game situation. Small-sided games are ideal for all skill development, as they allow players to practice their skills in a scaled-down game and gradually progress to using them in a full-sided game. It is best to start with more space and smaller numbers, then move toward using less space and higher numbers. The ratio of defenders to attackers should start low, then increase as players' skills develop. The more quickly a player can perform these skills, the more effective both he and his team will be. Decreasing space in any drill will decease the time a player has to work with, thereby forcing him to play quicker soccer. The same is true for increasing the ratio of defenders to attackers, but this approach will succeed only with advanced players. Once players are succeeding—and not before—the coach can also decrease the touch limit for the attacking players. One- and two-touch soccer quicken the play. Coaches can adjust several conditions as players develop: space, number of defenders, and touch limit.

It is not advisable to play keep-away games with a large number of players. The larger the number, the fewer touches on the ball for each player and the less effective the practice. If group size goes much above 12, then players who are not especially confident will tend to hide, see very little of the ball, and therefore miss out on the benefit of the practice. For a squad with 18 players, two groups of 9 will work much better for keep-away than the full group. It is okay, however, to play with the full squad on occasion.

Ball Control

It is legal to control a soccer ball with any part of the body other than the arms and hands, but certain parts of the body are easier to use than others. The feet, of course, are used most often, but the thighs, chest, and head are also important. Players should understand four principles of ball control.

The first principle is to move the controlling body surface into the ball's line of flight (figure 3.11*a*), which requires moving one's feet quickly. It is very difficult to control a ball when stretching for it with the foot, and it is almost impossible using any other part of the body (figure 3.11*b*). When using their feet, players should develop the habit of controlling the ball and creating a better passing angle in one movement. This approach normally requires the receiver to control the ball to the left or right of his body in order to widen the passing angle. Players should be able to use both the inside and outside of each foot. They should keep their head up and look for teammates before the ball arrives, but must get their heads back down to control the ball. Their heads should come back up as the players look for a pass.

Figure 3.11 Staying behind the flight of the ball: *(a)* her body is directly behind the ball, and her feet move to stay underneath the ball; *(b)* her feet have not moved quickly enough to keep her body behind the ball, and she must stretch to reach it.

Next, the player must select the controlling surface. The flight of the ball will probably determine which surface the player chooses, but it is generally best to use the feet whenever possible. Two main techniques are the wedge and the cushion. The wedge control involves trapping the ball between the foot and the ground, using either the sole or side of the foot (figure 3.12); it is also possible to use the chest by moving the chest down to force the ball quickly down. The cushion control involves withdrawing the controlling surface from the ball immediately on contact (figure 3.13). The idea here is to absorb force with the body, thus taking pace off the ball so that it falls lightly at one's feet.

Third, the receiving player should be sure to relax. If the body goes stiff—not uncommon due to the stress of the situation—ball control of any kind will be difficult to achieve. Players should try to relax and be as confident as they can throughout the process.

Finally, the player must keep her head steady (figure 3.14). The head acts like a rudder on a ship: If it moves, so does the rest of the body. Thus, holding one's head steady is a good principle to follow in almost every aspect of the game, especially when controlling the ball.

When controlling the ball away from defensive pressure, the first touch of the attacking player should be at an angle away from the defender. The ball is then played away from the defender and out from under the attacking player's feet (figure 3.15*a-b* on page 37).

Ball control should initially be practiced in pairs, so that each player can learn the techniques, but as soon as possible, pressure from another player should be incorporated to make the exercise more gamelike (it is a completely different

Figure 3.12 Side of the foot wedge trap.

Figure 3.13 Thigh trap using thigh as a cushion.

Figure 3.14 Head position for correct ball control.

Figure 3.15   Controlling ball away from defensive pressure: *(a)* the attacking player's first touch; *(b)* the ball is played away from the defender.

skill when performed under pressure). This activity can be done in threes, with one player serving the ball, one receiving it and working on control, and one defending by moving toward the controlling player to pressure her.

Goal Scoring

Scoring simply means putting the ball into the back of the net. In most cases, it is done with a shot—striking the ball with the instep in much the same manner used for the instep pass—but goals can also be scored in many other ways. If, for example, the ball bounces off a shin bone and into the net, it can hardly be considered a shot, but it still counts. Goal scoring is more about being in the right place at the right time, and it is probably one of the most difficult tasks in the game. It is necessary to learn the skill of shooting—striking the ball with one's foot—and forwards in particular had better be good at it!

To some degree, shooting is more an attitude than a skill. Players need to be prepared to shoot at any given opportunity, and most certainly need confidence in their ability. It is often said that goal scorers are born, not made, and there is some truth in that. It certainly helps, however, to use good shooting technique. The mechanics of shooting are very similar to those of passing, and in some cases shooting is in fact as simple as passing the ball past the goalkeeper into the net. Thus players should hold good passing technique in mind when shooting the ball, rather than thinking they have to break the net every time they shoot.

The shooter should always know where the goal and goalkeeper are in order to shoot into the most open part of the net. Goalkeepers are often taught to cover their near post (the post closest to the ball), so as a rule of thumb it is a good idea for players to shoot for the far post. This also opens up the possibility that a mis-hit shot will turn out to be a very effective cross.

The shooter should generally concentrate on accuracy rather than power in order to at least make the goalkeeper save the ball: An off-target shot never scores, whereas an accurate one always has a chance. The shooter should keep his head down and steady, keep his eyes on the ball, concentrate on the center of the ball, and hit through that point. He should avoid lurching, trying instead to remain calm and strike the ball smoothly. An overly quick kicking action ("snatching") is often caused by slight panic, which leads the player to overfocus on getting the shot away quickly. Certainly this is sometimes necessary, but more often than not the shooter has more time than she thinks, so it is best to remain calm and smooth in her kicking action. It will produce better contact on the ball.

In game play, shooting requires the ability to strike the ball from different heights and directions. The ball may be on the ground, bouncing, or on the fly. It may be moving directly toward or away from the shooter, or coming in from the side. Each scenario requires certain techniques and needs to be practiced in and of itself. When the ball is moving away, the shooter should step into it with the nonkicking foot (figure 3.16). This can be a difficult maneuver—it is hard to catch up with a ball moving away from one's body—and the resulting shot may lack power. In addition, if the nonkicking foot is too far behind the ball, the shot will rise and probably sail over the bar. Ideally, then, the nonkicking foot should be placed next to the ball, and with a ball that is moving away from the body this requires extra effort.

Figure 3.16 Stepping into ball with non-kicking foot.

When the ball is moving *toward* the shooter, the problem often lies in keeping the shot down. It is very easy to get slightly under the ball and hit it over the bar. The shooter should concentrate on keeping her head and knee over the ball and kicking through the middle of the ball (figure 3.17*a-c* on page 39). In addition, when the ball is moving toward the shooter, it is easier for her to generate power (through the rebound action), so she must take care not to try and hit it too hard.

When a ball is coming in perpendicularly, or from the side, it requires more of a sweeping action than a powerful strike. The shooter must concentrate simply on redirecting the ball toward the goal by placing the closest foot against the ball and using a sweeping motion of the leg.

Figure 3.17   Shooting with the ball moving toward the shooter: *(a)* approach at a slight angle; *(b)* step into the ball with the nonkicking foot while keeping the knee and head over the ball; *(c)* kick through the center of the ball.

Team Attacking Tactics

The individual attacking skills needed in order to create goal-scoring chances must be worked on continually. They are never truly mastered, no matter the level of play; there is always room to improve, and players must be prepared to do some of this work in their own time. Beyond individual skills, however, coaches need to prepare players to incorporate individual skills into team play to form an effective attacking unit. This section covers team tactics for attacking, including attacking from wing or flank positions, blind-side runs, crossover plays, and wall passing.

Attacking From Wing or Flank Positions

It is normally easier to penetrate a defense from wide or wing positions than it is down the middle. Organized defenses tend to concentrate their players in more central positions to protect their goal. It is impossible, however, to cover the whole width of the field with defensive players—there is just too much space—so defenders are taught to protect the middle and "give space" away in the wide or flank positions. Thus attacking teams should try to take advantage of this space; whatever defenders try to accomplish tactically, attackers should do the opposite.

Crosses are more dangerous—and more successful—if they are played into the back of defenders, between them and their goal, where it is very difficult for them to clear the ball. Players and coaches should be aware that defenders are most comfortable when they are facing forward, with the ball in front of them. They are much less comfortable when a ball is played behind them, forcing them to turn and face their own goal. So, whenever possible in crossing a ball, players should try to play it into an area that will make defenders turn toward their own net.

The two positions most likely to cross a ball from the wide flank into the opponent's penalty box are the two wingers and the two fullbacks. Most good crosses are played into defined areas or spaces in the penalty box and are not necessarily direct passes to teammates. It is the responsibility of the attacking player to understand where these spaces are and to recognize that the ball is going to be played into them rather than directly to a player. From the coach's perspective, if a cross is played successfully into such a space and no attacker is there to meet it, then the problem lies not with the crosser but with the forward. Wide players should be prepared to play or cross the ball into four basic areas: the near post, midgoal, the far post, and the edge of the penalty box.

Near-Post Crosses

The post nearest the ball is the one area of the field where defending teams are most vulnerable. The goalkeeper's advantage of being able to use hands is often negated because he cannot get to this space in time; nor, likely, can defenders. Attacking this area, more so than any other, is a matter of timing. Initially, the crosser of the ball must determine whether he has enough space to play a ball around the pressuring defender. If there is no defender at all, then it is easy, but if there is good pressure from the defender then the winger needs to create enough space to be able to cross the ball into the near-post area. His main job is to put the ball into the front space. The ball needs to be played quickly, with as much force as possible, and should arrive no higher than head height.

It is sometimes easier, though more dangerous, to play the ball on the ground, and in this case the attacking player inside the box must time her run so that she meets the cross in the right place at the right time. It is *not* up to the player crossing the ball to pass it directly to the forward—she is simply required to put it in the right space, and the attacker in the box must get to the ball ahead of the defender. This requires good timing, commitment, and determination. Forwards should start the run into that space as late as possible, then move as quickly as possible, thus leaving the covering defender with less reaction time.

A near-post cross is illustrated in figure 3.18, where O4 begins with the ball, plays it into target player O1, then receives it back. Next, he passes to his wide player O3, who responsibly gets enough space past defender X3 to cross the ball into the near post. O1 spins, turns, and attacks the far post in hopes of taking the defender with him and clearing out the space at the near

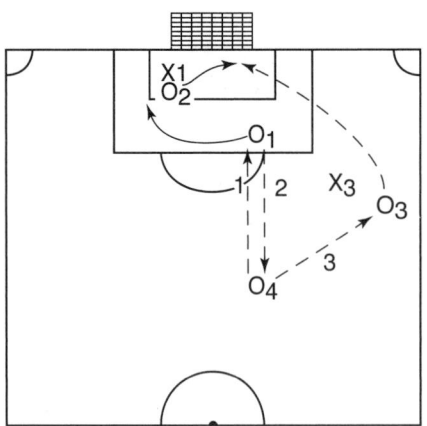

Figure 3.18 O3 creates room to play the ball past X3 and inside the 6-yard box level with the near post.

post. O2 has the responsibility of attacking the near post and winning the space in front of defender X1.

To be successful, near-post runs must be made at the correct angle. Players should run in the same path as the flight of the ball. In figure 3.19*a*, O2's run to the near post is nearly perpendicular to the flight of the cross. At this angle, O2 has little margin for adjustment; therefore, unless the cross is made right to her feet, her chance of scoring is low. In figure 3.19*b*, on the other hand, O2's run is much closer to the angle of the cross, giving her a much better chance to adjust on the run and correctly meet the cross.

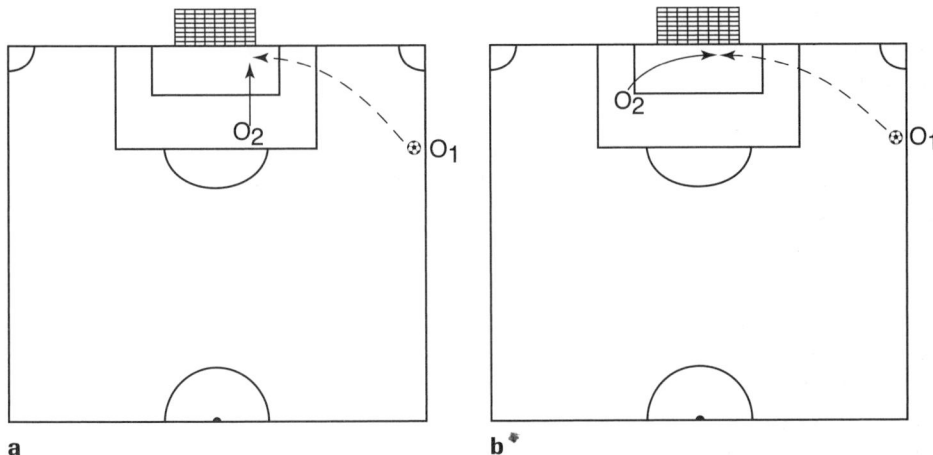

a   **b**

Figure 3.19   Meeting a near-post cross: *(a)* O2 attacks the cross from O1 at a 90° angle, allowing little room for error: *(b)* O2 attacks the cross at an angle almost directly behind the flight of the cross, giving O2 a better chance.

Midgoal Crosses

Ideally, the ball should be crossed to the middle of the goal at about the edge of the 6-yard box. This cross is usually made in the air; otherwise, it will not clear the first defender, who will be positioned toward the near post in front of the midgoal space. In order to attack this space, teams need to attempt to clear it of defenders. Intelligent runs by the forwards will pull defenders from these good defensive positions. In figure 3.20, O1 drifts away from the ball, toward the back post, and O2 makes a near-post run. O4 should then make a late run into this cleared space in hopes of meeting the cross at the

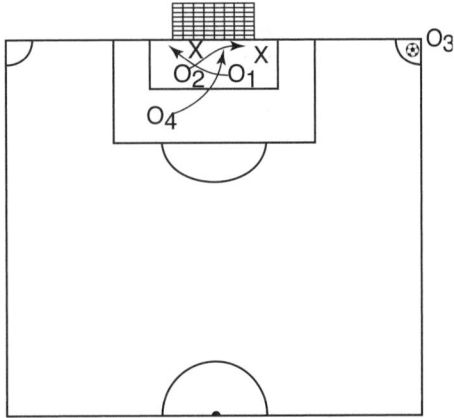

Figure 3.20   O4 attacks the midgoal space created by the movements of O1 and O2.

perfect time. Crosses played into this area have to be slightly more precise than in other areas, and they can be more difficult to complete since the opposition is likely to have more defenders in the area.

Far-Post Crosses

These crosses must be lofted in order to get past the goalkeeper and the defenders in the box. This can be done in two entirely different ways. The first is to loft a floating ball that needs to clear the far corner of the 6-yard box. This type of cross requires the attacking team to win the space with a good jumper and header of the ball. This type of cross is often fairly ineffective. The second type of far-post cross involves "pinging" or driving the ball. The crosser must make sure not to kick underneath the ball, because in that case it will float. Thus the ball must be driven through its center to get sufficient height but move faster and with a flatter trajectory. This is a much harder cross to hit, but if successfully played it is easier to win—and far more dangerous to the defense—than the lofted cross. In order to get a good forward run at the ball, as well as more height on the jump, the player attacking the ball on the far post needs to begin well away from the 6-yard box and back post.

Crosses into the box can be either in-swinging (moving toward the goal) or out-swinging (moving away from the goal). A ball delivered to the near post or midgoal can be very dangerous when played as an in-swinger. Since the ball is already moving toward the goal, all that is required is a minimal touch to direct it into the goal. This slight change in angle is often enough to fool the goalkeeper, and even if not touched, the threat of the challenge to the cross may be sufficient to freeze the goalkeeper and allow the cross to score directly. Crosses to the far post are more likely to be out-swinging, taking the ball away from the goal and the goalkeeper. This requires cleaner contact on the ball by the forward, who will have to generate power on the header through his own technique in order to direct the ball toward the net.

Balls Pulled Back to the Edge of the Box

If a winger has penetrated deep down the opposing flank and gotten close to the goal line, he will find it difficult to cross into the 6-yard box, and especially hard to get the ball in behind the defenders. The angle of the pass—not to mention the number of defensive players likely to be in the 6-yard box—simply will not allow it. Thus he needs to consider pulling the ball back toward the edge of the 18-yard box, which requires that a teammate pull away from the 6-yard box, back toward the 18-yard line, or that a player be holding on the edge of the penalty box. Balls pulled back into this area need to be struck firmly; otherwise, defenders will have time to close down the pass or the resulting shot.

Blind-Side Runs, Crossover Plays, and Wall Passing

Blind-side runs, crossover plays, and wall passing are all similar types of off-the-ball movement that allows attackers to either lose their markers or get into the back of a defender. Players that stand around with little activity are easy to mark defensively. Good movement away from the ball is much more difficult for the defender.

Blind-side runs are made by a player who, without the ball, runs behind defenders into a position where they are unlikely to see and react to him. In figure 3.21, O1 begins to run downfield with the ball, prompting defender X1 to come and challenge for the ball. At this point, O2 can make a blind-side run behind X1 to make himself available for a pass from O1.

Crossover plays occur when two players of the same team with one of them in possession of the ball, run across each other's

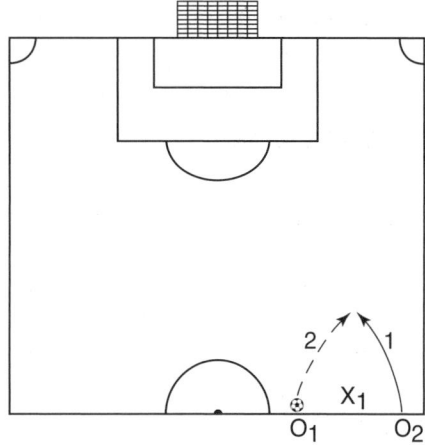

3.21 O2 makes a blind-side run behind defender X1, and makes himself available for the pass from O1.

paths. The player with the ball may release it to his teammate, who simply takes the ball from him, or keeps it himself using that player as a decoy. The defenders are not sure who is going to keep the ball and are momentarily confused. This split second can be enough for attacking players to lose their markers. Figure 3.22 *a-c* shows the technique used in a crossover play.

Figure 3.23 on page 44 shows the player movement involved in a crossover play. X1 runs toward teammate X2 and either releases the ball to X2 (who accelerates away) or uses X2 as a decoy while keeping the ball and accelerating away on her own. Thus the players cross over each other, leaving the defender unsure of who is going to keep the ball.

Figure 3.22   Crossover play protecting the ball from the defender with the furthest away foot: *(a)* the player with the ball protects it by keeping it on the foot furthest from the defender; *(b)* a teammate takes the ball; *(c)* the player accelerates in the opposite direction.

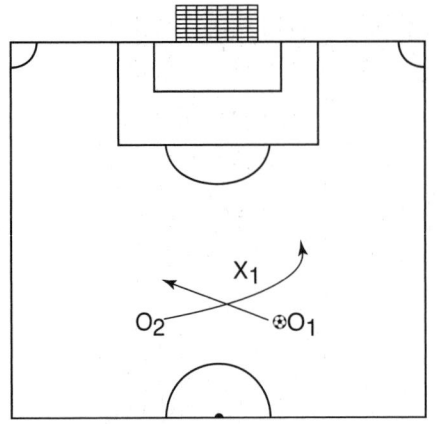

3.23 A crossover play where O2 takes the ball from O1 and accelerates away from defender X1.

The wall pass is one of the most commonly used passes in the game, and when done properly it is difficult to defend. It is a very effective way of losing the defensive marker and also allowing penetration to the back of defenders. A defender who goes to pressure the ball that is passed at the last moment will typically turn to look where it has been passed to. This often allows this same attacking player time to run by him and receive the ball back from the player he has just passed to, and he will have effectively lost his marker. Figure 3.24a shows a successful wall pass, where O2 dribbles the ball toward X1 and makes him commit.

Attacking player O2 should dribble the ball as close to defender X1 as he dare in order to make X1 commit. Otherwise, as seen in figure 3.24b, the defender, who has stayed well away from the player with the ball, will likely be able to stop the wall pass because he is already standing in the area where O2 is likely to want to run. Thus there is no penetration, and defender X2 still has the players and the ball in front of him. Teammate O1 can help by quickly moving closer to O2, thus decreasing the distance of the pass and speeding up its execution. When O1 releases the pass, he must accelerate as quickly as he can to the back of X1 to get the return or wall pass from O2. Figure 3.25a and b show an alternate view of a succesful wall pass.

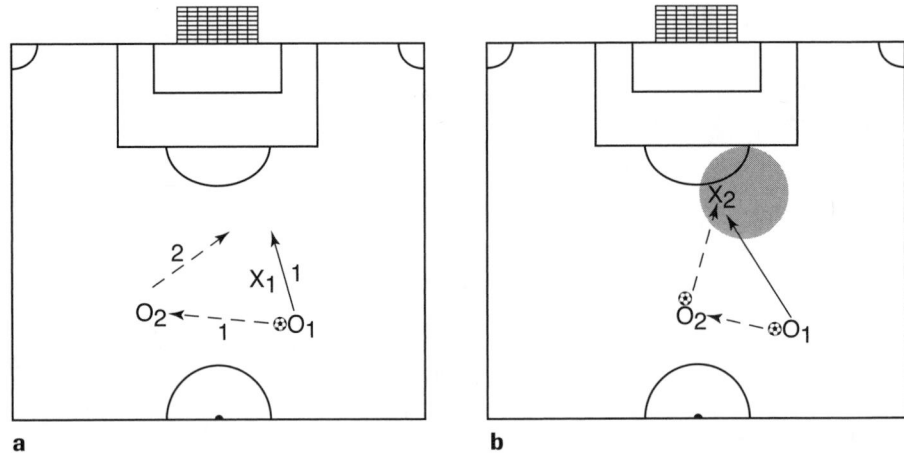

a   b

Figure 3.24 Wall passes: (a) O1 and O2 complete a wall pass around defender X1; (b) O2 has not taken the ball close enough to defender X2, and has not created enough space behind X2 for O1 to run into.

Figure 3.25   Wall pass making the defender commit: *(a)* the attacking player runs directly at the defender and makes him commit to the tackle, while the support player stays square to the ball; *(b)* the attacking player passes to the support, or wall, player and accelerates past the defender for the return pass.

DRIBBLING DRILLS

INDIVIDUAL DRIBBLING

FOCUS

Helping players become comfortable with a ball at their feet.

PROCEDURE

This drill is performed in a series of 8-by-8-yard (7.5-by-7.5-meter) boxes—or bigger if the players' skill level is poor. Each player has a ball and practices a specific move or moves in his individual box. The moves can vary widely, using different parts of both feet: inside of right to inside of left, or outside right to inside right, outside left to inside left, stepover right, stepover left, and so on.

MIRROR DRIBBLING

FOCUS

Creating a gamelike distraction by introducing a second player to the dribbling drill.

PROCEDURE

After a player is comfortable dribbling individually, She can pair up with a partner to do mirror work. This drill practice uses a 16-by-16-yard (about 15-by-15-meter) box formed by combining two of the 8-by-8-yard boxes used in the individual dribbling drill. The partners practice the target skill by simultaneously dribbling at each other, then each going to her right with the outside of the right foot, thus passing each other at the halfway point without colliding. Mirror work can be used to practice a wide variety of moves, as long as the players go to opposite sides so they do not collide.

1V1 DRIBBLING

FOCUS

Developing the skill of dribbling past an opponent.

PROCEDURE

Setup is similar to that for mirror dribbling. Each player stands in his own box, with one player as attacker and the other as defender. The attacker tries to dribble through the defender's square without losing the ball. Initially, the defender should exert merely token or partial defense, while the attacker improves his dribbling skill, but he can quickly move to regular defending in order to make it more realistic for the attacking player.

FIRST TOUCH

FOCUS

Receiving a pass and creating a first touch that gets the ball out from underneath the feet.

PROCEDURE

Working in pairs in 10-by-10-yard (about 9-by-9-meter) boxes, partners practice the push or side-of-the-foot pass with two touches while moving throughout the grid. The first touch must be made about a yard (or meter) away from the player's feet. Play should progress to one-touch, with both partners still moving within the grid. Remember: The fastest soccer one can play is one-touch soccer.

ONE-TOUCH PASSING

FOCUS

Passing with the use of both feet and an angled approach.

PROCEDURE

Working in a 10-by-10-yard (9-by-9-meter) box, partner A begins with a ball at her feet, standing outside the box. Partner B lines up in the corner of the box on the opposite side.

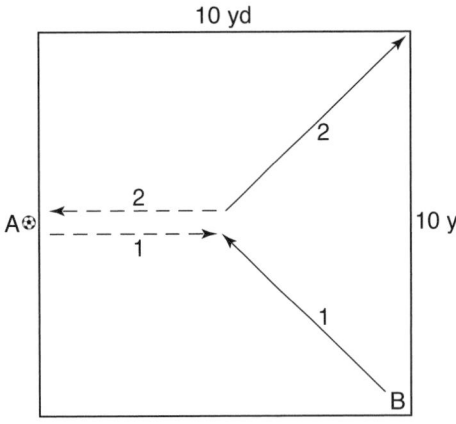

1. On the coach's command, partner B checks diagonally toward partner A, who serves her the ball.

2. B plays the ball back to A with her right foot, checks back to the opposite corner, then checks back at an angle, this time passing back with her left foot.

3. This pattern continues for about 1 minute. Then the partners switch roles.

The players should focus on using both feet, checking back at an angle to create space, and playing the ball back at a good pace (too fast and it will be hard to receive, too slow and it may never arrive).

PASSING FROM AN ANGLED APPROACH

FOCUS

Passing with both feet while approaching from different angles.

PROCEDURE

Work in a 10-by-10-yard (9-by-9-meter) box. With partner A outside the grid and a ball at his feet, partner B lines up in the middle of the grid adjacent to A.

1. On the coach's command, A plays the ball into the middle of the grid.

2. B runs straight across the grid and plays a one-time ball back to A, then repeats the process from the other side.

3. This continues for about 1 minute, then the partners switch roles.

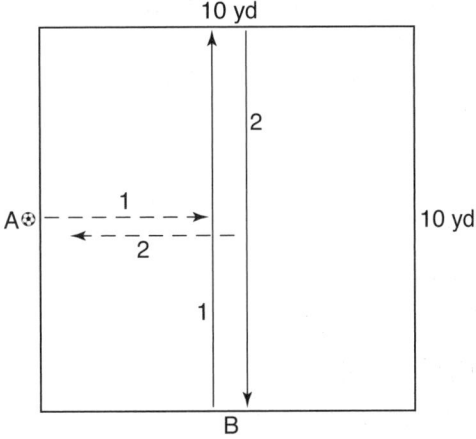

The players should focus on accuracy and pace of the pass, as well as changing speed after the pass has been made. They should pass the ball across the body, using the instep.

SUPPORT PLAY

FOCUS

Showing correct support play.

PROCEDURE

This drill involves four players working in a 20-by-10-yard (18-by-9-meter) area. Player A starts with the ball outside the grid.

1. Player B checks diagonally to receive a short pass from A, passes back to A, and then continues to run until exiting the grid on the other side.

2. Player A now plays a longer, first-time pass to player C at the very opposite side of the grid, 20 yards (18 meters) away.

3. B supports this pass, and C lays the ball to B, who in turn lays it back and runs out of the grid to the side she started on.

4. D begins the same process by receiving a ball from C.

5. This should continue for about 2 minutes, at which point the outside players switch with the players in the middle.

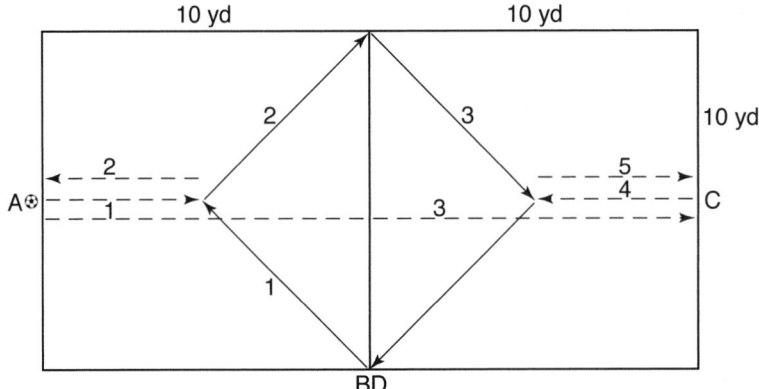

CONTINUOUS SUPPORT PLAY

FOCUS

Making support play more gamelike by having continuous movement.

PROCEDURE

This drill also involves four players working in a 20-by-10-yard (18-by-9-meter) area, but this time all four players work at once, two in the middle and two on the outside. Players A and C begin with balls on the outside.

1. On the coach's command, players B and D check to the appropriate partners to receive the ball, then turn with the ball, using a pivot-and-turn technique (making a half-turn with the ball so that they are facing the opposite partner on the outside of the grid).

2. Once they have turned, they make a longer pass to the opposite partner on the outside of the grid.

3. They continue to support this pass, receive it back, then turn and play another ball to their original partner. (Note that for clarity, only B's passes are shown in the diagram.)

4. This should continue for about 2 minutes. Then the outside partners change.

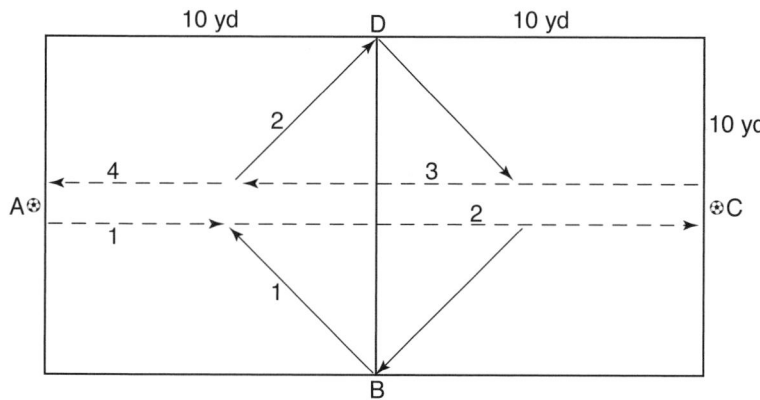

4V2 GRID

FOCUS

Improving passing skills under defensive pressure.

PROCEDURE

This is a possession or keep-away drill and begins to put passing into gamelike situations. If players' ability levels are low, it might be necessary to begin 5v2, thus providing the attackers with more passing options. The drill is performed in a 20-by-10-yard (18-by-9-meter) area.

1. On the coach's command, the attacking team tries to complete a set number of passes without turning the ball over to the defending duo.

2. If the ball is lost, it is given back to the attackers and the process begins again.

3. After 2 minutes, the two defenders should be changed. They will join the attacking group with two of the attackers becoming defenders. In this way everybody gets a taste of both attacking and defending.

The coach should emphasize passing skills and good support play. Speed of play can also be stressed by putting a two-touch limit on each player.

VARIATIONS

Coaches can initiate progressions by changing the numbers (e.g., adding defenders), the playing space, and even the rules to cater to the team's current needs. To increase the team's passing speed, the coach might put one player on a one-touch limit (and have him wear a different bib color), while the rest are allowed two touches. Another interesting variation is mandatory two-touch—the player receiving the ball must touch it exactly twice—which works well when a player needs to work on his first touch. He should make sure his first touch is smooth, away from the pressuring defender, and quick enough to get the pass or second touch under way before being tackled.

4V4 PLUS 2

FOCUS

Adding extra players to make passing more difficult.

PROCEDURE

This drill requires 10 players, divided into two teams of 4 each, along with 2 extras, in a 20-by-30-yard (18-by-27-meter) grid. In this keep-away drill, the two extra players are always on the team with the ball, so that in reality the drill is always 6v4, with the advantage to the side in possession of the ball. Remember the "plus two" always play with the four players who have the ball. When it is lost to the *defending* four, that defending four then become the attacking team, and are joined by the same "plus two" players again, providing six players against four. Periodically, change the "plus two" players; otherwise, they never have an opportunity to defend. The attacking six should try to complete as many consecutive passes as possible without turning the ball over to the defensive unit. The coach can change conditions or rules of the game to meet the team's needs.

4V4V4 DRILL

FOCUS

Working on passing skills and quick thinking.

PROCEDURE

In this drill players have to constantly recognize which team is on their side and who their passing targets are. This is quite a difficult drill—thus not a good one for beginning players. It is a variation of the keep-away drill, and in this case *three* teams (four players each) wear differently colored bibs. To accommodate the larger number of players, the playing area or grid needs to be extended slightly.

1. The coach determines which two teams first combine to form one team that attempts to keep possession of the ball.

2. The game begins with eight attackers facing four defenders and trying to get in as many passes as possible before losing the ball.

3. When the defending quartet finally wins the ball, they combine with the attacking four who did not lose the ball to form a new attacking team. In other words, when a player loses the ball, his quartet becomes the defending team. A ball kicked out of play is considered a lost ball.

FULL-FIELD KEEP-AWAY

FOCUS

Integrating passing skills with large numbers in order to practice getting numbers and getting into support positions around the ball; working on decision making about when to play short and when to play long.

PROCEDURE

The drill uses the whole game field, with the full squad split into two equal teams. A row of cones is placed 10 yards (9 meters) from each goal line across the field to mark the areas where the goalkeepers stand. If the team has two goalkeepers, then one is placed in each 10-yard zone; if the team has four, then two are placed in each zone.

1. The aim is to strike the ball from one's own half of the field to the goalkeeper *at the opposite end*. If he catches the ball before it bounces, the team is awarded 2 points. (This is difficult, as the pass will be at least 40 yards [37 meters], and it should not be attempted unless the player with the ball has plenty of time and space. The coach needs to work with players on correct decision making. The team should not be constantly forcing long passes down the field.)

2. If a team gets the ball past the halfway line, then puts together five consecutive passes in the opponent's half, it scores 1 point. The team should keep passing, since another point is awarded for each set of five consecutive passes.

3. When the opposition wins the ball back, the first team must now defend.

TARGET PLAY

FOCUS

Practicing passing skills involving a specific target.

PROCEDURE

This drill is executed in an area measuring 30 by 10 yards (27 by 9 meters) with either a 4v2, 2v2, or 3v3 game in the box (numbers depend on ability levels). Two additional target players, T1 and T2, are placed at the end and outside of the box. The aim is simply for one side to keep the ball by passing, and to get the ball into targets T1 and T2 as quickly and as efficiently as possible. A team should not use four passes if two will suffice. Players must make good decisions about when to play short and when to play long into the target. Once a target player has received the ball, the team should go in the opposite direction, toward the other target player. If the defenders win the ball, the game can be restarted by simply playing the ball to a target, and the game begins again.

VARIATIONS

The numbers and spacing of this activity can be changed depending on ability level. It can work just as well in a 30-by-15-yard (27-by-14-meter) area with a 5v3 attack-to-defense ratio. Normally, defenders are rotated and changed after a set period of time so that each player gets an equal amount of time defending and attacking.

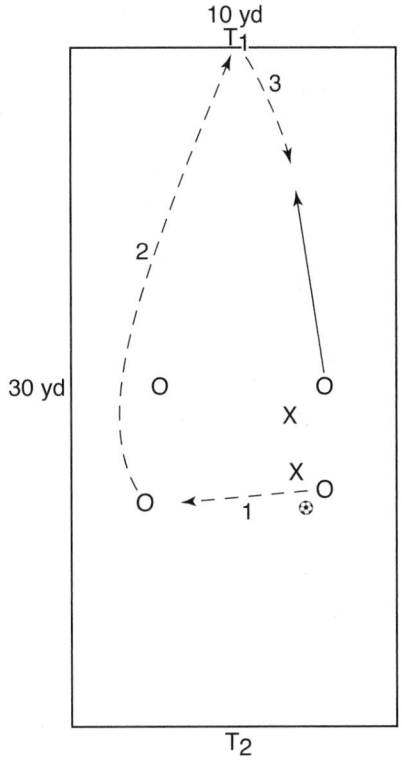

FOUR-TARGET GAME

FOCUS

Developing decision-making ability—whether to make a shorter or longer pass, and whether or not to support the ball.

PROCEDURE

The area of play measures 40 by 30 yards (37 by 27 meters). The drill works well with 12 players, with 6 working on passing and the remaining 6 acting as targets and support players. The object is to get the ball to the target's feet without making her move more than a couple of yards (or meters) from the corner.

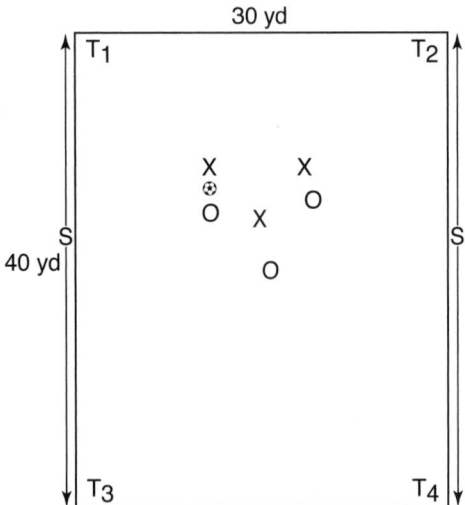

1. The Xs play toward targets T1 and T2, and the Os move toward T3 and T4.

2. The support players (S) stay outside the playing area but move up and down the sidelines, always supporting the team with the ball. Thus the game always pits five attackers against three defenders.

3. If T1 receives the ball from the Xs, a point is scored and the ball is then played by T1 across the grid to T2, who puts the ball in play to the O team.

VARIATION

One variation of this drill allows the team scoring the point to keep the ball when it is put back into play by T2. They now attack in the opposite direction, toward T3 and T4. The purpose is to ask players to be technically capable of playing a 30-yard (27-meter) ball into a target player rather than always playing the easier and safer ball of 10 yards (9 meters) to a support player—and especially to practice making good decisions about when to play short and when to play long.

ATTACKING THE DEFENSIVE WEAK SIDE

FOCUS

Practicing freeing a player by spinning off the wall.

PROCEDURE

O1 and O2 stand next to the ball for the free kick. O3 stands on the end of the wall farthest away from the goal, on the weak side.

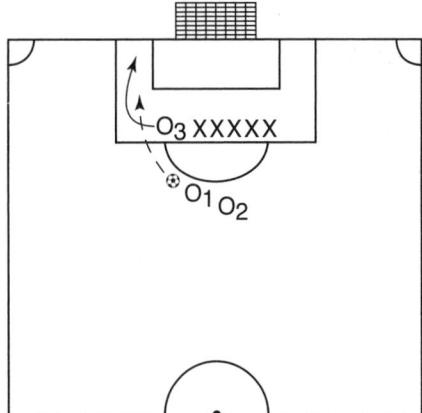

1. O3 spins off the wall and runs into the weak side space.

2. Either O1 or O2 plays the free kick into that area.

3. O3 can either cross or shoot.

FLANK OVERLAP

FOCUS

Practicing overlapping from a free kick.

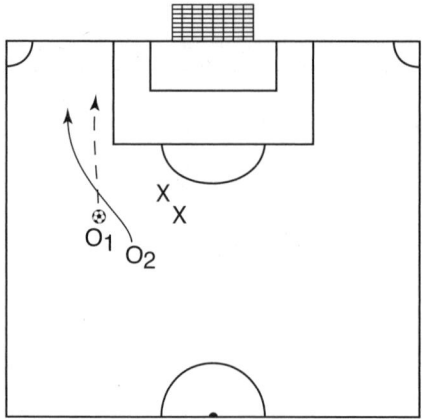

PROCEDURE

A similar concept to the previous drill but from a wing position.

1. O2 runs over the ball on the free kick and runs into space instead of crossing into the box as expected.

2. O1 passes the ball into this space. O2 can cross or shoot.

DECEPTIVE METHODS FOR FREE KICKS

FOCUS

Complicating free kicks.

PROCEDURE

It is best if this type of drill (or set play) is practiced on the game field itself, using its normal markings. This drill should be practiced a few yards outside the penalty box and slightly to the left or right of center.

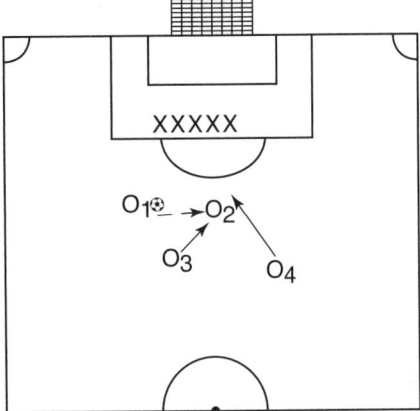

1. O1 passes ball to O2.

2. O2 stops the ball with the sole of his foot as if to suggest that O3 will shoot the ball.

3. O2 rolls the ball backward with the sole of his foot to O4 who comes in late to shoot the ball.

"PICK" THROW IN

FOCUS

Practicing releasing a player free to receive the ball from a throw in.

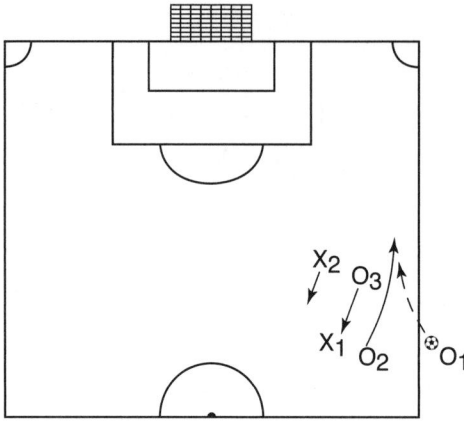

PROCEDURE

Start on the game field with three offensive players: One to throw the ball, one to receive it, and one to defend. After successfully practicing the drill this way, it should then be performed in 11v11 game play.

1. O3 throws the ball down the line; O2 runs to the ball.

2. O3 checks back toward O2 and sets a "pick," or blocks defender X1, thus releasing O2.

LONG THROW IN

FOCUS

Providing a goal-scoring opportunity from a throw-in situation.

PROCEDURE

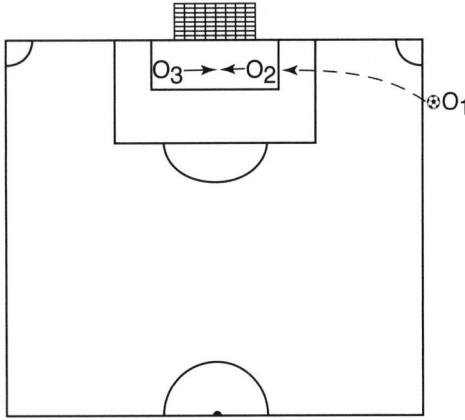

1. O1, who needs a long throw capability, throws the ball as close to near post distance as he can.

2. O2 posts up at that point and flicks the ball on toward the goal with his head.

3. O3 begins outside the far post and runs midgoal late and fast to receive the "helped" ball from O2.

BALL MOVING AWAY FROM AND TOWARD SHOOTER

FOCUS

Practicing shooting technique with maximum efficiency.

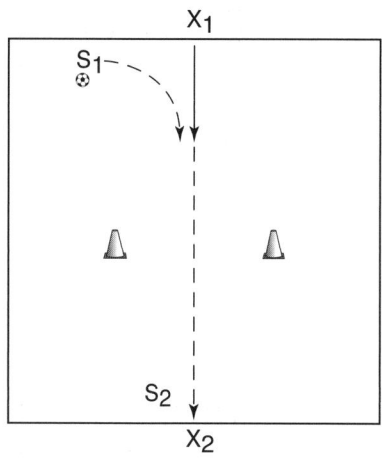

PROCEDURE

Players stand in pairs on either side of a mini goal marked by cones or flags. The distance away from the cones may be determined by the ability of the players. The better the player the further away. A distance of about 20 yards (18 meters) might be a good starting point with the cones or "goal" about 2 yards apart. One support player stands near each goal.

The support player serves the ball. The X player approaches the ball and shoots through cones or corner flags stuck in the ground to form a goal. This allows players to get plenty of shooting practice, and each can stop the ball after his partner has shot, thus shooting the ball back in his direction.

VARIATIONS

The drill can be made harder by adding defensive pressure or varying how the ball is served (e.g., on the ground or on the bounce). Players may also proceed to shooting at a full-sized goal with goalkeepers.

PRACTICE SHOOTING WITH MINIMAL STANDING

FOCUS

Practicing shooting technique.

PROCEDURE

Balls are fed from players who are lined each up at side of the field about 15 yards (14 meters) away from the shooter. The player who is in the front of this line will pass the ball to the shooter who is in front of the goal approximately 15 yards from the goal. He will then follow his pass so that he becomes the next shooter, and the player who has just shot the ball will join the end of that passing line. Both sides can go simultaneously as each shooter is going to opposite goals and should not get in each other's way. This will keep the practice moving, minimize standing, and offer every player plenty of shooting opportunities.

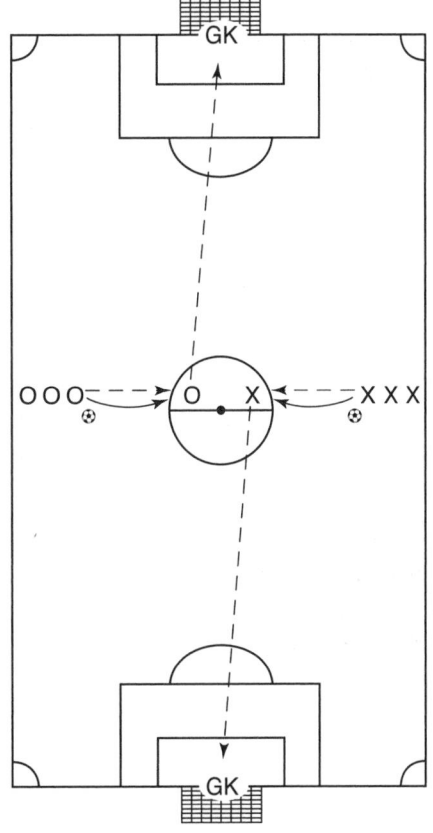

VARIATIONS

The easiest ball to handle is one received with the back foot (farthest from the passed ball, ensuring that the receiver is opened up). This would always be the right foot, since the ball is being served from the left side. The receiver should open up and shoot with her right foot. The drill can be reversed by keeping everything the same but asking the shooter to turn with the ball and shoot at the other goal. Many variations can be made by asking players to use different feet and turn in different directions (e.g., cutting the ball back with one foot and shooting with the other, or letting the ball roll past and then turning with the ball to shoot at the other goal). Balls can be passed on the ground, on the bounce, or in the air.

PRESSURE TRAINING FOR SHOOTING

FOCUS

Performing skills quickly, with no rest between serves of the ball, to encourage players to react instinctively.

PROCEDURE

Four servers stand in the corners of the penalty box, each with as many balls as possible. It helps to have ball retrievers standing behind the goal to get balls back to the servers efficiently.

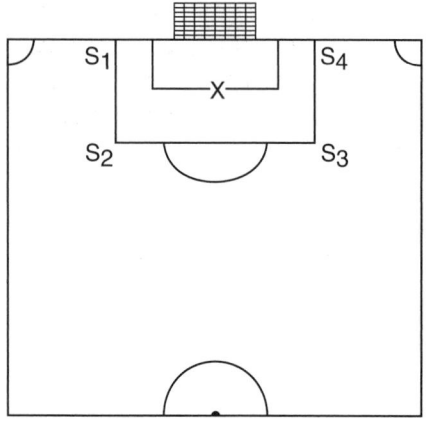

1. S1 begins the process by passing a ball to X, who receives it and shoots after one or two touches.

2. S2, S3, and S4 each pass the ball to X in turn. The timing is such that X never has the opportunity to stop or rest, and the drill does require a good number of balls to keep it going for any length of time.

Depending on the age and fitness level of the player, 2 minutes in the middle will likely be more than enough.

VARIATIONS

The drill can be varied by changing the height and speed of the passes and making the receiver use different parts of the body to control the ball.

GAME TRAINING FOR SHOOTING

FOCUS

Putting shooting into a realistic game situation.

PROCEDURE

This drill is played 5v5, with goalkeepers and full-size goals in a 30-by-20-yard (27-by-18-meter) area. Each team has three defenders and two attackers, none of whom can cross the halfway line (defenders must stay in their half of the box, and attackers must stay in the opponent's half). The sides play a regular game, with every player encouraged to shoot at every opportunity. Forwards can turn and shoot, but the game is more successful if they act as target players and drop the ball back to a teammate in the defensive half, who then tries to shoot. Players should work on angles and quick play. Defenders need to close quickly on the ball in order to prevent unrealistically easy shots. The coach can add conditions such as one- or two-touch limits.

MIDDLE THIRD GAME

FOCUS

Passing balls through different parts of the field.

PROCEDURE

The length of the field of play is from the edge of each penalty box (about 80 yards [73 meters] long), with the width 44 yards (40 meters) marked by extending the edge of penalty box outward parallel with the sidelines. Cones are used to divide the field into equal thirds, and two teams are formed for 8v8 play, with each team placing three players in the defensive third, three in the middle third, and two in the attacking third. Players are not allowed to leave their designated areas.

1. The goalkeeper throws the ball out to one of the wide defenders.

2. The defender is required to play the ball "down the channel" to the feet of the nearest forward in the attacking third. It is sometimes necessary to allow the forward to receive the ball by coming into the middle third (the defender is not allowed to follow) to stop the defender cheating by getting in front of the forward too early denying service to his feet. However, she must *begin* in the attacking third when the ball is played.

3. The forward plays the ball into the middle third to a supporting midfield player, who then plays it back into the attacking third.

As the play develops, it is often necessary for the coach to encourage players to switch the ball from side to side in both the defending and middle thirds before playing it forward.

VARIATIONS

1. To make this game a little more realistic, the coach can allow one attacking player to move from one third into the next, but only when he does *not* have the ball. The drill will not work well if a player is allowed to dribble through zones as this will defeat the object of the drill, which is to pass into the zones. This is excellent work for the two forward ("target") players, who have to learn how to play with their backs to the goal and hold the ball to allow support to arrive.

2. Ask the goalkeeper to throw the ball out to her defenders, but this time to any one of the three. The ball must be played into a target in the middle third of the field, switched, then played into the attacking third. This will force players to work on developing a play directly through the middle third. It is not a bad idea to stress a short-short-long philosophy when playing out of the back.

3. Open up the game to allow creativity and improvisation, with players asked to work the ball through any third they prefer, in any order. The coach should keep encouraging players to switch the play from side to side and play balls forward into targets.

MIDDLE THIRD PASSING

FOCUS

Developing the skill of playing through crowded areas in the middle part of the field.

PROCEDURE

An 8v8 game is played in an area measuring about 80 by 40 yards (73 by 37 meters). The playing area is divided into thirds, and all 16 players begin in the middle third.

1. The goalkeeper starts with the ball and either throws it out directly to his team in the middle third or gives it to a player who has come out of the middle third into his defensive area (no attacker is allowed to follow). Everybody else must remain in the middle third, with the exception of the defender getting the ball from the goalkeeper. If play begins this way, the defender who first receives the ball must pass it to a team-mate in the middle third; the defender is not allowed to dribble into the middle.

2. Once possession is gained, the team with the ball needs to pass it in the middle third, attempting to play it to an open player—a difficult task in this crowded area.

3. Once a player has received the ball in the middle third with enough space and time, he should pass it into the attacking third. If the pass is too direct, the goalkeeper will easily intercept, so the ball should be played diagonally where possible. No attacking player is allowed into the attacking third until the ball is passed into it.

4. One attacker may then run to the pass and be joined by a teammate. At this point, no defenders are allowed to follow, and the attackers should attempt to score a goal against the goalkeeper. No more than two attackers are allowed.

A touch limitation is recommended here—possibly one touch, or at least a one-touch finish Otherwise it becomes too unrealistic.

SHADOW PLAY

FOCUS

Developing a team style of play; teaching patterns of play, so that each player recognizes variations of when and where to pass the ball, how to attack and defend as a team, and, in general, what style of attacking play the coach wants the team to execute.

PROCEDURE

The drill involves all 11 players on a full field, with no opposition.

1. Play begins at the back, with a ball played to the back defenders. The coach then goes through the various ways in which the team is going to play the ball forward and attack the opposition's goal. It is sometimes helpful to work in thirds of the field, focusing first on how players are going to play the ball out of their defensive third (and to whom they are going to try to play it), then moving to the middle third, and finally the attacking third. In this format, the coach can show players where to run, where to support, when to play short passes, and when to play long, without the disruption caused by defenders.

2. The team should then go down the field and try to score a goal by incorporating all the patterns of play encouraged by the coach. At some point, it will be necessary to bring in defenders, which of course makes the task considerably more difficult, but the attacking players will at least have developed an idea of what they are trying to do as a team.

CHAPTER 4

Defending Skills and Tactics

Good defensive play is a must. Neglect this area of play at your peril! Many very good attacking players are eventually unsuccessful at a higher level because they have neglected the defensive side of the game. Very few teams have room for one-dimensional players; even a creative attacking player will be called upon to defend. Manchester United star Cristiano Ronaldo, recognized by many as the most exciting attacking player in the world, struggled initially because he was not good enough defensively. At the higher levels of soccer, games and championships tend to be won by well-organized defending rather than good attacking. Coaches are happier with a 1-0 win than a 2-1 win.

Good team defense requires all players to defend and to be proficient at both individual and team defense. Becoming a truly accomplished defender requires strength, courage, and discipline. It is unrealistic to expect all players to have all of these qualities, especially being brave in the tackle, but everyone on the team has a part to play. All players should at least be able to pressure the ball and shape the play so that defending becomes easier and more predictable for the defensive specialists behind them. Simple defensive pressure applied at the right time and place can often force the opposing team to give up the ball. Indeed, efficient defenses regularly win the ball by taking advantage of the other team's mistakes, without ever having to win it in a tackle.

This chapter covers the fundamentals of individual defending, then puts them in the context of team defending. This chapter stresses the importance of sound defensive principles for all players, not just defenders. (Note: Goalkeeping is not covered because it is such a specialized topic. I suggest *The Soccer Goalkeeper, Second Edition*, by Joseph A. Luxbacher and Gene Klein, 2002, Human Kinetics.)

Individual Defending Skills

Individual defending requires good 1v1 play and a good understanding of basic defensive principles. Defending requires far more than being tough and determined; it also demands intelligence and tactical awareness. Good positioning is crucial—the ability to pressure the ball at the right place and time will often suffice. Another vital role for defenders is to block crosses and shots. This requires no great technique—just being brave enough and close enough to block the ball—but it is sometimes difficult to encourage right and left defensive backs to get close enough to the ball to prevent it from being crossed into the box. Defenders who can do this are already well on their way to being successful. If this skill is combined with sound tackling ability and tactical awareness, then a player has the ingredients to be a good defender. If he is athletic to boot, then he is probably going to be a great defender.

The rest of this section looks first at individual defending skills (tackling, making recovery runs, pressuring, and tracking and marking), then at defensive principles, which apply to all defensive situations regardless of the technique used.

Tackling

The skill must be mastered by anyone who wishes to play effective defense. It is not always essential for attacking players, but even they need to be somewhat efficient. It is not the technique of tackling that is difficult, but the when, where, and timing of the tackle. To tackle successfully, a player must do as follows:

- Tackle from the front (figure 4.1 on page 71).
- Keep body weight low.
- Avoid stretching for the ball (the nontackling foot should be kept relatively close to the ball).
- Tackle through the ball with the side of the foot.

Tackling requires patience. It is normally a big mistake for defenders to go flying in at the first opportunity, because a good attacking player may use the defender's excessive forward momentum to play the ball by him. This approach also risks unnecessary fouls, since the defender cannot control his tackle.

Two developments in contemporary soccer put a premium on using prudence in tackling. First, as soccer has evolved in this country, the level of play has gotten better and better, with many more good youth players coming through to the higher

Figure 4.1 Front block tackle.

ranks. This evolution has created more parity between teams and, as a result, much closer games. Second, many teams in today's game gear their attack to set plays, which provide their best opportunity to score. Thus it is crucial that defenders do not give away silly free kicks due to poor tackling technique. Defenders need to be absolutely sure they can win the ball before trying to tackle, and even then they should do so only if they have defensive support behind them in the form of a covering defender. Poor decision making by defenders who are impatient in trying to win back the ball often leads to free kicks being given to the opponent in a dangerous area of the field. Players should try to win the ball in a tackle only if they are in position to get a clean strike at the ball. Any contact with the opponent's body before striking the ball will normally result in a free kick.

Defenders also need to take into consideration numerical advantage before deciding to tackle. The rule of thumb for defenders is this: If there are more attackers than defenders, don't tackle; simply retreat toward your own goal and protect your back. For the most part, defenders should not be drawn into tackles far upfield. Defenders who are in the opponent's half of the field should be thinking more of getting back to their own half than trying to win the ball in a tackle. That area of the field should be left to other players to defend.

A defender's angle of approach to a tackle is also vital; ideally, it should be from the front. Tackling from the side is very difficult, and from the back it is almost impossible without giving a foul away. Players must position themselves appropriately on the field so that they can approach from the front, and they need to do so as early as possible—*before* the ball is played to their opponent.

Recovery Runs

Most players understand that the closest player to the ball is the one who should challenge for it. But what about the rest of the players? What are they supposed to do? Clearly, standing and watching is not the answer. Once a player understands that she cannot effectively defend unless she is goalside of the ball, she will then grasp the necessity of recovering from a position on

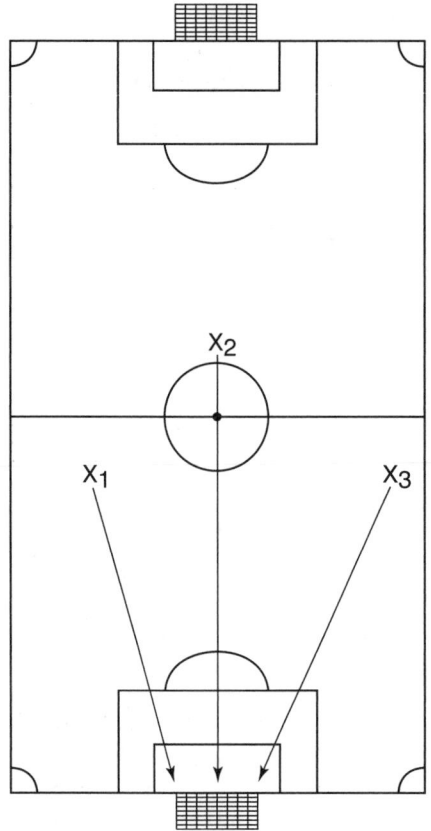

Figure 4.2 Recovery runs at an angle toward their own goal.

the wrong side of the ball. Recovery runs require effort, discipline, vision, and fitness. A player's inability to do them is often the reason that teams defend poorly. If the ball has been played past a defender, then his first responsibility to his team is to get into a position behind, or goalside to, the ball so that he can defend. If out on the wings, he needs to run back toward his own near post. If in the middle, he needs to recover toward the middle of the goal. He needs to recover downfield at these angles only until he has gotten to the goal side of the ball. At that point, he should stop and assess the situation, then decide how best to help the team defend. Figure 4.2 gives ideas for how and in which direction to recover.

Pressuring

This technique needs to be mastered by *all* players. Although forwards and midfield players are not necessarily expected to be able to win the ball in a tackle, they do need to be able to effectively pressure the ball. One must first get in behind the ball to be able to defend it. So the requirement is this: When out of position and not involved in the play, a player should recover backward toward her own goal, where she will be in a better position to pressure the ball.

Ideally, defenders should attempt to pressure the ball as soon as the opposing player receives it. To be able to do this, the defender needs to position himself near enough to his opponent that he can arrive at the same time the ball does. The attacking player will have his head down to receive the pass and quick pressure on him prevents him from getting his head up to look for teammates to pass to. The defender must be careful, however, not to get too close to the attacking player *before* the ball arrives. Though this may seem like a good idea—making it easier to defend and pressure the ball—in reality the ball is likely to be passed beyond the defender, allowing the attacker to run past the defender and on to the ball.

Once the opponent receives the ball, good pressure then requires being close enough to the ball so that if the opponent mishandles it, the defender can take it. More often than not, this is sufficient, negating the need to tackle. Good pressure also denies the attacking player an easy opportunity to play the ball forward.

Tracking and Marking Players

This work requires discipline, concentration, and physical and mental maturity. For any player to track an opponent, he needs good vision and awareness of activity away from the ball. It takes hard work and much coaching for players to develop constant awareness of what is happening away from the ball and to be capable of tracking attackers who are making good runs off the ball.

Marking principles are relatively easy to master. Defenders should be goalside of the opponent, and *between* the opponent and their own goal. In figure 4.3, X1, X2, and X3 are all in this relationship, and the farther

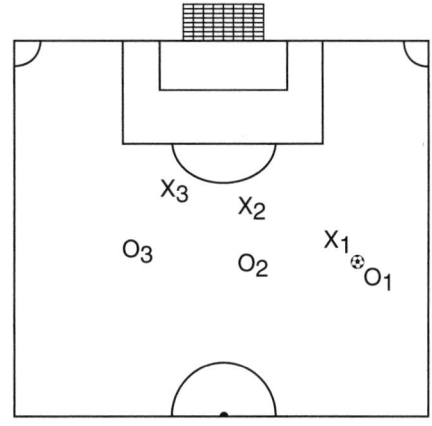

Figure 4.3 Correct marking placement.

they are from the ball, the farther they are from the opponent they are marking. Hence X1 is close to O1, X2 is farther from O2, and X3 is still farther from O3.

Tracking players is not so simple. Even when defenders are goalside of the ball, good attacking play and movement is likely to make their job difficult. It is the job of defensive players to mark their immediate opponent by positioning themselves so that they can quickly move to him should he receive the ball. Most young players understand how to mark their opponent but can quickly become confused when that opponent runs in behind them or makes diagonal runs across the field. Should they follow or should they stay? Have they even seen the run in the first place? Defenders who watch the ball at the exclusion of their opponent are likely to fail to see an opponent's forward run. Thus they must avoid exclusive ball watching and try to see both ball and opponent. An open body position facing downfield will help. Ball watchers tend to close their body and turn toward the ball, limiting their field of vision and often allowing them to see only the ball.

A defender will always feel comfortable when his opposite number remains in his set position (e.g., right wing, left midfield), but once the attack moves away from these positions the defender needs to understand how to mark his player, especially if the attacker is making cross-field or penetrating runs. Marking players who make runs without the ball requires defenders to be capable of tracking opponents. It will normally be necessary to follow or track the opponent until she moves into a position where she will no longer be able to receive the ball—in most cases, the wide areas of the wing. It is often possible to "pass on" the player you are tracking to another defender who does not have an opponent to mark, especially if the opponent is making a diagonal run. Good verbal communication is a must. Runs to an area in the back of defenders are more dangerous and much harder to track. Defenders dare not let attackers go unmarked. For defenders to track attackers effectively, they must keep goalside of the attacker, and in order to do this they must keep their opponent and the ball in view. Doing this while running at speed is difficult and requires much practice.

Marking players who have possession of the ball is, in many respects, much easier for the defender. Once a defender has taken responsibility and pressurized the player he is marking, he must stay with that player until the player either loses or passes the ball. The defender cannot allow the opponent to get away; he must stick to the task of following him, always remaining close enough to take the ball should he lose control.

Individual Defending Principles

There are four main principles a defender needs to understand in order to become a more accomplished defender. Ideally, the defender should deny the attacking player the opportunity to get the ball in the first place by intercepting it. Since this is not always possible, the defender must position himself to stop the attacker from turning with the ball and facing forward to run at him. Should this not be possible, then he must at least position himself to quickly pressure the ball. Finally, the defender needs to consider sending the attacking player in a defined direction, most often away from goal.

Deny the attacker the ball   Wherever possible, a defender should try to intercept the pass so that the attacking player never receives the ball. This is the simplest way to win the ball back. However, a defenders must be sure he can get to the ball first. If he miscalculates and misses the ball, the forward will be through on goal with little worry about the defender getting back to help. Thus he must be absolutely positive he can intercept the pass.

Stop the attacker from turning with the ball   If a defender fails to deny the attacker the ball, he may receive the pass with his back to the goal. The defender's job then is to stop that player from turning with the ball and facing forward (figure 4.4). Once the defending player has positioned himself to challenge for the ball, he must be

Figure 4.4   Stopping the attacker turning with the ball.

sure to watch the ball and not the player—that is, he must react to the movement of the ball rather than that of the player. In his challenge he must neither get so close to the attacking player that he cannot see the ball nor stand so far away that he cannot get a foot to the ball when the attacking player turns. Ideal position is usually 2 to 3 feet (about three-quarters of a meter) away from the attacker. The defender's body position should be low, with legs flexed or comfortably bent. Maintaining a low center of gravity helps not only in the tackle but also in balance and body adjustment, which is often necessary to counter the feints and deceptions of the attacking player.

When the attacking player has received the ball and the defender has moved into the correct position, the defender should concentrate and be patient, waiting for the right time to challenge. If he challenges for the ball too quickly, he is likely to foul the attacking player or overcommit on the tackle. The correct moment to tackle is when the attacker attempts to turn with the ball, because this is when he is most vulnerable. He can no longer protect the ball with his body, and his balance is not at its best.

Keep the play in front of oneself If an attacker does manage to turn with the ball, the defender's next task is to keep the player and the ball in front of him. Patience is needed to resist trying to win the ball too soon. When keeping the play in front of himself, the defender must decide when and where to put correct pressure on the ball, thus preventing the opponent from playing forward passes, crossing, or shooting on goal. Positioning is crucial. The defender not only needs to be goalside of the attacker, but also positioned in a direct line between the attacking player and the goal or passing target (figures 4.5 and 4.6).

The defending team can often win the ball back without tackling, simply by pressuring the ball. Defenders can apply good pressure by being quick to the ball and making up most of the distance to the forward who is receiving the ball while the ball is still in flight. As the defender approaches the player receiving the ball, he should take an angle that places himself between the opponent and his potential target, especially if the target is the goal. This helps deny the opportunity for that player to have an easy pass or shot on goal. When the pressuring defender is within a couple of yards (about 1.5 meters) of the attacker, he should slow down and creep forward. Failing to do this will probably result in overcommitting and being unable to stop in time. The defender should also watch the ball, as good attackers will try to wrong-foot defenders with swerves and feints. The defender should keep body weight low, which makes for a better

Figure 4.5 Correct position for tackle in relationship to the goal or potential passing target.

Figure 4.6 Incorrect position for tackle in relationship to the goal or potential passing target.

Figure 4.7 Sending a player down the line.

tackling position and allows the defender to turn more quickly should the forward knock the ball beyond him. He should have one foot forward and the other back, again allowing for a quicker turn and also helping him send the forward in a preferred direction.

Send the play in a certain direction When a defender cannot keep the play in front of him, it may be necessary to force the play to keep going in one direction, often down the sideline and away from the goal, but sometimes across the field (figure 4.7). By forcing the ball in a defined direction, the defender makes the play more predictable for the rest of his team. Support players and covering defenders then have a much better idea where the ball is going to go and can move into better position to help defend their goal. It's normally better for defenders on the wing to send the play down their sideline, which makes a direct attack on goal much more difficult since the ball is being forced away from goal. It also limits the attacker's passing options, and the defender can more easily receive help from teammates since they can better predict the attack.

Team Defending Tactics

Once a player is behind the ball and understands the fundamentals of defending—when and where to tackle, pressure, or force the play—the team is ready to defend. Correctly positioned players will be able to challenge for the ball, intercept passes, or pick up "loose" or "free" balls. The next concern for player and coach is putting these defensive skills to use in tactical team play. There are many different ways a team can defend, and these decisions are left up to the coach. The important thing is that all players understand their roles and responsibilities in the coach's tactical approach so that they are defending as a unit, not just in ones and twos.

This section covers team shape and the defense of key areas of the field, as well as how a coach should create a defensive system. One principle of team defense that doesn't need its own section is the numbers game, which is pretty simple: The defending team needs to have at least as many players around the ball as the attackers do, and preferably one more. Defending with numbers is vital and cannot be done unless players make the required recovery runs to stay compact rather than being overstretched. The numbers game is also integral to the other principles of team defense.

Photo courtesy of Willis Glasgow/WG Sports Photos.

Becoming a truly accomplished defender requires strength, courage, discipline, and determination to win the ball.

Team Shape

Good defending requires the team to be compact, with players spaced evenly over the field of play, especially around the ball. It's impossible for players to cover all of the field all the time—there is just too much space—and if they try to do so the team will get stretched, leaving large spaces between defenders and making it easier for attacking players to get positioned between them with enough space to avoid being quickly pressured. This, in turn, enables them to pass the ball out of trouble with relative ease. The correct positioning of the defending team's players is known as team shape. Good shape enables defenders to apply quick pressure as an opponent gets the ball and to pick up loose or second balls (i.e., balls that rebound unintentionally off of a teammate or an opposing player), and also allows them to limit the space between themselves, making it difficult for opponents to penetrate.

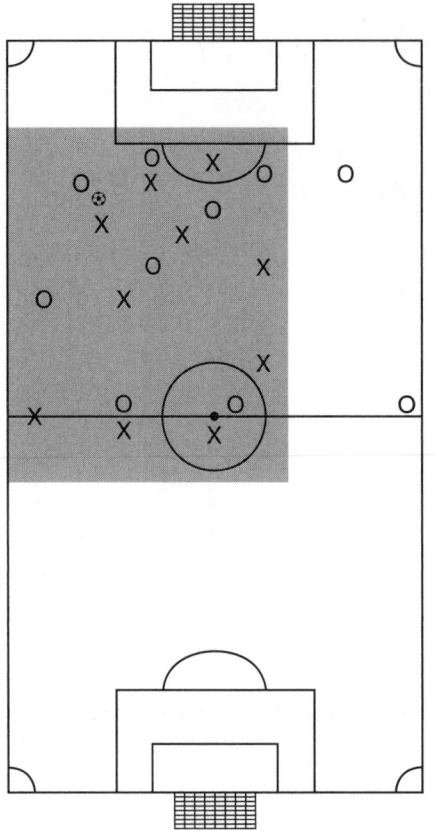

Figure 4.8 Sectional defending allows the defenders to cover less space.

Even with the best-laid plans, good team shape is not always a simple matter. Good attacking play and movement off the ball will often pull defenders out of position and make it very difficult to remain compact. If spaces develop between defending players and become too big, the defending team will have problems. The key is to have players recognize such spaces and fill them so that problematic holes do not develop. Defenders must not ball-watch! It makes recognition of shape problems even more difficult. Defenders must pay attention to what is happening "off the ball" and try their best to fill spots vacated by defenders who are tracking opposing forwards.

Figure 4.8 shows that by pressuring the ball as a team and remaining compact, the X defenders need to defend only the shaded area. The areas of the field left open are those that are least dangerous and would be most difficult to get the ball into. The shaded area shifts in relationship to the ball. As the ball moves downfield or across it, the shaded area moves as a block in the same compact manner along with the ball. Thus it is always very difficult for the opposition to play successfully out of this block. The key to success in using this method is to ensure that there is always quick pressure on the player with the ball, preventing him from ever getting his head up quickly enough to find passing opportunities outside the defensive block.

Key Areas of the Field

It is necessary to defend all over the field, but certain areas are most important. Defending the penalty area is a must. To do so, defenders need to be first to the ball, and when the ball is played into the box, they must know where the opponent is, concentrate on winning the space *in front* of him, and positively attack the ball. Determination and courage are essential, and when there is no teammate available to pass to, defenders should play the ball long, high, and wide.

When playing the ball long, a defender should always try to get distance on the clearance. Playing the ball well down the field will always relieve a team from pressure, if only temporarily. If the ball cannot be played long, then it should be played high. Defenders are much better off getting height on their clearance than trying to clear the ball on the ground. Playing a ball as high as possible gives defenders time to get into position regardless of where the ball goes. When all else fails, at least get the ball wide. Any poor clearance into central positions will increase the opponent's ability to score, whereas it is very difficult to score directly from a wide position.

In addition to defending the penalty box, it's critical that a team defend in its own half of the field. This is where defenders must get quick pressure on the ball and make sure that they mark and track any opponents in the area. The defending team needs to get as many players as possible back in behind the ball when it is in their half of the field, then keep the ball and the play in front of themselves. Many teams will try to defend in the opponent's half of the field, but the higher up the field they defend, the more difficult it is to remain compact, especially if the defensive unit stays back.

Creating a Defensive System

Creating a defensive style is both difficult and time consuming, with both players and coaches needing to contemplate many different factors before deciding on how best to defend. A team's system will depend on what formation it is playing. For example, playing with three forwards would require a much different defensive approach from playing with only one. Using three forwards might encourage a team to defend much higher up the field, since there are enough players available to put pressure on the defenders and perhaps deny them the opportunity to pass the ball upfield. Playing with only one forward, on the other hand, would likely require defending more toward the halfway line.

A team's system might also depend on the ability of the players—their level of play and their athleticism. A quick, athletic team might be encouraged to play a high-pressure game, trying to force opponents into errors. The system might even change in relationship to the opponent's skill level. A team might defend much higher up the field against a weak opponent in an attempt to force mistakes in their half of the field. Here are three factors that coaches and players need to consider in deciding the team's style of defending:

Should the team use high or low pressure? High pressure involves going after the ball in every part of the field, especially in the opponent's defensive third immediately after they get the ball. This type of defending requires all players to be active, especially those in the immediate vicinity of the ball. It will not work if only one or two players are quickly pressuring the ball, while the rest of the team is back watching from a distance.

If a team can make this style of defending work, the rewards are extremely high, because the ball can often be won back in great attacking position with a good opportunity to score a goal. High-pressure tactics are recommended when the opposition is technically fairly weak and can easily be forced into mistakes that create goal-scoring chances for the defending team. In addition, a team that is losing as time grows short might find it necessary to high-pressure the opponent in order to win the ball back well up the field. Even a low-pressure team has to make this change if down a goal late in the match.

Low-pressure defending is, of course, the opposite approach. This method gives opponents their half of the field, letting them bring the ball up the field toward the halfway line without pressure. The responsibility of the defending players here is simply to retreat goalside of the ball until they are in their own half of the field and get numbers behind the ball. This pretty well ensures that the defense is compact, with all 11 players in their own half, which makes penetration very difficult for the opposition. It also prevents the defensive unit from coming too far up the field and thus limits the space behind them, which makes it very difficult for opposing forwards to attack and create goal-scoring opportunities. The low-pressure approach might be used when facing an opponent that is technically superior but might get easily frustrated. It's extremely difficult to break down this type of defense when it is well executed.

Teams usually use a combination of high and low pressure, which means letting the opposition come up the field about 30 to 40 yards (27 to 37 meters) with little opposition, then defending the remaining two-thirds of the field with high pressure. This compromise allows benefits from both styles.

In which direction should the team force the play? As mentioned earlier, defending begins with the forwards. They do not need to be ball winners, but they do need to shape the play and send it in certain directions so that teammates behind them know where the ball is likely to be played. This is referred to as making the play predictable, and it lets teammates anticipate where and who they will need to defend next. Whenever players have to defend smaller segments of the field, it is easier for them.

Forwards typically have two choices: sending the play either outside or inside. In figure 4.9*a*, forward O3 is forcing right back X1 to the outside. This result could also be accomplished by having forward O1 do the same thing. The remaining defenders, especially left back O5 and central defender O6, squeeze the play to the left, anticipating that the ball will be played there. In figure 4.9*b*, O1 sits in the passing lane between X1 and X2, denying the pass and forcing the ball inside. The remaining defenders can react accordingly.

Should the team use zone or man-to-man marking? Man-to-man marking requires a defender to follow her opposite number and defend against her movement in all areas of the field. A coach can clearly define to the defender who she is supposed to mark. This simplifies defending but can easily allow the team's defensive shape to be disrupted as good attacking movement creates holes or spaces in the defense. Defenders will then be pulled into parts of the field they really should not be in as they follow their assigned attackers. A central defender, for example, should not be defending in the wide flank positions. If he is, there is sure to be a gap in the middle that may be exposed by a forward.

Zonal defending requires much more sophistication and player maturity and thus is much more difficult to apply. As the name suggests, a zone is a part of the field where it is the defender's responsibility to mark players who

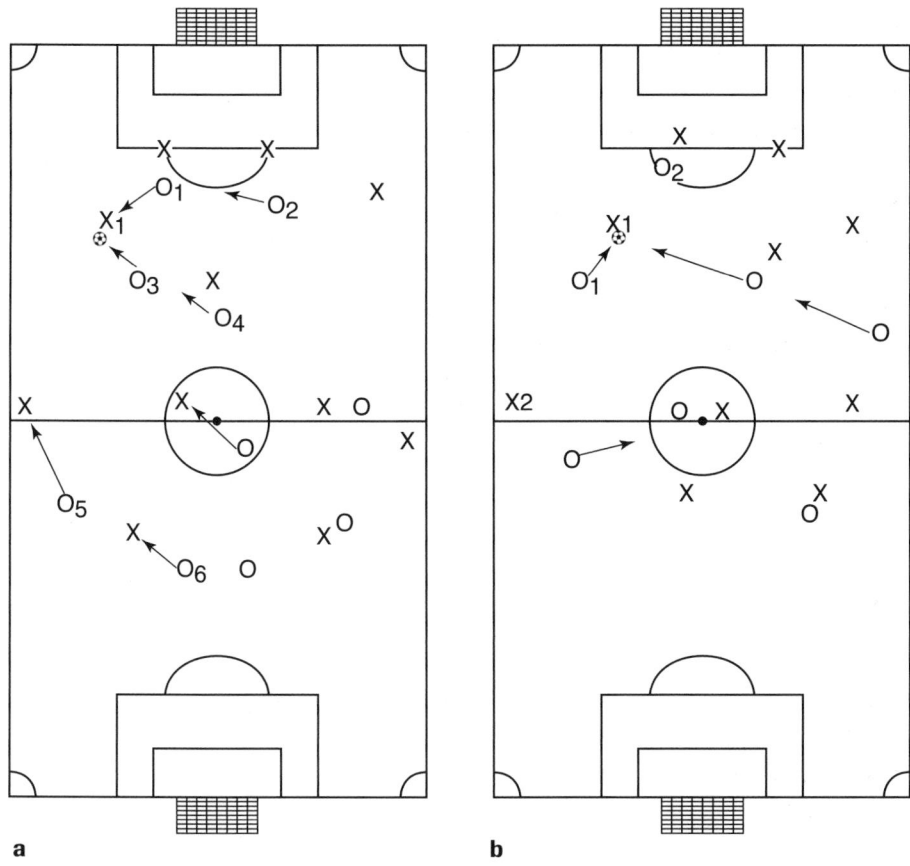

Figure 4.9 Forcing the play: *(a)* forward O3 forces defender to the outside; *(b)* forward O1 forces defender to the inside.

come into his area. It is unnecessary to follow an opponent all over the field, as the defender can release a player to a teammate once he moves out of his zone. The attacker will be picked up by another defender in the next zone. This approach clearly has the advantage of maintaining team shape, but is much more difficult to play, as it requires greater understanding of the game, greater organization, and excellent communication skills. It is also somewhat vulnerable in the seams of the zone and in the split second in which an attacking player is being passed on to her codefender. However, teams that learn to play zonal defense properly are likely to enjoy more success than those playing straight man-to-man.

In figure 4.10*a* on page 82, defender X1 goes to pressure the ball. Attacker O2 makes a diagonal run and is tracked by defender X2. As O2 continues his run, defender X2 must pass that player on to X3, who then continues to track him, allowing X2 to remain in his defensive area and possibly support X1. Communication is a vital part of this process, making sure that O2 is being watched and tracked by somebody at all times. In 4.10*b*, winger X7 is tracking opponent O1 down the left flank. It is not necessary for X7 to follow O1 all the way to her defensive third, because she can release her to defender X2 and thus be available to help defend in the midfield. This principal of passing on opponents to teammates applies mostly when defenders are tracking players who do *not* have the ball. If a defender picks up an attacker who does have the ball, she normally must stay with that player.

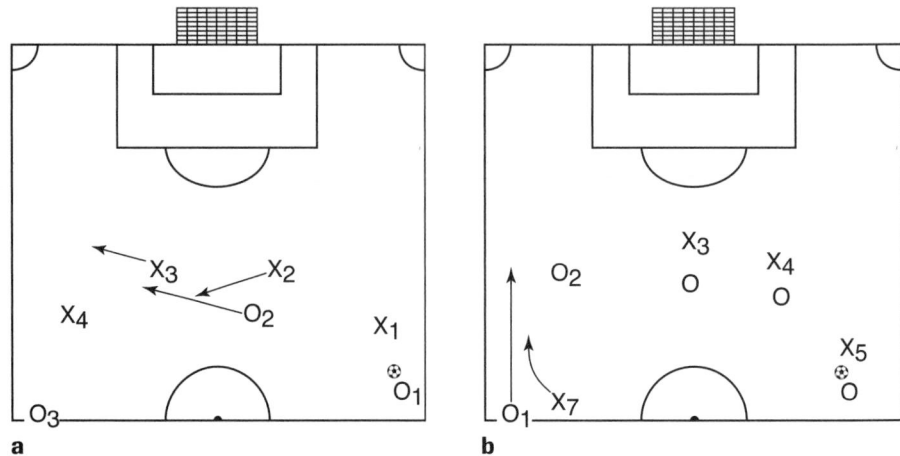

Figure 4.10 Playing zonal defense: *(a)* X2 passes O2 to X3, allowing X2 to support X1; *(b)* X7 tracks O1 down the left flank and then releases to O2.

Without question, it is much easier to play the man-to-man system of marking; therefore, it is more appropriate for most levels of soccer. I believe the advantage for most teams and players is that it assigns each defender a simplified role. At a high level, however, man-to-man marking can cause significant problems, as it leaves gaps that better opponents will exploit. A good compromise is to combine the two systems, playing man-to-man only in certain areas of the field. It can also make sense to make one defender responsible for man-to-man marking while others play a zonal scheme—for example, if the opposition has one especially good player who requires constant attention to limit the damage he might cause then a defender can be assigned to follow him all over the field. Another compromise is to have midfield players man-mark while the defenders zone-mark. This approach simplifies marking for the midfielders, who each match up with their opposite number with a clear directive about their defensive responsibility, and the risk is limited, since gaps created in the midfield are easier to cover and less serious than those at the back of the defense. For the defenders, however, the zonal approach is better since it is more important to avoid being pulled out of defensive position by good forward play. Gaps created here are much more serious than in the midfield.

STOP ATTACKER FROM TURNING

FOCUS

Stopping the attacker from turning with the ball.

PROCEDURE

In a 30-by-10-yard (27-by-9-meter) grid, O1 begins in the middle, with his back to defender X1.

1. S1 serves the ball to O1, who is checking toward the server.

2. X1 tracks and attempts to stop O1 from turning with the ball.

3. O1 attempts to turn with the ball and pass to S2.

4. If he is successful, S2 will now put the ball in play and the roles in the middle are reversed, with X1 checking the ball and O1 stopping him from turning.

Play continues for 2 minutes, then players change roles, with S1 and S2 taking a turn in the middle.

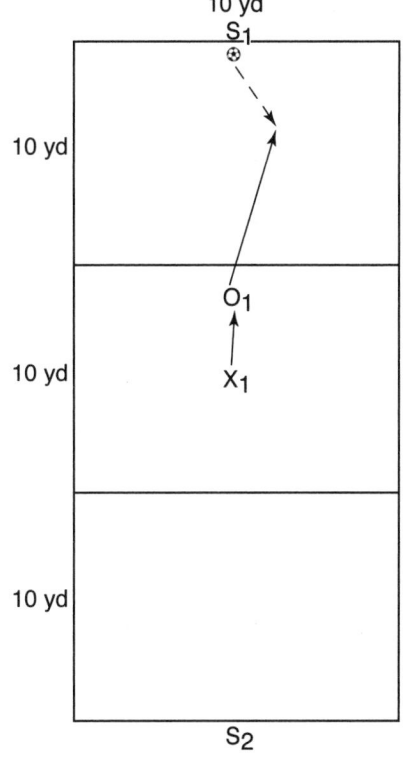

PRESSURE AND TACKLING

FOCUS

Putting quick pressure on the ball; denying the opportunity for attacking players to pass forward.

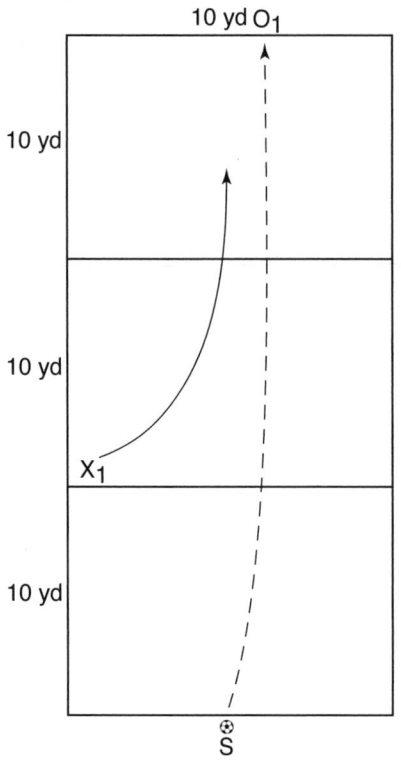

10 yd O$_1$

10 yd

10 yd

10 yd

X$_1$

S

PROCEDURE

In a 30-by-10-yard (27-by-9-meter) grid, S serves the ball on the ground to O1.

1. As soon as the ball is served, X1 moves to pressure and tackle O1, attempting to get to O1 at the same time the ball arrives.

2. O1 attempts to pass the ball back to S, with X1 trying to deny him that opportunity by either tackling or blocking the pass. X1 should attempt to place his body *between* the ball and the target S as quickly as possible. (This is referred to as getting into the passing lane.)

Players rotate roles every 90 seconds.

SENDING AN ATTACKER DOWN THE LINE

FOCUS

Sending an opponent away from the goal and into defined areas of the field.

PROCEDURE

1. S1 serves the ball to O1.
2. X1 approaches O1 at an angle designed to force O1 in one direction only—down the line.
3. O1 attempts to cut back inside so he can dribble the ball through cones placed 1 yard (or meter) apart in the opposite corner. X1 attempts to stop him.

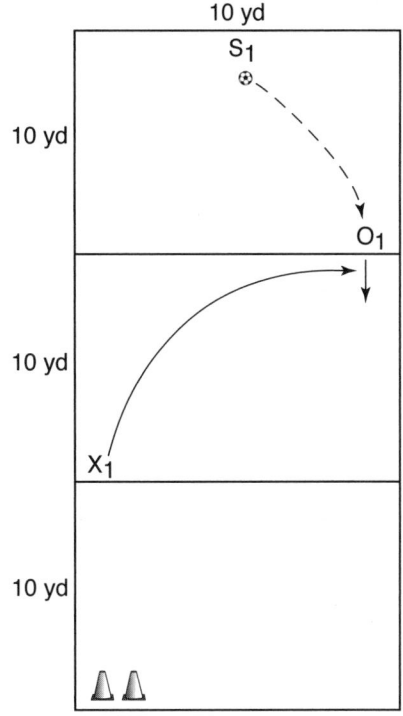

SUPPORT PLAY

FOCUS

Correctly supporting a defender who is pressuring the ball.

PROCEDURE

1. S passes to O1 *(a)*. O1 attempts to dribble the ball through cones placed one yard (or meter) apart in the opposite corner.

2. X1 pressures O1 at an angle that will force O1 down the line and is supported by X2, who positions himself to help X1 by supporting at a near-vertical angle so that he can pressure O1 if necessary.

VARIATION

In step 2, execute the drill so that the support position and approach of X1 and X2 are aligned across the field *(b)*, thus forcing O1 across the field.

Communication between X1 and X2 is vital: X2 should let X1 know which way to send O1.

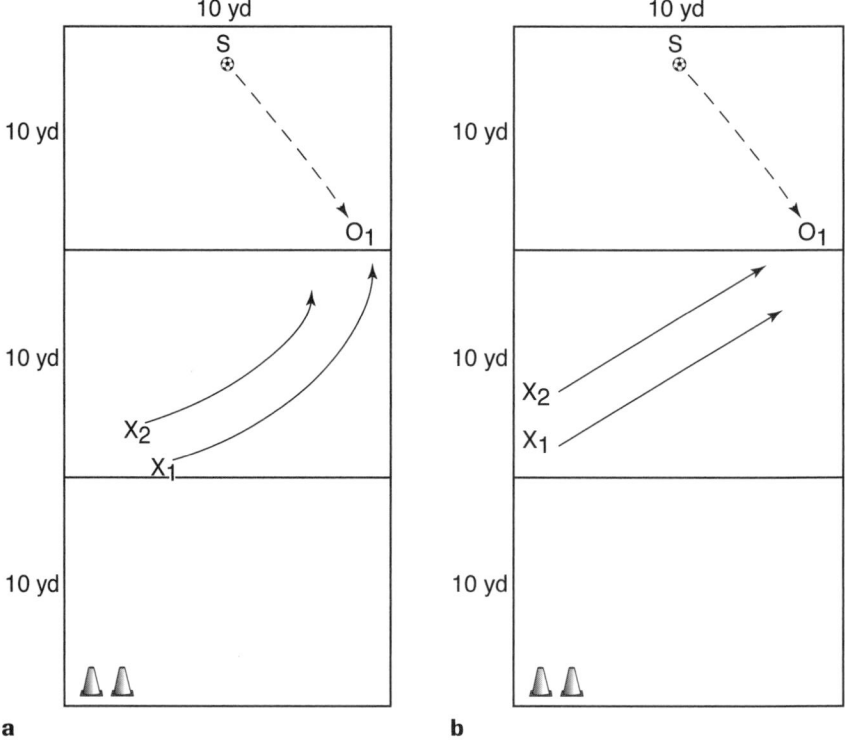

2V2 DRILL

FOCUS

Working on both good pressure of the ball and support play.

PROCEDURE

In a grid measuring 30 by 20 yards (27 by 18 meters), cones are placed 1 yard (or meter) apart on each end line. O1 and O2 play a game against X1 and X2, applying all defensive principles learned. Teams score by passing through the cones. The ball has to be on the ground to score. This drill should then be increased to 3v3 in an area measuring 35 by 25 yards (32 by 23 meters).

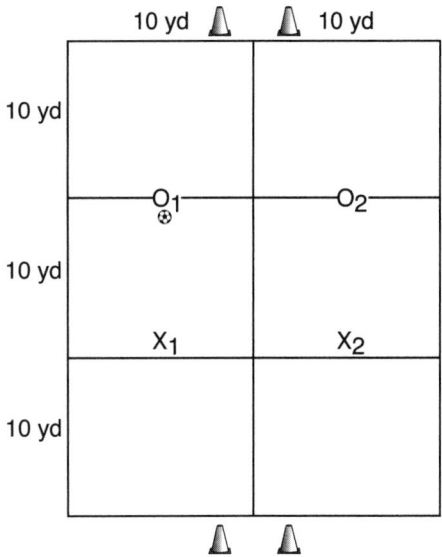

DEFENDING THE PENALTY BOX

FOCUS

Defending the most important area of the field, the penalty box; working on defensive principles to deny the opponents' goal scoring opportunities.

PROCEDURE

This drill requires 12 players, with 4 defenders and 4 attackers lining up inside the penalty box and 4 support players lining up outside the box.

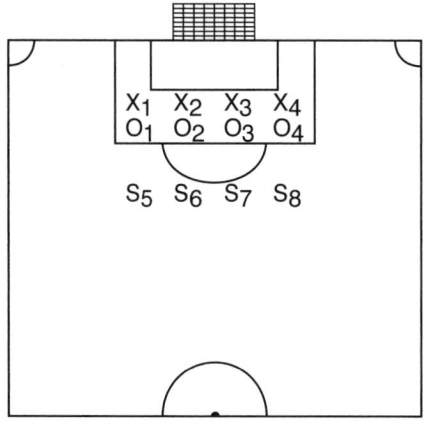

1. The support players are not allowed inside the box and they cannot shoot; they are responsible for passing to the 4 attacking forwards (O1–O4).

2. Defenders X1 through X4 are responsible for defending against the attackers inside the penalty box only.

3. The attackers (O1–O4) can pass the ball back outside the box to the support players (5–8), who then will pass it back into the box to an open forward.

Plenty of balls should be available for the support players outside the box.

VARIATION

Support players S5 and S8 can be placed into wide positions so that defenders will have to work on defending crossed balls.

ATTACK VERSUS DEFENSE

FOCUS

Applying all defensive principles.

PROCEDURE

This drill begins with 6 attackers against 5 defenders and a goalkeeper. Another defender can be added later. Attackers O6 and O5 begin with the ball and are restricted to two-touch soccer so as not to allow them to dribble the ball. Every other player has unlimited touches. If a sixth defender is added, the two-touch restriction on O6 and O5 is removed. The drill proceeds with a 6v6 attack. When defenders (X) win back the ball, they attempt to score through 2 sets of cones (2 minigoals 1 yard or meter apart) placed on the halfway line.

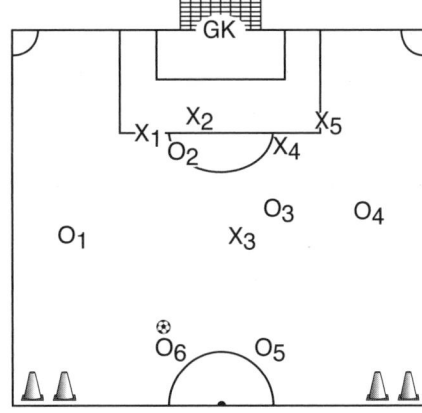

4-GOAL GAME

FOCUS

Adjusting to attacking play, which switches the ball quickly from side to side; understanding zonal play.

PROCEDURE

This game is played in an area 30 yards (27 meters) wide and 10 yards (9 meters) deep, with cones (1 yard or meter apart) serving as minigoals in each corner of the grid. Play a 4v4 game, with each team attacking two goals. This drill can be used defensively for pressure on the ball or offensively for switching the field of play.

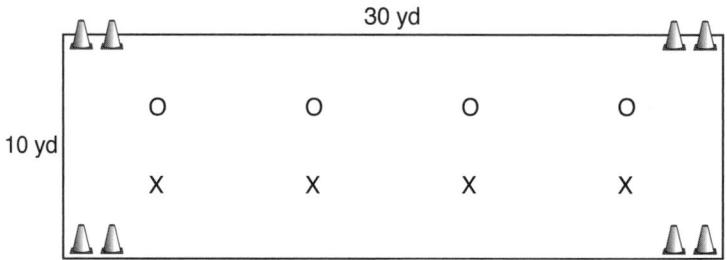

MIDFIELD GAME

FOCUS

Defending and correctly pressuring the ball, thus denying the easy option of attackers playing forward balls.

PROCEDURE

This drill uses the full playing field (though, depending on the number of players, it might be shortened by 10 to 20 yards [9 to 18 meters]). The playing length is divided into thirds, and play proceeds 6v6 in the middle third, with two defenders and a forward in each of the two attacking thirds.

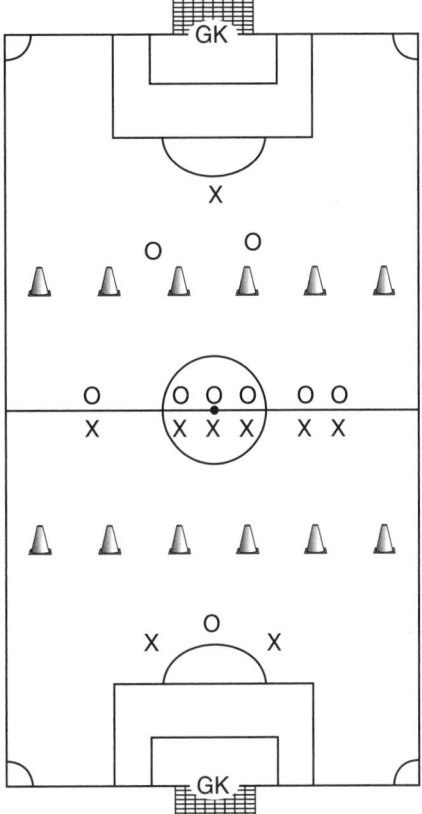

1. Play begins with the goalkeeper laying the ball to one of her two defenders, who must then pass it into the middle third. It is mandatory at this point to stay in one's third.

2. In the middle third, play is 6v6, with each team trying to deny the opposition the ability to play the ball forward to their target player in the attacking third.

3. If a team succeeds in getting the ball to its target player, one player is allowed to join her from the middle third, but no defenders are allowed to follow her from the middle third. The team with the ball now has a 2v2 situation in the attacking third with an opportunity to play for a goal.

4. Once this play is over, the midfield player in the attacking third must retreat back to her middle third. The ball starts with the goalkeeper again.

RECOVERY RUN

FOCUS

Practicing recovery runs to positions where defending can begin.

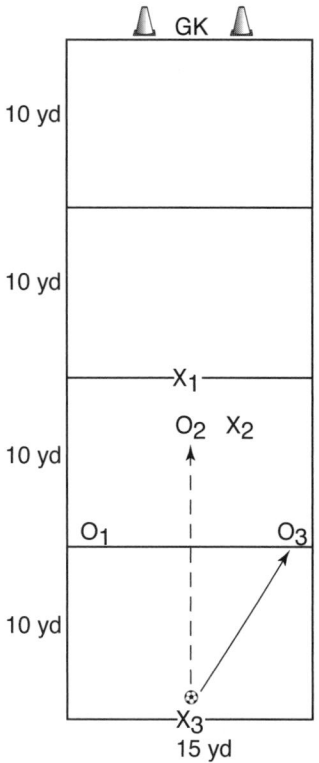

PROCEDURE

In a grid measuring 40 by 15 yards (about 37 by 14 meters), place three attackers (O1, O2, and O3) and two defenders (X1 and X2) in the third zone.

1. X3 begins the drill by passing to Os. O1 and O2 defend, but are outnumbered three to two.

2. Os attempt to take advantage of this numerical superiority by scoring between the cones past the goalkeeper.

3. X3 is allowed to recover the moment O receives the ball. He attempts to get goalside of the ball while X1 and X2 delay to give him time.

CHAPTER 5

Systems of Play

A system of play is a coach's plan for how he is going to use his 11 players. Formations are listed from the back in three basic groups: defenders, midfield players, and forwards. How many defenders, how many midfielders, and how many forwards does a coach believe he needs? For example, 4-4-2 indicates four defenders, four midfield players, and two forwards. This chapter covers some of the many options a coach has in deciding who plays where and, ultimately, what system is going to be used. It also discusses the pros and cons of different systems of play and how a coach can find the system that works best for the team.

Common Systems

Modern-day soccer can include any numerical formation adding up to ten (goalkeeper not included), but the most common formations are 4-4-2, 3-5-2, 4-3-3, and 3-4-3. This section explores the setup and the pros and cons of each system.

4-4-2

From a defensive point of view, this system has obvious advantages. It features eight potential defenders who can easily get behind the ball, and with four assigned defenders the full width of the field can be covered more easily. These four defenders can also easily match up with three attackers if playing against such a system. This system provides good team balance and fits naturally with playing zonal defense. It also works well for applying high pressure.

The system does, however, have its disadvantages. I will have fewer players in the midfield if playing against a 3-5-2 system using three central midfielders. Also, if either of the two central defenders go forward the team is left quite vulnerable to a counterattack, and the two forwards can become isolated as the mid four fall back to defend. But perhaps the most difficult problem is that oftentimes four defenders are marking only two forwards, leaving two defenders inactive. This can get confusing since young defenders are never quite sure whether to stay back and defend, or get forward into the attack.

This system's main attacking strength is that the team can attack out of the back with the two outside defenders, and also the two wide midfield players can be released to go forward with far less concern about defending, as the two backs are covering behind them. Attacking through the flanks is a key to success in using this system, and, even for the two forwards, a space is always available for running from central positions into wide positions. Switching the field of play is also relatively easy in this system. With four players across the back or midfield lines, the system's width means there are more options available for switching the ball from left to right, or right to left.

3-5-2

One of this system's main strengths is the number of players in the middle of the field, which gives a team great flexibility both for going forward and for defending. Games are often won or lost in midfield, and this system frequently allows a team to outnumber the opposition in that area. It allows midfield players to combine easily with the forwards; the proximity of three central midfield players allows constant and close support for the forwards. One or two attacking midfielders can also be given total freedom to attack without fear of being caught by a counterattack if the ball is turned over.

This system also has some disadvantages. Many high school coaches use it despite the fact that their teams often play in the school's football stadium, which typically houses a smaller field than is standard for soccer. On a narrow field, having too many players in midfield can cause them to get in each other's way. It's just too crowded. It should also be noted that some of those high school players will go on to play in college, where as many as three-quarters of the teams play with a flat back four, more than likely out of a 4-4-2 system.

The 3-5-2 system also creates problems for defenders. Playing with a back three rather than a back four requires certain capabilities, especially speed. It's quite dangerous to try to defend and cover with only three defenders, unless they are all quick. If the three defenders are playing with a sweeper back (a quick player assigned to provide roaming defense between the defenders and the goalkeeper), then the team is giving up one marking player, and the opposition is likely to have a numerical advantage somewhere else on the field. The sweeper is usually a purely defensive cover or support player, uninvolved in much else, which can lead to problems in other areas of the field. The system of three defenders can also be exposed defensively on the wings, especially if the ball is quickly switched by the opposition from one side to the other. Naturally, three defenders cannot cover the width of the field as well as four can. The space they have to give away is in the wide positions, allowing much room for the opposition to play a ball. It's also very difficult to use this system against a team playing with three forwards, since three defenders against three forwards is not a matchup any team would normally want.

4-3-3 and 3-4-3

Playing three forwards has definite advantages. It allows a team to pressure defenders who have the ball, making it very difficult for them to get the ball away. Attacking with three forwards can also force opponents to adjust, since very few teams are prepared to handle three attackers especially if they have only three defenders. Teams using this system can pressure and defend very high up the field, thus keeping the opposition pinned in its own half. The system is especially effective against weak opponents who have difficulty playing long balls up the field. It also makes it hard for opponents to play the ball sideways, thus encouraging them to play forward balls, often with little effect. The 4-3-3 system is much better suited to the size limitations experienced in high school football stadiums since the players are more evenly spread in the tight confines of this type of facility.

It is important to understand that this type of system must change in relationship to which team has the ball. A team will attack with a 4-3-3 formation, but is likely to have to defend with a 4-5-1 shape. This is done by withdrawing the two outside forwards back into midfield when the opponents win back the ball. These two forwards will join the middle three to form a group of five to defend the midfield thus creating the 4-5-1 shape. This system can be very effective but does require the two wide forwards to be disciplined enough to recover defensively.

Like all systems, playing three in the front has its disadvantages. Three players can be played out of the game with one successful pass by the opponent from the back, forcing a team to defend with only seven. Even more serious, teams can be easily out numbered in midfield if opponents play four or, worse still, five in that area (obviously, it is difficult to play three midfield players against five). This problem can be addressed by using a 3-4-3 system, which retains the advantage of three attacking forwards but gets an extra player into midfield to help with the numbers problem there, or as mentioned in the prior paragraph, by withdrawing the two outside forwards into midfield. This extra player is critical, because teams that control midfield tend to win games. The downside of using the 3-4-3 is that the team must defend with only three players.

A coach needs to choose systems that work with players' strengths and the team's style.

© Getty Images

Choosing Systems

Since each system has its pros and cons, it is impossible to generally recommend one over another. The choice of system depends on criteria including the types of players available, the formation used by the opponent, the tactical approach to a game, and the field conditions. What is most important is to use a system that fits the strengths of the players. A coach should get the best 11 players on the field, then find a system that meets their needs. Sometimes this requires moving a player to another position, and certain positions are easy to adapt to. For instance, most forwards can be taught fairly easily to play on the wing, and a midfield player can typically serve as a defender.

Next, the coach must consider team style. To play direct soccer and get the ball forward quickly with longer passes, it may be best to use more forwards. To focus on shorter passing through midfield, the coach might want an extra midfield player. To defend well, an extra defender might be the key. Whatever the case, the coach should play to the team's strengths, not to her own preference or comfort zone.

A coach may also consider changing a system to match up effectively with a particular opponent, but care must be taken in doing so, since teams should not regularly change how they play the game. The coach should be more concerned about preparing his own team to play to its strengths than about reacting to those of the opposition. Nevertheless, some consideration does have to be given to the opposition.

If pressed, I would say that the best system to use is generally the 4-4-2. Many coaches would disagree, but it's probably fair to say that this system places players across the field more evenly and covers the field better than any other. We have talked about team shape and its importance, and the 4-4-2 system is better suited than most to maintaining good shape.

Once a system has been chosen, there are many other considerations about how to play *within* that system. The following diagrams show some possibilities. In both the 4-4-2 and the 3-5-2 systems, the shape of the back unit is much the same. In both cases, defenders have to support each other, and the diagrams show how this is done. In the middle units, whether using four or five players, there are more options for team shape—again, as shown in the diagrams—and as with the back four unit, they still require depth in their shape.

Figure 5.1 on page 98 shows the Os lining up for the kickoff in a 4-4-2 formation, with the Xs in a 3-5-2. Figures 5.2 and 5.3 show that the 4-4-2 formation is used in two ways. Once play has begun, the formations change. Figure 5.2 on page 98 shows that the middle four players basically mirror the shape of the back four defenders when right back O has the ball. This is very much a zonal formation for both the middle four players and the back four. In figure 5.3 on page 99, the shape of the back four remains the same, but the middle four are different,

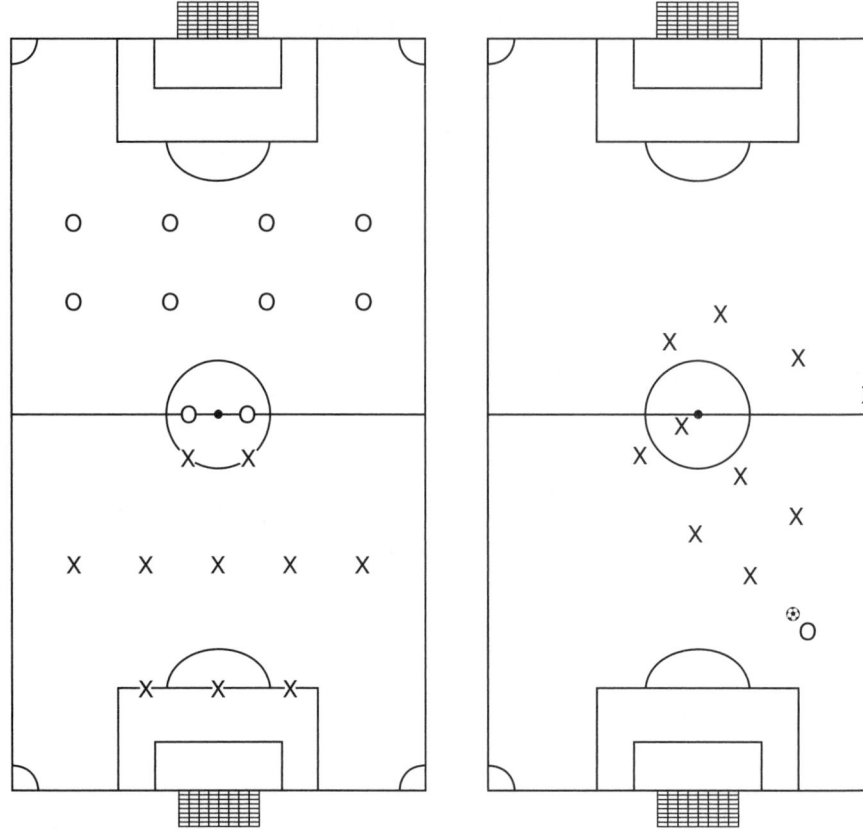

Figure 5.1 4-4-2 (Os) line up against 3-5-2 (Xs).

Figure 5.2 The defensive four and middle four both have an "L" shape.

giving the look of a diamond. This can make both defending and attacking a little simpler for the middle four. Players X7 and X11 are designated as the two wide players (wingers), with X8 being an attacking midfielder and X4 being a defensive or holding midfielder. Each player can mark and defend against his opposite number. This will only become a problem if the opposition is using three central midfield players, creating a numerical disadvantage, three against two. In this case teams may have to adapt by adding an extra midfield player.

Figure 5.4 shows a different look with a team defending in the 3-5-2 formation. X6 at the back is the sweeper or covering player, who normally has no direct marking responsibilities. X5 and X4 are man-marking the two forwards. The five defending midfielders could use many different looks, but in this case X8 has been given a holding or defending role, making the defensive unit at the back look like a diamond, with the remaining four midfielders playing in front and either man-marking their opponents or playing zone.

Regardless of the system used, the coach must consider how to defend and attack within that system. He can begin with defending and address the back four

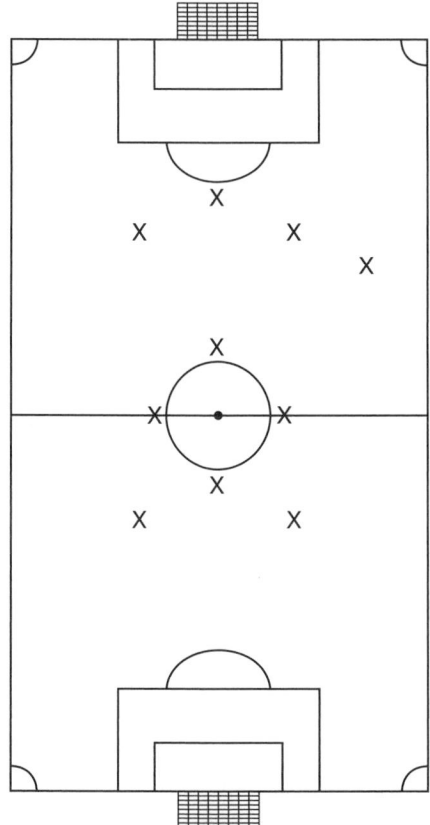

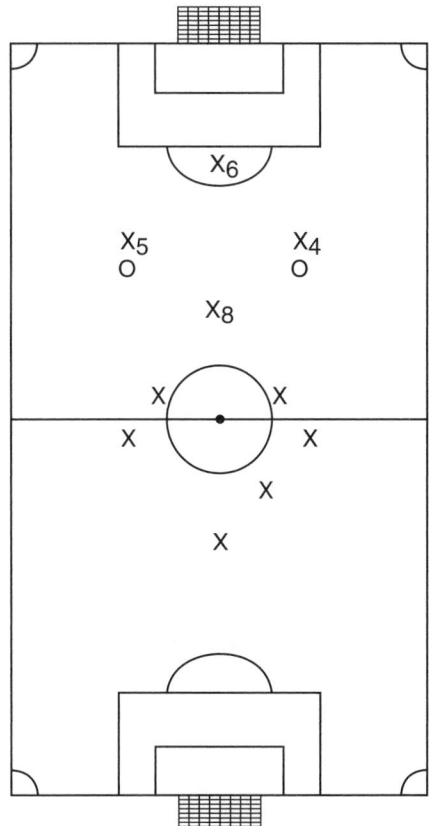

Figure 5.3   The back four have an "L" shape formation, while the middle four make a diamond.

Figure 5.4   A 3-5-2 formation with a diamond shape at the back.

only, working on shape, compactness, and defensive cover, both with and without attacking players working against them. He can then move to the midfield players, and finally the forwards. When satisfied with the defending of each unit by itself, the coach can put it all together, coordinating the three units to defend with all 11 players. The same process can be used for attacking—starting with concepts, then working in the three separate units before putting it all together. This part-to-whole method helps enormously in the early stages of system play.

Systems of play can be distracting, time consuming, and often frustrating. It is absolutely necessary to develop a system, but not at the expense of working on fundamentals of the game. The coach's time is well spent on teaching players to "sit" in the right part of the field at the right time and to recognize what is happening on the field—that is, to read the game and understand it. These points takes precedence over learning a system, as a smart soccer player will do well even when not taught a system.

Teams need to choose wisely when deciding on a system. The choice should always be based on the playing abilities of the team, but the system currently used the most, worldwide, is the 4-4-2, and adaptions of it. We have considered two shapes that can be used in the 4-4-2 system, but there are many variations. For example, a team may wish to hold one of its midfield players back in a defensive role to help protect its back four. Thus the 4-4-2 may look like a 4-1-3-2, with the middle unit of four split into a 1-3. Formations can also change depending on whether a team is attacking or defending. In the 4-4-2 formation, a team would attack with the two forwards, with midfield players coming forward to support them. However, when the ball is turned over a team may withdraw a forward toward midfield to help the middle unit defend. Technically, the formation then would look like a 4-5-1. A team playing in a 3-5-2 may defend with that shape but attack with a 3-4-3 formation by pushing a midfield player into the attack. Formations should be very fluid.

Once the team has chosen its formation and decided how it is going to play, players should be made aware of adjustments, if any, that they may have make when playing a team with a different formation. One key question is this: Should the team stick to its default mode and let the opposition worry about making adjustments, or should it change its system to counter the opposition? Making such decisions effectively will distinguish the good team and coach from the average ones, but there are no easy answers. The coach can begin by considering whether hers is the better team. If so, then it might be best to make no adjustments at all—to let the opposition worry and make their own adjustments. If the opposition is stronger, however, or if, say, the team is incapable of handling the extra player the opposition may have in midfield, then the coach might want to consider tactical changes designed to disrupt or upset the opponent's system. In its simplest form, this might mean just adding an extra midfield player if, for example, the opposition holds a numerical advantage or happens to be particularly strong in that area. If a team is using a 4-4-2 system and the opponent plays in a 4-5-1, options include the following:

- Withdraw a forward to match the opposition's 4-5-1.
- Withdraw a defender and play in a 3-5-2.
- Continue to play in a 4-4-2, but ask the weak- (opposite-) side midfield player to come inside toward the middle and mark one of the opposition's central midfield players. (This approach leaves a defensive gap that must be covered by the outside back on the same side.)
- Continue to play in a 4-4-2 formation, but since the opponent will likely have three central midfielders (thus overmatching the two central midfielders in the 4-4-2), the coach can compensate by trading one wide player (winger) for an extra central midfielder to even the numbers. In this approach, the outside *back* on the side with no winger must come forward in attacking situations to give the necessary width of play on that side.

- If a team plays three at the back and the opposition's strength is wing play or diagonal passing into the corners, then the coach should probably compensate by adding an extra defender and playing with four at the back.

Teams playing away from home often adjust their formation to a more defensive approach. It is more difficult to win on the road, which tends to make coaches more cautious in their approach to the game.

It is essential to remember that systems of play and specific formations are static concepts that often bear little resemblance to the fluidity of the game itself. They are merely starting points, designating potential positions for players to retreat to when defending or attacking to maintain good team shape. It can be effective to interchange positions, but players must understand that to retain the basic shape of the formation they are playing in they need to move fluidly to fill spots left by teammates who move elsewhere. These adjustments require excellent understanding of the game, and it usually takes a good deal of time and experience before players truly grasp the concept. Thus coaches have many decisions to make, and many options to choose from, and how they handle them can make the difference between winning and losing.

CHAPTER 6

Set Plays and Restarts

A set play can be defined as any start of play following the stoppage of the game by the referee. Examples include center kickoffs, goal kicks, throw-ins, corner kicks, dropped balls, and direct and indirect free kicks. The rewards can be enormous for developing an efficient and well-organized series of set plays. This is the only time in the game when the ball can be played without pressure from the opposition, and with the nearest opponent 10 yards (about 9 meters) from the ball. Set plays are also the only times in soccer when a team knows for sure what is going to happen, and they must take advantage of these chances, since a well-orchestrated set play often leads to a goal-scoring opportunity. This chapter addresses direct and indirect free kicks, corner kicks, and throw-ins from both the attacking and the defending perspectives.

I recommend devoting considerable time during practice games to set plays—both the attacking and the defending aspects. A full-sided practice game can be periodically stopped in order for the team to perform a set play. Doing this during practice game sessions feels more real than asking players to practice a set play in isolation from game play.

Attacking Set Plays

No matter where the restart is on the field, and no matter what type it is, teams should always be encouraged to play a positive ball, which usually means playing a forward ball. It is often a waste to play a ball backward, and it can even play a team into trouble. Several years ago at the Dallas Cup (the biggest youth tournament in the world), I saw a team take a one-goal lead in the first 12 seconds of the game without even touching the ball. Unlikely as this sounds, the opposition kicked off to begin the game and passed back to a midfield player. This player immediately came under pressure and passed back to one of his defenders, who also came under pressure and so passed back to his goalkeeper, who, unfortunately, was coming out too quickly and missed the ball. The ball entered the goal and his side was down 1-0 in an extreme example of negative passing.

Teams should attempt a direct shot on goal or at least play the ball into the danger zone inside the penalty box. Free kicks and corner kicks can and should be very productive. Most throw-ins are simply a method of putting the ball back in play and keeping possession, but still require some practice. This section covers several attacking set play situations: free kicks around the opponent's penalty area, corner kicks, and throws.

Free Kicks Around the Opponent's Penalty Area

Of all the set plays, direct and indirect free kicks around the opponent's penalty area are the most likely to produce goal-scoring opportunities. (That means this is also the most dangerous part of the field for a defending team to give away a free kick, and players need to be careful about how they tackle in this area.) As a result, players and coaches should spend a good deal of time on these plays in practice sessions. Players can also work on these kicks by themselves before or after practice.

The referee will determine whether an awarded free kick warrants a direct shot on goal or an indirect kick, wherein the ball must first be touched by a teammate before a goal can be scored. This can involve as little as touching the ball just enough to move it a yard (or meter) or less. With minor adjustments, the same set play can be used for a direct or indirect free kick. In some cases, a coach may want to consider taking an indirect kick even if a direct kick has been awarded. Moving the ball sideways just a bit changes the angle of the shot, possibly making the defensive wall and the goalkeeper's positioning less effective. Defensive walls are generally set by the goalkeeper so that they are protecting his near post. The angles are determined in relation to the placement of the stationary ball for the free kick. When the indirect free kick is taken, if it is now rolled a couple of feet to the side, and then struck at goal, the angle has been changed from that assumed by the wall and the goalkeeper's position, perhaps providing a better opening for the shot. Thus I will consider direct and indirect free kicks as the same thing for the purpose of this section.

Since most of these free kicks are easily within shooting range, it is realistic for the kicking team to anticipate a scoring opportunity with proper execution. The opposition will put up a wall that is likely to be set by the goalkeeper, and if the opportunity arises and the referee allows it, a quick shot on goal should be taken while the goalkeeper is out of position. Most referees will not allow such a quick shot, but it's worth trying. Taking the free kick before the defensive wall is properly set gives the shooter a much clearer look at the goal and thus a better chance of scoring.

Since this is usually not possible, a team needs to have a series of well-practiced direct and indirect kicks. If practice time for working on these kicks is limited, then I recommend keeping the number of options to a minimum, maybe three or four, and practicing them very well. This approach will be more efficient and less confusing for players. (In fact, one option may be as simple as shooting straight at the goal.) With this in mind, how can a team improve its chances of scoring?

© Sport The Library

Players should spend a good amount of time improving free kicks around the opponent's penalty area, as these kicks are likely to produce goal-scoring opportunities.

The goalkeeper will set a defensive wall of four to five players protecting one of her posts. She will then stand off-center toward the other post. The kicking team might want to start by considering whether to try blocking the goalkeeper's vision. This can be done in several ways, but basically they would be attempting to place their own players between the ball and the goalkeeper, in his direct line of sight (figure 6.1). Players' options for where to stand are limited, however, by the offside rule; obviously, they cannot stand directly in front of the goalkeeper. Here are a couple of options:

In figure 6.2, O2 and O3 are standing on the end of the defensive wall in front of the goalkeeper to block his vision. The kicker then shoots at these two players, who move out of the way as soon as the ball is struck. This ploy can also be used with just one player on the end of the wall. The opposition must stay 10 yards (about 9 meters) from the ball until the free kick is taken, but the attacking players can stand as close as they want. The advantage of putting players on the end of the wall is that they can both block the sight of the goalkeeper and, when the kick is taken, spin off the wall and thus be close enough to goal to look for any rebounds from the initial shot.

The disadvantage of putting the vision-blocking players at the end of the wall is that, at 10 yards from the ball, they will only partially block the goalkeeper's vision. The closer they stand to the ball, the more difficult it will be for the goalkeeper to see it. This limitation can be addressed by placing the two vision-blocking players immediately in front of the ball. They may also be involved in the play, either as part of a decoy or in the kick itself. An example is shown in figure 6.3.

At least two players should be placed on the ball in order to confuse the defending team, who will then be unsure which player is going to take the kick. The kicking team can augment this advantage by placing both a left-footed and a right-footed player on the ball, thus increasing the options for the angle of the kick. If the ball is to the right side of the goal, then the shot angle is better for the

Figure 6.1 Use an extra player to block the goalkeeper's vision.

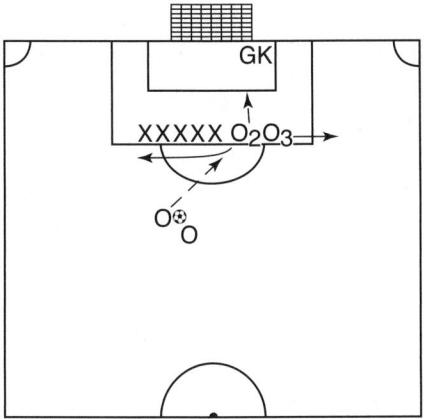

Figure 6.2 O2 and O3 are positioned on the end of the wall to block the goalkeeper's view of the ball.

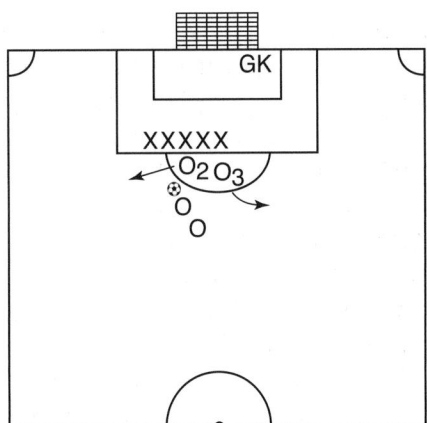

Figure 6.3 O2 and O3 are positioned directly in front of the ball.

left-footer, and vice versa. The opposition may realize this, so it is advisable for the kicking team to mix it up occasionally.

No matter how players are positioned for the free kick, certain fundamentals must be honored. The team must maintain good shape, which means considering what might happen should the kick fail and the opposition regain the ball and begin to counterattack. It's important to have enough defensive players behind the ball to protect in this case; thus the kicking team cannot send all players forward. Another consideration: What if the shot is partially saved or hits a goalpost and rebounds? Are enough players positioned to take advantage of a rebound? Does the team have the right *types* of players in the correct positions? Are the best defenders back from the ball, the best kickers around the ball, and the quickest in good position to corral a rebound?

Figure 6.4 shows one way to "set" players for the direct free kick. O11 and O8 are blocking the goalkeeper's view, along with O7, and should quickly move out of the way as the shot is taken. Any one of three players—O7, O6, and O5—can take the free kick (as predetermined by the coach), with O2 spinning off the wall and attacking the goal with an eye toward a rebound. O9 and O10 will do the same. O4 and O3 will remain back to maintain team shape and help protect against any counterattack. The free kick options in this scenario are limited only by the imagination of the coach and players, but it is worth remembering to *keep the free kick as simple as possible*. The simpler the kick, the more likely it is to succeed.

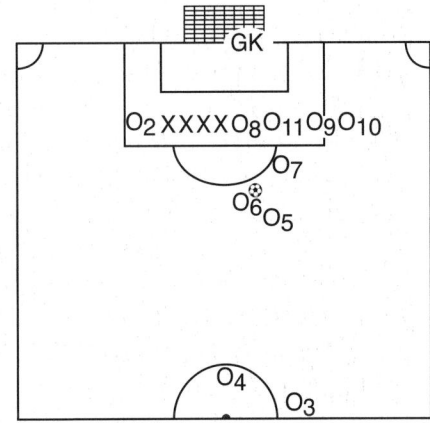

Figure 6.4 O7, O8, and O11 block the goalkeeper's view of the ball.

Corner Kicks

Though a bit less likely than free kicks to produce a goal, corner kicks still provide good scoring opportunities; in addition, they occur much more frequently (as many as seven or eight times a game, versus one or two free kicks outside the box), so they should be practiced on a regular basis. As with free kicks, the team's best dead-ball strikers should take the corner kicks. There is nothing more frustrating than having this set play fail due to a poor kick.

Corner kicks should be designed to play to the team's strengths, with the correct players in the correct positions. The best headers of the ball should be positioned in the penalty box to receive the cross from the corner kick. If these players are defenders, they should be brought forward for the corner kick (and replaced by an appropriate number of players remaining back to defend). Typically, the bravest of the headers should be placed in position to attack the corner kick.

In-Swinging Corner Kicks

The in-swinging, near-post corner kick appears to be in vogue in modern soccer. Successfully taken, it is very difficult to defend, since with an in-swinging cross the flight of the ball is already heading toward the goal and may need only the slightest of touches to direct it into the net. This type of cross is especially difficult for goalkeepers, who are already unsure of the ball's path due to the threat of a deflection, and thus are often deceived. Sometimes, just the threat of a player deflecting the cross is sufficient to confuse the goalkeeper. In addition, this type of firmly low-struck ball (preferably about head high), quickly whipped into the box with several players obstructing the goalkeeper' view, is very difficult to get to.

Another huge advantage with this type of kick is that success does not necessarily require great headers of the ball. The team needs to find a player who is brave and is good at winning the space in front of defenders. Winning this space is the key. The player must be first to the ball, which requires determination and courage. If she is first to the ball and the corner kick is well struck, it may well be that a mere touch from the attacker's head will produce devastating results for the defending team.

Once a coach has decided to use an in-swinging corner kick, the next step is to find the two best crossers of the ball. Both a right-footed and a left-footed player are needed, with the left-footer taking kicks on the right side of the field, and the right-footer taking those on the left side.

Like all good things, this approach does have its drawbacks. Consistently striking an in-swinging ball with the correct trajectory is difficult, and it can be hard to find a capable player. Another challenge arises when (as is not uncommon) the defending team places a player in front of the near post; it is difficult for this type of kick to clear that defender, but it must be done if the kick is going to be successful.

No matter what type of corner kick is used, a team should not become predictable. It's best to keep the opposition guessing where the ball is going to be played. One option is to make the first corner received in the game a short one (see figure 6.5). When the team receives its second corner kick, the opposition may expect another short kick, which makes it a good time to go with a longer one (see figure 6.6). In figure 6.5, O7 will play the ball on the ground firmly to O9, who is coming quickly off the near post. O9 will play the ball back to O7 at an angle, and O7 will whip it into the far post as a cross or shot. The far post is attacked by O6, O8, and O4, and all it will take is a deflection for the ball to end up in the back of the net. Easy! Figure 6.6 shows an in-swinging, near-post corner kick.

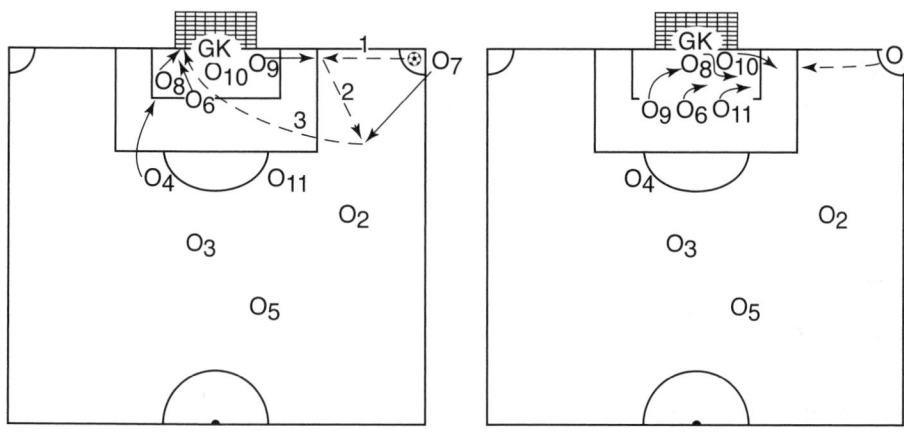

Figure 6.5   A short corner kick.

Figure 6.6   An in-swinging near-post corner kick.

Out-Swinging Corner Kicks

Out-swinging corner kicks can be just as effective as in-swinging kicks, but they require technically better headers of the ball. The ball will usually have to be played into a deeper part of the penalty box, either midgoal or toward the far post (it's difficult to play to the near post since the ball is curling away from the goal. In order to direct the ball into a deeper part of the penalty box, the kicker will need to give it more height on the cross, which means it will be in the air longer and tend to hang more than the firmly driven near-post ball. Heading this type of cross requires good technique, as well as the ability to jump high, time the jump correctly, and make excellent contact on the ball with the head. Central defenders are often the best bet for this role, since they tend to be big and to be good technical headers of the ball by the very nature of their position.

To make life more difficult for the defending team, all attacking players should be constantly moving inside the penalty box, checking in and checking out before the corner kick is even taken. Timing of runs is critical to the success of this approach, as the players need to be moving forward, toward the ball, at the moment it is kicked. Each player should be assigned a defined area of the penalty

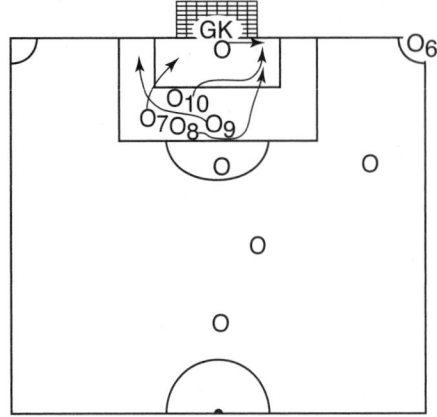

Figure 6.7 Attacking players begin in a cluster.

box to run into, and these runs should cover the most likely areas for the ball to be delivered into—namely near, midgoal and far post. The attacking players should arrive at the same time the ball does. Figure 6.7 gives an example of an approach to a corner kick where all players begin in the same part of the penalty area, then spread out and attack, making it very difficult for defenders to mark and track them. Os 7, 8, 9, and 10 will quickly attack near-post, midgoal, and far-post as the ball is served.

If the team is weak at heading, and therefore unlikely to be effective on corner kicks, the coach must consider how to compensate. He might consider making a short corner kick by bringing two players over to handle the kick; now, instead of playing the ball directly into the box, the team can play it short to the second player. If the opposition is slow to recognize and adjust to what is happening, the ball can be quickly kicked to the second player, who dribbles toward the goal before crossing or shooting. The opposition will probably wise up quickly to this ploy and send a defender over to stop it; by rule, however, she must be 10 yards (about 9 meters) from the ball until it is kicked. The attacking team still has two attackers on the ball for the corner kick, which creates a two-on-one advantage. The attacking team can play the ball short, draw the defender to the ball, then pass quickly to take the defender out of the play. The player receiving the pass can dribble and then shoot or cross.

Should the opponent position *two* players 10 yards (9 meters) from the ball to match the attacking two (and they should), the attacking team can simply play the ball short (perhaps 1 yard or meter in), thus slightly altering the angle of the cross, then immediately cross it into the penalty box before the two defenders can close on it. Thus if facing a well-organized defense that has had to send two defenders out to protect against the corner kick, the attacking team will have pulled two defenders away from the penalty box, which causes reorganization problems for the opponent and creates more space in the box for attacking the corner kick. This tactic helps a team that is not strong in the air, since it provides more space and time to operate, with fewer defenders in the box.

Throws

Since they usually do not produce immediate goal-scoring opportunities, throw-ins are probably the least important of all set plays. They should not, however, be totally ignored. If nothing else, a coach must make sure that players can put the ball into play in keeping with the rules of the game. Nothing is more frustrating than having the referee stop the game for an illegal throw and award the retake to the opposition. Both feet must be on the ground and *behind* the sideline when the ball is released. The ball should begin behind the head and be released in front, with equal pressure from both arms. The player making the throw-in should quickly pick an open teammate to throw the ball to. Opposition players tend to lose concentration momentarily when the ball goes out of play, and the attacking team can take advantage of this lapse by throwing the ball in a way that makes it easy to control, either with the head or feet. After the throw, the thrower should immediately become involved as a support player.

Where possible, the ball should be thrown forward, and on a throw-in that is close to the opponent's penalty box, a strong thrower might even consider a long throw-in to the box, which can lead directly to an opportunity on goal. A team can use this option like any other set play by organizing inside the penalty box so that players know who the target player is and where the other players should stand in relationship to the target. I recommend keeping this play very simple by asking the target player to flick the ball on with his head from the near post toward the far post, with players behind him ready to meet it on the far post.

Defending Set Plays

Set plays must be defended mostly in the defensive third of the field, and it's uncommon for teams to practice defending free kicks in the middle third, since a ball in this area poses limited threat on goal and is therefore deemed less important. Most good teams, however, will try to take quick free kicks in this middle area, and it is imperative to be quick in getting a defensive player in front of the ball to slow it down. Quick free kicks are less likely to be taken in the attacking third of the play, since teams will usually set up their practiced free kick and may more likely require the referee to restart the game with his whistle, but the defending team must be alert even in this area.

When the ball is whistled dead, many players on both sides of the field will lose concentration and stop playing (many players use this bit of time to rest). Either team can take advantage of this lull by reacting quickly to the restart of play, catching the opposition in a moment of disorganization . The most crucial defensive efforts always happen in the defensive third of the field, which can be subdivided into two areas: the middle or central positions (a very dangerous area), and the wide or wing positions (including corner kicks and throw-ins).

Defending Free Kicks in Central Positions Outside the Box

Teams should do their utmost to avoid giving away free kicks in this area, which is both the most dangerous and the most difficult to defend. The rules of the game require defending players to stand 10 yards (about 9 meters) from the ball while the free kick is being taken. It's a good habit to initially stand players closer than that and let the opposition ask the referee for the 10 yards. If necessary, the referee will then mark out the 10 yards, which will delay the free kick and give the defending team more time to get organized, especially in setting the wall.

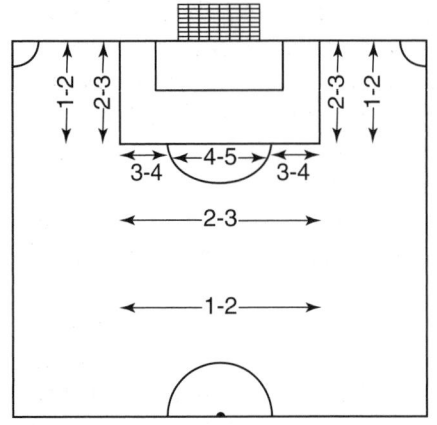

Figure 6.8 The number of players a goalkeeper should place in the wall depends on the ball's position.

Many teams have the goalkeeper set the wall, but a coach can use any player, especially a forward, from the upfield position. The wall should be positioned to cover one side of the goal, with the goalkeeper covering the other. It is the goalkeeper's responsibility to call out the number of players he wants in the wall. This number will be determined by angle of the free kick and its distance from the goal. Figure 6.8 suggests how many players to put in the wall in relationship to the distance and angle of the kick: the farther out and the wider the free kick, the fewer bodies are needed in the wall. The wall must be predetermined so that each player knows exactly where to stand.

It is not a good idea to put the team's best defenders in the wall, since its only purpose is to block shots, which anyone can do. It is better to leave the better defenders free to defend the kick. A coach might, however, consider placing an extra defender on the end of the wall closest to the goalkeeper to act as a "crusher" or "rusher," charging the ball the moment it is about to be struck, while the wall remains stationary and tightly packed. The wall should be set with one player overlapping the post (figure 6.9) and with the tallest player on the outside end of the wall (covering the post) and the remaining players arranged in descending order of size so that the smallest player is on the other end. This arrangement puts more height where the goal is most vulnerable, on the post furthest from the goalkeeper, and less height toward the middle of the goal in the area that is easier for the goalkeeper to see and cover. Figure 6.10 shows where the rest of

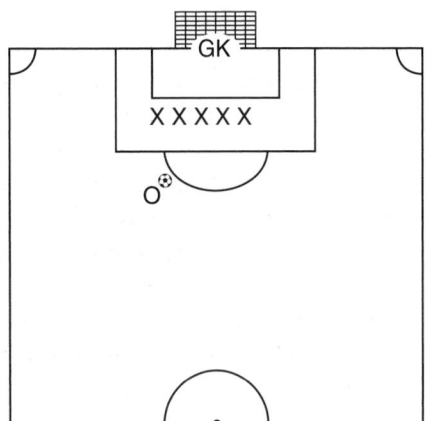

Figure 6.9 Wall set with one player overlapping the post.

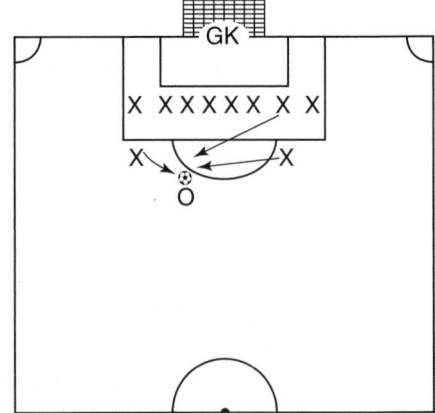

Figure 6.10 Remaining players sealing off the field.

the players should stand, sealing off the vital spots on the field. Two defensive players stand 10 yards (about 9 meters) from the ball on either side of it in order to challenge should the ball be played to the left or right. One can challenge the ball from the end of the wall, and the remaining two players stand in the space to either side of the wall to pressure any player or pass in this area. All players should be alert to the shot and to possible rebounds in the area behind the wall. Another option: Instead of positioning the two defenders to either side of the ball, they might be placed in positions to mark attacking players to the side of the wall.

Players need to be brave in the wall and stand tightly together for as long as possible as the shot is made. The worst thing that can happen is for the wall to split apart too soon, leaving holes for the ball to go through, which defeats the very purpose of the wall. Once the ball has been struck, these players should be alert and simply react to where the ball goes.

Defending Corner Kicks

Corner kicks are the most common restarts, so it's best to have that shop in order. As in most set-play situations, the critical elements are organization, discipline, and determination to be first to the ball. There are three ways to defend a corner kick: zonal coverage, man-to-man marking, and a combination approach. Each is covered later in this section. No matter which system is used, the positioning of the goalkeeper is crucial. If he stands too close to the far post, he risks being beaten at the near post; if too close to the near post, he will struggle to cover the back of the goal. In determining the best position, the keeper needs to anticipate how the kick is going to be taken, either as an out-swinger or an in-swinger. For an in-swinging kick, he needs to be tight on his line, favoring front of center. If anticipating an out-swinging kick, he needs to be off his line and slightly back of center.

Each team must also decide whether to put one or two defenders on the line to help the goalkeeper protect it. Most teams incorporate two defenders on the line, with one standing on each post, but some teams withdraw the player on the far post if the goalkeeper is strong in the air and can cover the back post without help. Having two players help the goalkeeper protect his goal line has obvious advantages—a shot or header on goal has to beat three players rather than two or one. The disadvantage lies in having fewer players available to help defend the cross, and it can be very problematic if the attacking team has more players in the penalty box than the defense does. If necessary, a team can bring all 10 players back, including the outlet forward, to defend the kick. (Normally, it makes sense to leave one player forward by the halfway line to pick up the ball should it be effectively cleared by the defenders.) In this way, a team can always leave two defenders on the goal line to help the goalkeeper (figure 6.11*a* and *b* on page 114).

Figure 6.11 Positioning of defenders to protect the goal line on a corner kick: *(a)* prior to a corner kick; *(b)* after the corner kick has been taken.

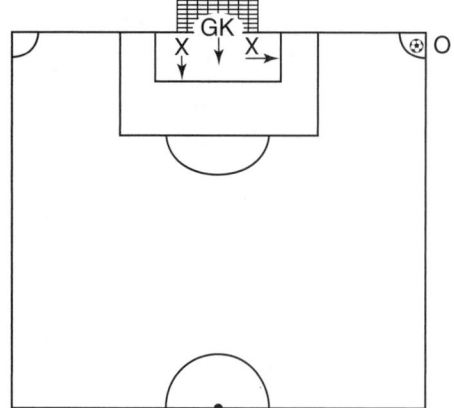

Figure 6.12 The goalkeeper and two defenders positioned on the line for a corner kick.

These players on the post should be positioned as follows: Figure 6.12 shows the goalkeeper shading slightly toward the front post. The goalkeeper must establish good foot position, with both feet on the goal line facing forward. This position requires the goalkeeper to look over his shoulder at the corner kick but gives him better vision of the total box. The defender on the near post needs to be off the line facing the corner kick, so that he can react to an in-swinging kick targeted for an attacker making a run past the near post. Attacking teams sometimes stand a player on this post in front of the covering defender. In this case, the defending team can consider bringing another defender to stand in front of him, thus covering his front and back.

Man-to-Man Marking

Other than the two players on the goal line, man-to-man marking means every defender matches up with a player on the attacking team. This straightforward approach is the simplest to organize and is probably the most effective for teams that do not have much time to spend practicing in these areas. Wherever possible, defenders should be matched in size to the attackers they will mark. This system is the easiest to learn and requires far less decision making than the others. It does have its problems, however, especially in trying to match up players, and it takes only one player who is insufficiently determined to win the ball in the air for the whole thing to break down. The system can also get confusing if the opposing team starts with all its players in one area, packed tightly together, before quickly dispersing to attack the ball. Where should defenders stand in this case? They have no choice but to gather with the attacking team and make sure they are extremely alert in deciding where to go and who to mark when the attacking team splits apart.

Zonal Coverage

In zonal coverage, aside from the goalkeeper and the two players protecting the goal line on each post, there will be seven or eight other players to help defend the corner. In most cases, a team will leave one player forward to be available if the corner kick is effectively cleared, meaning seven players are available to defend. Each defender is responsible for attacking the space in front of her. The defender must be alert and first to the ball. Some teams like to put one of the defenders in front of the ball, 10 yards (about 9 meters) from the corner kick, in order to disturb the kicker's service. I recommend against this, however, since that player can often be put to better use elsewhere.

In the case of a short corner kick, the defending team needs to send *two* defenders quickly out toward the corner flag to defend 2v2. The coach can take his pick as to which two players to send (not good headers of the ball), but whoever it is, the team will need to adjust its zonal coverage accordingly by moving players into slightly different areas and filling the areas left open by the players covering the short corner kick. In the situation shown in figure 6.13, I would suggest placing the two closest players, X2 and X3, 10 yards (9 meters) from the ball on the corner kick, thus matching two defenders with the attacking two. The two areas left by X2 and X3 now need to be covered, perhaps by moving X1 from the back post to the near post (leaving the back post for the goalkeeper and X5 to cover) and moving X8 into X3's zonal area. The attacking team

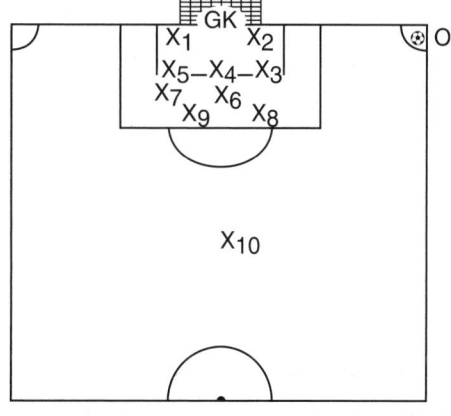

Figure 6.13 Team zonal coverage for a corner kick.

will often consider an in-swinging corner kick and put a player in front of X2 on the near post. The defending team might react by placing an extra defender (perhaps X3) in front of that player. Owning the space in front of the attacking player is always critical. It really does not matter which players are moved, so long as it is done quickly, efficiently, and in such a way that the key zones in the penalty area are still covered.

The huge advantage of zone coverage is that a team can effectively block off all the dangerous areas a ball may be crossed into, giving the opposition little chance to find space in which to attack the corner kick. The disadvantage is that this coverage is very difficult to master. In my experience, there have never been enough defenders with the ability to be effective in their designated zone area. They have to understand exactly what area they are responsible for and be first to the ball within their zone. In addition, it's very difficult to defend an attacking player who comes quickly and late into a given area. Nevertheless, this is a very effective system if done correctly.

Man-to-Man and Zonal Combination

I prefer a combination of man-to-man and zonal defense, which offers the best of both worlds by having players who *can* zone-cover play that way, and using the rest to man-mark. It is easier to find this combination of players, and the zonal coverage should help compensate for breakdowns in man-to-man marking in the key areas of the box, as an extra zone player can be placed in that area.

The combination approach requires the coach to find two good zonal players, who are placed on the 6-yard box, covering the area of front post and mid-goal—perhaps the two most dangerous areas for the ball to be. The job of these two players is to attack the space in front of them if the ball is played into that area. If it is played long into the space behind them, it becomes the responsibility of another player, either the second zone player or one of the remaining players marking man-to-man. Beyond these two, the rest of the team is responsible for marking man-to-man and following any attacking player inside the penalty box. Of course, the two zone players have no such responsibility. This approach provides double coverage in the most dangerous area of the goal—a much better situation than before. In figure 6.14, X11 is left as a forward for the defensive clearance, and X1 and X2 protect the goal line as before, with X4 and X5 acting as zonal players just inside the 6-yard box. The remaining five players will then match up man-to-man with the opposition. If for some reason there are not enough players to match up man-for-man, the defending team can always take a player out of zonal coverage.

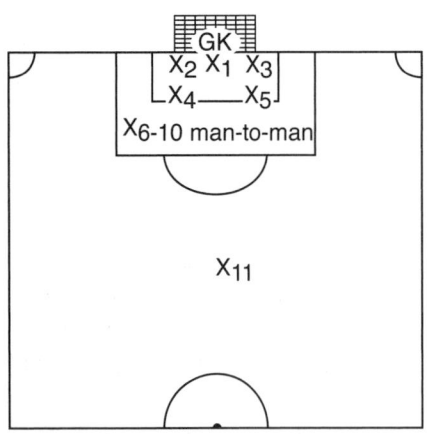

Figure 6.14 Positioning for a corner kick using both zonal and man-to-man coverage.

Defending Wide Free Kicks in the Defending Third

Free kicks from this part of the field are extremely dangerous and must be defended well. Unlike corner kicks, which are taken from the goal line, these free kicks have a much better angle toward the goal, and if the defending team is careless the attacker can score directly on the kick. The same principle applies to this kick as to the corner kick: An *in-swinging* ball struck at pace to an area toward the far post can cause chaos for the defense, especially the goalkeeper, who on many occasions may be guarding against the rush and possible deflection of the ball to the goal by a forward. This distraction and threat to the keeper can be enough to allow the kick to score directly from the free kick, with nobody else touching it. A ball struck as an *out-swinger* does not pose quite the same threat, as its flight is *away* from the goal.

Another danger is that of the attacking team setting all players toward the far post, leaving the area at the near post empty. This is a sign that the ball may be served into this empty area, with attacking players moving toward the near post at the very last second, making it difficult for the defense to react in time. To negate this problem, a team should place a defender in the near-post area before the kick, with no other responsibility other than covering this area.

Placing two defenders in a miniwall 10 yards (9 meters) from the free kick, between the ball and the goal, can distract the attacker and interfere with the free kick. For example, in figure 6.15, O7 is taking a free kick from the wide right area of the field. It would be prudent to put two players 10 yards from the kick to prevent attacker O8 from overlapping and attacking the space in the corner. Either X4 or X3 can go with that run, and the remaining player can try to alter the flight of O7's free kick. Most of the remaining players in the penalty box can mark man-to-man. It would be necessary to cover the near post area of the field with a zonal player (X2).

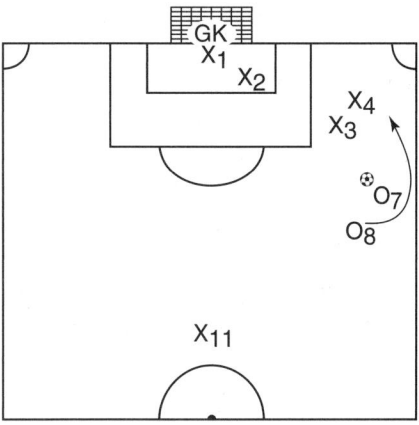

Figure 6.15 Key player positioning for defending wide free kicks.

Defending Throws

A throw-in is the most common restart of the game and therefore should not be neglected. Defenders must not lose concentration when the ball goes out of play. This is not the time to rest or "tune out." Instead, defenders should take the opportunity while the ball is out of play to mark the opposition, especially around the throw-in area, where marking needs to be very tight. Man-to-man marking is all that is required.

Long throws in the attacking third of the field need special attention. Many teams have players who can throw a ball into the opposition's 6-yard box, and if the defense is not careful this can be very dangerous. It's important to have a sense of the length of the throw, as well as the target player the thrower is aiming for inside the 6-yard box. Once this player has been identified, she should be marked from the front and the back. The goalkeeper should also be alert, normally beginning in the front half of her goal. As with all set plays, when the ball is launched into the penalty box, the key is to be alert and be first to the ball, then react quickly to all situations.

CHAPTER 7

Physical Conditioning and Nutrition

There is more to soccer than attending practices and games. In order to attain goals and maximize success, players must be willing to commit fully to a strength and conditioning program. The game of soccer has changed over the years, becoming much more athletic, with speed and strength playing big roles. To succeed at the higher levels, players must work on all aspects of their fitness. Training for strength and conditioning should be combined with a healthy, sensible diet to attain the best results. This chapter lays out a program for developing speed, strength, explosion to the ball, and fitness on the field, as well as nutrition guidelines for maximizing performance.

Elements of a Physical Conditioning Program

Excellent physical conditioning is necessary for excelling at high-level soccer. It must become part of a player's lifestyle, something he is prepared to work on every day, both in practice and in his own time. Physical conditioning involves six main components: warm-up, flexibility, agility, speed, cardiorespiratory fitness, and strength. The following sections detail each component and include drills that athletes can integrate into various phases of training. The drills are meant as starting points, and coaches and players can easily substitute their own activities. The key is to understand which types of activity can improve which facets of conditioning, then include them in one's workout.

Warm-Up

A warm-up should be performed daily to prepare the body for activity by elevating the heart rate and raising body temperature. A warm-up stimulates blood flow to the muscles, getting the body ready to perform high-intensity activity. Players should always begin with a vigorous warm-up; skipping it increases the risk of injury.

I recommend using dynamic stretches and movements to warm up because they mimic the types of movement used in soccer. Stretching with movement (as compared with static stretching) prepares the muscle more readily for activity. The following subsections offer suggestions for dynamic warm-up activities. After stretching, I recommend doing 5 to 15 minutes of ball work to get the heart rate up: Individual ball work, small-sided games, and keep-away all work well. Ball work can also involve technical and even tactical aspects.

A-SKIP

Start on your toes. Bring one leg up, so that your heel is tight to your buttocks, your thigh parallel to the ground, and your ankle locked, with your toes up. As you bring your heel to your buttocks, briefly hop off the ground and land (in a skipping motion) with your standing leg. Lower the raised foot back to the ground. Alternate sides.

B-SKIP

Start on your toes. As in the A-skip, bring one leg up, so that your heel is tight to your buttocks, your thigh parallel to the ground, and your ankle locked, with your toes up. As you bring your heel to your buttocks, briefly hop off the ground and land (in a skipping motion) with your standing leg. Now, however, rather than lowering the leg back to the ground, as in the A-skip, extend it out in front of you so that it is relatively straight. Finish by pulling it back down to the ground from its extended position. Alternate sides.

CARIOCA

Stand with your knees bent, back straight, and shoulders and hips square to your head. Start by moving to the right, crossing your left leg in front of your right and reaching for maximal distance. Now bring your right leg out from behind the left and reach farther to the right side of your body. Then cross the left leg behind the right and again move your right leg to the right of your body. You should cross left over right, then right over left. Do the opposite and move from side to side.

SIDE-TO-SIDE SHUFFLE

Stand with your feet a little more than shoulder-width apart, heels over your toes, knees slightly bent, torso straight, and head up. Start by sliding your right foot toward the left until it is centered under your body. Then drive off of the right foot and move your left foot until your feet are a little more than shoulder-width apart. Repeat. It will look like a side-to-side shuffle, leading with the left leg on every step. Alternate leading legs. Over 10 yards (9 meters), do 5 repetitions leading with the left, and 5 leading with the right.

HIGH-KNEE

Move slowly down the field, driving your knees up to your chest, with a slight forward lean of your body to propel you forward. (This will look like running in place.) Make sure that your ankles are locked, your toes up, your heel close to your buttocks, and your arms swinging from the shoulder, not the elbow.

SPRINT

Sprint at 75 percent of your maximum speed from the end line of the field to the edge of the penalty box. Repetitions can vary from 5 to 10, and they can also be added at the end of a fast footwork drill as a 10-yard (9-meter) run. You can also sprint at 100 percent of your maximum speed, with jog-recovery back to the starting point.

Flexibility

A flexibility program involves a series of stretches intended to increase range of motion in order to prevent injury, improve performance, and prevent muscle tightness after workouts. Flexibility is crucial to obtaining maximal speed and jump height, as well as preventing the tightness that can compromise proper performance. Integrating flexibility training into a conditioning program also greatly reduces the chance of injury. Flexibility exercises should be performed before any other activity and after every workout. It is particularly important to stretch after working in the weight room.

Each athlete needs a partner to perform the following stretches. Each stretch should be held for about 10 seconds. The first five stretches should be performed in order, using one leg, then repeated in order using the other leg. The quad stretch and hip flexor stretch should be performed in this way as well.

HEEL CORD

Lie on your back and have your partner grasp your foot. Your partner should raise your leg to a 45-degree angle (with your knee fully extended so that your leg is relatively straight), then push your toes toward your shin until you feel a good stretch.

FRONT OF SHIN

Lie on your back and have your partner grasp your ankle. Your partner should raise your leg to a 45-degree angle (with your knee fully extended so that your leg is relatively straight), then pull up on your toes until you feel a good stretch.

HAMSTRING

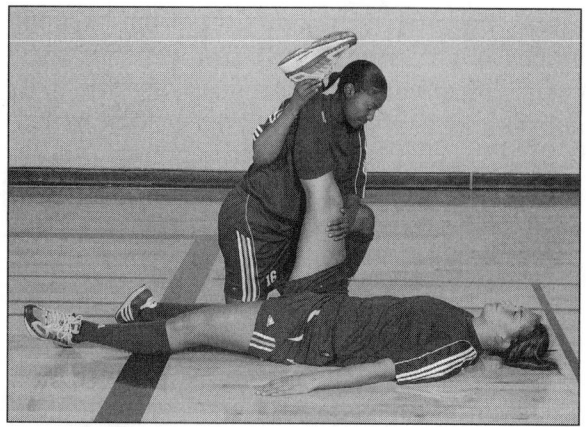

Lie on your back and have your partner grasp your ankle. Your partner should then raise your leg while you keep your knee fully extended (with your leg comfortably straight). Your partner should then push the whole leg back until you feel a good stretch in your hamstring.

SOFT KNEE

From the hamstring stretch position, have your partner put his or her thumb into the crease behind your knee. Your partner should push your knee to your chest with a bent leg, then extend your ankle outward until you feel a good stretch. Maintain the bend in your leg, and push your ankle toward your partner's chest.

KNEE ACROSS

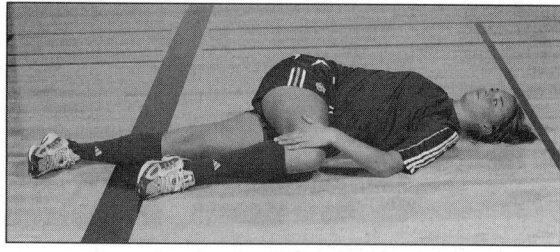

Lie on your back and keep your shoulders flat on the ground. Bend one leg, grasp the knee with your opposing hand, and pull it across your body. Your opposite leg should remain straight on the floor.

FIGURE-4

Lie on your back and place the ankle of your stretching leg on top of your opposite knee, so that your legs form a 4.

BUTTERFLY

Begin in a seated position, with your feet together on the ground and your heels pushed as close to the inside of your thighs as possible. Relax your legs so that your knees move toward the floor. Your partner should put light pressure on your knees to push them toward the floor.

QUAD

Lie on your stomach, with one leg straight on the ground and the other leg bent at the knee so that your ankle comes toward your buttocks. Your partner holds that knee up to 6 inches (15 centimeters) off the ground and pushes your ankle toward your buttocks.

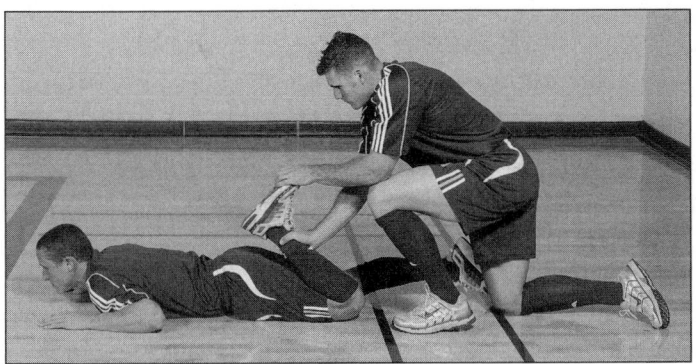

HIP FLEXOR

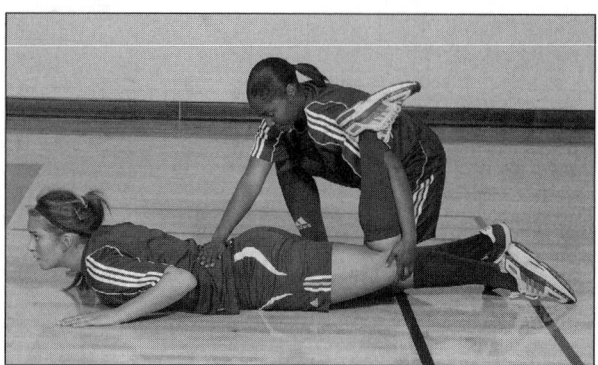

Lie on your stomach, with one leg straight on the ground and the other leg bent at the knee so that your ankle comes toward your buttocks. Have your partner put one hand into the small of your back and pull up on your knee with the other hand. Whereas pushing the ankle (in the quad stretch) stretches the quad, pulling the knee here stretches the hip flexors.

Agility

Agility is one of those characteristics that soccer players *must* have if they are going to be successful. By the very nature of the game, physical contact occurs constantly, and players who can stay on their feet and "ride" tackles when being physically challenged are at a big advantage. It also takes great agility and mobility to wriggle out of tight situations when surrounded by opponents.

The agility drills in this section are of two types: quick-feet drills and field agilities. The first eight drills in this section are quick-feet drills that should be performed as a series. In each one, the player jumps over the line as many times as possible in 10 seconds, resting for about 30 seconds between exercises. The remainder are plyometric drills—exercises that increase explosiveness by enabling muscles to achieve maximal quick contraction to increase vertical and lateral movement. They are intended to link maximal strength with maximal speed of movement. At the completion of each rep of a plyometric drill, players should sprint 10 to 15 yards (9 to 14 meters). Players should rest about 35 seconds between sets and get about 1 minute of rest between exercises.

SINGLE-LEG FRONT-TO-BACK

Hop forward over the line with your right foot. Then hop back across the line as quickly as possible. Do as many reps as you can in the given amount of time. Repeat with your left foot.

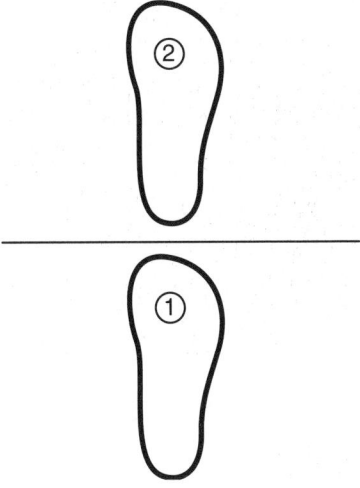

SINGLE-LEG SIDE-TO-SIDE

Hop sideways across the line with your right root. Then hop back across the line as quickly as possible. Do as many reps as you can in the given amount of time. Repeat with your left foot.

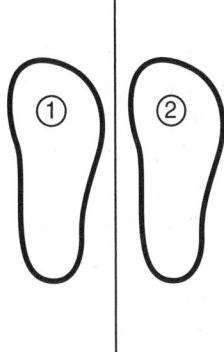

DOUBLE-LEG FRONT-TO-BACK

Hop forward over the line with both feet. Then hop back across the line as quickly as possible. Do as many reps as you can in the given amount of time.

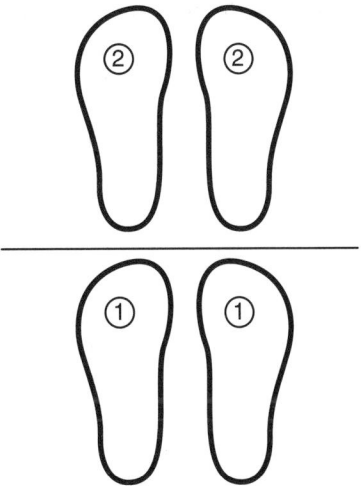

DOUBLE-LEG SIDE-TO-SIDE

Hop sideways across the line with both feet. Then hop back across the line as quickly as possible. Do as many reps as you can in the given amount of time.

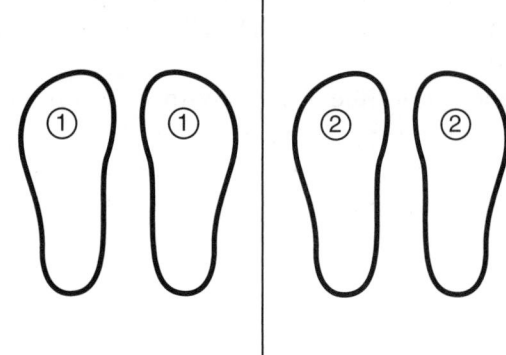

ON AND OFF THE LINE

Stand with both feet touching the line. Then hop and spread your feet apart. Upon touching the ground, quickly hop and bring both feet back together. Do as many reps as you can in the given amount of time.

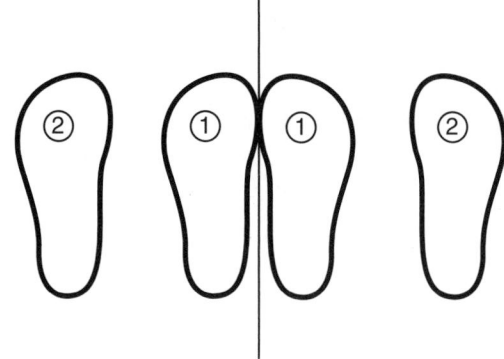

ALTERNATING FEET

Stand with your right foot in front of the line and your left foot behind it. Hop and quickly change foot positions, so that your left foot is in front of the line and your right foot is behind it. Do as many reps as you can in the given amount of time.

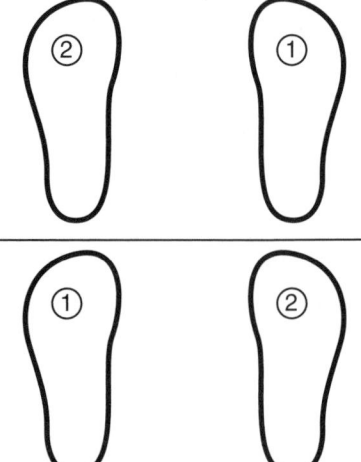

SCISSORS

Straddle the line with your feet spread apart. Quickly bring your right foot in front of your body and across the line, while your left foot goes behind you and across the line. Hop back to your beginning position, then reverse the activity so that your left foot goes in front of you and your right foot goes behind you. Do as many reps as you can in the given amount of time.

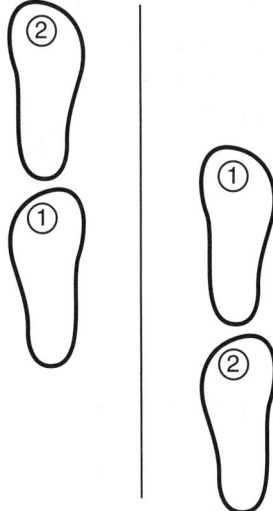

SHUTTLE RUNS A AND B

Place six cones 5 yards (4.5 meters) from each other in a line. For shuttle A, start at the first cone and sprint to the second, then backpedal back to the first cone. Next, sprint from the starting point to the third cone and backpedal back to the first. Continue in this pattern all the way through the cones. For shuttle B, start at the first cone and sprint to the second, then turn and sprint back to the first cone. Next, sprint to the third cone, then turn and sprint back to the first. Continue in this pattern all the way through the cones.

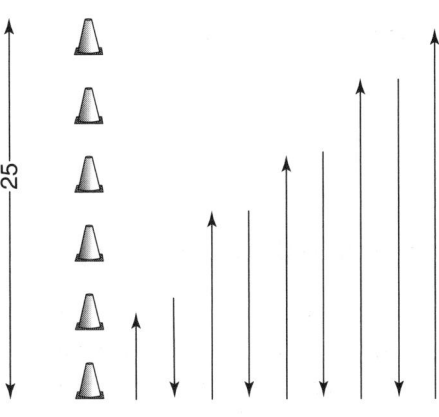

IN/OUT

Imagine five dots in the shape shown. Start with your left foot on dot A and your right foot on dot B. Hop and land with both feet on dot C. Then hop again and land with your left foot on dot D and your right foot on dot E. Hop back and land with both feet on dot C, then hop again and land with your left foot on dot A and your right foot on dot B. Repeat 5 times.

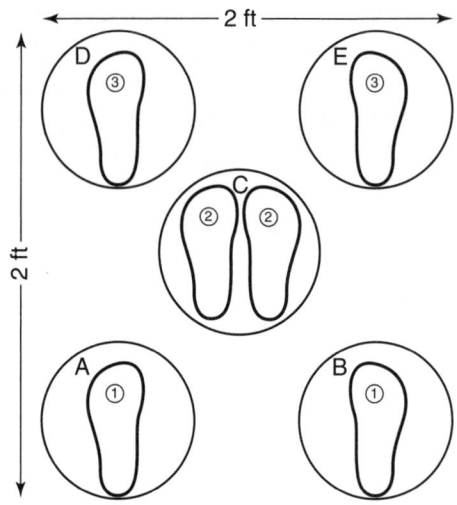

SINGLE-LEG HOURGLASS

Imagine five dots in the shape shown. Start with your right foot on dot B, then hop to dot C, to dot E, across to dot D, back to dot C, back to dot A, and over to dot B. This pattern draws an hourglass. Repeat 5 times, then switch feet and do the whole thing using your left foot. To execute a double-leg hourglass, hop from the dots in the same order but with both feet together.

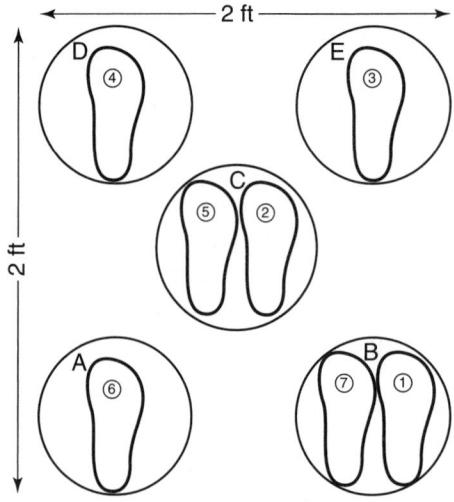

SQUAT JUMP

Stand in a squat position, with your thighs parallel to the floor, arms up with your hands on the back of the head, and feet shoulder-width apart. Jump up and out. You are trying to achieve maximal height on your jump. Land with your feet shoulder-width apart and your knees over your toes, moving slightly forward with each jump. As soon as you land, get back into the squat position and go right back up. Perform 5 consecutive jumps, then finish with a short sprint of 5 to 10 yards (4.5 to 9 meters).

THREE-CONE HOP

Place three cones 2 feet (0.6 meter) from each other in a line. Starting at one end of the line, hop with your right foot (lifting your knee as high as possible toward your chest) into the area between the first and second cones. As soon as you land, immediately jump into the area between the second and third cones. Then jump again to the other side of the third cone. Turn (still on your right foot) and jump through the cones going the other direction. As soon as you finish with the right foot, go through the cones with your left foot. Then jump through with both feet. Perform five reps for each leg.

SINGLE-LEG, SIDE-TO-SIDE CONE HOP

Stand beside a cone. Jump sideways over the cone with one leg, driving the knee of the jumping leg toward your chest. Upon landing, immediately jump back over the cone using the other leg. Jumping over and back completes 1 rep. Do as many as possible in a given amount of time (e.g., 30 to 60 seconds).

SINGLE-LEG HOP

Perform 5 successive hops on one leg, then sprint 10 to 15 yards (9 to 14 meters). Jog-recover back to the starting point. Switch legs. Perform 3 to 5 reps on each leg.

Speed

Speed kills the opponent! This might be the most significant factor in the game of soccer. Many coaches would take an average soccer player with great speed over a great soccer player with average speed. Each person is born with a certain genetically determined capability for speed, and players who lack good speed must try to compensate in other areas and hope for the best. The good news is that speed can be improved within a given range, so it is very important to work at it. Players who do so will get quicker.

The best way to improve speed is to sprint, which differs from cardio training (covered next) in that the object of speed drills is not to cause fatigue. Sprinting works on the body's anaerobic system, where the energy is pulled from storage in the muscles. Plenty of rest can be given between runs, so that the athlete does not tire. Speed work thus consists of shorter distances with more rest between runs.

BASIC SPRINT

Sprint three different distances: 20, 30, and 50 yards (18, 27, and 46 meters). After each sprint, walk back to the starting point in order to ensure a full recovery before the next repetition. Each sprint must be performed with maximum effort!

I like to put a variation or two into these sprints. For instance, on a 20-yard (18-meter) sprint, we may have players begin with their back turned toward the direction of the sprint, thus making it a turn-and-sprint. We may ask players to jump up and down on the same spot, then sprint on the whistle, or even sit down so that they must get quickly to their feet before they begin to sprint. Such variations are intended to simulate game situations before the sprint.

7-BY-30 SPRINT

Place four cones in a straight line, spaced evenly over 30 yards (27 meters). Stand at the first cone and sprint toward the last one. Accelerate between the first and second cones, so that you are at full speed by the second one. Maintain full sprint until you hit the third cone, then decelerate until you reach the fourth one. Turn and jog back to the first cone in 20 seconds, then repeat the process 7 more times.

5-BY-10 SPRINT

Place two cones 10 yards (9 meters) apart. Sprint back and forth between the two cones 5 times, there and back being one time. This is explosive, short-sprint work that develops quickness of turn, an important capability for soccer players. Take plenty of rest between reps.

© AP Images

In order to attain goals and maximize success, players must be willing to fully commit themselves to a challenging conditioning program.

ACCELERATION RUN

Athletes stand at the end of the field. On the coach's signal, they perform a half-field run, increasing speed from 25 percent, to 50, to 75, and finally to 100 percent during each quarter of the run. This is excellent speed work because the gradual build up of pace enables the athlete to run at his or her fastest at the end.

Cardiovascular Training

All players need to be physically capable of playing a 90-minute soccer game. Unfortunately, the large squad sizes and frequent substitutions used in the United States do not always require players to be as fit as they should be. The time may come when one needs to play for a full game, and players should prepare for this eventuality. The cardiovascular training program is intended to build a baseline of fitness, then train the aerobic system to the level needed to play the game. Unlike speed work, where the athlete rests between drills, cardio training requires running for distance until fatigued.

Players must have a strong cardiovascular base before any other fitness gains can be achieved, and this base should be established during the preseason. Once this is done, it is neither necessary nor beneficial to continue to work at a high-level cardio program. Game play (along with occasional cardiovascular training for maintenance) is sufficient.

1:1:1 RUN

Run as hard as you can for 1 minute, walk for 1 minute, then jog for 1 minute. Repeat in this order for at least 10 minutes.

120

Sprint the length of the field (120 yards) in the specified time, then jog back to the starting point in the allotted recovery time. Sprint and recovery times should vary depending on age and ability level of the group. For older players (15 and above), I suggest an 18-second sprint with a 42-second jog-recovery, repeated 10 times.

2-MILE RUN

You will need to perform this run on a track. Coaches should set time limits based on quality and age of athlete. I suggest that college athletes complete the run in 12 minutes, and scholarship athletes should be quite capable of that. For high school players, I suggest 12 1/2 minutes.

15:15 RUN

Sprint for 15 seconds, then jog for 15 seconds. Repeat for 2 minutes. Next, back-pedal for 5 seconds, turn and sprint for 10 seconds, then jog for 15 seconds. Repeat this sequence for 2 minutes. Then go back to the first pattern for another 2 minutes.

300-METER SHUTTLE

Place two cones 50 yards (46 meters) apart. Run from one cone to the other and back 3 times, for a total of 300 yards (274 meters). Coaches should adjust the allotted time according to age and ability, and I suggest test-running this sort of activity with a couple of the team's better athletes to get a sense of how much time to allow. The target for the whole group should be a little slower than the results of the test run.

Strength

The game of soccer has improved over the last decade or two. There are several reasons for this, most of which are connected to the improved athleticism of soccer players. The physical aspect of the game is very important, and the ability of an individual player to not only win a ball in a challenge but also maintain possession when challenged is enormous. This can be the difference in scoring or stopping a goal being scored, and will have a huge impact on the result of the game. Players cannot afford to be easily pushed off the ball.

Strength training for soccer should consist of total body activities that work all the major muscle groups in the legs, arms, back, abdominals, and chest. This program is done almost exclusively in the weight room. Most strength exercises can be adapted to the equipment available, whether barbells, dumbbells, or machines. Some strength exercises, such as push-ups and pull-ups, use body weight, with no equipment required.

In my program, weight training is very important. Not only does it provide our players with the necessary strength, but also it reduces the possibility of injury. We introduce some strength activities during the preseason in August to help new players learn our system, activities, and techniques, and we typically do three sessions a week for about 3 weeks. Once our season begins, however, we downshift into maintenance mode, lifting once or twice a week (and avoiding game day and the day before a game). At this point, the workout often consists only of light upper-body work, with no leg activity at all. Players' legs are tired enough from training and playing games.

Strength training is a complex subject, and safety is of the utmost importance. This section includes a sampling of exercises for both upper and body here to get you started. I recommend referring to *Encyclopedia of Muscle & Strength* by

Jim Stoppani (Human Kinetics, 2006) for exercises, complete technique descriptions, and safety considerations. It is also advisable to work with an experienced strength coach who can make sure that all safety measures are in place. Technique is crucial in weight training; if it is done incorrectly, the athlete risks injury. Athletes should never train by themselves, and they should always have a spotter when working with weights.

CALF RAISES

Begin standing on an elevated surface so that your heels are lower than your toes. Rise up onto your toes using only the strength of your calf muscles. Pause at the top of each rep and lower yourself slowly back to the start position until you feel a stretch in your calves. Do not bounce at the top or bottom.

STEP-UPS

You will need a 12-16 inch (1/3 meter) box for this exercise, or you can use the bottom row of a bleacher. Begin standing on the ground with a dumbbell in each hand with both arms hanging at your sides. Step up onto the box leading with the right leg and follow with the left leg until you are fully on top of the box. Step down with the left leg leading and the right leg following. Alternate which leg leads with every rep. Maintain erect posture throughout the exercise.

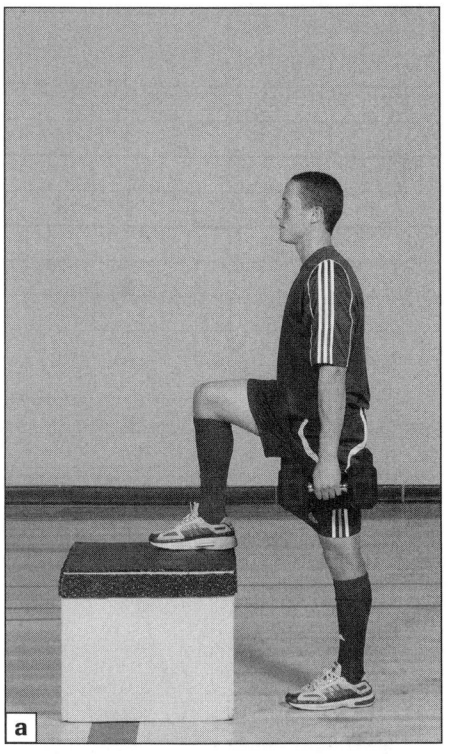

LUNGES

Stand upright, holding dumbbells in both hands with both arms hanging at your sides. Step forward with your right foot and bend your right knee until your right thigh is parallel with the floor. Maintain erect posture: torso near vertical, chest out and shoulders back, and chin up. Push yourself back to a standing position by straightening the right knee. Repeat the lunge with the other leg.

BENCH PRESS

This can be performed with a barbell, dumbbells, or nautilus type machine. Lie on your back on a flat bench and place your feet flat on the floor. Grasp the weight slightly wider than shoulder width with palms facing away from your body. Begin with arms extended so they are perpendicular to your body. Bend the elbows out to the side of your body and lower the weight under control until it almost touches your chest. Press the weight all the way back up so that the arms are back in the extended starting position. Be sure to keep your back straight throughout the exercise, and do not bounce the weights when lowering or raising them.

INCLINE PRESS

This exercise is the same as the bench press except it is performed while lying on an inclined bench. This can be performed with a barbell, dumbbells, or nautilus type machine. Lie on your back on bench that is inclined 30 to 45 degrees and place your feet flat on the floor. Grasp the weight slightly wider than shoulder width with palms facing away from your body. Begin with arms extended so they are perpendicular to your body. Bend the elbows out to the side of your body and lower the weight under control until it almost touches your chest. Press the weight all the way back up so that the arms are back in the extended starting position. Be sure to keep your back straight throughout the exercise, and do not bounce the weights when lowering or raising them.

SHOULDER PRESS

Use dumbbells for this exercise. Sit with erect posture on a bench with support behind your back and place both feet flat on the floor. Grip the weights with palms facing away from your body. Begin with the elbows bent by your sides and the weights near your shoulders. Straighten your arms and press the dumbbells straight over your head until your arms are fully extended. Slowly lower the weights back to the original position.

Nutrition

What we eat and drink plays a significant role in accomplishing our athletic goals and maximizing our quality of performance. Food provides us with energy, and water is the cornerstone of proper functioning in all of our bodily systems. Without these building blocks, our bodies have a hard time growing. Hard-training athletes must be properly fueled in order to reach their physical potential. With proper nutrition, all of the work that we do in our conditioning programs will pay maximum benefit.

Unfortunately, many athletes are not fully aware of what they are putting into their bodies, or they simply do not know what choices to make to best serve their needs. Misinformation and fad diets abound in magazines, and it can be difficult to tell which have merit. Perhaps the most important thing to know about nutrition is that there simply are no miracles or shortcuts. Good nutrition is about leading a healthy lifestyle and creating consistently proper eating habits. Athletes should not get caught up in the hype of supplements; they simply do not need the stuff. Much of it is unnecessary--just commercial hype. Athletes will achieve the most success by learning how to plan their nutrition and make the best choices possible. This section provides guidance on how to use water and food to optimize the internal environment that is the human body.

Water

The human body needs water to function properly and to grow. Water constitutes 55 to 60 percent of an adult's body weight. It provides the environment in which nearly all the body's activities occur, plays a part in almost all metabolic reactions, lubricates joints, and acts as a shock absorber. Drinking water is even the best treatment for fluid retention (retained fluid shows up as excess weight that players must carry in training and competition): The body tends to hold onto certain substances it lacks or is not supplied with, and as fluid, specifically water, is supplied through the diet, the body tends to let go of any excess it may have been storing. Water also helps maintain proper muscle tone by giving muscles their natural ability to contract.

Thus it is vital that an athlete stay hydrated. Thirst causes us to provide needed water, but it lags behind the body's need. By the time one feels thirsty, the body is already in need of water. As a result, it is important for athletes to include a large amount of water in their diet--6 to 8 cups (about 1.5 to 2 liters) per day. Preferably, the water should be cold, as cold water is absorbed into the system more quickly than warm water (Jane Pentz, *Nutrition Specialist Manual*, 6th edition, LMA Publishing, 2000). The easiest way to stay hydrated is to carry a water bottle and sip from it throughout the day, particularly following workouts. Intense workouts use a large amount of fluid that must be replaced. Caffeine should be avoided altogether. Soda, tea, and coffee are *dehydrating,* thus undercutting one's efforts to provide the body with sufficient water.

Diet

This section gives general guidelines on macronutrients, along with sample menus. Individual application will vary, but the section is intended to provide concrete examples of what and how an athlete should eat in order to optimize training and game performance. For more information, I recommend *Nancy Clark's Sports Nutrition Guidebook* (Human Kinetics, 2008).

Good eating should follow these general guidelines:

Grains (e.g., bread, cereal, rice, pasta)	6 to 11 servings per day
Fruits and vegetables	5 to 9 servings
Meat, beans, eggs	2 or 3 servings
Milk, yogurt, cheese	2 or 3 servings
Fatty foods and sweets	Use sparingly!

These guidelines form a useful tool in planning daily meal allotments. Athletes should remember that they require a higher caloric intake than sedentary individuals and will sometimes benefit from breaking down their diet into carbohydrate, fat, and protein requirements in order to optimize performance gains through nutrition. The following breakdowns are recommended:

Carbohydrate	55% to 60% of daily caloric intake
Fat	20% to 25%
Protein	12% to 20%

Carbohydrate is the first energy source the body will use, and there are two types: simple and complex. Simple carbohydrate is found in fruits, vegetables, and table sugar. Fruit and veggie sugar is different from table sugar in that it can consist of both simple and complex carbohydrate. Complex carbohydrate, which is more readily stored by the body for use as energy, is found in grains (e.g., cereal, bread, pasta, rice), vegetables, and fruit. Eating fruits and vegetables is a good way to get simple carbohydrate. Refined or processed food such as candy and sugar-coated cereals should be avoided as it will quickly spike your energy level, but then drop fast.

Although fat has something of a bad reputation these days, it is an essential nutrient in a diet. The key is to choose the right sources of fat. Examples of foods with high fat content are cheese, oil, butter, whole milk or ice cream, bacon, and sausage. Athletes should avoid fried foods and foods high in animal fat—that is, saturated fat and trans fat—and look instead to get their fat from cheeses, nuts, milk, and unsaturated oils such as olive oil. Be aware that many cheeses and whole milk contain animal fat, and if they are part of your diet, then you should choose reduced fat dairy products.

Protein is the third macronutrient. It consists of amino acids, considered to be the building blocks of muscle. In fact, protein is so essential for building muscle that the body will break it down and use it for energy only if no other source of energy can be found. Good (lean) sources of protein are fish, chicken, lean beef, beans, and eggs.

Carbohydrate and protein provide 4 calories per gram of food, while fat provides 9 calories per gram. Athletes should be aware of their daily caloric intake. Though it may not be necessary to count calories on an ongoing basis, it is a good exercise to do when one first gets serious about nutrition as an important part of training. Reading labels of prepared foods is another important exercise.

Eating regular meals and snacks is essential to maintaining optimal energy and fitness levels. Skipping meals is *not* recommended, since it causes the body to begin using muscle as fuel. Breakfast is especially important, since skipping it forces the body to go 18 hours (from one evening to lunchtime the next day) without fuel. If a person does not have time to eat a complete breakfast, it should still be possible to eat 400 or 500 calories in fruit and bread. In addition to meals and snacks, it is important to consume a small amount of carbohydrate and electrolyte after a workout to replenish what was lost. Eating 200 to 400 calories of an energy bar, bread, or fruit will help the body recover and allow it to get on with building muscle.

Breakfast should generally consist of grains—that is, carbohydrate. A bit of protein in the form of eggs is not a bad choice, either. Lunch should be a more balanced meal, with some protein and some carbohydrate, and it should include fruits and vegetables. The contemporary American diet is woefully lacking in fruits and vegetables, and lunch is a good time to get them. Snacks should also consist largely of these nutrient-filled foods. Finally, dinner should involve mostly carbohydrate in the form of bread, potatoes, pasta, and vegetables, along with some protein. Table 7.1 offers good food choices for each meal and for snacks. Tables 7.2–7.4 provide sample daily meal plans that incorporate healthful foods. They should be used as a starting point for athletes learning how to plan their own meals. And it is worth remembering that eating a variety of foods keeps a person from getting bored and also provides a wide range of nutrients.

Table 7.1 Good Food Choices for Meals and Snacks

Breakfast	Lunch	Dinner	Snacks
Pancakes, waffles, or French toast with syrup but no butter	Baked potato (toppings limited to a little butter or low-fat ranch dressing instead of sour cream)	Rice	Fruits
Egg sandwich (egg on bread)	Green salad with low-fat or light dressing	Pasta with marinara sauce or light oil	Fruit juice (100% fruit)
Toast and jelly	Turkey, chicken, or lean roast beef sandwich (lots of veggies but light on mayo and cheese)	Potatoes (baked or broiled, with no fatty preparations)	Breads
Bagels (light on the cream cheese—honey or jelly can be used instead)	Pasta with marinara or meat sauce	Vegetables	Yogurt
Low-fat yogurt	Baked or broiled lean meats	Baked, broiled, or grilled lean meat	Pretzels
Cereal (in a bowl or bar)	Broth-based soups		
Fruit	Veggie pizza (cheese okay in limited amount)		
No bacon, sausage, or cheese	Pretzels		

Table 7.2 4,000-Calorie Sample Menu

	Serving	Calories	Carbohydrate calories	Fat calories	Protein calories
Breakfast					
Raisin bran	1 cup	139	120	5	14
Bagel	1	198	152	18	28
Cantaloupe	1/2 medium	92	81	3	8
Hash browns	1 cup	362	180	163	19
Poached egg	1	80	2	52	26
Wheat bread	2 slices	127	92	14	21
Jam	1 tbsp	115	112	2	1
Orange juice	250 ml (8 oz.)	111	100	4	7
Skim milk	375 ml (12 oz.)	131	75	3	53
Meal totals		**1355**	**914**	**264**	**177**
Lunch					
Orange juice	250 ml (8 oz.)	111	100	4	7
Diet soda	375 ml (12 oz.)	0	0	0	0
Fruit cocktail	1 cup	207	200	3	4
Green beans, cooked	1/2 cup	19	14	1	4
Mixed vegetables	1/2 cup	64	50	2	12
Spaghetti with meatballs	1 cup	334	155	105	74
Dinner roll	2	233	156	54	23
Reduced-fat cheese	90 g (3 oz.)	154	7	59	88
Sweet potato, baked	1	120	112	0	8
Meal totals		**1242**	**794**	**228**	**220**
Dinner					
Tea	375 ml (12 oz.)	3	3	0	0
Baked potato	2 medium	296	260	4	32
Peas, canned	1/2 cup	70	51	3	16
Steak, lean	150 g (5 oz.)	284	0	108	176
Whole wheat bread	2 slices	191	145	18	28
Gelatin with fruit	1 cup	194	115	68	11
Meal totals		**1038**	**574**	**201**	**263**
Snacks					
Apple	1	105	96	9	0
Chocolate pudding	1 cup	320	216	72	32
Meal Totals		**425**	**312**	**81**	**32**
Daily totals		**4060**	**2594 (64%)**	**774 (19%)**	**692 (17%)**

Table 7.3 3,000-Calorie Sample Menu

	Serving	Calories	Carbohydrate calories	Fat calories	Protein calories
Breakfast					
Scrambled egg	2	164	8	108	48
Oatmeal	1 cup	142	100	18	24
Raisins	1/4 cup	111	105	1	5
Orange juice	250 ml (8 oz.)	111	100	4	7
Bagel	1	198	152	18	28
Skim milk	375 ml (12 oz.)	131	75	3	53
Meal totals		**857**	**540**	**152**	**165**
Lunch					
Turkey, light	250 g (8 oz.)	142	0	30	112
Lettuce	1 piece	2	2	0	0
Tomato	3 slices	10	8	0	2
Mustard	1 tsp	4	1	2	1
Pita bread	1	165	132	9	24
Yogurt, low-fat	1 cup	230	172	18	40
Beef noodle soup	2 cups	274	114	97	63
Fruit punch drink	375 ml (12 oz.)	176	176	0	0
Meal totals		**1003**	**605**	**156**	**242**
Dinner					
Ham, lean	200 g (7 oz.)	290	0	95	195
Collard greens	1 cup	28	20	0	8
Cornbread	1 piece, medium	116	104	0	12
Black-eyed peas	1 cup	201	140	9	52
Wild rice	1 cup	223	191	5	27
Carrots, raw	1 cup	53	44	3	6
Water	375 ml (12 oz.)	0	0	0	0
Meal totals		**911**	**499**	**112**	**300**
Snacks					
Fig bars	4	212	168	36	8
Banana	1	107	100	2	5
Meal totals		**319**	**268**	**38**	**13**
Daily totals		**3090**	**1912 (62%)**	**458 (15%)**	**720 (23%)**

Table 7.4 2,000-Calorie Sample Menu

	Serving	Calories	Carbohydrate calories	Fat calories	Protein calories
Breakfast					
Grape-Nuts cereal	1/4 cup	104	92	0	12
Skim milk	175 ml (6 oz.)	69	38	4	27
Whole wheat bread	2 slices	129	94	14	21
Margarine	2 pats	70	0	70	0
Cantaloupe	1/2 medium	91	80	3	8
Meal totals		**463**	**304**	**91**	**68**
Lunch					
Corn tortillas	3	207	156	27	24
Ground beef, lean	90 g (3 oz.)	228	0	144	84
Lettuce	1/4 cup	6	6	0	0
Tomato	1 medium	40	32	0	8
Onion	1/4 cup	16	14	0	2
Spanish rice	1 1/2 cup	200	149	35	16
Root beer	375 ml (12 oz.)	155	155	0	0
Meal totals		**852**	**512**	**206**	**134**
Dinner					
Scallops, steamed	125 g (4 oz.)	120	0	14	106
Whole wheat roll	2	191	145	18	28
Broccoli	1 cup	57	32	9	16
Baked potato	1 medium	224	204	0	20
Corn	1 ear	97	76	9	12
Tea	375 ml (12 oz.)	3	3	0	0
Meal totals		**692**	**460**	**50**	**182**
Snacks					
Reduced-fat cheese	60 g (2 oz.)	102	4	40	58
Grapes	30	61	49	8	4
Meal totals		**163**	**53**	**48**	**62**
Daily totals		**2170**	**1329 (61%)**	**395 (18%)**	**446 (21%)**

CHAPTER 8

Practice Sessions

High-quality, interesting, and informative practice sessions are the lifeline for all programs. If a team does a good job in this area, good things are going to happen. I don't know how many times I've heard players complain about how boring practice has been (not talking about my own sessions, of course!). Naturally, players have to spend a lot of time improving their technical ability, which does require a lot of repetition, and for some players it's a tedious process. There is no reason it should be. With a little imagination, skills can be presented in different ways to create variety in a session. This chapter offers advice to both players and coaches on approaching practice, setting up a practice session, and organizing it. Practice sessions are seasonal and thus will change, sometimes considerably, depending on the time of year, so the chapter also addresses modifying a session to meet players' current needs.

Players' Attitudes Toward Practice

Even before they attend their first practice session, players have to realize they will get out of a session only what they put into it. It's all about attitude. Players have to maintain a positive attitude toward the session and work hard at whatever is being asked of them. It is the players' responsibility to go to every training session and attempt to make it the best one they have ever done—every time! They should not settle for second best.

Several years ago I was fortunate enough to coach an Under-16 (Olympic development) national team at an international tournament in France. A week before traveling, the team met for a 3-day coaching session at the IMG Academies in Florida. What impressed me about those boys was not so much their ability, though it was good, but more their attitude. It struck me then, as it still does today, that there was a reason those boys were representing their country, and it was far more than just their talent. I have seen many players who had more talent than some of those boys but were nowhere near as good. That group never had to be told anything twice. They listened intently to everything said to them; in fact, they were like insatiable sponges unable to get enough information. Every minute of every session was special to them. They cared and strived for perfection. That's why they were at the top.

Players should understand that it is the coach who picks the team, and that players need to make a positive impression on that coach in order to be selected. Again, this sometimes takes more than sheer ability. A coach can be very influenced by seeing a player always pay attention when he speaks. Players should look him in the eye when he talks. They should do their best to be in the top group in fitness sessions, and when the coach asks for help in setting up the field for the session, they should be available and eager. All these traits make a difference in how a coach perceives a player—perhaps even the crucial difference in getting selected.

It is possible to work very hard, yet retain the ability to be lighthearted and find amusing moments. Training sessions need a positive atmosphere, which is a major ingredient for successful learning. So how do we get it? It takes effort from both sides—player and coach—but having a sense of humor and a pleasant demeanor is a good way to begin. A session must include fun; it cannot be deadly serious the whole time. Players and coaches should be able to smile at each other and not take mistakes too seriously. In fact, players *have to* make mistakes to get better. I prefer players who are amused easily and play with smiles on their faces because it improves the atmosphere and makes for a more enjoyable session, and I believe players get much more out of it.

In the end, though, it is up to each player to get mentally prepared for the training session, and this requires effort, mental toughness, and focus. Players must not allow themselves to go into any session with a casual approach. Though it is sometimes difficult, they should approach each training session with the same focus they bring to a game. Coaches who demand nothing but a player's best—and who see to it that everything is done well every time—will help players in this quest.

Elements of Practice

Most of the time, when I walk up to a training session and the players are there before me, it is a fair bet that one of two things is happening: Either they are sitting around doing nothing, or they are shooting on goal. At least with the latter, some soccer activity is taking place, but neither is what I really want. The easy way to ensure a productive beginning in a coaching session is for the coach to arrive early and have the session already set up so that it can begin on time. When players arrive, they can immediately change their shoes and be told by the coach how best to get ready for the session. Possibilities include jogging, stretching, and doing individual ball work. In fact, it is best if the coach puts a system in place so that players understand what is expected of them if they arrive early at practice. And coaches should have the session ready to go and begin on time!

Over the years, I have been asked to do many clinics for teams and players, and I am always shocked when asked to do a 3-hour session. I do not believe that even a highly motivated professional can concentrate for that length of time. Practice should be about quality, not quantity, and after countless training sessions over the years I have settled on 90 minutes as the optimal length. A coach should end a session even sooner if the practice quality has deteriorated and he cannot motivate the group to get it back. There is no point in training if players are getting little out of it—all that does is risk a silly injury. I would recommend a clinic last no longer than two hours. It may be necessary to go a little longer than ninety minutes during the pre and early season stages while players are building fitness and getting organized.

The same basic structure should apply to all training sessions: a warm-up segment, followed by a tactical and technical section, and, to end the session, some type of game. Depending on the time of year and the level of play, it might also be necessary to do a fitness session. Most of the time, this should be done at the very end of the training, but on occasion it can be done on the front end in order to simulate late-game fatigue in the practice game at the end of the session. Fatigue is the main cause of mistakes on the field, and a fitness session at the beginning will help a coach and player gain awareness of this problem and perhaps prepare better for handling it in actual games. However, since the quality of the practice will drop considerably when fitness is done at the beginning, it is not a good idea to take this approach on a regular basis.

The worst sessions are usually the ones where too much time (or even a whole session) is spent on technical drills. When this approach is coupled with the fact that coaches like to talk—which stops the session much too often—players might be left feeling like they are getting very little out of a session, and they will most likely lose interest before the end. Thus it is advisable to allow time for game play toward the end of a session. Players love to play the game, and they will learn a lot just by doing that; in addition, they will at least get enjoyment from this segment even if the rest of the session has been a bore. Find time to play a game every practice session, even if it is only for a few minutes.

Warm-Up: 15 Minutes

The purpose of warming up is to increase the heart rate and get blood flowing to the muscles so they are loose and ready to perform. Players should not be fatigued by the warm-up, but they certainly should have a sweat on. Warming up can include stretching, jogging, and, if possible, an activity related to the main theme of the session. If you are not incorporating the dynamic stretching systems, and are using static stretches, then at least do some jogging before going into the stretches. Stretching cold muscles can be detrimental. Many coaches and players also like to incorporate "keep-away" games, where players are asked to complete as many passes as they can within a confined area (see chapter 3) in their warm-up sessions.

Static stretching involves stretching a particular body part without any movement, typically while sitting on the ground. In contrast, dynamic stretching, where the muscle is put through a range of movement while being stretched, has been found much more effective in preparing the muscles for soccer activity because it is much more explosive in nature. Whatever technique is used, players should make sure they have loosened their main muscle and ligament groups and raised their heart rates before proceeding.

Main Theme: 30 Minutes

The coach should select one topic for the session and focus on it exclusively. He should avoid getting sidetracked into other problem areas. It is always tempting to try to correct all problems at once, but this can lead to information overload and far too much stoppage of the game. I suggest that during the early season, coaches systematically go through the technical and tactical areas that they think need to be covered, perhaps beginning with passing and ball control, then moving through the various technical skills of the game.

As the season progresses, these sessions need to be related to correcting problems the team has encountered in the previous game. Sessions can also be used to help prepare the team for an upcoming game by making tactical adjustments. Themes can vary widely. Table 8.1 lists problems that may arise, along with possible session themes to help players solve those problems.

It is also helpful to use this time with the team to cover potential game scenarios: How would the team react if trailing 1-0 with 15 minutes to go? What would the coach want the players to do, and how would they play? What if they

Table 8.1 Suggestions for Themed Sessions

Problem	Possible themes
Not enough ball possession	• Passing: keep-away sessions or conditioned games such as two-touch • Technique sessions on passing • Good support play, creating angles to receive the ball • When to play long and when to play short
Too few goal-scoring opportunities	• Correct movement off the ball • Penetration down the flanks • Penetration down the middle • Crossing • Runs in the box • Shooting
Poor ball control	• Technical work on ball control • Quality of the first touch • Ball control both under and away from pressure • Mandatory two-touch (forces players to work on a good first touch)
Incorrect team shape	• Shadow play • Playing positions in mandatory segments of the field (players must play only within a designated area)
Weak defense	• Individual defending technique • Team defending in segments (back defenders, midfielders, and forwards) • Team defending as a whole unit • When to tackle and when not to • Heading

are reduced to 10 players? Or winning 1-0 as time winds down? Many times over the years I have regretted being less prepared for this last scenario than I should have been. Every player and every coach has had the displeasure of blowing a 1-0 lead late in the match by doing all the wrong things, only to see the other team tie or even win the game. It is well worth the time and effort to be prepared for *all* potential situations by covering them well in practice. Every player will know her roles and responsibilities for various scenarios, which allows a much better response in the game than having the coach scream instructions and try to make adjustments on the fly.

Game-Related Play: 30 to 40 Minutes

Players love to play the game, and I believe in allowing the team to play some type of game every day. This does not mean they simply play an unrestricted 11v11 game (though it is beneficial to do this once a week if the facility is available), but this activity should involve some form of competitive play, even if it is just a small-sided 5v5 game. Small-sided games (using full-sized goals) are excellent for game development. The reduced player count allows for more touches on the ball, and players still get the full benefits of a regular game, both tactically and technically. The full-sized goals allow all players to practice shooting, and they can never do enough of that, since, in the end, the game is about scoring goals. The coach should be wary of spending too much time on keep-away drills, where there is often no direction or end product of the game.

Small-sided games can be used to develop almost any skill or tactic. Coaching can easily be done in this format (versus the often overly elaborate drill setup); this approach is simple but very effective, with plenty of learning going on. For example, the coach can integrate the theme of the day into 5v5 game play. The key might be something as simple as a two-touch regulation, if the theme is passing. Or it might be much more complex if the theme is a tactical issue from a recent game. Perhaps the team struggled to score goals, so the emphasis is on having wingers cross the ball into the goal mouth and having strikers make late runs to "get on the end" of the cross and put the ball in the net. Whatever the problem, it can be covered in the 5v5 game.

Integrating a theme into game play can begin at a very basic level. The coach might break a particular skill or tactic into its fundamentals, requiring players to start with partner practice or even solo work. The intensity can then be slowly built up into more gamelike situations by adding numbers and conditions, so that players are performing it in the midst of more distractions. Begin with small numbers, achieve some success, and then increase the difficulty. As the numbers increase, so does the difficulty, and incremental increases in size may be best, perhaps from 3v3 to 5v5, to 8v8, to 11v11, always working on the same skill. Success in the small-sided environment will not guarantee the same progress and success in the full-sided game, so care should be taken to progress as slowly as needed.

Fitness

Finally, a session should address the issue of fitness. After all, a 90-minute soccer game played with effort requires a high fitness level. If a team trains and plays with intensity, the players will *maintain* their fitness level with minimal extra work. Preseason work, however, focuses on *achieving* the base fitness level; once game-level fitness has been reached, fitness work can then be kept to one or two sessions a week, depending on game schedule. Extra fitness work should not be done during the 2 or 3 days just before a game. Here are some fitness activities that can easily be incorporated into a practice session.

Shuttle Runs   This activity works on endurance with speed. Place six cones 5 yards (about 4.5 meters) apart, for a total distance of 25 yards (about 23 meters). Two players can work together with this set of cones; thus, a group of 16 players will need eight rows of cones. One player is timed as he runs to each cone and back without stopping. The run should be completed inside 32 seconds. The player then rests as his partner runs. The coach should decide how many reps each player does; I usually set a target of 10. If a player does not succeed in the allotted time, the coach decides what consequences should apply. The allotted time should be adjusted to the level of athlete.

Acceleration Runs   This activity involves excellent speed work. The best distance is probably 60 yards (about 55 meters). Players should slowly accelerate to the 60-yard mark, running at quarter-pace for the first 15 yards, half-pace for the second 15, three-quarter pace for the next 15, and finally full sprint for the last 15. They should jog or walk back for recovery. Repetitions are decided by the coach but should be in the range of 6 to 12.

Full-Field Runs   This is endurance work using the length of the soccer field, probably 110 to120 yards (about 100 to 110 meters). All players should run at once, with a target time of perhaps 25 seconds, then jog back to the starting point in 35 seconds. If they get back early, they may stop and rest. Each run will proceed on the 60-second mark, decreasing by 1 second each round. Thus the next run would be inside 24 seconds with a 36-second recovery, then 23 seconds with a 37-second recovery, and so on. Reps are decided by the coach or determined by ability level.

Pavlovs   This activity involves endurance and speed work. It is a partner activity, with each partner standing on the halfway line, outside the field of play and on opposite sides from each other. The coach may wish to partner a stronger runner with a weaker one to make the teams more equal. This exercise is not timed. On the whistle, the first partner runs halfway around field on the outside of the lines (i.e., outside the field of play) until he touches his partner's hand on the other side of the field. The partner then takes off on her half-field run (again, outside the field), while the first partner jog-recovers across the middle of the field along the halfway line. He needs to be back at his original starting point by the time his partner (the second runner) arrives to touch his hand. The process is repeated, as partner 1 begins his second rep while partner 2 jog-recovers back across the middle to her starting point. Reps are decided by the coach.

European Drills   This endurance activity is an all-time favorite used by many coaches. Paired up and running in two lines close to each other, the group runs on the outside of the field, constantly doing laps. The activity is controlled by the coach, who runs with the players. It is a timed run that should probably go for 20 minutes without stopping. The coach integrates a variety of activities into the run. He can slow the pace, increase it, or add push-ups, squat thrusts, piggyback runs, and so on. The point is to integrate many different physical activities and challenges intermingled with the run.

Lappers   This is very much an endurance activity, disliked by players because it is tough to do, but quite useful. As in the European drills, players are partnered and running in two lines, but here the group is also split in half at the middle point of the pack. At the coach's command, players in the front half of the pack take off as fast as they can go. They must stay outside of the field lines. The second half of the pack continues its jogging pace, also outside the field. The first pack continues to run as hard as they can until they catch up to the jogging pack a lap or two later. They will arrive into the back of the jogging pack. When the whole group is back together, the second group, now at the front, follows the same procedure the first group did, running as hard as they can until they catch up with the first group, who have been jog-recovering from their first run. Thus 1 rep is completed. Reps are decided by the coach, and 2 or 3 will likely be enough.

Cool-Down: 10 Minutes

A cool-down can consist of light jogging and stretching, which help remove lactic acid from the muscle groups (it is the buildup of lactic acid that causes muscle soreness the next day). It is important not to neglect this activity, especially after a particularly hard physical session. More experienced players should be capable of doing this cool-down themselves, but it is not a bad idea for a coach to direct this session too.

Coaching During Practice

To begin with, understand the difference between "coaching" and "directing" the session. Directing requires information to be given throughout the whole session about how to set up and do various activities. This is basic leadership and organization of the session by the coach. On the other hand, coaching is providing information to the player about how, why, and when to do an activity. This is normally provided in the theme section of the session but will likely carry over into the game play.

Once in the coaching phase of the session, coaches must be careful not to give too much information, and, in particular, not to try covering too many topics. Rather than giving in to the temptation of trying to correct all problems at once, the coach should focus a session on one or two predetermined topics. Overcoaching can be a huge problem. Many coaches simply talk too much, offer too much advice, and constantly stop the game so that there is very little flow. It is better to let the kids play the game, and the younger they are, the more they need to play—and the less they need to stand and listen.

A soccer player who is challenged can make only two kinds of decisions: good ones and bad ones. It is a coach's job to stop the game when necessary, *explain* to the player why he made a given decision, and, if it was a bad one, offer an alternative. This is coaching: being able to recognize a problem, then efficiently articulate and demonstrate a solution to the team or player. Any visual

© AP Images

Successful coaches allow players to play the game during practice but are also prepared to analyze drill performance and make corrections when necessary.

aid the coach can provide for the player will be helpful, and I have found that the "stop-and-freeze" technique works well. When the coach sees a situation that needs to be discussed, he stops the game with a whistle and insists that the players freeze on the spot. This is like taking a snapshot of the action, and it allows the coach to visually point out a specific problem. Used correctly, this is a great tool.

One common misconception is that coaching is all about setting up appropriate drills for a specific theme, then letting the drills *be* the session. If that were the case, coaching would be easy: Just buy a book of drills, explain them to the team, and let them work it out for themselves. In reality, coaches must be prepared to analyze performances in the drill, stop it when appropriate, and make necessary corrections. With this in mind, it is best to resist the urge to spend long periods of time on drills, especially if they are repetitive. It must be understood that a specific drill is only a means to an end. It is just the beginning.

Many of the problems and issues a coach has to address in practice are game-related, but not all. Some problems emerge off the field, and if not corrected they can hurt performance on it. Fixing problems on the field is a multitask problem, but if a coach goes about it in a systematic fashion, it is not as difficult as it seems. A team's program should cover these basic needs: fitness-related, technical, tactical, and psychological. Problems will arise in any of these areas, and a coach should be able to identify problems and set forth a program for correcting them—one at a time! The type of correction is often determined by the level of play. Less experienced players will need more time on technical matters, whereas more experienced ones will deal with tactical issues.

Seasonal Practice Sessions

The season needs to be broken into four segments: preseason, early regular season, late regular season, and, if relevant, postseason. The material covered and the activities used in these segments will differ as the needs of players and of the team as a whole change throughout the season. Early on, the coach might think in terms of quantity of work so that players will have a workable base level of fitness, then shift toward a quality focus later on so that the team is sharp.

Preseason

The purpose of the preseason is to achieve two major objectives: build a fitness level that provides a good base for the season, and begin the on-field organization process for the season. In some cases, there will be the additional need to select and identify players. The length of the preseason depends on many factors, some of which are out of the players' and coaches' hands. The starting date for the preseason is typically affected by issues including availability of players and facilities, family commitments, coach's schedule, and rules of the relevant soccer association. Generally speaking, the longer the preseason the better, not so much to allow more fitness work but to be able to work at a slower pace. Crowding a preseason fitness schedule into a few days is an invitation to injury. If fitness work is too intense—if too much is done too soon—the body will break down. A good time to start training is 2 to 3 weeks before the season. Coaches might try to cram several sessions into a day, which, again is not a good idea. The maximum should be two sessions, with some days involving only one. (This number may have to vary due to individual circumstances.)

The preseason can be a brutal time of year for players. Physical demands are high, and sessions can be painful and fatiguing. The key is to come into the preseason prepared. It helps if the coach has posted or forwarded to players a fitness schedule to be followed in the lead-up to the preseason, but even if not, players can still prepare themselves for preseason with a fitness regime of their own. It should begin with distance running to work on aerobic capacity, then move toward interval training (shorter distances that involve changes of speed, intensity, and distance). These sessions may go as long as 2 hours; going longer typically diminishes quality and increases the risk of injury.

I am a big believer in fitness work with a ball, which serves well in two ways. First, it is easier to get more fitness work from players if there is a ball involved, because it tends to distract them from the unpleasantness of the work. Second, it provides some technical training, since the ball is involved. It will be necessary to do some fitness work without the ball, since using a ball can reduce the speed and intensity of the activity. I suggest that initially 50 percent of the work be done with the ball. Integrating the ball into fitness work is not hard; it just requires a little imagination. It can be as simple as doing 5 reps of a 20-yard (about 18-yard) run ending with a shot on goal, or 30 jumps heading a ball back to a partner on each elevation, which is great leg work. One activity my players dread, because it is quite fatiguing, is to place one player on the outside of each side of a 10-yard (9-meter) box, with two more players in the middle of the box. The two in the box play 1v1 soccer, using the players on the outside as passing outlets. The aim is for either player in the middle to keep possession as long as possible by dribbling or passing to the outside players, who are always supporting the player with the ball. The game goes for 60 seconds, after which two more players replace them. Doing several reps gives players a considerable workout.

This time of the season is also a perfect opportunity to put your players through a battery of physical tests to assess speed, agility, and endurance. This information can tell a coach a great deal: Who is the quickest? The fittest? The strongest? Such information can help the coach select players for the team. I tend to rank players with these scores and post them, so that players know where they stand in relation to the rest of the team and where they need to improve. I also file the scores, so that if a player returns I can compare results from one year to the next. I use a battery of five tests and do one of these every other day.

Cooper Test   I use a simple adaptation of this test that is basically a 2-mile run within a given amount of time. We use 12 minutes as the target, but this would be too fast for younger players. Each coach should set his own target time based on age, but in the end the time is less important than who finishes where.

Stinkers   Two flags are posted 40 yards (about 37 meters) apart. Each player teams up with a partner, and they time each other's runs. Each player runs around the flags (there and back) 4 times, then rests while her partner runs. They alternate for 3 reps, and each player's times are then combined for an overall result.

4-8-4 Test   A player runs 400 yards (about 365 meters) with a 5-minute rest, 800 yards (about 730 meters) with another 5-minute rest, then another 400 yards. The three times are combined for a complete score.

Beep Test   This is a repetitive 20-yard (about 18-meter) run marked out by two cones and prompted by a repeating beep that begins slowly but gets more frequent with every 8 runs. The player runs from one cone to the other on every beep. Players are eliminated when they cannot complete the repetition on pace with the beep. This activity requires a prepared recording that is readily available via soccer catalogs and stores; it may be worth the trouble of finding one.

40 Yards Times 10   These are simple 40-yard (37-meter) sprints with no set recovery time. The coach records the player's quickest time and the combined total of all 10 times. As the fitness base is being established, the coach needs to begin preparing his team technically and tactically. This can be done simultaneously, although fatigue from fitness sessions limits the level of quality the coach can expect from a coaching or technical session. Time restraints for most coaches preclude sessions that are purely fitness-based, so a combination of fitness and coaching will probably be necessary. Once the fitness base has been established (about 2 weeks in), the coach's priority should switch to preparing the team for the season tactically and technically, with maintenance fitness sessions interspersed from time to time.

Early Regular Season

This period will probably last through the first five or six games of the season, assuming a 20-game season. It is a continuation of preseason work but with fewer fitness activities and less endurance work. Sessions during this phase should be limited to approximately 90 minutes, since the preseason work to build up players' base fitness levels has been completed. Each session should still be very intense.

This is the time to get players to play within the tactical organization of the team's system. This work probably began during preseason, but the bulk of team preparation should be done during this early part of the regular season. Players should work hard on team play, spending much time on both defensive and attacking principles. I prefer to begin with defending and spend as long as needed on this area before moving on to attacking principles. Game days will begin to interfere with coaching sessions, and it is best also not to do much on the day before a game. However, if the team is not fully prepared—and in the early season it is likely not to be—then some compromises have to be made.

An extra segment of the season, referred to as midseason, could be carved out after several games have been played. It would serve as an interim period between the early and late regular season periods and would involve characteristics of both.

Late Regular Season

This period involves the last few games of the regular season. The exact number depends on how many games the team plays, but in any case it definitely refers to a time when the coach should have an established starting 11 and a settled team. These sessions should be tailored to the current state of the team. If the team is successful and winning games, then very few changes will be needed; the team should mainly keep doing things as usual. If all is not well, and the team is not firing on all cylinders, then changes need to be made. For the most part, tactical sessions will now be less frequent because it is more important to make sure players are physically ready for the next game.

It is important to make sure players are healthy and revitalized for the next game. Fatigue and injury will play a part, as long seasons do take a toll. It is more important to rest a player and allow him to recover than it is to ask that player to participate in a hard training session. Oftentimes, a coach might hold a light training session for some players and a more difficult one for others. During preseason and early season training, all players tend to be equally fit, but as the season progresses those who play less will go backward and fall behind the rest, especially in terms of fitness. The only solution is to do extra fitness and training sessions with this group. In my program, the day after a game, the players who played a significant part in the game are required only to jog, stretch, and possibly do some light ball work. The remaining group has a normal practice session, perhaps even including some fitness work. This split can be a challenge for the coach, because the motivation level of players in this group may well be down. They need to be challenged, not forgotten, and it is important to attend to their needs, because their participation at a competitive level is crucial during the latter part of the season. Their role is to help the starting team get sharp for possible postseason play, and they must be helped to realize that this role is every bit as important as anyone's in the starting 11.

Postseason

This is the time of year that everybody plays for. Being here probably means the team has been successful and is now playing for bigger and better things. This is the really fun part of the year, something I always look forward to. It makes all the hard work well worth it.

Interestingly enough, some teams get better as the season goes on and consistently do well in the postseason, while others seem to fail at this stage. Although the quality of players can have a lot to do with this dichotomy, training sessions can affect it as well. Some coaches are very good at getting their teams to play well at just the right time. It is important for coaches to try to peak their teams at this time of year, to enable them to play their best soccer of the year in the postseason. The main principle is to avoid overworking them. Rest can be more effective than anything. The coach must decide carefully when to do a practice session, making sure that any higher-intensity work takes place well before game day. I would suggest that teams need at least 2 or 3 days of light workouts before a big game, with attention also given to lifestyle habits during this period.

When the team does practice, it is quality, not quantity, that is essential. The coach must demand nothing but the best from her players and stop the practice if she is not getting it. As soon as the quality drops, she should finish the session. Most of what can happen at this stage is bad, with frustration setting in, and perhaps a key player getting injured. The coach must help players stay sharp, alert, and focused on doing things well.

Speed work, not endurance, is needed at this point. After a grueling season, players' game fitness should be solid. Sharpness of play is now vital, because it can make the difference between winning and losing games. If the team is sharper than the opponent, it is more likely to win the game. The coach should insist that everything be done quickly, and quick short runs should be encouraged at the end of practice, with plenty of rest time between runs. This is not the time to fatigue the players. They will be tired enough from the long season.

Off-Season

This is always an interesting time of year, because each player has different needs and desires during this period, and it is impossible to suggest a general approach that is best. Without question, some complete rest from soccer is critical in order to avoid getting stale, and I believe players should have a few weeks of break time. This does not necessarily mean that they should do nothing physically, and playing another sport or doing another activity would be okay.

I do have a concern about today's youth players, particularly the better ones. I believe they are being forced to play too much. It is not unusual for a player to have high school soccer in the fall, with practice every night and games once or twice a week, plus possible weekend involvement with a local club team (which might include games). Typically, once the high school season finishes, club ball begins, often going from late fall through the spring. Throughout this time, some of these same players may participate in an Olympic development program (an extra activity involving representing one's state, region, or national team), which also involves more practice and games. That could then be followed by Super Y-League play, which runs all summer. This is too much soccer. It may be best to take a break in the summer and avoid the temptation to do everything. Players' needs vary—some enjoy playing almost year-round, while others need a break—but no player should truly play year-round. It is detrimental in the end.

Depending on the length of the break, players should begin getting ready for the new season about 2 to 3 weeks before it begins. They will probably need to do this on their own, but their local coaches should be able to help them with suggestions.

CHAPTER 9

Matches

After the hard work of selecting and preparing the team, match day finally comes around, and for most of us this is what it's all about. I don't think there is a bigger thrill than match day for either the player or the coach. With it, however, come all the pressures of feeling the need to win. While fun and enjoyment are integral to playing the sport, in the end it is about the result. All players, no matter at what level they are playing, go into each game with the objective of winning. I have not met a player yet that starts a game with the goal of losing. Match day is when a team's winning attitude and preparation are put into practice. This chapter covers game-day routine for both the individual player and the team, and it discusses how a coach can prepare a game-day strategy for her team itself, as well as one for playing against the day's opponent. The chapter also looks at the types of adjustments that both the team and the individual player might have to make in order to win the game.

Game-Day Routine

Game-day routines can vary considerably, depending on the age and level of the team. They are also affected by whether the team is playing at home or on the road. But no matter what the situation is, some form of routine is necessary. Human beings are generally creatures of habit and feel much more secure when in a comfortable, regular environment doing familiar activities. Routine helps create a comfort zone and, without question, better prepares players mentally for the task at hand. Game-day routine has two facets: the individual's routine, which should begin at least the day before the match, and the team's pregame routine, normally set by the coach.

Individual Routine

An individual player's routine should begin with a good night's sleep for the two nights leading up to a competition. It's also a good idea to get game equipment packed the day before so that it doesn't become a stress factor immediately before leaving for the game. The pregame routine should be kept as calm as possible, with no surprises. Cleaning one's boots the night before gets the mind focused on the upcoming game. It might sound somewhat old-fashioned, but it does have a positive mental effect, and if nothing else the player will look good on game day! Players should also pay close attention to what they eat, even on the day before the game. It is best to stay away from greasy foods such as burgers and bacon and focus instead on lean foods that provide good amounts of carbohydrate and protein.

On the day of the game, players should do what feels comfortable to them. The idea is, if it works, stick with it. Each player has his own idiosyncratic ways of preparing psychologically for a game. Some players like to listen to certain types of music, whereas others prefer quiet. I have known players who like to sit by themselves and visualize how they are going to play the game. Some stay busy, while others like to rest. I coached an All-American player (later drafted to the MLS) who got upset if he could not fit in a nap 3 or 4 hours before the game. To each his or her own.

Sometimes a player's game-day routine is not working; she does not feel mentally or physically ready for the game. This often indicates a lack of mental readiness, but not always. It may be that the pregame warm-up (though for the most part this will be a team routine) is not quite right for the player and needs to be tweaked. She may need to stretch longer than the rest of the team, or do more sprints, or be on the field warming up earlier. Each player should find the routine that works best for her, even if it means experimenting a little.

Team Routine

A team's routine can start the day before a match. I have always encouraged teams to be close off the field as well as on it—this is great for team chemistry, and good team chemistry helps win games. Players might consider getting together as a team the night before a big game, whether for dinner or another activity. Teams do not necessarily need to do this for every game, but it's a good approach to use before a big game.

The team's game-day routine will normally be established by the coach, who of course has his own idiosyncrasies and team requirements, but it is also prudent for the coach to allow some flexibility in the routine for individual differences. The important thing is to be ready to play right from the whistle. Teams that start slowly will live to regret it. A good pregame routine should include the following features:

1. A tactical talk covering major issues for the game
2. Individual warm-up time (personal routine)
3. Motivational talk by the coach (if he is uncomfortable with this, it may be turned over to an assistant coach, guest, former player, or current player)
4. Team warm-up
5. A few minutes of personal time
6. Team sprints: 10-yard (9-meter) repetitions for about 60 seconds immediately before kickoff

My team's routine is as follows: Two hours before the game, we meet in a classroom to discuss game tactics. One hour before kickoff, we allow players to go onto the game field and do their own thing for 15 minutes. Most players stretch lightly or jog, then kick a ball around. The team returns to the field with about 35 minutes remaining on the pregame countdown clock for a formal warm-up with the coaching staff. We keep the warm-up routine consistent. It begins with team stretching and running, followed by two groups of players playing keep-away in a confined area—typically the starting 10 in one group and the rest in another group, while the goalkeepers do a separate warm-up by themselves. If the team has sufficient staff, I recommend having a coach involved with the goalkeepers' warm-up, as otherwise they will get neglected. Just before kickoff, time is allowed for players to collect their own thoughts. Finally, 60 seconds before the game begins, we finish with 5 or 6 sprints of 10 yards (9 meters) each.

It is easier for a coach to get teams ready physically than mentally. The coach has control over the physical side of the warm-up but may not be as successful with the mental aspect. Hopefully he has done a pretty good job of this in the locker room before the warm-up, but it's not a bad idea to get the team together one last time just before kickoff and, if nothing else, give a final reminder of the keys to the game. If the coach is good at motivating, he can give it one more go.

Scouting

Modern-day game preparation has changed enormously in just the last few years. Though unlikely to be used at the younger levels, video cameras and computers are now widely used in upper-level programs. Many teams record their games or the opponent's games and have either the entire team or individual players watch the video. The coach can use it to analyze the opposition, identifying not only their style of play but also how and where they play. What side of the field do they tend to attack? Who are their key players, and who gets the ball in which areas of the field? Do they tend to attack with long passes or short ones? When the central defender has the ball, what are his passing tendencies? This kind of analysis can help a team enormously in preparing to face a particular opponent.

Computer software is now available to help a coach break down every aspect of the game. Coaches can record a live game and use the software to mark any area they are interested in. For instance, if a coach wants to look at all goal-scoring opportunities created by the forwards, he can use the software to mark or tag a player every time he receives the ball in the attacking third of the field, then call up these situations later for analysis. Such software tends to be quite expensive, and initially it can be difficult to use. It took many hours of trial and error for us to get comfortable with our system. Indeed, most teams do not have the staff or time to scout opponents in this way, so scouting is still much more likely to be done in the old-fashioned manner of physically scouting opponents and taking notes. However, for those who have the resources and wish to become the very best (player or coach), this type of analysis should be considered. It's beneficial for a player to see himself on a professionally prepared video tailor-made for analyzing his strengths and weaknesses.

Modern technology aside, most team situations will still be pretty basic, so it would be prudent to scout a game by going to watch your opposition play—the closer to game day the better (current information is, obviously, more valuable). It is always useful to have a handle on the opposition before the game. In particular, a coach should take note of who the opponent's key players are and generate ideas for how her team might play against them. I suggest using the following checklist for scouting:

- What formation are they using? (Chart the starting team as it lines up for the kickoff. Write down their shirt numbers in the formation they are playing, and next to each number note any substitute that comes on to replace that player.)

- Who are the key individual players, the go-to players, and what are their tendencies when they get the ball?
- What are the team's tendencies? Style of play? Do they play through midfield or go more directly to the forwards? What do the forwards do when they get the ball? Does the team play balls over the top for the forwards to chase or do they play shorter, to the forwards' feet?
- Which side of the field do they like to attack? Do the wingers go down the line or cut inside? Cross to the near post or far post?
- Are they playing a flat back four, and if so do they hold a high or low line? Is there space to get into the back of the defense? Who are the weaker players defensively (thus indicating possible areas to attack)?
- How is their team speed? Is there a slow player who can be isolated and attacked by a quicker player?
- Who is their main playmaker, how do they go through him, and how can he be stopped?
- What does their main playmaker do when she gets the ball?
- Do their defenders attack and get forward, or do they tend to stay back? If one goes forward, can the space behind him be attacked?
- What do they do on their set plays and restarts? (Chart them.)

Once a coach has all this information, he needs to sit down and identify the most relevant parts for his team. He must take care not to use too much, since in the end he must prepare *his* team the way he wants them to play. If he over focuses on how to respond to the other team, his own squad may be overwhelmed, and it will almost certainly be disruptive to their style. A coach must focus on his own players and the way they play the game, then identify selected elements of the opponent's profile and consider ways to play effectively against them. This part may constitute as little as 10 percent of weekly preparation for very strong teams. Weaker teams may have to pay more attention to this area as they may feel they have to do something differently to win a game against much stronger opposition. They may have to spend as much as 40 percent of preparation time considering their opponent.

The coach's main job, then, is to get his team ready to play its next game. Once he has scouted the opposition and processed and applied that information, he needs to work on his own team's play. Experienced coaches sense the strengths and weaknesses of each player and of the team as a whole—especially the team tendencies. But even an experienced coach can use specific and detailed information about his team, and an inexperienced one will definitely need it. So how should a coach go about getting such information? It's actually quite simple, requiring only a little help and a little time.

The coaching staff should write the squad list on a notepad and in practice begin to chart information in columns next to each player's name. If the team has had trouble keeping possession of the ball, one column might be designated for passing tendencies, and a checkmark could be added each time a midfield player makes a pass. Others columns might track balls passed forward, balls passed backward, balls passed longer or shorter than 20 yards (about 18 meters), and so on. The results might show something like the following: Nearly 7 out of 10 passes by the center midfield player went forward more than 20 yards, and 5 of 10 went to the opposition. This might suggest that she is forcing the ball forward too much, which could be one reason the team is losing so many possessions. Or perhaps 8 of 10 passes are going to the left side of the field, thus neglecting the right-side players and often allowing the opposition to anticipate the play. Or, if the coach wants to concentrate on midfield play, she need only have someone chart the passing success rate of the four midfield players by marking a check for a successful pass and an X for an unsuccessful one. This charting of players' performance can be done both in practice and in games.

The information gained can be used in practice and should in fact constitute the main material used by the coach to help the team improve: What do we do well? Keep doing it! What do we do poorly? Change it! This information can also be quite valuable to individual players, who are often unaware of their tendencies and thus can be enabled by this kind of analysis to identify and work on areas of need. If a coach is not available to do the charting, then a parent might do it, and the coach or player can take it from there.

Game-Day Strategy

Once game day arrives, it is time to put everything together like a well-oiled machine. The game day itself is broken into distinctly separate stages: pregame, the game itself, halftime, and postgame. Each stage requires different things from players and coaches.

Pregame

This stage varies depending on the team. Most middle school soccer programs report about an hour before kickoff, whereas high school and college teams likely gather earlier. Ideally, the coach begins with a meeting to discuss technical and tactical issues, rather than focusing on motivation. One of my assistant coaches brought the use of handouts to our program a couple of years ago, and they act as reminders of points we have talked about in the days just before the game: what the opposition may try to do against us, key opposing players, issues we have been working on, and perhaps a mention of the importance of that particular game. This really is just a summary of what we have focused on in the past week. I have found it quite useful, and it is yet another strategy for getting the coach's points across to players.

As far as chalk-and-talk is concerned, I use it very sparingly and probably only in the meetings prior to kickoff or occasionally at halftime. I almost never use it in coaching sessions, as I believe the carryover value is not high and the time can be better spent on the field showing teams what to do rather than drawing it on a board.

© AP Images

A player's winning attitude, preparation, and determination are put into practice on game day.

During the Game

Once the game starts, coaches need to be extremely careful in how much they coach and what kind of coaching they do. They should observe the game closely and try to figure out what is working and what is not, and in particular what the opposition is doing to make life difficult. If things are not going well, then something needs to change, and it's the coach's job to figure out what. Many coaches get so caught up in yelling instructions to players that they miss out on what is really happening. The time to do most coaching is in practice sessions during the week before the game, not in the game itself. Players need to be able to think for themselves, and the coach must hope they have been adequately prepared. Some coaching from the sidelines is appropriate, but a coach should not have players relying on him to talk them through almost every game situation. Besides, during a game, by the time he shouts instructions and the player processes them, then physically reacts, it's probably too late. Game coaching from the sideline should generally be kept to the occasional tactical adjustment, in moments when it will not distract the players. The occasional motivational comment is sometimes also appropriate.

It is sometimes difficult for an inexperienced coach to identify her team's problems and generate suggestions to share with the team during halftime. Here are some points to watch for as the game progresses:

- Does the team have an adequate number of players *behind* the ball?
- Is there adequate defensive depth?
- Would the offside trap work better?
- Is tight marking necessary? Should there be more pressure on the ball at midfield?
- Do the midfield players need help in marking players?
- Would zonal coverage work better, especially if the opposition is sending a lot of players forward?
- Is the covering defender free?
- Are the front runners pressuring the opposition's defenders?
- Are chances being taken in the final third?
- Are available shots being taken?
- Is there adequate support of the ball?
- Are players overlapping when appropriate, thus getting forward?
- Would overloading help the attack?
- Are players too rigid in their positions or are they practicing fluid mobility?
- Is the ball on the ground enough?
- If the opponents are weak in the air, is that being exploited?
- Is more direct (or indirect) play needed?
- Are the midfielders supporting the strikers?
- How is the team's shape, and are the players "sat" in the correct parts of the field at the correct times?
- Need more high or low pressure?
- Does there need to be more communication between players?
- Does the attack need more diagonal runs?
- Is the timing of runs okay, or are players are getting forward too soon and taking their own space away?
- Is there a need for more combination play?
- Is the team sufficiently exploiting the goalkeeper's weaknesses?

Halftime

This is when a good coach needs to go to work. Once in a while, when things are going really well, I can go to halftime and simply tell the team to keep everything the same, but that does not happen as often as any of us would like.

Most of the time, adjustments need to be made, and it is helpful if the coach takes a small notepad to the game and makes a couple of notes about problem areas during the first half. The coach who relies on memory is likely to forget something important. Points should be specific and few—too often, coaches talk in generalities, and talk too much. Telling a player he needs to work harder doesn't get it done. He needs to know where and when he needs to work harder. Often, the problem is on the team level; for example, perhaps the opposition has an extra player in midfield who is causing difficulties. The coach must help her team know exactly how, and with whom, they can negate that player. The coach should hit three or four critical points. Any other problems will have to be taken care of the next day, on the practice field.

Sometimes the half-time talk needs to be more motivational than tactical. Every player, and every team, has experienced a first half of playing flat, with little emotion or effort. I've often wished I could figure the preparation level of teams before the game has started, and not have to leave the motivation until halftime, but I've never been able to come up with that secret. Motivational half-time talks are an art in themselves, with widely varying approaches (depending in part on the players' age) and varying results. Some coaches rant and rave, while others use cutting language and words. Some take a calm approach. It's difficult to recommend definitively how to handle this task, and much depends on the coach's personality. Negative criticism and personal insults rarely work, and I do not recommend this approach. The coach must be careful not to let his own frustrations get in the way of what should be said, and he must recognize the difference between motivating a team and motivating a single player. When dealing with a single player, he must decide whether to address the problem in front of the whole group or pull the player aside for a private talk. The player's age can make a huge difference here. Players who are 13 or 14 are still too sensitive for—and rarely would respond well to—any form of personal insult or negative criticism, especially in front of the team. Thus, half-time comments to such a player should be made mostly to that individual only. As the player gets older, the approach can change. I would expect an 18-year-old college player to be able to handle a rough half-time exchange with a coach, especially if it is justified. Players should try not to take these situations personally. I know this can be difficult, but almost always these comments are not personal attacks, which is well worth remembering when a coach is "having a go" at a player.

Postgame

I have always felt that postmatch talks should be kept to a bare minimum. Emotions are probably still running high, and match analysis (and especially individual player analysis) should probably be saved for the next day. A poor performance needs to be left as is and addressed later, when emotions have subsided and players are more receptive to criticism and better prepared to improve their performance. If the team has played well, it should be complimented on the spot. Positive feedback always feels good, especially after an important win, and the coach should let players know they have done well. Even these comments, however, should be kept fairly brief. I have seen coaches keep a team for 30 to 40 minutes after a game, and believe me, players hate it and cannot wait to get off the field. A tired, unresponsive player is not who a coach needs to be talking to.

It is important, in the end, that everything be kept in perspective. Make sure that the highs are not too high, and the lows are not too low. Here, players may need guidance, and a coach's response to a big win or loss often sets the tone for the team. I can remember taking days, as a young coach, to get over a bad loss, and being unable to sleep for a couple of nights. Players may respond in the same way. Today, I am over it by the next day and take a much healthier approach. One should feel down after a bad loss, and excited after a big win, but neither should be overdone.

A coach should also attend to lifestyle habits and try to know what her team does before and especially after games. Most dedicated players realize that it is important to live correctly before a game, but some can get a little carried away after one. It may be necessary to set some rules. This is unlikely to be an issue for younger players, who are probably going home with their parents, but older players are going to go out, and guidelines may be useful.

Postgame Analysis

The next day is always a good time to analyze the game and meet with players to discuss their performance. In most cases, this can be done on the field during practice. This is not always ideal, since in this setting most information will be expressed in verbal terms, not always providing the clearest analysis. As discussed earlier in this chapter, video can be a great addition to the verbal analysis delivered on the practice field. The coach does not have to have software to do this; a simple game tape will do the trick.

This postmortem should be followed by light activity on the field—perhaps 40 to 50 minutes of jogging, stretching, and easy ball work (technical activities or keep-away). Players who did not play, or who played very little, need to do more, and it may be necessary to set up a separate practice for this group.

It is crucial to gear subsequent practices to the needs of the team as determined by the postgame analysis. Typically a coach should look for the following:

• Did the team perform in a fashion that resembled practice sessions leading up to the game? Did the team follow through on the game plan? If not, why? (It is important to practice in an environment as close as possible to the game situation in order to maximize carryover value.)

• Did individual players do the job expected of them? Either way, they will need feedback and guidance. This tactical analysis of a player's performance is likely to result in a need for time in practice sessions to work specifically on problem areas. For example, the team may have had insufficient width and attacked down the middle too often. A likely cause is that the two wingers were not providing the width (were not staying out toward the sidelines). This problem can be corrected by perhaps setting a playing field with two channels about 10 yards (9 meters) wide from the sidelines down the length of the field. Participants play a normal game except for the requirement that each of the two wide players must play in the channel when her team has the ball. They may come out of the channel only to defend when the other team has the ball.

- Did the team look defensively weak? It is vital to pinpoint where the problem was. It may have been a midfield issue, with players failing to track their opponents' runs off the ball. Or perhaps there were not enough players to defend in midfield. It may have been a problem with the back four. Perhaps they were too flat, with very little defensive cover. Whatever the cause, it must be identified and corrected.

- Did the team play with too little energy and get outworked by the opposition? Is the team fit enough, or do they need more fitness sessions? Was the team mentally prepared to start the game? Often, the solution to this problem can be found in the stage of the game when the problem occurred. If at the beginning, it's likely to be a mental issue. If late in the game, it's probably physical. If for the whole game, then back to square one, beginning with the fact that it's simply not acceptable—period!

- Did the team create goal-scoring opportunities? If not, the coach may have a difficult problem to resolve, since it may mean the team simply lacks sufficiently creative players. Nevertheless good coaching and good tactics should allow the team to create scoring chances. Are players passing the ball into the back of the opposition's defense? Are forwards running into positions in the back of the defense? Are enough players making forward runs? Again, the coach must consider many possible causes, identify the real ones, and find ways to address them.

- Is the team failing to convert goal-scoring opportunities? Two words: Shooting practice!

Addressing any issues that were problematic in the previous game will help the team work on its weaknesses and start preparing itself for the next match.

Every coach and every player has their own unique style, and their approaches to coaching and playing can differ enormously. There is no absolute way to do anything in the world of athletics, but there are some time-tested approaches that are sure to work, and hopefully we have covered some of these in this book. There is no substitute, however, for enthusiasm and effort, and though sometimes the best-run coaching sessions or most talented player will struggle, both coaches and players should bring their best effort to *every* session.

For many, winning is not what it is all about. Soccer is a great game, in my opinion the greatest game in the world. Enjoy it. It is a fun-filled activity that will challenge you. Accept that challenge, have fun, play with passion, and you too can consider that you have had success from this great game.

INDEX

Note: The italicized *f* and *t* following page numbers refer to figures and tables, respectively

ABOUT THE AUTHOR

Michael Parker, the wins leader among active Division I men's soccer coaches, has won six national titles in 30 years of collegiate head coaching experience spanning all three NCAA levels. He has been at University of North Carolina at Greensboro since 1984, taking a club program and leading it to success in Division III (two national titles) and Division I (fourth among Division I active coaches with a winning percentage of .736).

His teams have made 19 NCAA tournament appearances, and in 1993 he became the first men's soccer coach in NCAA history to lead a team to the tournament in all three divisions. During his tenure, UNCG has won 10 conference titles, including six during its Division I era. Parker's 2004 team was ranked No. 1 in polls for much of the season. Parker also won three national titles while head coach at Lock Haven in 1977 and 1978 (Division III) and 1980 (Division II) and three national titles at the semipro level with the USISL's Greensboro Dynamo in 1993, 1994, and 1995.

Parker resides in Greensboro, North Carolina.

Gain the competitive edge!

Optimum training translates to optimal performance with the help of the *Sports Performance DVD Series*. With four DVDs that cover development of speed, power, strength, and flexibility, this series will help you build a program for your specific needs.

Each DVD begins with a series of assessments, which identify your strengths and weaknesses and establish a baseline for customizing training programs. From there, numerous exercise options and sample workouts are provided, all of which may be tailored to address the demands of your sport.

Flexibility for Sports Performance
ISBN 978-0-7360-6422-4 • 57-minute DVD

Power for Sports Performance
ISBN 978-0-7360-6528-3 • 37-minute DVD

Speed for Sports Performance
ISBN 978-0-7360-6525-2 • 56-minute DVD

Strength for Sports Performance
ISBN 978-0-7360-6421-7 • 25-minute DVD

 View a clip at
www.HumanKinetics.com!

To place your order,
In U.S. call **1-800-747-4457**
In Canada call **1-800-465-7301**
In Europe call **+44 (0) 113 255 5665**
In Australia call **08 8372 0999**
In New Zealand call **0064 9 448 1207**
or visit **www.HumanKinetics.com**

 **HUMAN KINETICS**
The Premier Publisher for Sports & Fitness
P.O. Box 5076, Champaign, IL 61825-5076

Contents

Grammar and Punctuation

Writing Skills

Creative Writing

Contents

Contents

Grammar and Punctuation

Spelling

What is Covered in this Topic?

This topic covers...
- forming plurals of **nouns**
- commonly confused words.

Forming Plurals

Your **spelling** should be **accurate** to make your writing as effective as possible.

Spelling mistakes often happen when making **singular** nouns into **plurals**. Plurals are formed in different ways.

Regular Plurals

Many nouns are made plural simply by adding an 's', for example...
- car(s)
- computer(s)
- floor(s)
- window(s)
- chair(s)
- desk(s)
- pencil(s)
- tree(s).

tree

trees

Sibilants

Nouns ending with 's' or 'sh' sounds are called **sibilants**. Add 'es' unless the word ends in 'e'. If the word ends in 'e', then only an 's' is needed. For example...
- torch(es)
- prize(s)
- fox(es)
- house(s)
- bus(es)
- hose(s).

fox

foxes

Spelling

Nouns Ending in Y

To find the ending for nouns that end in 'y', look at the letter before the 'y'.

If the letter is a **consonant** (any letter other than 'a', 'e', 'i', 'o', 'u'), change the 'y' to 'ies', for example...

- body – bodies
- party – parties
- lady – ladies
- century – centuries
- baby – babies
- puppy – puppies
- city – cities
- army – armies
- sky – skies
- apply – applies.

(Note that this rule doesn't apply to proper nouns.)

If the letter before the 'y' is a **vowel** ('a', 'e', 'i', 'o', 'u'), add 's', for example...

- alley(s)
- tray(s)
- key(s)
- play(s)
- ray(s)
- donkey(s)
- chimney(s)
- day(s).

donkeys

donkey

Nouns Ending in O

You need to learn which words end in 's' and which end in 'es' with this kind of plural.

If a singular noun ends in 'o', normally the word is turned into a plural by adding an 's', for example...

- piano(s)
- auto(s)
- logo(s)
- solo(s).

There are some exceptions when 'es' is needed, for example...

- echo(es)
- tomato(es)
- hero(es)
- torpedo(es)
- potato(es)
- tornado(es).

Nouns Ending in F and Fe

If a singular noun ends in 'f', change the 'f' to 'v' and add 'es', for example...
- loaf – loaves
- thief – thieves
- half – halves
- yourself – yourselves.

If a singular noun ends in 'fe', the plural ends in 'ves', for example...
- knife – knives
- life – lives
- wife – wives.

Not all words follow this pattern, for example...
- roof – roofs
- handkerchief – handkerchiefs
- chief – chiefs
- belief – beliefs.

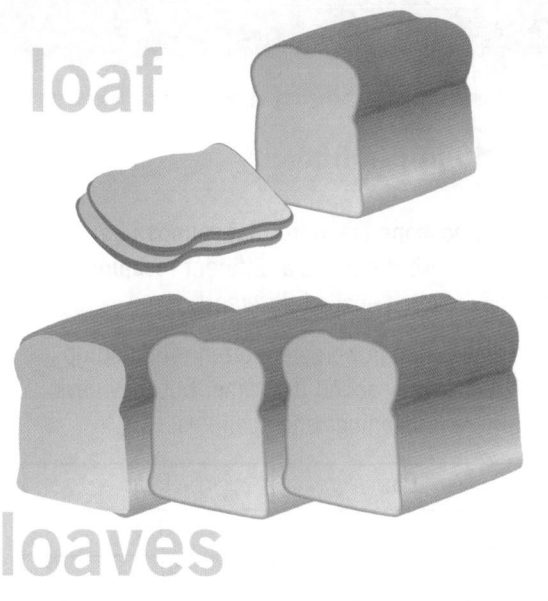

loaf

loaves

Unusual Plural Nouns

Not all plural nouns end in 's' or 'es'. With some nouns the word can be used to mean either the singular or plural, for example...
- I saw a deer in the wood (singular)
- I saw three deer in the wood (plural).

Some other examples of this kind of singular or plural noun are...
- sheep
- trout
- salmon.

Some nouns change their spelling when they're changed to plural, for example...
- foot – feet
- tooth – teeth
- mouse – mice.

Other nouns are only ever used in the plural, for example...
- scissors
- trousers
- clothes.

Collective nouns are unusual because they're singular nouns that mean a group of things, for example, a herd (singular – one herd) of cows (plural – more than one cow).

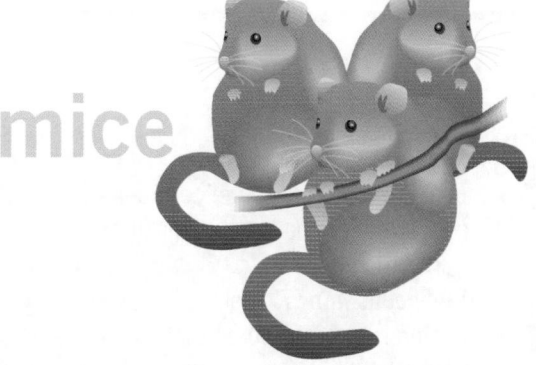

mice

mouse

Spelling

Homophones

A **homophone** is a word that **sounds** like another word but has a different **meaning**. They're often spelled differently.

Some common words are often muddled up because they sound the same, but they have different meanings and spellings:

Pair	Pear
Tow	Toe
Waist	Waste
Here	Hear
There	Their
Manor	Manner
Flower	Flour
Fowl	Foul
Bear	Bare
Whether	Weather
Seems	Seams
Hair	Hare

Look up the meaning of each of the words in a dictionary.

flour

flower

Quick Test

1. Compete the following sentence: Spelling mistakes are often made when making singular words into _plural words_ .
2. What are nouns with 's' or 'sh' sounds called? _sibilants_
3. What name is given to words that sound the same but have a different meaning? _Homophone_
4. What is the plural of deer? _deer_
5. What should you do if in doubt about the spelling or meaning of a word? _use a dictionary._

KEY WORDS

Make sure you understand these words before moving on!

- Noun
- Spelling
- Accurate
- Singular
- Plural
- Sibilant
- Consonant
- Vowel
- Collective noun
- Homophone
- Sounds
- Meaning
- Dictionary

Choose the correct options in the following sentences.

1. When writing, your spelling should be as **interesting** / **accurate** / **detailed** as possible.

2. If you're writing about one person or object, you're writing in the **plural** / **first person** / **singular**.

3. The letters 'm', 'p', and 't' are all **vowels** / **adjectives** / **consonants**.

4. A noun that names a group of people or object is called an **abstract** / **proper** / **collective** noun.

5. It's important that your **spelling** / **sentence** / **dictionary** is correct so that your writing is clear.

6. The words 'weather' and 'whether' are examples of **proper nouns** / **homophones** / **sibilance**.

7. The letters 'a', 'e', 'i', 'o', and 'u' are **vowels** / **consonants** / **homophones**.

8. The word 'sibilance' describes a certain kind of **image** / **meaning** / **sound**.

9. Words that name things are called **verbs** / **nouns** / **adjectives**.

10. You use **spellings** / **singular** / **plurals** when writing about more than one person or thing.

11. Good spelling helps to make your **vowels** / **nouns** / **meaning** clear.

12. If you're unsure about a spelling, use a **book** / **sound** / **dictionary** to check it.

13. The phrase 'the slithering, slinky snake' uses **onomatopoeia** / **sibilance** / **noises** to create sound effects.

Spelling

1 Complete the plural ending in each of the following sentences.

a) Sophie always found the English <u>class</u> really interesting. *classess*

b) The removal men loaded all the <u>box</u> into the van. *boxes*

c) The geography teacher asked Alex to give out the <u>atlas</u>. *atlases*

d) All the <u>table</u> were ready in the restaurant. *tables*

e) Jim was very hot, so he opened all the <u>window</u>. *windows*

f) The <u>house</u> were empty and due to be demolished. *houses*

g) Tim was three <u>inch</u> shorter than his brother. *inches*

h) The <u>ray</u> from the sun were very strong. *rays*

2 Correct the spellings in the following sentences.

a) The <u>boyes</u> both had several <u>hobbys</u>, including football and skateboarding. *boys hobbies*

b) One of Alice's <u>qualitys</u> was that she was hardworking and always made the best of her <u>opportunitys</u>. *qualities opportunities*

c) My mother made a delicious curry with <u>mangos</u> and <u>tomatos</u>. *mangoes tomatoes*

d) The <u>soldieres</u> were all <u>heros</u> in their own ways. *soldiers heroes*

e) There were lots of mosquitos, as the <u>whether</u> was to hot. *weather*

f) Alan's <u>trouseres</u> were a little tight on his waste after he ate a huge pile of <u>potatos</u>. *trousers potatoe*

g) The ship was being <u>toed</u> and steered a careful course between the boys. *towd*

h) The <u>sopranoes</u>, singing <u>beautifully</u>, were dressed like angels with their <u>halos</u> gleaming in the <u>lightes</u>. *sopranos haloes lights*

3 Write out the following passage, correcting all the spelling mistakes as you do.

> Todd and his friendes followed the path into the valley. The heards of cattle roamed freely and there were lots of sheeps too. All manor of birdes flew in the sky and Todd and his frends felt the sun on there faces and the wind gently ruffle there hare. They had herd that bares roamed these hills but they didn't sea any and so thought they must be in there lairs. In the streams they sore trouts swimming and salmons jumping.

Working in small groups, look through the exercise book or folder of work of each member of your group. Pick two or three pieces to look at.

Step 1: Look at pieces of work that have been marked and corrected by your teacher. Make a list of all the spelling mistakes that have been spotted.

Step 2: Try to put the mistakes into groups according to what the problem is, for example...
- plural endings
- homophones
- confused words
- a wrong spelling for some other reason.

Step 3: Make a table or graph showing the most common spelling mistakes.

Step 4: Produce a large poster showing...
- each spelling error (give the word in its context of a phrase or sentence)
- the correct spelling
- pictures or illustrations to add impact and effect to your poster.

Choose a problem from this topic that can occur in spelling (e.g. making plurals of nouns, homophones).

Prepare a PowerPoint presentation, illustrating the kinds of mistakes that are often made and say why. Your presentation should...
- give examples of words that are often spelt wrong
- give the correct spellings of these words in a sentence
- include a short spelling test.

Give your presentation to your class or a small group.

Include the spelling test and see how well your audience does.

Grammar

This topic looks at...
- word classes
- written forms of language.

Word Classes

The term 'word classes' is the name given to the basic types of words that the English language is made up of.

It will help you to use English correctly if you can identify the different kinds of words you use when writing and understand what they do.

Word Classes	What it Does
Noun	Nouns name things, such as people, places, things, and ideas.
Pronoun	Used instead of a noun (for example, 'he', 'she').
Verb	Describes some kind of action (it's sometimes called a 'doing word').
Adjective	A word that describes a noun.
Adverb	A word that describes a verb.
Conjunction	Joins two words or parts of a sentence together (it's sometimes called a 'joining word' or connective).
Preposition	Usually used with nouns or pronouns and shows a connection between the noun or pronoun and the rest of the sentence, e.g. The man put his book on the table – *on* tells you where he put the book.
Interjection	A word that expresses emotion or surprise (for example, 'Ouch!', 'Hurry!').
Article	Used to introduce a noun (for example, 'the', 'a', 'an').

Word Classes in Action

Here are all the word classes working together in a sentence:

Noun — **Tom ran quickly to the corner shop but it was closed, oh no!**

Verb   Preposition   Adjective   Conjunction   Verb   Interjection

Adverb   Article   Noun   Pronoun   Adjective

Nouns and Pronouns

There are different kinds of nouns:
- **Common nouns**: these name general everyday things and objects around us (for example, 'table', 'car', 'dog', 'river', 'computer', 'sky').
- **Concrete nouns**: a kind of common noun which describes something physical that you can see, hear, smell, taste or feel (for example, 'pen', 'chair', 'water').
- **Abstract nouns**: things we can't see or touch, like feelings and emotions (for example, 'love', 'fear', 'pride', 'confidence', 'generosity').

- **Proper nouns**: the names of specific people, places, times, events, books, etc. (for example, 'Sandra', 'York', 'Tuesday', 'the Great Fire of London', 'River Thames', '*Great Expectations*').
- **Collective nouns**: the names of groups or collections of things (for example, 'a herd of cows', 'a flock of birds', 'a swarm of bees').

Pronouns take the place of a noun in a sentence. They can save a lot of repetition of nouns (for example, 'I', 'he', 'she', 'they', 'it', 'me', 'you', 'us', 'them').

Verbs

Verbs are one of the most important parts of speech. It's not possible to have a sentence without a verb. In fact, a verb can make a sentence all on its own, for example, 'Run!'; 'Stop!'; 'Go!'; 'Jump!'; 'Sit!'

Verbs are doing words – they describe actions, such as 'Jane *kicked* the ball'. They are *being* words and describe states such as, 'The radiator *was* very hot', or 'Your dog *seems* friendly'.

Adjectives and Adverbs

Adjectives tell you more about (or describe) the nouns or pronouns. They usually come in front of the noun or pronoun, for example...
- the *blue* boat ploughed through the *heavy* sea
- the *tall*, *powerful* man had *short*, *cropped* hair.

Adverbs tell you more about verbs – they tell you where, how or when something was done. For example...
- the burglary happened *here*
- he looked at me *angrily*
- you shouted at me *yesterday*.

Grammar

Conjunctions

Conjunctions (or connectives) join parts of a sentence together, as in the following examples:

- 'He jumped for the ball. He missed it.' becomes 'He jumped for the ball *but* he missed it.'
- 'Do you want an ice-cream? Do you want a lollipop?' becomes 'Do you want an ice-cream *or* do you want a lollipop?'

Commonly used conjunctions:
- And
- But
- Or
- Although
- As
- That
- If.

...although

Prepositions & Interjections

Prepositions show the relationships between two parts of a sentence. For example…
- he sat *on* the sofa
- you can't leave the classroom *without* permission
- we stayed *near* Scarborough
- the text message was *from* David.

Interjections are exclamations, short phrases or single words that express feelings such as surprise, shock, disgust and anger. For example…
- Ah! Ow! Yippee!
- Hooray! Phew! Ouch!

Articles

Articles come before a noun. There are three words that are normally called 'articles':
- 'A' and 'an' are **indefinite** articles.
- 'The' is the **definite** article.

Note the difference that the use of an indefinite or a definite article can make:
- *The* car broke *a* speed limit as it tore down *the* road.
- *A* car broke *the* speed limit as it tore down *a* road.

Quick Test

1. True or false – an adjective tells you more about a noun.
2. True or false – Manchester is a common noun.
3. True or false – an interjection joins two parts of a sentence together.
4. True or false – a pronoun can replace an adjective.
5. True or false – 'run' is a preposition.
6. True or false – 'a', 'an' and 'the' are articles.

Work out the key words from the clues below, then copy and complete the crossword.

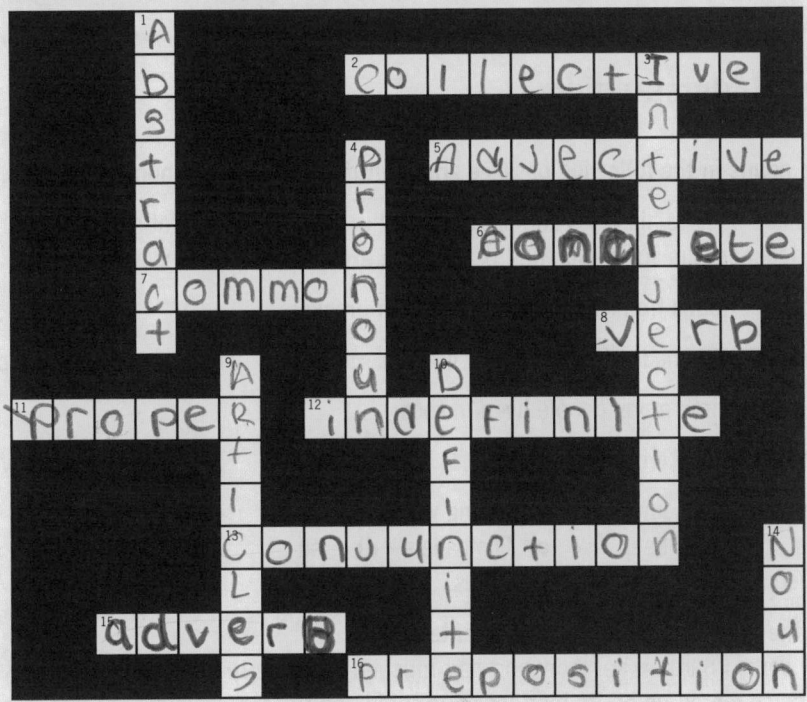

Across

2. 'Flock' and 'herd' are examples of this kind of noun. (10)

5. A word that describes a noun. (9)

6. 'Table' is an example of this type of noun. (8)

7. This type of noun describes an everyday object. (6)

8. 'Run' is an example of one of these. (4)

11. 'John' and 'River Avon' are examples of this type of noun. (6)

12. 'A' and 'an' are this kind of article. (10)

13. Joins two parts of a sentence together. (11)

15. A word that describes a verb. (6)

16. 'On', 'in', and 'at' are examples of this. (11)

Down

1. 'Pride' and 'kindness' are this kind of noun. (8)

3. Ouch! is an example of one of these. (12)

4. 'Him', 'her', 'we', and 'them' are examples of this. (7)

9. 'The', 'a', and 'an'. (8)

10. 'The' is called the _Definite_ article. (8)

14. A word that names something. (4)

Grammar

1 Find the nouns in the following passage and identify what kind of noun each one is.

Harry walked back to his class and sat down at his desk. He felt great satisfaction in the fact that the teacher, Mrs Tompkins, had praised the excellence of his essay.

2 Form abstract nouns from the following words in brackets.

a) Sean's face beamed with (proud) _pride_ when he received the prize.

b) In Dickens' time many people lived in (poor) _poverty_ .

c) Rachel showed a lot of (confident) _confidence_ before taking her driving test.

3 Give the collective nouns for the following words.

a) Lions _Pride_   b) Sheep _Flock_   c) Footballers _team_   d) Fish _shoal_   e) Cows _herd_   f) Sailors _crew_
g) Soldiers _Regiment_   h) Ants _colony_   i) Ships _Fleet_   j) Eggs _clutch_   k) Flowers _bunch_   l) Wolves _pack_

4 Identify the pronouns in the following sentences.

a) Kate worked hard on her story and had finished it before the end of the day.

b) The horse reared up on its hind legs and threw the rider, but luckily she was unhurt.

c) The family packed their belongings, even though they were unsure about moving to their new home.

5 Identify the adjectives in the following sentences.

a) We went on holiday last week and the weather was beautiful.

b) The grey sky looked threatening as the bitter, icy wind blew hard across the barren landscape.

6 Find the adverbs in the following sentences and say which verbs they describe.

a) I will work hard to pass my exams. =pass

b) Todd grimly hung on to the rope. =todd

c) Kim smiled happily at the news. = smiled

7 Which words are conjunctions and which are prepositions in the following sentences?

a) The boy slammed his book on the desk and walked out of the room.

b) I tried to write a story about the weather but I couldn't think of any ideas.

c) Billy went out to the field and joined in a game of football.

8 Identify the definite and indefinite articles in the following sentences.

a) This is the book I told you about.

b) I had a lovely sleep.

c) The teacher ate an apple.

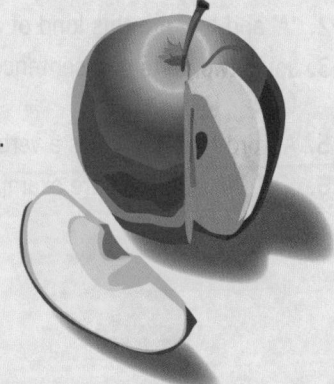

Working with a partner, design a poster for the wall of your classroom, explaining the basic word classes.

You should…
- make your poster eye-catching
- keep it simple – don't try to explain too much, but give the basic explanation of each word class
- think carefully about the layout.

Now design a series of information leaflets to accompany your poster:
- Each leaflet should give information about each word class.
- Include examples to illustrate the key ideas.
- Present the information in an interesting way.

With your partner, prepare a presentation designed to teach the key ideas of word classes.

You could use PowerPoint or slides to illustrate the presentation.

Record a sound commentary to go with your presentation.

VERB (doing word)

NOUN (naming word)

Example:

Tom ran quickly

Sentences 1

What is Covered in this Topic?

This topic looks at...
- different kinds of sentences
- simple sentences
- the verb in a sentence
- verb and subject agreement.

Different Kinds of Sentences

There are four different kinds of sentences. Each type of sentence has a particular purpose.

Most of the sentences that you use in your writing are statement sentences.

Note that sentences that are exclamations end with an exclamation mark.

Some commands can also end with exclamation marks.

Type of Sentence	Purpose	Examples
Statement	To make a statement	• I love reading novels. • It is sunny today.
Command (sometimes called **imperatives**)	To command, order or request	• Come down here now. • Pass me the milk please. • Go over there.
Question	To ask a question	• Did you enjoy the film? • Have you finished your work yet?
Exclamation	To express surprise, anger, pleasure, etc.	• What a lovely day it is! • How clever you are!

Did you enjoy the film?

Simple Sentences

The most basic kind of sentence is the **simple** sentence.

Simple sentences have...
- a **subject**
- a **verb** (a verb that has a subject is called a **finite** verb).

Lots of problems that can occur when writing sentences are to do with these parts of the sentence. It's important that you're able to identify the subject and the verb in your sentences so that you can check that you're using correct grammar and English in your writing.

Identifying the Subject

The subject tells you who or what the sentence is about. The position of the subject in a sentence can vary.

Usually the subject comes at the beginning of a sentence:

Subject Verb

Tom trains hard on his mountain bike.

Sometimes the subject comes a little later:

Subject Verb

On the whole Samira likes science.

Occasionally the subject comes after the verb:

Verb   Subject

In the middle of the pitch lay an injured player.

The subject can be a single word, e.g. 'Tom' or 'Samira' or a group of words, e.g. 'an injured player' – this group of words is called a **phrase**.

Sentences 1

Identifying the Verb

In a statement sentence the verb normally comes immediately after the subject:

Subject Verb

David thinks that computer games are really fun.

Sometimes, though, there are one or more words between the subject and the verb:

Subject Verb

Nick, surprisingly, did better in the test than Susie.

What Verbs Tell You

The verb tells you about the subject and can give different kinds of information:
- It can describe an **action**, e.g. 'trains', 'works'.
- It can describe a **state** or **condition**, e.g. 'likes', 'hates'.
- Some verbs simply link the subject to the rest of the sentence, for example:

Subject Verb Rest of sentence

Helen is on holiday in Cornwall.

Here is another example:

Subject Verb Rest of sentence

Kate was very happy with the money.

Other linking verbs that work like this include 'seems', 'appears', 'becomes', 'am', 'are'.

The verb in a sentence can consist of one word, e.g. thinks, or a group of words (called a verb phrase), for example:

Subject Verb phrase

George shouldn't have been going on the trip.

Subject and Verb Agreement

When writing a sentence the subject and verb must **agree**. Mistakes often happen in written sentences because there isn't agreement.

Look at these two sentences and see if you can see what is wrong with them.

I were walking to the shops.

My books is on the table.

You might have noticed that in these two sentences, the subject and verb do not agree.

I were (✗) walking to the shops should be:

I was (✓) walking to the shops.

My books is (✗) on the table should be:

My books are (✓) on the table.

In spoken English, it's quite common for verbs and subjects not to be in agreement, but in written English it's not considered correct.

Quick Test

1. How many kinds of sentences are there? 4
2. What is another name for a command? order
3. A group of words is called a ~~Phrase~~ Phrase.
4. A verb that has a subject is called a Finite verb.

KEY WORDS
Make sure you understand these words before moving on!

- Sentence
- Statement
- Command
- Imperative
- Question
- Exclamation
- Simple
- Subject
- Verb
- Finite
- Phrase
- Action
- State
- Condition
- Agree

Sentences 1

Complete each sentence by finding the missing word.

1. The most basic kind of sentence is called a _simple_ sentence.

2. A group of words without a verb is not a _sentence_.

3. For a sentence to be written in correct English the verb and subject must _agree_.

4. A verb that has a subject is called a _finite_ verb.

5. 'Are you ready yet?' is an example of a _question_.

6. When a verb tells you what someone is doing it describes an _action_.

7. If the verb in a sentence is made up of more than one word it is called a verb _phrase_.

8. Apart from describing actions a verb can also describe a ~~statement~~ or _condition_.

9. 'Oh no, I've torn my coat!' is an example of an _exclamation_.

10. Every sentence must have a _subject_ and a _verb_.

11. A sentence that issues an order is called a _command_ or an _request_.

12. 'I like school.' is an example of a _statement_ sentence.

Testing Understanding

1 **Identify the types of sentences:**

a) Clean up your room immediately! *co*

b) I think autumn is my favourite time of the year. *statement*

c) Could you lend me five pounds to go out tonight, please? *question*

d) Pass me that pan, would you? *question*

e) The sun was shining brightly and I felt happy and free. *statement*

f) That plate was very hot! *exclamation*

g) Please make sure that you wipe your feet on the mat. *request*

h) What a silly boy you are! *exclamation*

2 **Identify the subject and verb in these sentences:**

↓ = subject
J = verb

a) <u>Joe</u> <u>ran</u> as quickly as he could to the bus stop.

b) It was hard but <u>Rachael</u> <u>passed</u> her exam.

c) In the corner of the room <u>sat</u> an evil old <u>witch</u>.

d) <u>Harry</u> and <u>Mario</u> <u>camped</u> by the river.

e) In the middle of the table <u>stood</u> a large, silver <u>candlestick</u>.

f) <u>Annie</u> <u>is happy</u> with her watch.

g) <u>Sam</u> <u>threw</u> the ball into the middle of the <u>crowd</u>.

h) <u>Gasping</u> for breath <u>Kim</u> crossed the finish line.

i) The <u>boat</u> <u>sank</u> in the stormy sea.

j) <u>Sandra</u> and <u>Steph</u> <u>are from</u> <u>Durham</u>.

3 **Identify which of these sentences are incorrect and write out the corrected sentence.**

a) We are going on a long walk tomorrow.

b) You ~~is~~ *are* a good student and work very hard.

c) I am a keen cyclist.

d) I thought you ~~was~~ *were* going to help me tidy up.

e) I ~~were~~ *was* going to go out tonight but I haven't ~~any money.~~ *got*

f) My dogs ~~has~~ *have* two meals a day.

g) There ~~is~~ *are* lots of people queuing for tickets. *sure*

h) We ~~was~~ *are* going to the seaside. *sure*

Sentences 1

Work with a partner to design a poster to show the four different kinds of sentences.

Your poster should...
- be eye-catching
- be clear and easy to understand
- give an example of each kind of sentence
- use layout effectively to display information.

Now create a second poster that shows how simple sentences are structured and how to identify the subject and verb.

Your poster should...
- give clear information
- show examples
- present the information in an interesting way.

Present your posters to your class and ask them to comment on how effectively they think that you have presented the information.

Ask them to give examples of the ways you might improve the posters (if there are any).

What is Covered in this Topic?

This topic looks at...
- compound sentences
- phrases and clauses
- complex sentences.

Compound Sentences

When two or more **simple sentences** are joined together by connectives (also called conjunctions), **compound sentences** are formed.

The conjunctions that join simple sentences together are called **coordinating conjunctions** or coordinators.

simple sentence

Jasmine worked hard on her essay.

She got full marks for it.

simple sentence

compound sentence

Jasmine worked hard on her essay and she got full marks for it.

coordinating conjunction

Here are some more examples of simple sentences made into compound sentences by connecting them with conjunctions:
- I want to go to the party *but* I haven't finished my homework.
- Amy found delivering papers hard work *yet* she enjoyed it.
- We got a bus to town *then* went to the cinema.

Sentences 2

Types of Conjunctions

Conjunctions that join simple sentences together are: 'but', 'or', 'nor', 'then', 'yet', 'for', 'so', 'and'.

Sometimes you can slightly change the meaning of the sentence depending on which coordinating conjunction you use. For example...

- I am going to visit Todd. I will see Michaela.
  - I am going to visit Todd *and* I will see Michaela.
  - I am going to visit Todd *then* I will see Michaela.
  - I am going to visit Todd *so* I will see Michaela.

💡 *Think about the differences in meaning of these sentences depending on which coordinating conjunctions have been used.*

Phrases and Clauses

A **phrase** is a group of words that doesn't contain a finite verb and so doesn't make complete sense on its own. For example...

- at great cost
- cycling furiously
- to my great relief
- with a silly grin.

A **clause** is a group of words that contains a finite verb. A simple sentence contains one clause.

Multiple Sentences

Sentences that contain more than one clause are called **multiple sentences**.

Compound sentences contain two clauses, so are multiple sentences. Every clause must contain a finite verb.

Look at this example of a multiple sentence:

Mallory rushed to the window but he saw nothing

finite verb   finite verb

To check whether a sentence is a simple sentence or a multiple sentence, you need to pick out the finite verbs. If there is only one, it's a simple sentence. If there is more than one, it's a multiple sentence.

Main and Subordinate Clauses

Some clauses can make complete sense on their own. These are called **main clauses**. Other clauses can't stand on their own because they are **incomplete**. These are called **subordinate clauses**.

subordinate clause   main clause

(**Although he tried hard**) (**Mark failed his driving test.**)

The main clause is '*Mark failed his driving test*' as it makes complete sense on its own.

The subordinate clause is '*Although he tried hard*' as it's incomplete and can't make sense on its own.

Differences Between Sentences

Look at these two simple sentences:

The band played well. They lost the competition.

The same information in a compound sentence could read:

The band played well but they lost the competition.

A **complex sentence** has one main clause and one or more subordinate clauses. Complex sentences join the different parts of a sentence in a way that gives you more information than if you wrote in simple sentences.

BATTLE
of the Bands

Friday, 29th May, 9pm

Sentences 2

Writing Complex Sentences

A complex sentence can present information in several ways, each of which gives a slightly different meaning.

💡 *Think about the different meanings of these complex sentences.*

main clause | subordinate clause

(The band played well) (even though they lost the competition.)

subordinate clause | main clause

(Even though the band played well) (they lost the competition.)

subordinate clause | main clause

(Although the band played well) (they lost the competition.)

Each sentence has one main clause that can stand on its own and one subordinate clause that can't because it's incomplete.

Interesting and varied writing makes use of a variety of sentence types, and in order to write accurately and express your ideas well you need to use sentences correctly.

Quick Test

1. What is a phrase?
2. When writing why should you use a variety of sentence types?
3. What joins two simple sentences together to make a compound sentence?
4. How many main clauses does a complex sentence have?

Match each key word with its definition.

Complex sentence	A sentence with one main clause and any number of subordinate clauses.
Main clause	A group of words that doesn't contain a finite verb.
Phrase	A sentence made up of two simple sentences.
Simple sentence	Joins two sentences together.
Coordinating conjunction	A sentence with just one finite verb.
Compound sentence	A group of words with a finite verb.
Multiple sentence	A clause that doesn't make complete sense on its own.
Subordinate clause	A sentence that contains more than one finite verb.
Clause	A clause that has a finite verb and subject and makes complete sense on its own.

Clause

Phrase

Sentences 2

1 Use suitable coordinating conjunctions to change these simple sentences into compound sentences.
   a) I didn't know about the problem. I can't explain it. *—so*
   b) She ran for the bus. She missed it. *—but*
   c) Shall we go to the cinema? Shall we go bowling? *—and*
   d) We must leave now. We will miss the start. *—or*
   e) I will tidy up my bedroom. I don't want to. *—but*
   f) I will see you tonight. I will pick you up at 7.00pm. *—and*

2 What is the difference in meaning between these pairs of sentences?
   a) Sam didn't revise much for his exam and he got a grade C.
      Sam didn't revise much for his exam but he got a grade C.
   b) We went to drama club and had some hot dogs and pop.
      We went to drama club then had some hot dogs and pop.

3 Which of these are phrases and which are clauses?
   a) swerving round the bend *P*   b) I love going on trips *C*   c) you did well *P*
   d) coming out *P*   e) you drive me mad *C*

4 Identify the main clause and subordinate clause in the following sentences.
   a) I put on my coat because it was raining. *SC*
   b) As the door was locked he couldn't get in. *S*
   c) Before opening his notebook he
      sharpened his pencil. *SC*
   d) He was slumped in the chair staring
      vacantly at the television. *SC*
   e) I paid the bill although the
      food was disgusting. *E*

RESTAURANT
(309) 688-8828
S0071MH115 04-20-01

Shepherd's pie
Spaghetti bolognese   8.99
Blueberry muffin   7.99
Double Choc muffin   1.50
Cappuccino   1.50
Cappuccino   1.99
                          1.99

SUBTOTAL: 23.96
SERVICE CHARGE @ 10%   2.39
BALANCE DUE: 26.35

CASH: 30.00
CHANGE: 3.65

8:32 REF#12

Menu

Work with a partner to devise a set of worksheets explaining compound sentences and complex sentences.

Your worksheets should…

- explain things accurately
- be clear and easy to understand
- give an example of each kind of sentence
- use layout effectively to display information
- contain at least three questions to test understanding.

Write an answer sheet to go with your test questions.

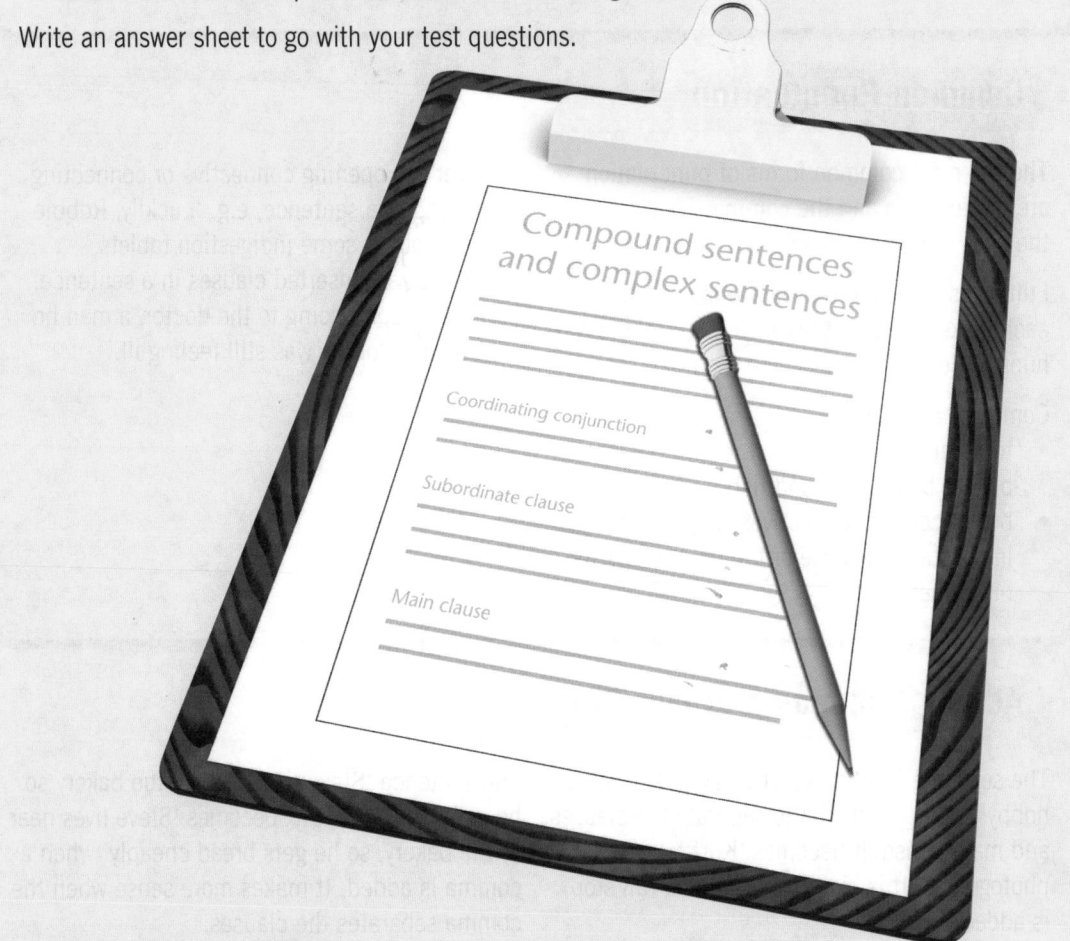

Compound sentences
and complex sentences

Coordinating conjunction

Subordinate clause

Main clause

Exchange your worksheets with another pair and try doing each other's worksheets.

When you've finished the worksheets, join up with the other pair and discuss how you got on.

Talk about how successful you felt the worksheets were in explaining the ideas and how useful you found the questions that were designed to test your understanding.

Punctuation 1

What is Covered in this Topic?

This topic looks at...
- common forms of punctuation
- common word errors and confusions.

Common Punctuation

The two most common forms of **punctuation** are the **full stop** and the **comma**. They are also the ones that get mixed up the most.

Full stops are used to separate clauses that each make sense on their own, e.g. Robbie was hungry. He went to buy some food.

Commas are used...
- to separate items in a list, e.g. 'Robbie bought beans, rice and fish for his dinner.'
- before certain connectives, e.g. 'Robbie got indigestion, because of the food he ate for his dinner.'
- after the opening connective or connecting phrase in a sentence, e.g. 'Luckily, Robbie had bought some indigestion tablets.'
- to separate inserted clauses in a sentence, e.g. 'Despite going to the doctor, a man he trusted, Robbie was still feeling ill.'

Adding Commas and Full Stops

The sentence 'Kurt takes photographs it is his hobby' needs a full stop to separate the clauses and make sense. It becomes 'Kurt takes photographs. It is his hobby.' when a full stop is added.

The sentence 'Nick loves to travel he visits the USA at least twice a year' needs a full stop to make complete sense. It becomes 'Nick loves to travel. He visits the USA at least twice a year'.

The sentence 'Phil eats a lot of vegetables although he is allergic to sprouts' needs a comma to separate the clauses, to become 'Phil eats a lot of vegetables, although he is allergic to sprouts'.

The sentence 'Steve lives near to the bakery so he gets bread cheaply' becomes 'Steve lives near to the bakery, so he gets bread cheaply' when a comma is added. It makes more sense when the comma separates the clauses.

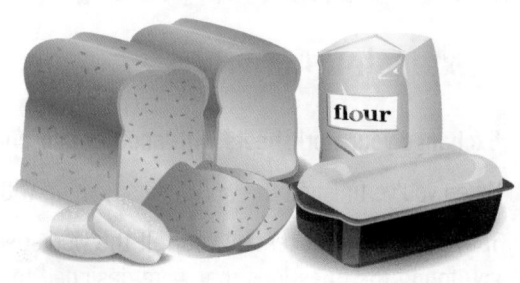

Semi-Colons

Semi-colons are used to...
- separate complicated lists, e.g. 'In the meeting we have Dr. Dave Moreman, Steffs University; Professor Norbert Scragg, Keile University and Mr. Fred Halfbiscuit, University of Palos Park.'
- separate closely-related clauses instead of a full stop, e.g. 'New Mexico is a beautiful place; the land is varied and the people are friendly.'

Colons

Colons are used to...
- introduce an idea, e.g. 'There's one thing you need to know about cabbage: it tastes vile.'
- introduce a list, e.g. 'Jambalaya contains many ingredients: rice, beans, meat and tomatoes.'
- introduce a quotation, e.g. The teacher's statement read: 'It's not what you write; it's how you write it that counts.'

Hyphens and Dashes

A hyphen is a mark used to separate two parts of a combined word, e.g. self-obsessed.

A hyphen is used in these examples:
- The award-winning writer thanked the audience.
- The man lacked self-confidence.

A dash is a mark used to act like brackets around an inserted clause, e.g. 'My friends – Darren, Debbie and Donna – all like sport.

Punctuation 1

Apostrophes

There are two kinds of **apostrophe**:
- Apostrophes of **omission** – they replace the missing letters in shortened forms of words, e.g. can't = cannot.
- Apostrophes of **possession** – if a word ends in anything but *s*, add *'s* to show possession, e.g. the girl's book (there is only one girl, so add *'s*).

If a word ends in *s*, place the apostrophe after the *s*, e.g. James' book; the girls' book (there are several girls so put the apostrophe after the *s*).

This rule sometimes causes confusion, because we might write 'James' book', but we might say 'James's book'. Both are acceptable.

Here are some examples where apostrophes of omission are needed:
- Fred wasn't guilty of the crimes he was charged with.
- Too much time on the internet isn't good for you.

Here are some examples where apostrophes of possession are needed:
- Sir's hair was the shortest in class.
- 'Will you help me fix Phillip's bike?' asked Sarah.

There, Their, They're

'**There**', '**their**' and '**they're**' are often confused, especially 'there' and 'their':
- Their – belonging to them, e.g. 'It was their car.'
- There – indicating a place, e.g. 'There is a man over there!'
- They're – shortened version of 'They are', e.g. 'They're coming to see us tonight.'

Here are some examples in using the correct form of 'their', 'there' and 'they're':
- The pupils wanted to do their homework straight away.
- 'They're not paying attention!' moaned the teacher.
- 'Is there a doctor in the house?' shouted the man.
- 'Look over there. They're playing with their new football.'

To, Too and Two

The words 'To', 'Too' and 'Two' are commonly confused.

'To' is used...
- like 'towards', e.g. 'I am going to the shops.'
- with the **infinitive** form of verbs, e.g. 'I am going to run.'

Too means 'also' or 'as well', e.g. 'Are you going? Can I come too?' 'Is it too much?'

Two is the number 2.

Here are some examples of 'to', 'too' and 'two':
- Is it too late?
- Do you want to know who won the lottery?
- You two are too alike to be true!

to, too
and two

It's and Its

The use or omission of the apostrophe in 'its' and 'it's' is a common error:
- It's – 'It is' or 'It has', e.g. 'It's going to rain'. 'It's been a long time since I had beans for tea.'
- Its – belonging to 'it', e.g. 'The monkey scratched its chin.' 'The river burst its banks.'

Here are some examples of 'it's' and 'its':
- The cathedral got its name from the area it was originally built in.
- Whether it's true or not, it still seems strange that aliens would be interested in Earth.
- It's hard to be humble when you're brilliant.

it's and its

Quick Test

1. Insert a comma or a full stop:
   'Donna gets on with everyone, she is a very understanding person.'
2. Add a hyphen or a dash:
   'The well-dressed man caught the train.'
3. Add a colon or semi-colon:
   'Dan's favourite saying was often repeated; "Don't do anything that I'd do!"'
4. Add apostrophes of omission and possession:
   'The Prime Minister's policies didnt please everyone.'
5. Choose the correct form of each word in the following sentences:
   a) There / their / they're is the man who took there / their / they're money.
   b) The dog was licking it's / its paw. It's / Its a sure sign that it was hurting.
   c) There are to / too / two many people who want to / too / two play football.

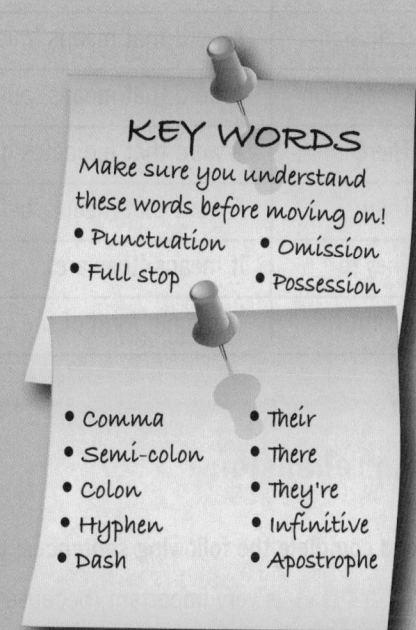

KEY WORDS
Make sure you understand these words before moving on!
- Punctuation
- Full stop
- Omission
- Possession

- Comma
- Semi-colon
- Colon
- Hyphen
- Dash
- Their
- There
- They're
- Infinitive
- Apostrophe

Punctuation 1

Which key word definitions are correct and which are incorrect?

Keyword	Definition
a) Punctuation ⊕	The use of standard marks and signs in writing and printing to separate words into sentences, clauses and phrases in order to clarify meaning.
b) Full stop Ⓕ	A punctuation mark indicating the end of a clause that doesn't make sense on its own.
c) Comma Ⓕ	A punctuation mark indicating the end of a clause that makes sense on its own.
d) Semi-colon ⊕	A punctuation mark used to sometimes separate complicated lists.
e) Colon ⊕	A punctuation mark used to sometimes introduce a quotation.
f) Hyphen Ⓕ	A punctuation mark used to act like brackets around a clause.
g) Dash Ⓕ	A punctuation mark used to separate two parts of a combined word.
h) Apostrophe ⊕	A mark used to show speech.
i) Omission Ⓒ	A word that means 'missed out'.
j) Possession ⊕	A word that means 'put an apostrophe after the s'.
k) There Ⓕ	A word that indicates direction.
l) Their Ⓕ	A word that means 'belonging to us'.
m) They're ⊕	It means 'they are'.
n) Infinitive ⊕	The main form of the verb.

Comprehension

Copy and complete the following sentences, using some of the key words above.

1. _Punctuation_ is very important, because your writing will not make sense without it.

2. Be careful that you don't mix up _commas_ , which separate clauses, and _full stops_ , which separate sentences.

Comprehension (cont.)

③ Apostrophes of _Ommisions_ for missed-out letters need to be put in the correct place, as do apostrophes of _Possesion_, which show that something belongs to something else. These are the basic forms of punctuation that people tend to mix up.

Testing Understanding

Correct the following passage, which has punctuation missing and contains spelling errors.

The soil below Londons streets holds many secrets. It's true to say that people have been living in London for thousands of years, but London has kept many of its secrets until now this is one of the secrets, 'An ancient Roman road beneath there garden' was what the headline in the London newspapers said. Mike Fredrickson whod lived in Southwark for many years always wondered what the bits of tile were that he kept digging up and assembling in his shed.

After many years of collecting these tiles, Mike and his wife took them to they're council office where they heard that their was an archaeologist an archaeologist whod tell them what theyd found. Mikes decision too take the bits two the council proved to be inspired they turned out to be part of a Roman mosaic from a selfcontained villa beneath his back garden Mikes hoping that his discovery will mean that hell not have two buy a lottery ticket in future.

True or False?

Are the following statements true or false?

① 'There' means 'belonging to them'. (F)

② Apostrophes are used for more than one reason. (T)

③ Hyphens and dashes look similar, although they have different uses. (T)

④ It's stands for 'it is', but not 'it has'.

⑤ Commas can separate sentences. (T)

⑥ Colons can be used to introduce an idea. (T)

⑦ Commas separate items in a list, but only the first two. (F)

⑧ You put an apostrophe on any word ending in s. (F)

⑨ 'To' is the number 2. (F)

⑩ Commas are used after the opening connective in a sentence.

Punctuation 1

Skills Practice

Your brief is to create information posters for primary school pupils on the following topics:

- **How to use apostrophes.**
- **Commonly confused words – 'there / they're / there', 'it's / its' and 'to / two / too'.**
- **The differences between commas and full stops.**
- **How to use semi-colons, colons, hyphens and dashes.**

Step 1: Look back over the topic and write your own versions of the rules and definitions you've learned. Simplify the language to make the explanations clearer to younger children.

Step 2: Make up three examples of each rule or definition to go onto each poster. Make sure they're correct.

Step 3: Try to think of catchy ways of remembering the rules. Can you make up any rhymes, pictures or other ways of making people remember the rules that you can put on your posters? Trying to think of ways of remembering the rules is a good way to remember them yourself.

Extension Activity

Design some more posters, but this time choose a different target audience.

a) Adult learners:
- How would you change the text so they didn't feel that you were talking down to them?
- How would you change the font and the pictures on the poster to make it more appealing to them?

b) Your own age group:
- What examples would you choose to make your peers interested?
- How might you use humour to attract their attention?

c) People learning English as a foreign language:
- How would you use images to get round the problem of the readers being new to the language?
- Why might you need a very clear font?

Use the prompts to make sure your posters are appropriate for the audience and get your message across clearly.

Punctuation 2

What is Covered in This Topic?

This topic looks at...
- direct speech
- reported speech
- play scripts.

Direct Speech

Direct speech is when the actual spoken words are used in a piece of writing. This kind of writing speech has its own special kind of **punctuation**.

Look carefully at the way the following piece of speech is punctuated.

The Hobbit by J.R.R. Tolkien

'Something strange is happening,' said Thorin. 'The time has gone for the autumn wanderings; and these are birds that dwell always in the land; there are starlings and flocks of finches; and far off there are many carrion birds as if a battle were afoot!'

Suddenly Bilbo pointed: 'There is that old thrush again!' he cried. 'He seems to have escaped, when Smaug smashed the mountain-side, but I don't suppose the snails have!'

Sure enough the old thrush was there, and as Bilbo pointed, he flew towards them and perched on a stone near by. Then he fluttered his wings and sang; then he cocked his head on one side, as if to listen; and again he sang, and again he listened.

'I believe he is trying to tell us something,' said Balin; 'but I cannot follow the speech of such birds, it is very quick and difficult. Can you make it out, Baggins?'

'Not very well,' said Bilbo (as a matter of fact, he could making nothing of it at all); 'but the old fellow seems very excited.'

'I only wish he was a raven!' said Balin.

'I thought you did not like them! You seemed very shy of them, when we came this way before.'

① Speech marks only go around the words that are actually being spoken.

② A comma is needed to separate the spoken part from the part telling you who is speaking, unless a question mark or exclamation is used.

③ If an exclamation mark or a question mark is used, then a comma's not needed to separate the spoken words from the rest.

④ A capital letter isn't needed here because this is a continuation of the spoken sentence.

⑤ Speech begins with a capital letter at the beginning of the spoken sentence.

⑥ A new paragraph's needed every time a different speaker begins speaking.

Punctuation 2

Speech Layout

There are three different kinds of speech layout (the spoken words are highlighted in italics):

- The part telling you who is speaking comes at the end, e.g. *'Are you coming to my party, Kim?'* asked Jane.
- The part telling you who is speaking comes at the beginning, e.g. Kim said, *'Yes, I'm really looking forward to it.'*

- The part telling you who's speaking comes in the middle of the speech sentence, e.g. *'That's great,'* said Jane, *'because you'll know lots of the others that are coming.'*

If in doubt where to place the **speech marks**, ask yourself what words are being spoken. These are the words that need speech marks (also called **quotation marks**) around them.

Indirect Speech

Indirect speech (sometimes called **reported speech**) is a different way of writing down things that have been said. The following conversation is written in direct speech:

'What are you doing?' the farmer asked Matt and his friends.

'We know we shouldn't be here,' answered Matt, 'but we're not doing any harm.'

'Where are the rest of your friends now, and what are they doing?' The farmer looked at him suspiciously.

'I don't know, but I expect they're hiding in the woods.'

'What are you doing in this barn?'

'We're looking for shelter from the rain.'

'But you shouldn't be on my land at all,' said the farmer, beginning to get angry. 'The police are on their way.'

'I'm sorry,' Matt said.

Here is the same conversation written in indirect speech:

The farmer asked Matt what he was doing. Matt answered that he knew they shouldn't have been there but they weren't doing any harm. The farmer asked him where the rest of his friends were and Matt replied that he didn't know, but that they'd probably hidden in the woods.

The farmer then asked Matt what they were doing in the barn and Matt replied that they were looking for shelter from the rain.

The farmer began to get angry and told Matt that they shouldn't have been on his land at all and that the police were on their way. Matt apologised.

Think about the changes that have been made to change the direct speech version into the indirect speech version.

Changing Pronouns

When the conversation is converted from direct speech to indirect speech, several changes occur.

First and second person personal **pronouns** are changed to the third person.

Direct Speech	Indirect Speech
You (singular)	He / She
Your	His / Her
We	They
I	He / She
You (plural)	They
My	His / Her

Changing Tense and Adverbs

The **tense** is changed, mainly from the **present** (direct speech) to the **past** (indirect speech), for example...
- 'What are you doing?' (direct); What he was doing (indirect).
- 'Shouldn't be on my land' (direct); Should not have been on his land (indirect).

The **adverbs** that refer to time and space change. Phrases such as 'said the farmer', are changed to 'The farmer said that...,' for example...
- here (direct) – there (indirect)
- now (direct) – then (indirect)
- this (direct) – that (indirect).

Word order can change and some information can be summarised:
- Direct speech – 'I'm sorry,' said Matt.
- Indirect speech – Matt apologised; speech marks aren't used.

Punctuation 2

Play Scripts

Play scripts (sometimes called **drama** scripts) are another way of presenting speech.

Look at the following example of a short play script.

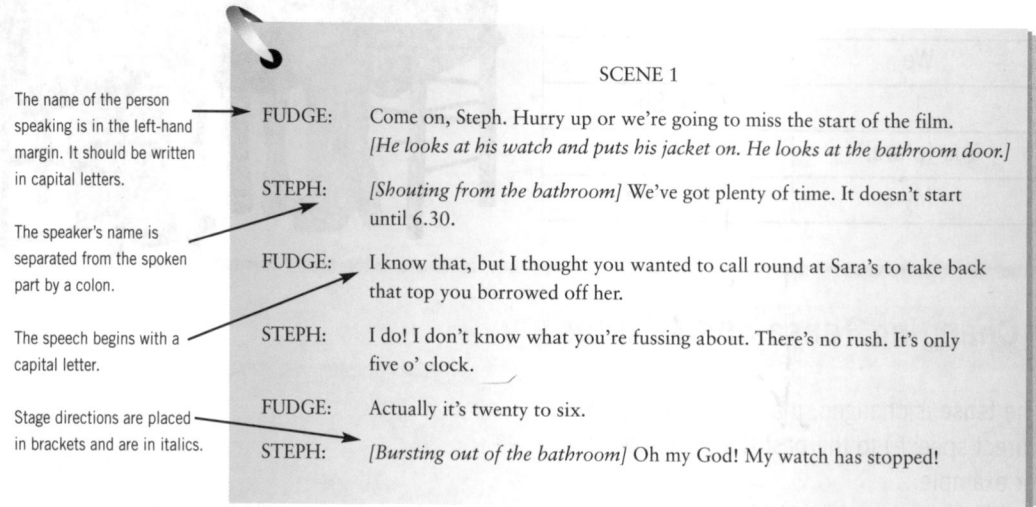

The name of the person speaking is in the left-hand margin. It should be written in capital letters.

The speaker's name is separated from the spoken part by a colon.

The speech begins with a capital letter.

Stage directions are placed in brackets and are in italics.

SCENE 1

FUDGE: Come on, Steph. Hurry up or we're going to miss the start of the film. *[He looks at his watch and puts his jacket on. He looks at the bathroom door.]*

STEPH: *[Shouting from the bathroom]* We've got plenty of time. It doesn't start until 6.30.

FUDGE: I know that, but I thought you wanted to call round at Sara's to take back that top you borrowed off her.

STEPH: I do! I don't know what you're fussing about. There's no rush. It's only five o' clock.

FUDGE: Actually it's twenty to six.

STEPH: *[Bursting out of the bathroom]* Oh my God! My watch has stopped!

The example shows that...
- speech marks aren't used in play scripts
- the name of the character speaking is on the left-hand side
- the speaker's name is separated from the spoken part by a colon
- the speech begins with a capital letter
- **stage directions** are used to describe actions, scenes and anything else happening on the stage; they're usually brief and aren't spoken, so they're put in brackets and in italics.

Quick Test

1. What are used in direct speech, but not in indirect speech and play scripts?
2. When writing direct speech, when should you begin a new line?
3. In what tense is indirect speech usually written?
4. In a play script, what separates the speaker's name from what they say?
5. What do stage directions do?

Key Words Exercise

Unscramble these anagrams to find the key words, then match them to the right definition.

Anagram	Handwritten answer	Definition
Credit cheeps	*Direct speech*	Speech that reports what's been said.
Auctionpunt	*Punctuation*	Words that stand in place of the noun.
Crinedt secpeh	*Indirect speech*	Past and present are examples of this.
Deporter hecspe	*reported speech*	A play is written in this.
Snoopurn	*Pronouns*	Speech that uses the exact words that are spoken.
Enset	*tense*	These marks help to make written English readable.
Restpen	*present*	These tell you what's happening on stage.
Taps neets	*past tense*	Another term for 'play script'.
Verbsad	*Adverbs*	This describes things that happened yesterday, for example.
Layp prisct	*play script*	Another term for 'speech marks'.
Amard crispt	*Drama script*	The tense that describes things that are happening now.
Peshce krams	*speech marks*	These only go round the words that are spoken.
Tuqootain skarm	*quotation mark*	Another term for 'indirect speech'.
Getsa creditsoin	*stage directions*	Words that tell you more about the verb.

Punctuation 2

1 **a)** Write out the following passage, putting in the speech marks where necessary and laying the speech out correctly.

A Merry Christmas, Uncle! God save you! cried a cheerful voice. It was the voice of Scrooge's nephew, who came upon him so quickly that this was the first intimation he had of his approach. Bah! said Scrooge, Humbug! He had so heated himself with rapid walking in the fog and frost, this nephew of Scrooge's, that he was all in a glow; his face was ruddy and handsome; his eyes sparkled, and his breath smoked again. Christmas a humbug, uncle! said Scrooge's nephew. You don't mean that, I am sure? I do, said Scrooge. Merry Christmas! What right have you to be merry? What reason have you to be merry? You're poor enough. Come, then, returned the nephew gaily. What right have you to be dismal? What reason have you to be morose? You're rich enough.

A Christmas Carol by Charles Dickens

b) Now try writing out the passage again, converting it into indirect speech.

c) Convert your direct speech version of this extract into play script form.

Record a short conversation between yourself and a friend, or with a member of your family.

Step 1: Write out the conversation in direct speech. Think about...
- the layout – use a new paragraph for a new speaker
- where the speech marks should go
- the use of capital letters
- the use of punctuation marks such as commas, full stops, question marks and exclamation marks.

Step 2: Write another version of this using indirect speech. Remember to think about...
- your use of tense
- changing pronouns
- changing adverbs
- changing phrases such as 'said the girl'
- removing speech marks.

Step 3: Compare the differences between your two versions.

Working with a partner or small group, write a short scene for a play.

The scene can be about anything you like. Focus on...
- the layout of the speech
- the use of stage directions
- using the correct tense.

When you've finished writing the scene, try performing it. Use your script to act it out, with each person taking a part and one person acting as director to take control of the action.

You need to...
- capture a sense of the characters' voices
- make use of your stage directions.

Remember that you'll need to practise this several times and experiment with different ways of speaking the lines and acting out the action.

Punctuation 3

What is Covered in this Topic?

This topic looks at...
- contraction apostrophes
- commonly confused words
- possessive apostrophes.

The Apostrophe

There are two main reasons for using **apostrophes** in your writing:

1 To shorten a word or to combine two words together into one shortened form by missing out a letter or letters. Apostrophes used like this are called contraction apostrophes (or apostrophes of omission).

2 To show that someone owns something, i.e. to show **possession**. Apostrophes used like this are called **possessive** apostrophes.

These two reasons for using apostrophes are completely separate and you shouldn't muddle the two up.

Contraction Apostrophes

In some **contractions** two words are combined to create a new single unit. Note how an apostrophe replaces the dropped letters in each example:
- they're – they are (the 'a' is dropped)
- you've – you have (the 'h' and the 'a' are dropped)
- didn't – did not (the 'o' is dropped)

You'll be very familiar with these contractions and lots more like them. The mistake that is sometimes made, though, is to put the apostrophe where the two words join rather than where the letter(s) have been missed out.

For example:
- did'nt (✗) didn't (✓)
- had'nt (✗) hadn't (✓)

He didn't like flying

He hadn't got used to the noise

Commonly Confused Words

Sometimes contracted forms are confused with words that sound the same or are similar to other words. Words that sound the same but have different meanings are called homophones.

Here are some of the most commonly confused homophones:

Contracted form	Meaning	Homophone
It's	It is It has	Its (e.g. The dog lost *its* bone)
Who's	Who is	Whose (e.g. *Whose* bag is this?)
They're	They are	Their (e.g. *their* ball) or there (e.g. over *there*)
You're	You are	Your (e.g. *your* book)

Can you think of any other homophones that are created by contractions?

You might have thought about the following that are often confused too:

- we're = 'we are', sometimes confused with...
  - were (e.g. We *were* going to the cinema)
  - wear (e.g. What are you going to *wear*?)
  - where (e.g. *Where* are you going?)
- here's = 'here is', sometimes confused with...
  - hears (e.g. He *hears* a sound.)

their ball

Punctuation 3

Possessive Apostrophes

Possessive apostrophes are probably more misused than any other punctuation mark:

1. Sometimes apostrophes are used when they should not be.
2. Sometimes an apostrophe is needed but is put in the wrong place.

Is An Apostrophe Needed?

The possessive apostrophe is used to show **ownership** or possession of something. For example:

The boy's book = The book belonging to the boy.

Apostrophes are never used on words that are simply plurals and are not indicating ownership. For example:
- The boy's went to town. (✗)
- The boys' went to town. (✗)
- The boys went to town. (✓)

If in doubt about whether or not an apostrophe is needed, ask yourself 'what belongs to the boy?' (as in this example). If you can't identify anything described as belonging to the boy then an apostrophe isn't needed.

Have a look at these sentences and see if you can identify those that need an apostrophe and those that don't.
- The mans hat was blown off.
- The girls pen fell on the floor.
- The trees bent with the force of the wind.
- The trees branch snapped off.

Here are the ones that needed an apostrophe:
- The man's hat was blown off.
- The girl's pen fell on the floor.
- The tree's branch snapped off.

Where Does the Apostrophe Go?

Once you've decided that an apostrophe is needed, the next question is 'where does it go?' There are two ways that you can work this out and if you use these checks, you should always get your apostrophes in the right place.

cat's tail   cats' tails

Method 1	Method 2
If the 'owner' is **singular** the apostrophe goes before the s ('s), e.g. 'The boy's house was in darkness'. (*one* boy)	Always put the apostrophe straight after the name of the 'owner'.
If the 'owner' is **plural** and the plural ends in s the apostrophe goes after the s (s'), e.g. 'The trees' roots were very deep'. (*more than one* tree)	For example: • The woman's bag (owner – the woman) • The women's party (owners – the women) • The cat's dish (owner – the cat – one cat) • The cats' bed (owner – the cats – more than one cat)
In cases like these where the plural ends in s the apostrophe actually tells you whether one boy or tree is meant or more than one.	Sometimes the ownership isn't clearly stated because the phrase is shortened, e.g. we often drop the word 'shop', 'house' and 'surgery' from phrases and use a shortened version such as butcher's meaning 'butcher's shop' or dentist's meaning 'dentist's surgery'. Watch out for these because these need apostrophes too, e.g. I'm going to the doctor's (doctor's surgery), I'll call at the baker's (baker's shop), I'm going round to Jim's (Jim's house).
If the plural doesn't end in s then the apostrophe goes before the s ('s), e.g. 'The men's minibus broke down'.	
Here 'men' is the plural and doesn't end in s. In cases like this the actual word tells you that there is more than one man and so the apostrophe doesn't need to go after the s to show this.	

Quick Test

Complete the sentences below.
1. Apostrophes that indicate ownership are called _____ apostrophes.
2. Shortened forms of words are called

   _____
3. Words that sound the same but have different meanings are called

   _____ .

Punctuation 3

Key Words Exercise

Unscramble these anagrams to discover the key words and then find the key words in the word search.

C	R	C	O	N	T	R	A	C	T	I	O	N	S	S	T
R	I	U	F	S	P	O	S	S	E	S	S	I	V	E	Q
K	D	E	L	H	B	O	B	I	T	F	B	Y	P	M	S
P	H	Y	G	H	O	O	W	L	D	D	B	P	V	P	J
O	A	E	H	S	R	M	Q	E	S	T	K	L	R	B	B
S	P	D	Y	Z	H	T	O	N	Y	K	J	U	I	B	U
S	A	P	O	S	T	R	O	P	H	E	S	R	O	Y	Z
E	A	B	J	G	M	M	G	B	H	R	M	A	W	T	J
S	I	K	T	J	N	E	S	L	C	O	N	L	N	N	H
S	E	D	T	B	O	A	I	B	O	U	N	Y	E	G	W
	M	Y	L	C	D	N	N	U	N	V	H	E	R	T	L
O	W	X	P	E	Y	I	G	R	F	O	T	H	S	Z	R
N	B	M	M	H	Q	N	U	S	R	J	R	T	H	M	M
E	G	N	X	J	B	G	L	T	S	K	S	R	I	N	Q
L	A	C	X	J	B	S	A	R	T	D	U	S	P	V	H
R	Q	M	H	O	M	O	R	C	O	N	F	U	S	E	D

1. lapurl - Plural
2. whisperno - ownership
3. spiesnosos - Possesion
4. raccoontints - contraction
5. snailrug - Singular
6. henhopmoos - homophones
7. focusend - confused
8. evesissops - possessive
9. nameings - meanings
10. shapetroops - apostrophes

1 Complete the following sentences correctly using it's or its.

a) I know ___It's___ raining and the forecast says ___its___ going to get worse.

b) The car has just had ___its___ annual service so, with a bit of luck, ___it's___ going to get us to Cornwall without a problem.

c) The way that dog is baring ___it's___ teeth and snarling, I think ___its___ going to turn nasty.

d) ___Its___ always been an ambition of mine to become a film star but I don't think ___it's___ going to happen.

e) The eagle swooped down onto ___its___ prey, grabbed it in ___it's___ talons and flew back to ___it's___ nest.

2 Complete these sentences using who's or whose; they're, their or there; your or you're.

a) ___They're___ coming to stay this weekend and ___They're___ bringing ___their___ nephew with them.

b) I went ___there___ last year and saw ___their___ carnival procession but I've heard ___they're___ not having one this year.

c) ___Who's___ coming with me to see ___their___ performance and ___whose___ car are we going in?

d) If ___you're___ short of money again ___you're___ going to have to use ___your___ savings.

e) If you've lost ___your___ book ___you're___ not going to borrow mine.

3 Put the possessive apostrophes in these sentences.

a) The cars' headlights were not very bright and the roads' twists and turns made driving difficult.

b) The boys' changing room was very noisy and the teacher's voice could hardly be heard.

c) The young childs' painting won the competition and was displayed in the towns' art gallery.

d) The suns' rays shone through the window and the old ladys' eyes were dazzled for a moment.

e) I'm going to the doctors' tomorrow so I'll get a prescription then.

Punctuation 3

Create a series of information sheets for Year 8 or Year 9 students explaining clearly how to use apostrophes correctly.

One information sheet should cover using contraction apostrophes.

One information sheet should cover commonly confused words.

One information sheet should cover using possessive apostrophes.

Try to make your information sheets informative, entertaining and eye-catching so think carefully about how you're going to design them. It would be useful, for example, to use illustrations to help present the information.

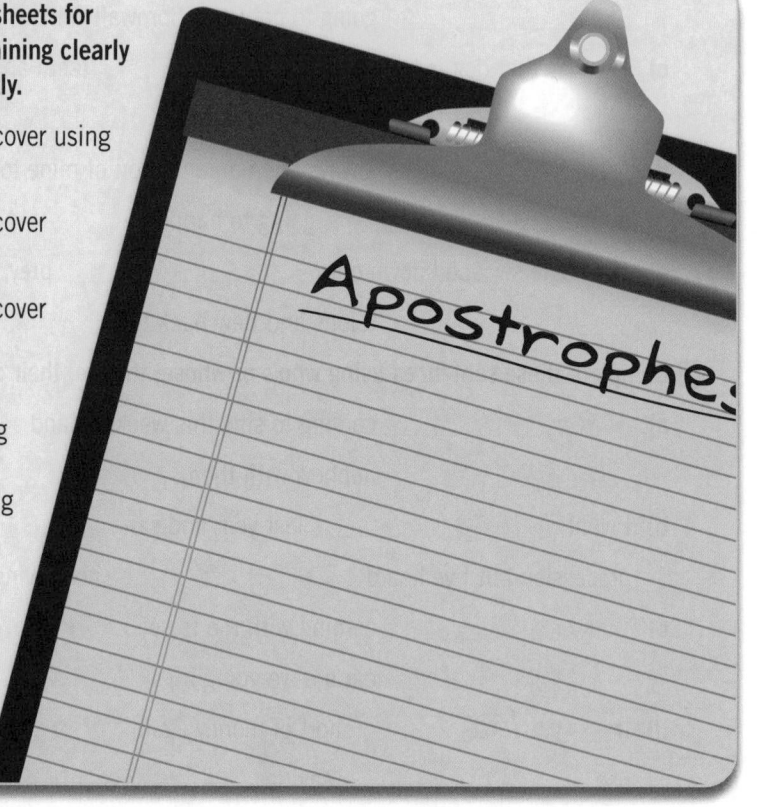

Extension Activity

When you've finished your information sheets, create a worksheet to go with each information sheet in which you set questions or puzzles based on the use of apostrophes. Again, think about the design to try to make your worksheets as interesting as possible.

Work with a partner and exchange both information sheets and worksheets.

Read each other's worksheets carefully and make notes on...
- how easy to understand you found them
- how effective the presentation was
- any suggestions for improvement.

Try doing the work that your partner set on the worksheets and note how well you felt this work helped to reinforce how to use apostrophes.

Discuss your thoughts and ideas on each other's work.

Writing Skills

The Writer's Craft 1

This topic looks at...
- descriptive techniques
- how to use words more effectively
- how to use descriptive techniques to make writing more interesting
- how to develop original similes and metaphors.

The Way You Write

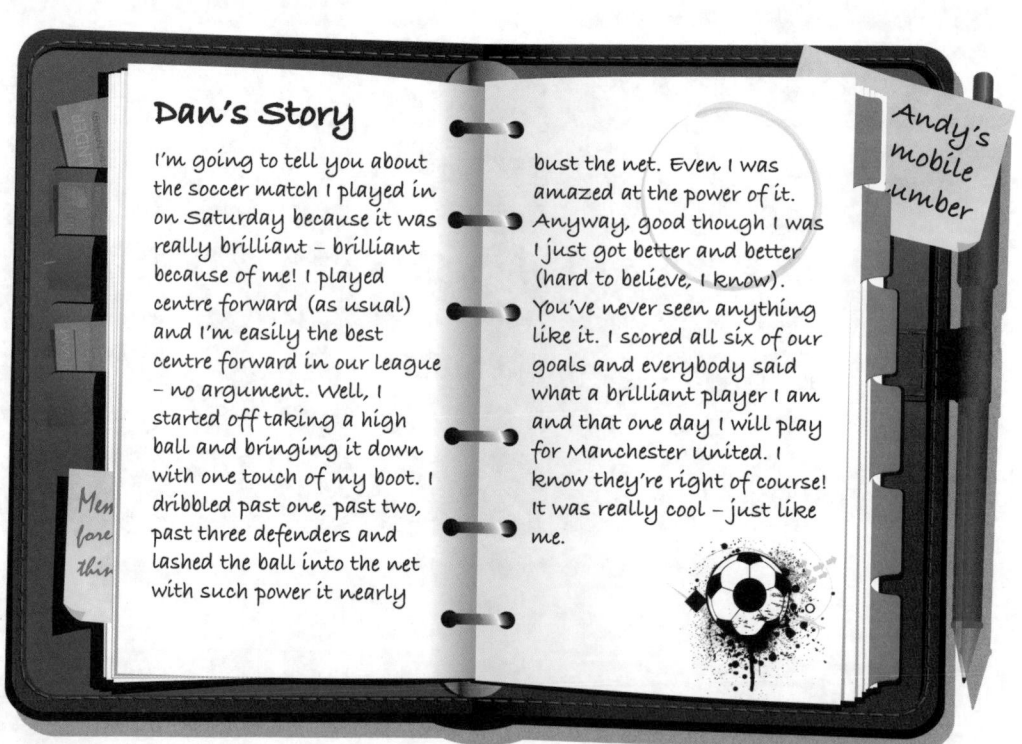

Dan's Story

I'm going to tell you about the soccer match I played in on Saturday because it was really brilliant – brilliant because of me! I played centre forward (as usual) and I'm easily the best centre forward in our league – no argument. Well, I started off taking a high ball and bringing it down with one touch of my boot. I dribbled past one, past two, past three defenders and lashed the ball into the net with such power it nearly bust the net. Even I was amazed at the power of it. Anyway, good though I was I just got better and better (hard to believe, I know). You've never seen anything like it. I scored all six of our goals and everybody said what a brilliant player I am and that one day I will play for Manchester United. I know they're right of course! It was really cool – just like me.

It's not just what you write, but how you write it that's important. Here is an example of a piece of writing. It might not have the effect that the writer intended it to have!

Dan clearly enjoyed writing his story and wanted to put across how good he is at football but instead he sounds big-headed and silly.

Where do you think Dan went wrong?

A good writer uses descriptive techniques. Using original versions of the following techniques will improve your writing further.

Adjective – a word that describes and adds extra information to a noun. For example, 'Henry always wore *dark* clothes.'

Simile – a comparison that generally uses 'as' or 'like'. For example, 'Henry's dark clothes made him look as *gloomy as a broken lightbulb*.'

Metaphor – a comparison where one thing is given the qualities of something else. For example, 'Henry *was a pit of gloom after realising he had failed his tests*.'

Similes

The following similes are common:
- Deaf as a post.
- Solid as a rock.
- As different as chalk and cheese.
- As quiet as a mouse.
- As wise as an owl.

Common similes aren't as effective because they're overused and don't put a precise picture in the reader's mind.

You don't have to think of a totally original simile to develop your writing, although it helps if you can. You might begin with common similes to help you develop into writing original ones.

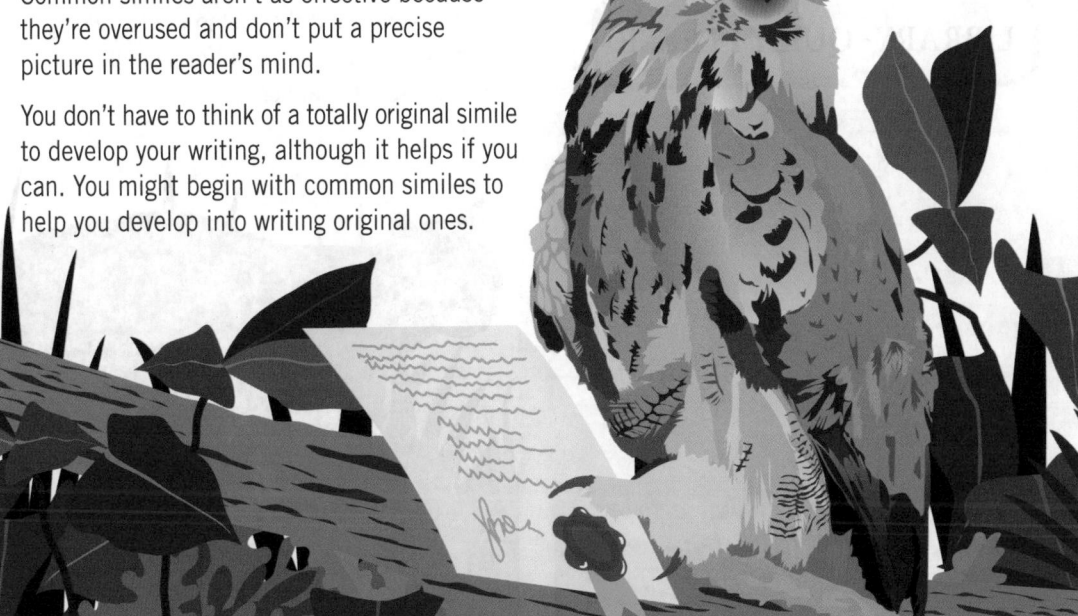

The Writer's Craft 1

Developing Common Similes

Here are some more common similes:
- As pale as a ghost.
- As blind as a bat.

To improve these similes, you can add an adjective or adjectives before the final noun. For example…
- as pale as a painted ghost
- as blind as a hooded bat.

To improve them further you might add an extra clause – extra information in the form of a phrase – after the main simile:
- As pale as a painted ghost, who's been faded by sunlight.
- As blind as a hooded bat, that's been locked in a darkened cell.

Try to develop the following similes by adding extra adjectives and clauses.
- *As quiet as a mouse.*
- *As wise as an owl.*

Making Metaphors

Metaphors are a more powerful way of describing events in a story's opening or ending, or at important moments in the story.

Look at the difference between these two sentences:

Simile	Donna was as scared as a timid, trembling mouse, hiding from a fearsome cat.
Metaphor	Donna was a scared, timid, trembling mouse, hiding from a fearsome cat.

The metaphor is stronger because it's not saying Donna is 'like' the mouse – it's saying she 'is' the mouse, so it has a more powerful effect on the reader.

Notice how the same ideas have been used in the simile and the metaphor. By taking the words 'as' or 'like' out of a simile, you can make a metaphor.

Sound Effects

Alliteration is the repetition of the same letters or sounds at the start of words that are close together. For example, 'The <u>cr</u>acked, <u>cr</u>azy footpath <u>cr</u>umbled beneath his feet.'

Alliteration should be used sparingly – only when you want the sounds of the letters to create a feeling, or perhaps to copy the sound of something.

Onomatopoeia is when words sound like the things they're describing, for example, 'moo', 'crack' and 'plop'.

Onomatopoeia should be used sparingly, for sound effects. If you overdo it, your writing could end up sounding cartoon-like and immature.

Assonance – the repetition of similar or identical vowel sounds, for example, 'R<u>ough</u>, t<u>ough</u> <u>u</u>ncl<u>u</u>ttered st<u>u</u>ff.'

This is similar to alliteration in the way that you should use it – for example, to emphasise a feeling or a sound effect.

Personification and Pathetic Fallacy

Personification is when you apply human qualities to something that isn't human, or is **abstract**. For example…
* the chair rocked back on its heels (The chair is described as though it's acting like a human)
* fear wrote its name in their hearts (Fear is being described as though it's a person).

Pathetic fallacy is a form of personification, but one where you give human qualities to something in nature. For example, 'The sky cried.'

Personification and pathetic fallacy are good techniques that make your descriptions more powerful. They can have the same strong impact as metaphors.

Quick Test

1. Complete these common similes:
   As cold as i…; As flat as a p…; As hard as n…
2. What do you call a comparison that uses 'as' or 'like'?
3. What do you call a comparison where one thing is said to be another?
4. What do you call words that are positioned close together and begin with the same letter or sound?
5. What is onomatopoeia?
6. Convert this simile into a metaphor:
   Tara was as nervous as a trembling child at the dentist's.

KEY WORDS
Make sure you understand these words before moving on!
* Adjective
* Simile
* Metaphor
* Clause
* Alliteration
* Onomatopoeia
* Assonance
* Personification
* Abstract
* Pathetic fallacy

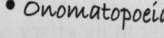

The Writer's Craft 1

Match each keyword with its definition.

Keyword	Definition
Adjective	A comparison where one thing is said to be another.
Simile	A group of words close together that begin with the same letter or sound.
Metaphor	Repeated use of similar or identical vowel sounds, in words that are close together.
Clause	A phrase that forms part or all of a sentence.
Alliteration	A kind of metaphor where abstract or non-human things are given human qualities.
Onomatopoeia	A word that describes a noun.
Assonance	Not real – an idea or concept.
Personification	A comparison using 'as' or 'like'.
Pathetic fallacy	A word that sounds like the thing it's describing.
Abstract	A kind of metaphor where things from nature are given human qualities.

Comprehension

Choose the correct options in the following sentences.

1. If you use *an adjective / onomatopoeia / assonance* to describe a noun, it will add extra detail to it and tell the reader more about it.

2. If you add a *simile / metaphor / adjective* to a description by comparing, using 'as' or 'like', you will put a picture in the reader's mind, which will help them to understand what you're describing.

3. A *simile / metaphor / adjective* is also a comparison, but stronger in its effect because it's saying that one thing is another.

as...

like...

Testing Understanding

Read the diary extract below and find all the examples of the following techniques.

1. Alliteration
2. Adjectives
3. Similes
4. Metaphors
5. Personification
6. Pathetic fallacy
7. Assonance

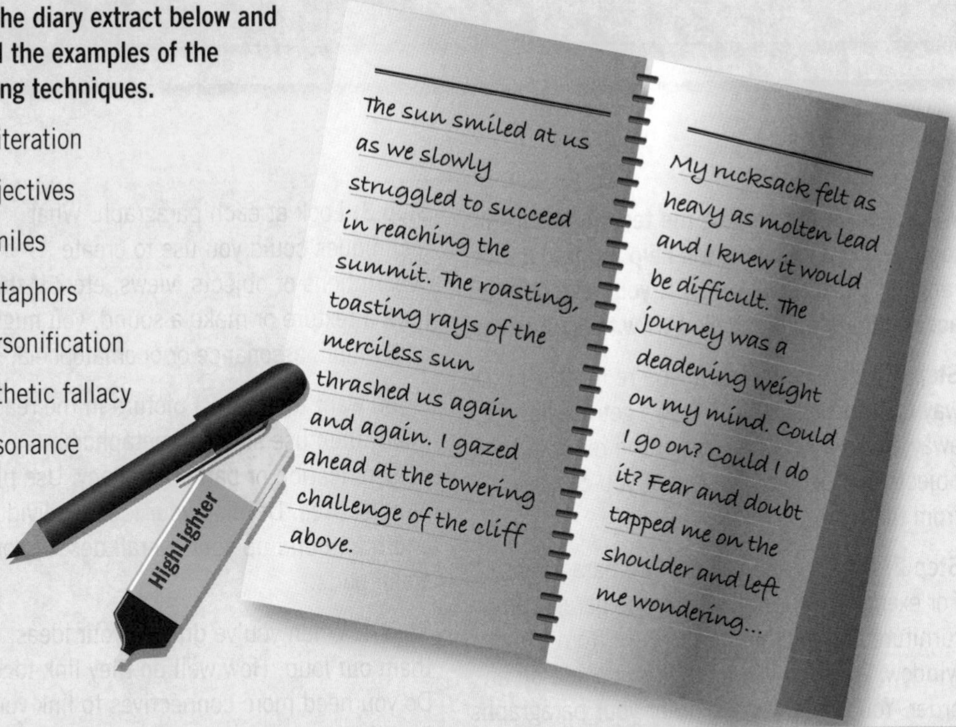

The sun smiled at us as we slowly struggled to succeed in reaching the summit. The roasting, toasting rays of the merciless sun thrashed us again and again. I gazed ahead at the towering challenge of the cliff above.

My rucksack felt as heavy as molten lead and I knew it would be difficult. The journey was a deadening weight on my mind. Could I go on? Could I do it? Fear and doubt tapped me on the shoulder and left me wondering...

Techniques

Name the techniques used in the following sentences.

1. The moon smiled down at us as we walked in its light.

2. His mood was as heavy as a lorry-load of bricks.

3. The mad, bad dad ran through the sand.

4. The rugged, rough, ramshackle cottage was finally theirs.

5. The desk did a back-flip and landed on Lisa's foot.

6. Boom! Crack! The ship exploded, disintegrated and sank.

7. The smooth, silky structure was as unreal as a dream.

8. Glug... Kelli deftly drank the delightful drink.

The Writer's Craft 1

Skills Practice

Write a description using the techniques in this topic. Using a thesaurus will help you find a wider range of descriptive words. If you have internet access, there's a site called www.thesaurus.com

Step 1: Describe the room you're in. It's a good way to start because you won't get carried away. Make a list of what's in the room, all the objects and people. Note what you can see from the room.

Step 2: Organise your ideas into paragraphs. For example, you might have one paragraph on furniture and another on the view from the window. When you've done this, decide on an order. You might want to order your paragraphs by their importance to you, or by the order you see them when entering the room.

Step 3: Look at each paragraph. What techniques could you use to create descriptions of objects, views, etc.? If they have a texture or make a sound, you might use alliteration, assonance or onomatopoeia.

If you want to create a picture in the reader's mind, then use similes, metaphors, personification or pathetic fallacy. Use plenty of adjectives. Develop your ideas individually and then build up your overall description from small parts.

Step 4: When you've drafted your ideas, read them out loud. How well do they link together? Do you need more connectives to link your ideas? Have you used similar techniques too often, or too close together? If you have, redraft until you get the result you want.

Extension Activity

Choose either Dan or Peigi's story at the start of this topic on page 24. Keep to the same facts, but rewrite the story using a range of descriptive techniques to make it more interesting for the person who reads it.

The Writer's Craft 2

What is Covered in this Topic?

This topic looks at...
- ways to make your writing more descriptive using verbs and adverbs
- how to vary sentences
- how to target parts of your writing to achieve the best effect.

Verbs and Adverbs

A **verb** is a word that **indicates** an action, such as 'run', 'wait ' or 'snore'. Verbs are often referred to as 'doing' words.

The sign of a good writer is more to do with their choice of verbs than adjectives. The following passage uses unadventurous verbs that don't tell the reader much about the character or events:

> Effin <u>ran</u> to the shops but <u>walked</u> the last few yards. He <u>walked</u> into the shop and <u>got</u> some food. He <u>put</u> it in his bag and <u>went</u> home.

By choosing more unusual verbs, you grab the reader's attention. The choice of verbs starts to create a more exciting story:

> Effin <u>raced</u> to the shops but <u>strolled</u> the last few yards. He <u>ambled</u> into the shop and <u>stole</u> some food. He <u>stuffed</u> it in his bag and <u>sprinted</u> home.

💡 *Can you think of verbs to improve the following passage? Is your version more interesting than the original?*

Andy got out of bed and walked into the kitchen. He got a cup out of the cupboard and made a cup of tea. He touched his head because it hurt.

Adding Adverbs

Adverbs are words that describe how you do something i.e. they describe verbs. They often end in 'ly', but not always – examples include 'quickly', 'lazily' and 'fast'. In a passage that contains a lot of action, using adverbs is a good technique because they describe what's happening in greater detail.

Compare this passage to the versions above.

> Effin raced <u>quickly</u> to the shops but strolled <u>lazily</u> over the last few yards. He ambled <u>nervously</u> into the shop and <u>secretly</u> stole some food. He <u>quickly</u> stuffed it in his bag and sprinted home <u>speedily</u>.

The Writer's Craft 2

Finding Verbs and Adverbs

Look at this passage from *Buddy* by Nigel Hinton. At this point, Buddy and his friends have just peeped through the door of a derelict house and have seen something spooky and unexplained.

💡 *What verbs can you find? Think about what they have in common and what feelings they create?*

💡 *Why do you think Nigel Hinton only uses two adverbs in this passage?*

Charmian screamed and together they flew down the steps in terror. Dashing across the gravel Charmian tripped over the edge of the lawn. She crashed against Buddy and they both fell onto the wet grass. They stumbled up and ran blindly towards the gate. Buddy banged his elbow as he squeezed through, and a half-sob, half-laugh, shook him. His legs felt weak with the pain and the panic but he forced himself to run. Charmian could hardly keep up with him but he grabbed her hand and pulled her after him.

Positioning Adverbs

The adverb doesn't always have to come before the verb that it's describing.

The **positioning** of the adverb can come in the following places:
1. At the start of the sentence – 'Quickly, Bob caught the train after work to get to the theatre'.
2. After the verb – 'Bob caught the train quickly after work to get to the theatre'.
3. Before the verb – 'Bob quickly caught the train after work to get to the theatre'.

You can create different effects and emphasis by placing the adverb in different places. The first version above seems hurried. The second one makes the act of catching the train more important, whereas the last one makes Bob seem more important!

💡 *The following sentences have the verbs underlined:*
1. *Holway <u>ran</u> to the camera shop.*
2. *Kristina <u>dug</u> the plants in her back garden.*
3. *Ed <u>used</u> the video camera to <u>film</u> the band.*
4. *Preston <u>watched</u> his dad <u>performing</u> at the show.*
5. *Andrea <u>yawned</u> when she <u>walked</u> into the room.*

Add your own adverb, either before or after each verb, to make the sentences more interesting.

Word Order

Changing the word order can affect the tone and effect of a sentence. This works best with **complex** sentences and some **compound** ones.

For example...

- 'Will didn't want to go back home, because it was raining and it was too far to travel' – the main clause is first, suggesting it's the most important thing in the sentence.
- 'Because it was raining and too far to travel, Will didn't want to go back home' – the main clause is at the end, suggesting that the reasons in the sentence are more important.
- 'Will, because it was raining and too far to travel, didn't want to go back home' – the main clause is split in two, suggesting that all parts of the sentence are of roughly equal importance.

Try reordering the following sentences with either the main clause at the end or a split main clause.

1. *Lisa didn't want to leave the house, because it was cold and she was ill.*
2. *Michelle bought the presents early, as it was Christmas and she was well organised.*
3. *Emma didn't like her photograph, because of the bad lighting and the spot on her nose.*
4. *Rachel ran the marathon, despite getting blisters and a leg injury the previous time.*
5. *Silvana ate the pizza, although it was dry and she didn't like the taste.*

Writing for Effect

A good writer chooses when and where to use a particular technique to create the best effect. All writers focus on...

- openings
- endings
- key moments.

The writers of the three extracts in the following section have chosen techniques carefully to achieve the effects that they wanted to place in the readers' minds. As a good writer, you will need to do the same.

Creating Imagery

John Steinbeck uses lots of adjectives to create a vivid, almost photographic, picture to get the reader's attention in the opening of *Of Mice and Men*.

> A few miles south of Soledad, the Salinas River drops in close to the hillside bank and runs deep and green. The water is warm too, for it has slipped twinkling over the yellow sands in the sunlight before reaching the narrow pool. On one side of the river the golden foothill slopes curve up to the strong and rocky Gabilan mountains, but on the valley side the water is lined with trees – willows fresh and green with every spring, carrying in their lower leaf junctures the debris of the winter's flooding; and sycamores with mottled, white, recumbent limbs and branches that arch over the pool.

How many adjectives are used in this opening passage? What do you notice about the kinds of adjectives he uses?

The Writer's Craft 2

Creating Imagery (cont.)

The following passage uses a simile and a **cliffhanger** (a suspenseful ending) to create an interesting end to the story.

💡 *Can you find the simile and the cliffhanger?*

'Fred,' she shouted, 'that's quite enough – I want to get out of here.' Fred turned round, his dark hair shining in the sunlight like glossy silk. She looked at him and smiled, picked up her bags, walked over to the doorway, went down the path and away...

Finally, look at this key moment from *The Lottery* by Shirley Jackson. The writer uses **repetition**, an adverb, questions and **ellipsis** (…) in this extract. All have been combined to build up the tension.

After that, there was a long pause, a breathless pause, until Mr. Summers, holding his slip of paper in the air, said, 'All right, fellows.' For a minute, no one moved, and then all the slips of paper were opened. Suddenly, all the women began to speak at once, saying, 'Who is it?', 'Who's got it?', 'Is it the Dunbars?', 'Is it the Watsons?' Then the voices began to say, 'It's Hutchinson. It's Bill… Bill Hutchinson's got it.'

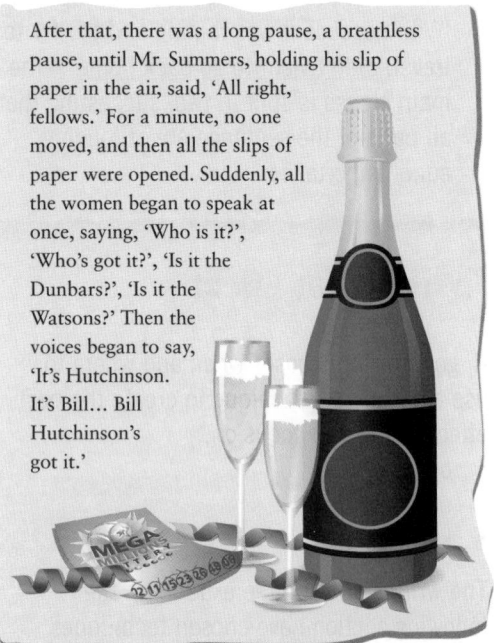

Quick Test

1. What do most adverbs end in?
2. Do adverbs go after the verb or before?
3. What is the effect of using a lot of similar verbs, close together in a text?
4. Why is word order in sentences important?
5. What effect might you achieve by leaving the main subject of a sentence until last?

KEY WORDS
Make sure you understand these words before moving on!
- Verb
- Indicates
- Adverb
- Positioning
- Complex
- Compound
- Cliffhanger
- Repetition
- Ellipsis

Key Words Exercise

Work out the key words from the clues below, then copy and complete the word search.

E	P	H	S	O	H	E	G	U	H	C	L	X	T
N	E	V	L	A	T	M	O	A	Y	L	S	O	P
C	L	T	E	M	I	C	M	D	L	I	P	N	T
R	I	S	C	R	H	E	K	V	D	F	C	V	A
E	P	A	B	D	B	F	S	E	T	F	S	E	S
G	T	B	S	G	A	N	N	R	E	H	S	R	E
N	I	H	Q	I	L	R	G	B	F	A	T	C	P
A	N	I	S	E	T	A	C	I	D	N	I	T	I
H	D	Y	J	P	I	N	H	J	U	G	C	A	L
F	O	A	C	O	M	P	L	E	X	E	N	Z	O
F	N	S	I	S	P	I	L	L	E	R	I	B	N
I	A	D	N	U	O	P	M	O	C	V	N	I	Y
L	P	O	S	I	T	I	O	N	I	N	G	L	Z
C	E	R	E	P	E	T	I	T	I	O	N	K	O

...shows

placing...

doing...

1. A word meaning 'shows'.

2. A series of three dots used to build up suspense or tension.

3. A 'doing' word.

4. A word meaning 'placing'.

5. A type of sentence that has more than one clause, where one clause depends on the other for it to make sense.

6. A word that describes how you do something.

7. A type of sentence that's usually made from a couple of simpler sentences, joined by simpler connectives like 'and' or 'but'.

8. A technique where a word or phrase appears more than once.

9. Ending a story with suspense.

The Writer's Craft 2

1 **Identify the verbs and adverbs in the following passage.**

Ruth ran quickly towards Neil, who dashed nervously out of the way. Cautiously she glanced around, but couldn't see where he'd gone. Breathing deeply, Neil hoped that she wouldn't find him. She'd picked on him in the past, cruelly – and he didn't want her to hurt him again.

2 **Use either verbs or adverbs to make the following passage sound like a quick, exciting event.**

    a) Don _____ to the train station _____ . Nicolas, his grandson, was

        _____ there, _____ with the car engine revving away. _____ ,

        there were no traffic wardens _____ there, so he didn't get _____ for

        parking in a restricted area.

    b) **Now use different verbs and adverbs to make the passage sound slow and lazy.**

        Don _____ to the train station _____ . Nicolas, his grandson, was

        _____ there, _____ with the car engine revving away. _____ ,

        there were no traffic wardens _____ there, so he didn't get _____ for

        parking in a restricted area.

3 **Say whether the following sentences have the main clause...**
* **at the start**
* **at the end**
* **split between the start and the end.**

    a) Grant played his guitar badly, because he had a headache.

    b) Grant, because he had a headache, played his guitar badly.

    c) Mike painted the picture because he was inspired by the weather.

    d) Because he was inspired by the weather, Mike painted the picture.

    e) Gerald scratched his chin, because it itched.

    f) Gerald, because it itched, scratched his chin.

Write a key passage of the middle of a story, using the techniques you have learned in this topic.

The hero of your story discovers something that scares them and they must quickly escape. Build up the tension first and then, after the discovery, create a fast-moving description to describe the feeling of escape.

Step 1: This passage should be made up of three parts, or paragraphs:
a) The build-up of tension.
b) The discovery.
c) The escape.

Jot down your ideas for each section. Where will the passage be set? What will be the discovery? What will your hero have to escape from? Where will he or she escape to?

Step 2: Draft your ideas. Try to use the following techniques:
a) Use sentences with the main clause at the end to build up tension. Use short sentences and questions.
b) Make the discovery short and perhaps use ellipsis.
c) Use lots of fast, active verbs and adverbs to create the feeling of someone rushing to escape.

Step 3: Read your draft out loud. Can you see differences in style, tone and mood between the different parts? If you can't, try adding more of the techniques that you've developed, or change those you've included until you're happy with the overall effect.

Try writing the opening or the ending for the same story. How might you create the 'right' kind of mood using...
• varied sentences?
• verbs and adverbs?

Creative Writing

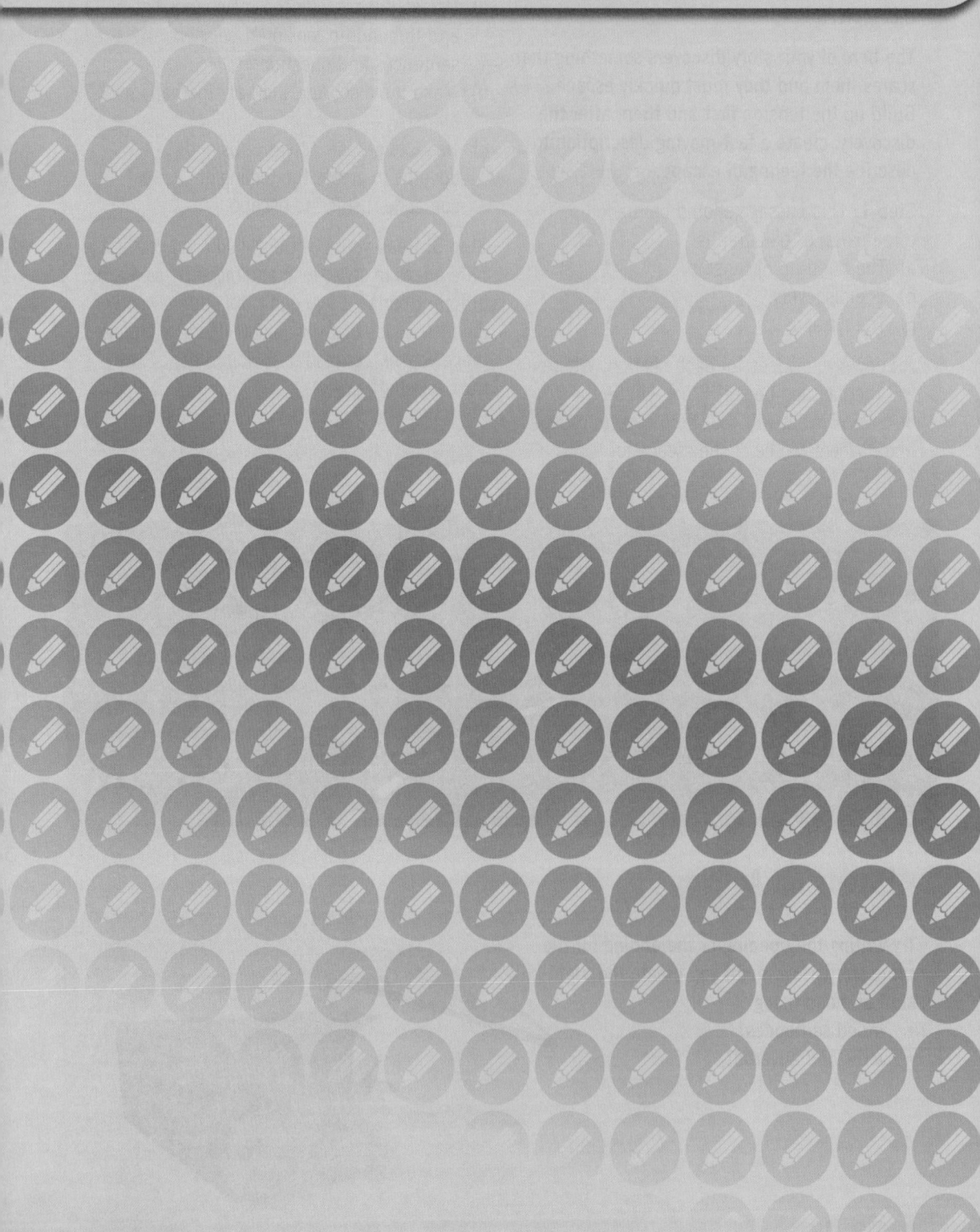

Writing Fairy Tales

What is Covered in this Topic?

This topic looks at...
- how to write to entertain
- how to use conventions of the fairy tale genre.

Features of Fairy Tales

Most of us experience fairy tales at some time, either by having them read to us, reading them ourselves, or watching film adaptations.

Fairy tales have evolved over time so we don't know who wrote many of them – even the Brothers Grimm and Hans Christian Andersen developed their versions from earlier tales that had been passed down.

Nowadays, new versions of fairy tales are created, which use the conventions of these earlier stories – films such as *Shrek* or *Enchanted* are two good examples of this.

As there are various versions of some fairy tales, the details of the story may vary. There's no 'right' version – just a different way of telling the story.

Fairy tales share many common features, such as...
- characters
- ideas
- plot-lines.

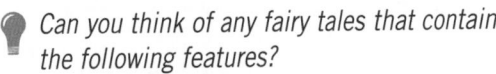 *Can you think of any fairy tales that contain the following features?*
- *Fairy godmothers.*
- *Wicked stepmothers.*
- *Handsome Princes.*
- *Animals coming to life.*
- *Woods and forests.*
- *A princess – or a beautiful but hard-done-to young woman.*
- *Giants and monsters.*
- *Spells and curses.*
- *Happy endings.*

Writing Fairy Tales

Different Versions

There are many different versions of fairy tales. For example, the story of Cinderella has different versions that come from different **cultures** and **traditions**.

The following extract is from a Scottish version called *Rashin-Coatie*.

💡 *What typical fairy tale features can you see in this passage?*
- *What types of characters are there?*
- *How is the story typical?*
- *How is the language typical?*

Rashin Coatie

Once, a long time ago, there was a gentleman had two lassies. The oldest was ugly and ill natured, but the youngest was a bonnie lassie and good; but the ugly one was the favourite with her father and mother. So they ill-used the youngest in every way, and they sent her into the woods to herd cattle, and all the food she got was a little porridge and whey.

Well, amongst the cattle was a red calf, and one day it said to the lassie, 'Gee that porridge and whey to the doggie, and come wi' me.'

So the lassie followed the calf through the wood, and they came to a bonnie hoosie, where there was a nice dinner ready for them; and after they had feasted on everything nice they went back to the herding.

Every day the calf took the lassie away, and feasted her on dainties; and every day she grew bonnier. This disappointed the father and mother and the ugly sister. They expected that the rough usage she was getting would take away her beauty; and they watched and watched until they saw the calf take the lassie away to the feast. So they resolved to kill the calf; and not only that, but the lassie was to be compelled to kill him with an axe. Her ugly sister was to hold his head, and the lassie who loved him had to give the blow and kill him.

She could do nothing but greet [weep]; but the calf told her not to greet, but to do as he bade her; and his plan was that instead of coming down on his head she was to come down on the lassie's head who was holding him, and then she was to jump on his back and they would run off. Well, the day came for the calf to be killed, and everything was ready – the ugly lassie holding his head, and the bonnie lassie armed with the axe. So she raised the axe, and came down on the ugly sister's head; and in the confusion that took place she got on the calf's back and they ran away. And they ran and better nor ran till they came to a meadow where grew a great lot of rashes; and, as the lassie had not on many clothes, they pu'ed rashes, and made a coatie for her. And they set off again and travelled, and travelled, till they came to the king's house. They went in, and asked if they wanted a servant. The mistress said she wanted a kitchen lassie, and she would take Rashin-Coatie...

Alternative Fairy Tales

Some fairy tales make fun of the **genre**, as seen in the following version of *Little Red Riding Hood* by James Finn Garner.

There once was a young person named Red Riding Hood who lived with her mother on the edge of a large wood. One day her mother asked her to take a basket of fresh fruit and mineral water to her grandmother's house – not because this was womyn's work, mind you, but because the deed was generous and helped engender a feeling of community. Furthermore, her grandmother was not sick, but rather was in full physical and mental health and was fully capable of taking care of herself as a mature adult...

...On the way to Grandma's house, Red Riding Hood was accosted by a wolf, who asked her what was in her basket. She replied, 'Some healthful snacks for my grandmother, who is certainly capable of taking care of herself as a mature adult.'

The wolf said, 'You know, my dear, it isn't safe for a little girl to walk through these woods alone.'

Red Riding Hood said, 'I find your sexist remark offensive in the extreme, but I will ignore it because of your traditional **status** as an outcast from society, the stress of which has caused you to develop your own, entirely valid, worldview. Now, if you'll excuse me, I must be on my way.'

Red Riding Hood walked on along the main path. But, because his status outside society had freed him from **slavish adherence** to **linear**, Western-style thought, the wolf knew a quicker route to Grandma's house. He burst into the house and ate Grandma, an entirely valid course of action for a **carnivore** such as himself. Then, unhampered by rigid, **traditionalist** notions of what was masculine or feminine, he put on Grandma's nightclothes and crawled into bed.

Although the writer is having fun with the features of the genre, he is still using those same features. The story has been changed to make it less offensive and politically-correct, and this has made it funnier.

💡 *How has the story been changed to make it less offensive?*

💡 *What fairy tale features can you see in this version?*

Writing Fairy Tales

Creating Your Own Fairy Tale

Fairy tales can be changed in many ways to entertain the reader.

A fairy tale could be created by picking one feature from each category below to create the outline for an original story. You might come up with a strange story to fit these features together, but it would be recognisable as a fairy story because it would contain traditional features.

Good Male Character
Prince Charming, Jack, Buttons, Aladdin, Any random handsome prince!, Dick Whittington

Good Female Character
Snow White, Cinderella, Rapunzel, Sleeping Beauty, Red Riding Hood, Princess Jasmine

Evil Character
Wicked witch, Wicked stepmother, Ugly sisters, Magic talking mirror, Old woman, Sheriff of Nottingham

Random other Character
Woodcutter, Cute animal(s), Dwarf, Cat, Wizard, Dragon

Magic
3 wishes, Kiss, Poisoned apple, Magic Word, Lamp, Magic Beans

Setting
Cottage, Wood / Forest, Castle, Garden, Dungeon, Cave

Common Features

Fairy tales can also use several other common styles and features:

- They often use **clichéd** phrases, beginning with 'Once upon a time' and ending with 'Happily ever after'.
- They're often written in the **third person**.
- They contain sentences that begin with, or use, **adverbs**, e.g. 'Suddenly, Cinderella noticed that it was nearly midnight…'
- There will be a problem at the start of the story – a **crisis** – which will be solved after many trials.
- Good people end up happy and bad people end up unhappy.
- Characters make good and bad choices, but they learn from them to become better people.

 How true are these features of the fairy tales that you know?

Quick Test

1. What are conventions?
2. There are different versions of most fairy tales – true or false?
3. What is a cliché?
4. What is meant by a 'crisis' in fairy tales?
5. What is an adaptation?

Key Words Exercise

Match each key word with its definition.

Key Word	Definition
Convention	Different patterns of behaviour or life, resulting in overall ways of doing things.
Evolved	Basic storyline.
Cultures	A problem.
Status	The passing down of some elements of a culture from generation to generation.
Carnivore	Believing something without questioning it.
Third person	A meat eater.
Genre	Typical ways of writing that have developed.
Plot-line	A format or style.
Tradition	A person who believes in the passed-down ways of doing things.
Slavish adherence	Different changed versions.
Traditionalist	Noticeable qualities.
Adverb	Grown.
Adaptation	The use of 'he' 'she' or 'it' in sentences.
Feature	Words that describe how things are done.
Linear	Rank.
Clichéd	Repeated so often that it's become boring.
Crisis	In a straight line.

Writing Fairy Tales

Testing Understanding

Read the following fairy tale, *The Real Princess*, by Hans Christian Andersen.

There was once a Prince who wished to marry a Princess; but then she must be a real Princess. He travelled all over the world in hopes of finding such a lady; but there was always something wrong. Princesses he found in plenty; but whether they were real Princesses it was impossible for him to decide, for now one thing, now another, seemed to him not quite right about the ladies. At last he returned to his palace quite cast down, because he wished so much to have a real Princess for his wife.

One evening a fearful tempest arose, it thundered and lightened, and the rain poured down from the sky in torrents: besides, it was as dark as pitch. All at once there was heard a violent knocking at the door, and the old King, the Prince's father, went out himself to open it.

It was a Princess who was standing outside the door. What with the rain and the wind, she was in a sad condition; the water trickled down from her hair, and her clothes clung to her body. She said she was a real Princess.

'Ah! We shall soon see that!' thought the old Queen-mother; however, she said not a word of what she was going to do; but went quietly into the bedroom, took all the bed-clothes off the bed, and put three little peas on the bedstead. She then laid twenty mattresses one upon another over the three peas, and put twenty feather beds over the mattresses. Upon this bed the Princess was to pass the night.

The next morning she was asked how she had slept. 'Oh, very badly indeed!' she replied. 'I have scarcely closed my eyes the whole night through. I do not know what was in my bed, but I had something hard under me, and am all over black and blue. It has hurt me so much!'

Now it was plain that the lady must be a real Princess, since she had been able to feel the three little peas through the twenty mattresses and twenty feather beds. None but a real Princess could have had such a delicate sense of feeling.

The Prince accordingly made her his wife; being now convinced that he had found a real Princess. The three peas were however put into the cabinet of curiosities, where they are still to be seen, provided they are not lost.

Wasn't this a lady of real delicacy?

Look at the table below.

a) **Identify all the features that appear in the story of *The Real Princess*.**

b) **Which features are not present?**

Beautiful girl / Princess	Handsome Prince	Helpful animals	Set in a wood / forest / castle	Helpful magic
Contains a crisis / problem	Characters make bad choices	Wicked stepmother / witch	Starts with 'Once upon a time'	Bad magic
Ends 'Happily ever after' or similar	Characters make good choices	Giants and / or monsters	Written in the third person	Uses adverbs

Write your own fairy tale for a younger child. It needs to be a traditional one, like those by Hans Christian Andersen. It should be recognisable as a fairy tale, containing the features seen in this topic.

Step 1: Using the lists of features, choose suitable characters and settings for your story. Try to give the characters romantic, old-fashioned names.

Step 2: The basic plot contains a problem that is created at the start – for example, a curse is put on someone. The remainder of the story is about how the victim comes to solve the problem and learns important lessons in the process. Decide what the problem is going to be at the start and which characters are going to be affected.

Step 3: The victim then has to undergo a series of tests, or go on a journey in order to solve their problem. Decide what those tests are, or what the journey will involve.

Step 4: Before the problem is resolved, the victim has to undergo one last test – they may fail, but then be saved, like Snow White, or they may pass it. Decide what that test is and what the result is. After that, it's quite easy to finish the story, because we know how it will end… happily ever after!

Step 5: Remember to write in the third person and use plenty of adverbs and adjectives to create an appropriate style. After writing it, try reading it to a younger relative to see what reaction you get – based on their reaction, you might wish to redraft and improve it.

Write a politically-correct fairy tale like James Finn Garner's, or update a traditional story with modern references. For example, you might have Cinderella marrying the lead singer of a boy band and her ugly sisters could be rejects from a reality TV show!

Imaginative Writing

This topic looks at...
- planning your story
- structuring your story
- first person and third person narratives
- ways to open and end your story.

Planning a Story

An interesting story that keeps the attention of the reader needs careful planning.

That's because many parts need to work together to create the overall effect of your story, which you need to think about before you start writing.

Plot, Structure

Story, Setting

Style, Language

Characters, Themes

Your story needs to have the following:
- **Plot** – what happens in your story (sometimes called the storyline).
- **Structure** – the order the events happen in your story and the way they link together; the way the story is built.
- **Characters** – the people (or animals, etc.) that you create and that your story centres around.
- **Setting** – the place, situation, circumstances, world, etc. that your story is set in.
- **Language** – the kinds of words (vocabulary) you use in your story.
- **Style** – the way in which you write your story.
- **Themes** – the ideas you put forward or draw attention to in your story (e.g. a story about someone being picked on at school might explore ideas about bullying).

Planning Your Approach

Here are two ways you can approach planning your story:

1. Think up your character or characters and create a story for them.
2. Think up your plot, then create your character(s) to fit in with the storyline.

Structuring a Story

In order to write an effective story, it's important to think about the structure and how the events that make up your plot will develop and link together.

When you plan your story you need to think about...

CHAPTER 1
Once upon a time...

- the **beginning** – this needs to capture the reader's attention and make them want to read on
- the **middle** – in which you develop your plot, characters and ideas
- the **climax** – usually the story builds up to some kind of climax, key moment or event that leads to the ending
- the **ending** – this brings the story to some kind of conclusion.

The Beginning

You can begin a story in different ways. Here's how four different writers begin their stories.

What do you notice about how they begin?

Captures the reader's attention with an unexpected idea.

> You can call me Link. It's not my name, but it's what I say when anybody asks, which isn't often. I'm invisible.
>
> *Stone Cold* by Robert Swindells

Begins with direct speech, which captures the reader's attention. The mention of a ghost arouses interest and makes the reader want to read on to find out what's happening.

> 'I can assure you,' said I, 'that it will take a very tangible ghost to frighten me.' And I stood up before the fire with my glass in my hand.
>
> 'It is your choosing,' said the man with the withered arm, and glanced at me askance.
>
> *The Red Room* by H.G. Wells

Describes and sets the scene.

> On the morning of the third day, the sea calmed. Even the most delicate passengers – those who had not been seen around the ship since sailing time - emerged from their cabins and crept on to the sun deck where the deck steward gave them chairs and tucked rugs around their legs and left them lying in rows, their faces upturned to the pale, almost heatless January sun.
>
> *Someone Like You* by Roald Dahl

Focuses on introducing and describing a character.

> When Farmer Oak smiled, the corners of his mouth spread till they were within an unimportant distance of his ears, his eyes reduced to mere chinks, and diverging wrinkles appeared round them, extending upon his countenance like the rays in a rudimentary sketch of the rising sun.
>
> *Far from the Madding Crowd* by Thomas Hardy

Imaginative Writing

Deciding How to Begin a Story

The important thing to do is capture your reader's interest at the beginning of the story. You could...

- begin with an unexpected and intriguing idea
- set the scene through vivid description
- begin with **dialogue** (**direct speech**) between your characters
- focus on a **description** of a character or characters
- give your reader information about the characters or situation
- begin with a dramatic event.

Developing Ideas

You need to plan the structure of your story carefully. Think about...

- how the events of your story unfold and link together
- how your characters develop and relate to one another
- creating a series of ideas to keep your reader interested and make them want to read on
- building up to some kind of climax or key moment in your story
- varying your use of language to keep your story interesting, lively and vivid.

Remember to...

- keep the action moving
- make your characters convincing – try to bring them to life
- use dialogue (speech) at various points to give added interest and make your story more interesting
- make your description vivid by using well-chosen **adverbs** (words that describe verbs) and **adjectives** (words that describe nouns), but don't overdo it or your writing will sound false and 'flowery'.

Points of View

Before beginning, you need to decide which point of view to use to tell your story. This is called the **narrative viewpoint**.

The two most commonly used points of view are **first person** narration and **third person** narration.

First and Third Person Narratives

In a first person narrative the **narrator** is actually a character in the story, so the 'I' narrator tells the story. This style of telling the story gives the feeling that the narrator is talking to you directly and tells everything from the point of view of the narrator character.

In third person narratives the narrator is outside the story and describes the characters and events as if they know everything that's going on. They can describe what's going on in the minds of all the characters and make comments on characters and events.

Third person

David woke up this morning

I woke up this morning

First person

Ending Your Story

Sometimes, story endings are disappointing. They can seem flat and lacking excitement or interest, or can just fizzle out leaving the reader thinking, 'So what?'

You should decide on the ending of your story as part of your planning. It's as important to think carefully about how to end your story as it is to think about how to begin it.

The ending should leave the reader feeling or thinking about something – they might feel satisfied, angry, puzzled, amused, intrigued, or any other emotion.

There are various ways to end your story. Here are some examples:

- End with a dramatic event.
- The story comes to a natural end based on the way the plot has developed.
- End by revealing some information or knowledge that throws light on the events or characters.
- An unexpected twist.
- An ending that leaves things up in the air and keeps the reader guessing or drawing their own conclusions – a cliffhanger.

Quick Test

1. What is meant by the 'setting' of a story?
2. What are the ideas explored in a story called?
3. What is the key event or high point of the story called (it usually comes towards the end)?
4. Give two types of narrative viewpoint.

KEY WORDS

Make sure you understand these words before moving on!

- Planning
- Plot
- Storyline
- Structure
- Character
- Setting
- Language
- Vocabulary
- Style
- Theme
- Beginning
- Middle
- Climax
- Ending
- Dialogue
- Direct speech
- Description
- Adverb
- Adjective
- Narrative viewpoint
- First person
- Third person
- Narrator

Imaginative Writing

Work out the key words from the clues below, then copy and complete the crossword.

ACROSS

3. The point of view a story is told from. (9, 9)
4. This allows the reader to imagine the scene or character. (11)
5. These live in your story. (10)
8. The way in which you write your story. (5)
11. The 'twist in the tale' is one kind of this. (6)
13. Key moment of a story. (6)
14. The words used in the story. (10)
18. Another word for speech. (8)
19. Type of speech, spoken. (6)
20. _____ person narrative uses 'I'. (5)
22. Stories are usually told in the first or third _____ narrative. (6)
23. Another name for the plot of a story. (9)

DOWN

1. The words you use to write your story. (8)
2. Part of story where characters are developed. (6)
6. A word that describes a verb. (6)
7. Opening to a story. (9)
8. Where the action of a story takes place. (7)
9. You need to do this before writing your story. (8)
10. Another word for storyline. (4)
12. They tell the story. (8)
15. A word that describes a noun. (9)
16. The ideas you explore in your story. (6)
17. The way that events of the plot link together. (9)
21. In a _____ person narrative the narrator is not a character in the story. (5)

1. Why is the opening of a story important?

2. Give three ways in which you could begin a story.

3. What is the structure of a story?

4. Why is the ending of a story important?

5. Give two ways in which you could end a story.

6. Read the following sentences and identify whether they're written in the first person or in the third person.
   a) I turned slowly to look at Zoe and felt that our efforts had been worthwhile.
   b) My uncle was the strangest man I had ever known, but he thought that I was the odd one.
   c) Sam thought she would never finish her story – she just could not think of an ending she was happy with.
   d) We seemed to have been waiting for hours but Jim said that we had only been there for fifteen minutes.
   e) She opened the door carefully, feeling very frightened about what she might find.

7. What is an adverb?

8. What is an adjective?

9. Read the following sentences and identify the adverbs and adjectives.
   a) The old man hobbled slowly up the dusty road.
   b) 'Not that one!' shouted Kim loudly. 'You need the blue folder.'
   c) The sun slipped slowly below the skyline, leaving only a golden glow in the darkening sky.
   d) The wind blew violently and the rain rattled against the trembling windows.
   e) He leapt quickly out of the way as the smoking car veered suddenly off the road and mounted the pavement.

10. What do you think is wrong with the following paragraph?

> The deep, rich blue of the bright, clear, sparkling summer sky with its fluffy, delicate cotton-wool white clouds added to the calm, beauty and tranquillity of the lovely, peaceful scene. The golden, warming, smiling sun shone down on the green, gold-spattered, empty fields.

Imaginative Writing

Skills Practice

Look at the opening page of three novels or short stories that you have read. Look at the technique each writer used to begin the story and make notes on them. Think about how the stories begin:

- Does the writer set the scene?
- Are characters introduced and / or described?
- Is speech used?
- Does the writer use a 'shock' or 'surprise' opening?

Write a short analysis of how each writer begins their story. Make sure that you support your ideas with some examples from the story openings.

Extension Activity

Work with a partner and swap notes with them. Read each other's notes.

Compare the ways in which the stories begin and discuss your ideas about how effective each opening is and give reasons for your views.

Draw a table in which you rate the openings of the stories you looked at, from the most effective to the least effective. For example, here are some comments on this opening to a story:

'Halloa! Below there!'

When he heard a voice thus calling to him, he was standing at the door of his box, with a flag in his hand, furled round its short pole. One would have thought, considering the nature of the ground, that he could not have doubted from what quarter the voice came; but instead of looking up to where I stood on the top of the steep cutting nearly over his head, he turned himself about, and looked down the Line. There was something remarkable in his manner of doing so, though I could not have said for my life what. But I know it was remarkable enough to attract my notice, even though his figure was foreshortened and shadowed, down in the deep trench, and mine was high above him, so steeped in the glow of an angry sunset, that I had shaded my eyes with my hand before I saw him at all.

The Signalman by Charles Dickens

Novel or Short Story	How it Opens	Comments
The Signalman by Charles Dickens	Direct speech (someone shouting), then a description of how the man acts and a description of the scene.	The opening exclamation, 'Halloa! Below there!', immediately captures the reader's attention. The man acts strangely, which makes the reader want to read on and find out why. The 'angry sunset' creates an ominous note.

Character and Atmosphere

What is Covered in this Topic?

This topic looks at...
- using language effectively
- creating convincing characters
- setting the scene
- creating atmosphere.

Creating Characters

Characters are a very important part of a story and they come in all shapes and sizes. They may not even be human – in some stories the characters are animals or aliens from space.

The characters you create for your stories are made up from your imagination. Sometimes, though, writers create new characters using ideas from their own experiences and people they have met.

Creating Believable Characters

The key points to remember when creating characters are to...
- avoid stereotypes (unconvincing 'cardboard cut-out' characters)
- make them believable and convincing.

The table contains some techniques and ideas you could include in your story.

Technique	Ideas
Description	• Give some information about your characters. • Describe how they look. • Give ideas about their attitudes and feelings. • Describe their actions.
Dialogue	• What the characters say and how they speak tells the reader a lot about them. • What other characters say about them can be revealing.
Thoughts and feelings	• Letting the reader know what's going on in a character's mind.
Actions	• How the character behaves and reacts to other characters.

Character and Atmosphere

Introducing Characters

In the following two passages the writers use two different approaches to introducing characters.

 What do you notice about them?

Nightmare Stairs by Robert Swindells

She's Mum's big sister, Auntie Anne, but they're not a bit alike. Or if they are I can't see it. Mum's nice, you know? A really nice person – the sort who'll go out of her way to do someone a good turn, even a complete stranger. Auntie Anne isn't. No way. I'll tell you the sort of person she is. Suppose she's in the car park and it's Saturday afternoon and the place is full, right? She's loaded her shopping into the boot and she's ready to leave when she notices someone waiting for her space. Instead of starting up and pulling away like she meant to, she'll find a cloth and get out and start working her way round the car, really slowly, doing the windows and mirrors. They don't need doing – she's making the guy wait, that's all. And if he gives up and moves on she's really glad. I know she's my auntie but I've no time for her. In fact I hate her and I always have.

The Secret Passage by Nina Bawden

When John and Mary and Ben Mallory first saw their Aunt Mabel they thought she looked very disagreeable. She was tall and thin with a long, thin face and grey hair insecurely fastened in a straggly bun at the back of her neck. Whenever she turned her head, a little shower of hairpins fell out. When she met the children at London Airport, she was wearing a faded brown coat and stockings that wrinkled on her skinny legs as if they had been intended for a much fatter person.

John thought she probably looked like that, so shabby and cross, because she was a widow. His father had told him that her husband, Mr Haggard, had been drowned at sea.

In *Nightmare Stairs* the writer...
- uses first person narration
- uses a comparison between her mother and Auntie Anne to tell us straightaway that her auntie isn't a nice person – a detailed example of her auntie's behaviour is given to illustrate this.

In *The Secret Passage* the writer ...
- uses third person narration
- gives the names of the characters
- describes what Aunt Mabel looks like
- gives an idea of what John thinks about her.

Settings

The **setting** is an important part of your story. You need to think carefully about how you're going to describe it. Here's an example of a writer describing a setting.

💡 *How does the writer create an impression of the setting?*

The Lord of the Flies by William Golding

The shore was fledged with palm trees. These stood or leaned or reclined against the light and their green feathers were a hundred feet up in the air. The ground beneath them was a bank covered with coarse grass, torn everywhere by the upheavals of fallen trees, scattered with decaying coco-nuts and palm saplings. Behind this was the darkness of the forest proper and the open space of the scar. Ralph stood, one hand against a grey trunk, and screwed up his eyes against the shimmering water. Out there, perhaps a mile away, the white surf flinked on a coral reef, and beyond that the open sea was dark blue. Within the irregular arc of coral the lagoon was still as a mountain lake – blue of all shades and shadowy green and purple.

The writer uses several techniques in the extract:

- The use of **adjectives**, such as *green* feathers, *coarse* grass, *fallen* trees and *decaying* coco-nuts.
- The use of **metaphors** – the shore was 'fledged' with palm trees (fledged is a word used to describe a young bird with feathers that's ready to leave the nest) and the trees' leaves are described as 'green feathers'.
- The use of a **simile** – 'still as a mountain lake'.
- He describes the setting as it is seen through the character Ralph's eyes.

💡 *How many more adjectives can you spot?*

Adding Detail

When writing your own story you can help your reader to 'see' the setting in their mind by...

- adding small touches of detail as you develop your story
- using longer passages (as in the example above) in which you give a more detailed description of the setting.

Character and Atmosphere

Atmosphere

The **atmosphere** of a piece of writing is closely linked to the **mood** or **tone** created. Words that might come into your mind when you think about atmosphere could include these: peaceful, friendly, happy, tense, frightening, spooky, exciting, sad, edgy, creepy.

Creating an Atmosphere

Atmosphere is the special feeling created by a writer's description of the action or setting in a story. It creates the mood of the writing or the feelings created in the reader's mind.

💡 *How would you describe the atmosphere created in this extract from* Dracula *by Bram Stoker?*

Soon we were hemmed in with trees, which in places arched right over the roadway till we passed as through a tunnel; and again frowning rocks guarded us boldly on either side. Though we were in shelter, we could hear the rising wind, for it moaned and whistled through the rocks, and the branches of the trees crashed together as we swept along. It grew colder and colder still, and fine, powdery snow began to fall, so that soon we and all around us were covered with a white blanket. The keen wind still carried the howling of the dogs, though this grew fainter as we went on our way. The baying of the wolves sounded nearer and nearer, as though they were closing round on us from every side.

The passage creates a feeling of tension or fear, which the writer creates through his use of the **language** or vocabulary. For example…
- 'hemmed in with trees' creates the sense of being in a tunnel
- 'frowning rocks' creates a threatening feeling
- 'the rising wind' and 'moaned and whistled' add to the creepy atmosphere
- 'It grew colder and colder' adds to the tense atmosphere
- 'the howling of the dogs' and 'the baying of the wolves' creates an eerie and ominous sound effect.

Quick Test

1. What kind of narration is used in each of these sentences?
   a) My name is Joe and I'm thirteen years old.
   b) The boy's name is Joe and he is thirteen years old.
2. Complete the following sentences:
   a) You should try to make your characters _____ and _____ .
   b) In creating your characters you need to use your _____ .

Key Word Exercise

Complete each sentence by finding the missing key word.

1. In order to create a convincing picture of your characters you need to use

   _____ effectively.

2. You use your _____ to create your characters.

3. Making your characters convincing will prevent them being _____, or

   'cardboard cut-outs'.

4. You might create an eerie _____ when writing a ghost story.

5. Atmosphere in writing is closely connected to _____ .

6. _____ can make your description more vivid by telling you more about

   the nouns in your writing.

7. Another useful way of making your description more vivid is by using a

   _____ to compare the thing you're describing to something else.

8. A _____ is like a simile but doesn't use 'like' or 'as'.

9. The things that characters do are called their _____ .

10. You can describe what characters think about other characters and events, which reveals

    their thoughts and _____ .

Character and Atmosphere

1 The following passage from *Oliver Twist* by Charles Dickens describes Oliver's first meeting with the Artful Dodger. Dickens concentrates on the physical description of The Dodger. Pick the word from each group that you think best fits in with the description of the character.

> He was a **bent / snub / sharp**-nosed, flat-browed, common-faced boy
> enough; and as **dirty / small / strange** a juvenile as one would wish to see;
> but he had about him all the airs and **tricks / ideas / manners** of a man.
> He was short of his age: with rather **round / bow / barrel**-legs, and little,
> **glassy / sharp / tired**, ugly eyes. His hat was stuck on the top of his head
> so **firmly / lightly / tightly**, that it threatened to fall off every moment –
> and would have done so, very often, if the wearer had not had a knack
> of every now and then giving his head a sudden **twitch / nod / shake**
> which brought it back to its old place again. He wore a man's coat,
> which reached nearly to his heels. He had turned the **material / cuffs /
> lapels** back, half-way up his arm, to get his hands out of the sleeves:
> apparently with the ultimate view of **pushing / thrusting / placing** them
> into the pockets of his corduroy **trousers / shirt / vest**; for there he
> kept them.

2 What kind of atmosphere do you think is created in this passage from *The Watch House* by Robert Westall?

Write down any word or phrase that you think helps to create this atmosphere and explain your choices.

> As they reached the door, Anne gave one last look back. In the dusk at
> the far end of the room, Arthur's model lighthouse had begun flashing
> at last.
>
> 'Run back an' switch it off – there's a good lass. Then turn the key in
> the lock an' fetch it when ye come.' Arthur started towards the
> cottage, whistling.
>
> Anne suddenly wished Arthur had waited. The rocket-hall was very dark,
> now the lights were off. She hurried down it with her eyes on the floor.
> Her footsteps sounded hollow on the bare boards. Hollow, and too loud
> in that private place. But who could be listening?
>
> She pushed the switch over, and the lighthouse stopped flashing. As she
> turned back, she made the mistake of looking up. All around her, the
> twisted dusty blackened gear of foreign dead men hung. Too much of it.
> Personal, intimate as a sea-boot, and old.

Plan the first stages of a story of your own.

Stage 1: Decide on the type of story you're going to write, e.g. an adventure story, a ghost story, a school story, etc.

Stage 2: Decide on your narrative viewpoint.

Stage 3: Write down the key points of your plot (don't have too many – try to summarise it in a maximum of 10 points).

Stage 4: Structure the events of your story, expanding a little on the key points of your plot. Remember that you will need...
- an effective opening to capture the interest of your reader
- interesting events that keep your reader's interest and build up to a climax or key moment
- an effective ending (think carefully about the effect you want to achieve at the end).

Stage 5: Make a list of your characters and make notes on them. Remember:
- Don't have too many characters. In a short story you don't have the space to develop too many characters. It's better to have a small number of well-developed, convincing characters.
- Give your characters individual characteristics or features to make them more interesting and convincing.

Stage 6: Decide on the setting or settings of your story. Think carefully about how you're going to present it. Remember to describe your setting effectively to help make your story convincing and interesting to read.

After you've planned your story, prepare a short talk to give to a small group of friends or students in your class. In your talk you should...
- **explain the decision you made when planning your story**
- **explain the effects that you want to achieve**
- **answer any questions that they might have.**

You should try to be as clear as possible when presenting your ideas to the group.

ideas

Friends lost
haunted house
no electricity

Descriptive Writing

This topic looks at...
- using description to create setting, atmosphere or mood
- using description to help develop characters.

Descriptive Writing

The purpose of descriptive writing is always the same – to create a picture in words of whatever you're describing so that you give your reader a vivid impression of the place, event, characters, etc.

Descriptive writing can be used in two main ways, both in imaginative and non-fiction writing:

1. It can be used as the main focus of a piece of writing, e.g. if you're writing a description of a place you visited on holiday or describing something that has happened to you.
2. It can be used to make a particular part of a piece of writing more vivid, e.g. to give a detailed impression of a character or scene.

Effective Description

An effective description should...
- capture and hold the reader's attention
- be convincing, whether it's based on reality or made up out of your imagination
- be based on observation
- use language effectively.

Choosing your Words

To make your description effective it's really important to choose your words carefully. Remember that words don't just have a specific meaning; they can also suggest different kinds of feelings and emotions.

For example, 'frightened' and 'terrified' both have the same basic meaning, but the feelings or impressions they give aren't quite the same.

💡 *What do you think the difference is between 'frightened' and 'terrified'?*

You might feel that 'terrified' suggests a stronger, more intense kind of fear than the word 'frightened'.

To help you pick the right word to convey the meaning you want, you might find a **thesaurus** useful (this is a book that gives you lots of alternative words to describe a particular meaning).

Making your Description Vivid

There are various **techniques** you can use to make your descriptions more vivid and original so that you capture your reader's interest and give them a really good sense of what you're describing.

Here are some ideas:
- Use various senses to create a strong impression – lots of descriptions focus on what can be seen, but don't forget that touch, taste, sound and smell can add vivid details to description too.
- Use **adverbs** (words that describe verbs) to add to the description of actions.
- Use **adjectives** (words that describe nouns) to make a real difference to the vividness of the description.

- Use **similes** (which compare one thing to another), **metaphors** (which say that one thing *is* another), and **onomatopoeia** (words that sound like the sound they're describing, e.g. bang, crash).
- Use a varied **vocabulary** (here's where your thesaurus can help – a good **dictionary** is very useful too to check the meanings of words you find in your thesaurus).
- Use **dialogue** to help bring characters or situations to life.
- Use a variety of sentence lengths to make the description more interesting to read, e.g. short sentences to add tension / complex sentences to build description.

Descriptive Writing

Describing Scenes

Read these two descriptions of the same scene. Which do you think gives the most vivid impression of the scene and why?

You might have found the second version more effective because it gives a more vivid impression of the state of the room.

💡 *Can you see what techniques the writer has used to create this effect?*

Here are some ideas:

- Adverbs have been used, e.g. to describe how Jane's parents looked – looked *angrily*.
- Adjectives have been used to add to the description, e.g. *terrible* mess, *unidentified* liquid, *beige* carpet.
- Similes have been used, e.g. 'it looked as if someone had emptied several dustbins over it'.
- Dialogue has been used to create a sense of Jane's father's reaction to the scene.
- Use of the senses.
- Long, complex sentences to build description.

> When Jane's parents returned home they looked at the state that they found in the living room. They were shocked by the mess it had been left in after the party. The floor was littered with rubbish and there were cans everywhere. Some kind of liquid had been spilt on the carpet and had left a large stain on it and the dining table had a scratch across it. The air was stale and stuffy. Jane's dad shouted for her to come down straight away.

> When Jane's parents returned home early they looked angrily at what they found in the living room. They were visibly shocked by the terrible mess it had been left in after the party the previous evening. The floor was so littered with rubbish it looked as if someone had emptied several dustbins over it and there were coke and lemonade cans everywhere. Some kind of unidentified liquid had been spilt on the beige carpet and had left a large, purple stain on it, which had spread like a big blot on blotting paper. The dining table had a deep scratch right across the middle of it. The air was stale and stuffy and smelt like a rugby team's changing room after a particularly hard match. 'I don't believe this!' exclaimed Jane's dad, in disbelief. 'Jane! Get down here. Now!'

Setting and Mood

Language can be used in different ways to create a sense of setting and mood. Look at the following description and think about the kind of setting and mood the writer creates and the ways he uses language to create his effects.

Coming up for Air by George Orwell

Thursday was market day. Chaps with round red faces like pumpkins and dirty smocks and huge boots covered with dry cow-dung, carrying long hazel switches, used to drive their brutes into the market-place early in the morning. For hours there'd be a terrific hullabaloo: dogs barking, pigs squealing, chaps in tradesmen's vans who wanted to get through the crush cracking their whips and cursing, and everyone who had anything to do with the cattle shouting and throwing sticks.

You might have noted some of these ideas:
- The setting described is that of a busy cattle market and the writer creates a mood of the bustle and action taking place there.
- As well as describing the visual scene, the writer uses sound and onomatopoeia, e.g. 'barking', 'squealing', 'cracking'.
- Adjectives are used, e.g. *red* faces, *huge* boots.
- A simile is used: 'faces like pumpkins'.

Characters and Actions

The following writer adopts a different style to create a picture of his subject.

💡 *How do you think this differs from the previous extract by George Orwell?*

Return of the Native by Thomas Hardy

Along the road walked an old man. He was white-headed as a mountain, bowed in the shoulders, and faded in general aspect. He wore a glazed hat, an ancient boat-cloak, and shoes; his brass buttons bearing an anchor upon their face. In his hand was a silver-headed walking stick, which he used as a veritable third leg, perseveringly dotting the ground with its point at every few inches' interval. One would have said that he had been, in his day, a naval officer of some sort or other.

You might have noticed here that the writer focuses simply on the visual detail of what the character looked like and what he was doing.

Some adjectives are used to give more detail, e.g. *old* man, *ancient* boat-cloak, and a simile is also used to make this visual description more vivid: 'white-headed as a mountain'.

Quick Test

Complete the sentences below.
1. Adverbs might be used in descriptive writing to tell you more about the
   _____ .
2. You use onomatopoeia in writing to create a sense of _____ .
3. Description can be used to create an impression of setting and
   _____ .

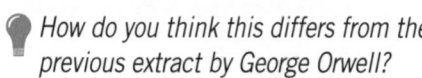

KEY WORDS

Make sure you understand these words before moving on!
- Characters
- Description
- Convincing
- Observation
- Language
- Thesaurus
- Techniques
- Adverbs
- Adjectives
- Similes
- Metaphors
- Onomatopoeia
- Vocabulary
- Dictionary
- Dialogue
- Setting
- Mood

Descriptive Writing

Key Words Exercise

Work out the key words from the clues below, then find them in the word search.

1. Another word for speech.

2. Description can help create a sense of _____ and _____.

3. Description can help you create convincing _____.

4. Good description is often based on careful _____.

5. Effective description can make your characters more _____.

6. Vivid _____ can create a strong impression of setting and mood.

7. To write descriptively you need to choose your _____ carefully.

8. A _____ and a _____ can help you choose the right words to use.

9. Your writing is more effective if you use a variety of _____.

10. These words describe verbs.

11. Both _____ and _____ use comparisons to make writing more vivid.

12. These words describe nouns.

13. _____ is used to create a sense of sound.

14. Another word for the words you use is _____.

C	H	A	R	A	C	T	E	R	S	N	A	T	Y	S
V	O	N	O	M	A	T	O	P	O	E	I	A	R	W
Q	L	M	E	T	A	P	H	O	R	S	M	F	A	I
P	D	S	Y	O	W	G	J	U	T	J	H	O	N	A
O	E	T	E	C	H	N	I	Q	U	E	S	X	O	U
O	S	A	T	S	E	T	T	I	N	G	E	T	I	D
B	C	V	O	T	B	U	L	A	T	C	V	H	T	G
S	R	Q	L	A	T	N	U	I	S	O	O	E	C	A
E	I	V	B	N	G	I	B	Y	O	N	C	S	I	D
R	P	S	O	M	T	M	N	I	R	V	A	A	D	J
V	T	B	M	A	Z	A	T	G	E	I	B	U	C	E
A	I	K	S	I	M	I	L	E	S	N	U	R	Y	C
T	O	C	M	L	E	R	S	T	U	C	L	U	C	T
I	N	N	L	I	Y	M	I	L	E	I	A	S	Y	I
O	L	A	D	V	E	R	B	S	S	N	R	W	R	V
N	D	I	A	L	O	G	U	E	I	G	Y	H	L	E
I	O	H	I	T	U	L	A	N	G	U	A	G	E	S

1 Look at the following passage from *The Trumpet Major* by Thomas Hardy, which describes a character, Anne. Make a list of the techniques that Hardy uses to make his description of Anne vivid and effective. Give an example from the passage of each technique you have listed.

> Anne was fair, very fair, in a poetic sense; but in complexion she was of that particular tint between blonde and brunette which is inconveniently left without a name. Her eyes were honest and inquiring, her mouth cleanly cut and yet not classical, the middle point of her upper lip scarcely descending so far as it should have done by rights, so that at the merest pleasant thought, not to mention a smile, portions of two or three white teeth were uncovered whether she would or not. Some people said that this was very attractive. She was graceful and slender, and, though but little above five feet in height, could draw herself up to look tall. In her manner, in her comings and goings, in her 'I'll do this,' or 'I'll do that,' she combined dignity with sweetness as no other girl could do; and any impressionable stranger youths who passed by were led to yearn for a windfall of speech from her, and to see at the same time that they would not get it. In short, beneath all that was charming and simple in this young woman there lurked a real firmness, unperceived at first, as the speck of colour lurks unperceived in the heart of the palest parsley flower.
>
> She wore a white handkerchief to cover her white neck, and a cap on her head with a pink ribbon round it, tied in a bow at the front. She had a great variety of these cap-ribbons, the young men being fond of sending them to her as presents until they fell definitely in love with a special sweetheart elsewhere, when they left off doing so. Between the border of her cap and her forehead were ranged a row of round brown curls, like swallows' nests under eaves.

2 Now look at this passage (also from *The Trumpet Major*) in which Hardy describes the setting. Make a list of the techniques he uses to create an impression of the setting and a sense of the atmosphere.

> Immediately before her was the large, smooth mill-pond, over-full, and intruding into the hedge and into the road. The water, with its flowing leaves and spots of froth, was stealing away, like Time, under the dark arch, to tumble over the great slimy wheel within. On the other side of the mill-pond was an open place called the Cross, because it was three-quarters of one, two lanes and a cattle-drive meeting there. It was the general rendezvous and arena of the surrounding village. Behind this a steep slope rose high into the sky, merging in a wide and open down, now littered with sheep newly shorn. The upland by its height completely sheltered the mill and village from north winds, making summers of springs, reducing winters to autumn temperatures, and permitting myrtle to flourish in the open air.
>
> The heaviness of noon pervaded the scene, and under its influence the sheep had ceased to feed. Nobody was standing at the Cross, the few inhabitants being indoors at their dinner. No human being was on the down, and no human eye or interest but Anne's seemed to be concerned with it. The bees still worked on, and the butterflies did not rest from roving, their smallness seeming to shield them from the stagnating effect that this turning moment of day had on larger creatures. Otherwise all was still.

Descriptive Writing

Write a piece of descriptive writing of your own on each of the following ideas:

- **A person you have met.**
- **A view or place you have seen.**
- **An experience you have had.**

Try to make each of your pieces of writing as vivid as possible by using some of the following techniques:

- Imagery such as similes and metaphors to help your readers re-create your description in their own minds.
- The use of the senses to create a vivid impression of the sights, sounds, tastes, smells and feelings.
- The use of adverbs and adjectives.
- The use of dialogue.
- A range of sentence lengths.

Extension Activity

When you have written your pieces, read each one aloud to a partner and discuss with your partner how effectively your description came across.

Ask your partner to comment on the following:

- Your use of language.
- The techniques you have used to describe your subject.
- Ways that you could improve your description.

When you have done that, switch roles and listen to your partner's descriptions and comment in the same way on their piece of writing.

Non-Fiction Writing

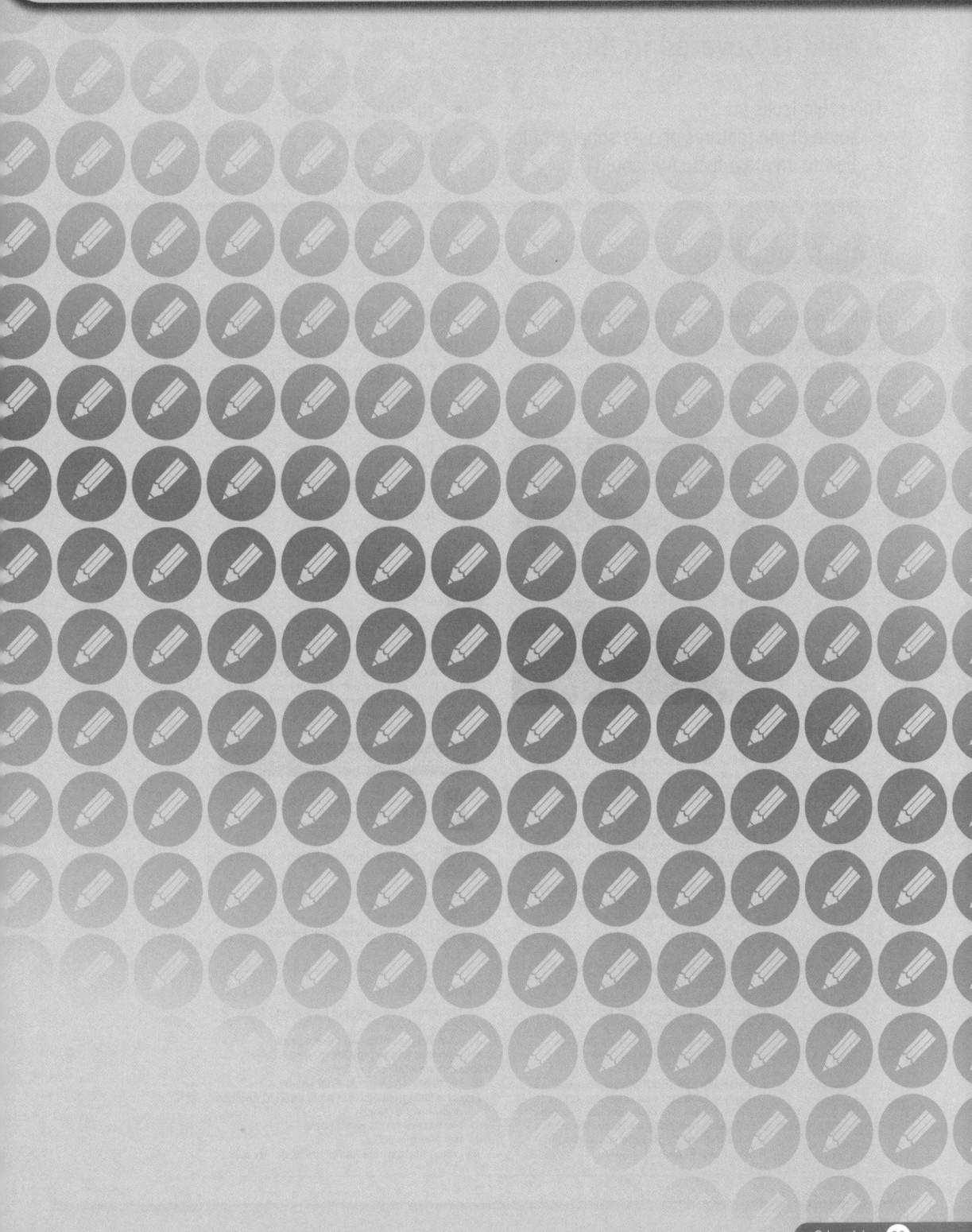

Personal Writing

What is Covered in this Topic?

This topic looks at...
- some of the features of a personal profile
- how to create a factual account
- the use of opinion
- how to write for a real audience.

All About Me

This is an example of a **personal profile** from a **social networking** website. You can put your details into a page, send messages to other members and make new friends.

Other people will get an idea of what you're like from...
- the information you decide to include
- the way you describe yourself.

Mybook.com

About me

My name is Robbie and I'm from somewhere in Europe. I'm a pretty ordinary person of my age and like doing the usual stuff like watching footy, chatting with mates and relaxing.

I get bored if I have too much work to do. I'd much rather be out playing football with my mates Grant, Mike and Gerald. Mike is in the year above us at school but he's a laugh.

I have a brother who I don't see very often because he's away at University, which means I get his room – Yay!

My likes

I'm a big fan of Port Vale FC. They're in Division One but they haven't been doing very well lately. I support my local team because I can go and see them with my dad. I can't go and see Premiership teams because they are too far away from where I live.

I also like junk food! My school gives us healthy food so I can only have chips once a week, which is horrible. I would eat chips every day if I could. My mum says that would give me spots, though, which would be bad...

Robbie
..is having to do his English homework (updated 2 minutes ago)

Name: Robbie Fulks

Birthday: 29th September

Interests: Aeroplanes, sport, music and reading.

What I did today

Today I was given loads of English homework by my teacher – it wasn't even homework night on the timetable, but he said that it would be good for us! I've also got loads of Science and Maths to do and I've got to get my ingredients for Food Tech for tomorrow. I won't be able to watch the football on the telly or go on MSN!

Messageboard

Rob, are you playing against Martyrs United tomorrow?
Grant

Have you done your Maths homework? It's solid!
Mike

I won't be in school tomorrow. Can you tell me what I miss?
Gerald

My top ten facts

1. My name is Robbie, but I answer to 'Rob'.
2. I have no pets.
3. I am strange because I like school.
4. I am learning to play the guitar.
5. I am very tall for my age.
6. My favourite singer is Kate Rusby.
7. I like foreign holidays. I have been to America and Holland (twice).
8. My brother has a weird name.
9. His name is Jubal.
10. I once ate a whole loaf of bread on my own.

Features of a Personal Profile

Personal profiles are all different, but they share similar features:

- Name / title.
- Personal information.
- Sections and headings.

- They are usually written in an **informal style**.
- They may contain photos, pictures, music and / or videos.

💡 *Which of these features can you see in Robbie's profile?*

Know Your Audience

When you put together your personal profile you will need to think about who might see it – your **audience**.

You need to ask yourself some questions:

- Who do you want to read it, and who else might read it?
- Why are you writing it? Is it to let your friends know more about you, or to make new friends?
- What are you going to include in your profile?

Look at Robbie's profile again. He wanted his profile to be read by his friends and also to help make some new friends.

💡 *Which parts of his profile were meant to be read by his friends? How can you tell?*

💡 *Which parts of his profile might be to attract new friends? How can you tell?*

Being Safe

You need to be careful about the information that you put online because you don't know who might read it.

The reason why you're writing it may not be the reason why someone else is reading it.

You need to be careful about what you write so that you don't give information out that someone else might use for bad reasons.

💡 *Look at Robbie's profile again – is there anything that you would tell him to take out? Why?*

Personal Writing

The Content of Profiles

The content of a profile...
- is mainly **factual**
- may include **opinions**.

💡 *Why do you think the content is mainly going to be factual?*

💡 *Why might your profile be boring if you don't include opinions?*

Look at these extracts from Robbie's profile. The parts highlighted in red are facts and the parts in blue are opinions.

> I'm a big fan of Port Vale FC. They're in Division One but they haven't been doing very well lately. I support my local team because I can go and see them with my dad. I can't go and see Premiership teams because they are too far away from where I live.

> I also like junk food! My school gives us healthy food so I can only have chips once a week, which is horrible. I would eat chips every day if I could. My mum says that would give me spots, though, which would be bad...

Quick Test

Complete the sentences below.
1. Headings are used because...
2. Don't put your full name on a web page profile because...
3. Use a mixture of facts and opinions about yourself because...
4. Give reasons for your opinions because...
5. Lists of facts are useful because...

KEY WORDS
Make sure you understand these words before moving on!
- Social networking
- Personal profile
- Informal style
- Audience
- Factual
- Opinion

Key Words Exercise

For each question, select the correct option to complete the sentence.

1 Social networking means...
   a) mixing with other people and making new contacts
   b) removing your information from a web page
   c) being careful
   d) working out how to use a computer properly.

2 A personal profile is a...
   a) website
   b) collection of facts and opinions about you
   c) form that you fill in
   d) booklet.

3 Informal style means...
   a) writing in a serious manner
   b) writing in a relaxed manner.

4 The audience of a piece of writing is...
   a) the people who write it
   b) the people who read it.

5 'Factual' describes...
   a) things that are made up
   b) things that are false
   c) things that can be proven
   d) things that someone has said.

6 Opinions are...
   a) always false
   b) ideas that someone has made up that are true
   c) ideas that someone has made up that may be true or false
   d) the same as facts.

Personal Writing

Here is a personal profile from the same site, but filled in by a very different person.

Mybook.com

Alex

A guitar superstar. Bow down and worship me! (updated 2 minutes ago)

Name: Alex

Birthday: 1st December

Interests: Me, me and… me! (Oh – and guitars)

What I did today

Today I learnt some new chords for the guitar. The bass player in our band is just rubbish though and couldn't play the amazing new song I wrote. Why can't he see how good my ideas are? I'll have to sack him.

About me

My name is Alex and you'd better remember it cuz I'm gonna be famous. Got no time for time wasters or posers cuz they're gonna stop me from getting to the top where I deserve to be.

I am the best guitar player for my age anywhere and anyone who doesn't agree with me is a waste of space. If you want my autograph then e-mail me and send me a fiver and then I'll post it to you if I can be bothered.

My likes

I like me because I'm great. I have loads of girls who fancy me and I'm not surprised because, well, who wouldn't?

I like playing the guitar – as you should know if you've actually bothered to pay any attention to my profile. I can't be bothered with school though. I don't need to try hard because I'm going to be famous when I grow up anyway.

Messageboard

Alex – you're sacked from the band.

Steven

How many chords do you know now? Three?

Amy

Can I have my guitar back, please?

Jimi

My top ten facts

1. I'm great
2. I'm great
3. I'm great
4. I'm great
5. I'm great
6. I'm great
7. I'm great
8. I'm great
9. I'm great
10. Did I tell you that I'm great?

1 a) Which parts of Alex's profile are meant to be read by people he knows? Explain your answer.

b) Which parts of his profile are intended for people who don't know him? Explain your answer.

2 a) Find two examples of slang in Alex's profile and write them down.

b) What impression does his use of slang create?

3 Find three examples of facts and three examples of opinions in Alex's profile.

4 Now compare Alex's profile to Robbie's.

a) Which features do the two profiles have in common?

b) How are the two profiles different?

c) What do these differences tell us about Alex?

d) Does Alex give more or fewer opinions than Robbie?

e) Does Robbie appear more or less reasonable than Alex? Explain your answer.

5 Which of the two boys would you most like to be friends with? Explain your answer.

Now that you know what a personal profile is like, have a go at creating your own.

Step 1: First of all, plan and decide...
- who you're going to write it for – who do you want your audience to be? Everyone? Just a few friends?
- why you are going to write it. Do you want to tell the world about your hobbies and skills? Do you just want to stay in touch with your friends?
- what you are going to include.

Step 2: Now draft your ideas – sketch them out in rough and work out what goes where. Check your spelling, punctuation and your use of slang. If you make lots of mistakes, just think what sort of impression you're going to give.

Step 3: Write up your final version. Get other people to read it and ask them whether they think it gives a fair impression of what you're like. Listen to their suggestions. Redraft it to make it even better.

Write personal profiles for these people:

1 Your teacher – he/she wants to come across as trendy and fashionable and wants to be noticed by the general public. What would you include?

2 Your best friend – he/she wants to come across as a really nice person to the pupils at their new school. What would you include to create a good impression of them?

3 A well-known person who has a bad reputation – what would you include to change people's opinion of them?

Forms of Persuasion

What is Covered in this Topic?

This topic covers...
- techniques of persuasion
- when and how to use these techniques in a formal or an informal setting.

Persuasive Techniques

Here is a begging letter sent by someone claiming to be down on their luck:

Dear Sir,

A fabulous person like you will surely understand my sad, pitiful predicament. I have no money or family. You must help me. Isn't it only fair that poor, hard-done-to and underprivileged people like me should receive support? Don't we deserve it? Haven't you ever felt like me? In a recent survey, over 95% of people nowadays have financial problems. There must be millions – no billions – of people who are suffering like me. Please, please, please try to understand my difficulties.

Think back to before you started work. You probably had no money. You probably had to rely on others to help you. We've all been in that situation, haven't we?

What if you don't help me? I might starve. I might even die. You wouldn't want that to happen now, would you? Think once – think twice – think help.

What about those people who say that people like me are a drain on society? They simply don't understand how people have suffered. They are cruel, heartless and uncaring. A thoughtful person like you wouldn't want to be considered to be one of them, would you?

Imagine me at Christmas. People will be sitting in their warm, cosy houses, feasting on delicious food and wine, while I will be alone, cold and shivering, picking up the festering scraps at the local bus station, hoping that someone will give me fifty pence to buy a cup of tea.

I'm not asking you to help me because I'm selfish. I'm not asking you to help me because I'm poor. I'm asking you to help me, to save my life.

If you don't, I'll come round your house and steal your telly.

Persuasive Techniques (cont.)

The begging letter on the previous page uses a number of techniques of **persuasion**:

1. **Flattery** – being nice to someone, in the hope that they'll agree to your suggestions.
2. Gaining sympathy / sob stories / **guilt** – make the other person feel sorry for you to get them on your side.
3. **Rhetorical questions** – questions that imply an answer without it being stated.
4. **Statistics** – if you use facts and figures, how can someone disagree?
5. **Repetition** – repeat what you want until the person you're working on gives in. This is used a lot by small children.
6. **Empathy** – putting yourself in the other person's place.
7. **Shock tactics** – scare people into doing what you want.
8. Twisting arguments so that they support your views – this shows that you're thinking of all the views and, therefore, come across as being reasonable.
9. **Emotive** words – often used along with gaining sympathy / sob stories / guilt.
10. Rule of three – three ideas, sequenced so that the final one makes the listener or reader feel as if they're getting a good deal, bargain, or extra value, for example, 'I'm not selling this plate for £10, I'm not selling it for £5, I'm only asking for £2.50…' It's probably worth 50p, but it sounds as if you're getting a bargain.
11. Threats and **blackmail** – a sinister way of 'persuading' someone.
12. Making deals / **compromise** – meet someone halfway if it means that you'll get most of what you want.

Can you see these persuasive techniques in the begging letter on page 106?

I'm not selling this plate for £10, I'm not selling it for £5, I'm only asking for £2.50…

Plates **£2.50** Plates

Persuading Effectively

To persuade someone effectively, it's not simply a case of using as many techniques as possible.

You need to consider who you're trying to persuade and what you're trying to persuade them to do. You will need to decide whether your persuasion needs to be…
- formal
- informal.

Forms of Persuasion

Techniques of Formal Persuasion

Sometimes you might have to use a more serious and **formal** tone if you're trying to persuade someone in authority, or writing for a serious reason.

For example, you might use a formal tone if you're...
- writing to persuade an authority figure to change their mind about their decision
- writing to persuade a company to give you a refund
- writing to protest about something that you don't like and want changed.

Remember that you need to sound sensible, serious and reasonable.

💡 *Can you use persuasive techniques in a formal situation? Examples are given for the first two.*
1. *Flattery – an experienced, well-respected person of your status...*
2. *Gaining sympathy / sob stories / guilt – the poor, downtrodden pensioners who will suffer from this decision...*
3. *Rhetorical questions*
4. *Statistics*
5. *Repetition*
6. *Empathy*
7. *Shock tactics*
8. *Twisting arguments so that they support your views*
9. *Emotive words*
10. *Rule of three*
11. *Threats and blackmail*
12. *Making deals / compromise*

💡 *Why do you think you have to be careful in a formal situation when using...*
- *shock tactics?*
- *repetition?*
- *emotive words?*
- *threats?*

```
      HARDWARE STORE
        (309) 688-8828
             -SALE-
SALE #: S0071MH115  04-20-08
93258 STCK LMP-ANT      29.97

           SUBTOTAL:    29.97
         TAX 38560:      1.50
 INVOICE 458 TOTAL:     31.47

       BALANCE DUE:     31.47
  _____

          REFUND:       31.47

            CASH:       00.00
          CHANGE:       00.00
 0071 04/20/08 13:18:32 REF#12
ALL RETURNS MUST BE ACCOMPANIED
   BY A VALID SALES RECEIPT.
     SEE STORE FOR DETAILS.
 THANK YOU FOR SHOPPING WITH US.
```

65 Vale Road
Southam
Warwickshire
WW14 1EG

9th July 2009

Hardware Store
23 Biggs Avenue
Leamington Spa
Warwickshire
WE3 6TU

Dear Sir/Madam

I recently purchased a circular saw from your store. However, when I opened the box I found that the saw was damaged – there are deep scratches down one side and one of the attachments is missing.

I would like a full refund for this product. Please find enclosed my receipt showing proof of purchase.

Yours faithfully

Tim Carpenter

Tim Carpenter

Techniques of Informal Persuasion

The situations in which you might want to use **informal** persuasion could include…

- getting a friend to do something they might not want to – for example, go on an outdoor pursuits holiday
- asking your parents for a favour – this might not be written down, but you'll still be using persuasive techniques
- persuading a brother or sister to lend you some money.

The same techniques can be used for informal and formal persuasion.

💡 Can you use persuasive techniques in an informal situation? Examples are given for the first two.

1. *Flattery* – Debbie… a gorgeous wonderful friend like you would surely lend me that top.
2. *Gaining sympathy / sob stories / guilt* – But Mum, I'll be the only person in my entire class who won't be able to go!
3. *Rhetorical questions*
4. *Statistics*
5. *Repetition*
6. *Empathy*
7. *Shock tactics*
8. *Twisting arguments so that they support your views*
9. *Emotive words*
10. *Rule of three*
11. *Threats and blackmail*
12. *Making deals / compromise*

💡 Why might you have to be careful with informal persuasion when using…
- flattery?
- repetition?
- threats and blackmail?

Quick Test

1. What is flattery?
2. What are emotive words?
3. How do statistics convince someone?
4. What are rhetorical questions?
5. Why is blackmail a risky persuasive technique?

KEY WORDS
Make sure you understand these words before moving on!
- Persuasion
- Formal
- Informal
- Flattery
- Repetition
- Statistics
- Shock tactics
- Emotive
- Blackmail
- Rhetorical questions
- Empathy
- Guilt
- Compromise

Forms of Persuasion

Unscramble the key words in the left-hand column, then match each one with its definition.

UPRAISESON	Questions that only have one implied answer.
LAMFOR	Using complimentary words to someone.
FAILNORM	The technique of getting someone to do what you want.
RATTYELF	Numbers.
LUGIT	Serious and following standards of politeness.
ASQUELCHIERIRONSTOT	What you use when you want to demand someone's attention straight away.
CATSITSSIT	Saying something again and again.
PETITIONER	Not serious – relaxed.
APEMYTH	Technique that involves threatening to reveal bad things about someone, or do bad things to them.
CATCHCOTKISS	Meeting someone halfway.
VIEMOTE	A word that describes the feeling you have when you make someone feel sorry.
LABMALICK	Putting yourself in the other person's place.
CRIMPMOOSE	Descriptive words that tug on the emotions.

Key Words Exercise

Choose the correct options in the following sentences.

1. It's good to start a persuasive letter with *flattery / blackmail / repetition* because it puts the reader in a good mood and gets them on your side. Try to make the reader feel *confused / guilty / happy* so that they want to help you.

2. Be careful if you use *slang / casual description / emotive words* because if you go over the top, your reader will think you're exaggerating and not being serious.

3. A good way to end a persuasive letter is by using some form of *threat / three part repetition / empathy* because it ends on a catchy, punchy, memorable statement.

Read the script below, which is an example of informal persuasion.

1. Identify and name the techniques used in the script.

2. What other techniques might the *Little Darling One* have used more successfully?

(Little Darling One is trying to pester a parent to allow him to go to the local Safari Park.)

LD1: Mum?

Mum: Yes dear?

LD1: I think that you're the most intelligent and kind mother a son could wish for. When I see you smile, I feel as I though I've been blessed in having you as my parent. Thank you for being my mother.

Mum: That's very nice dear. Pass me the pork scratching mix would you?

LD1: (Shouting) Mum! YOU'RE NOT LISTENING TO ME! I'M TRYING TO BE NICE – IF YOU DON'T LISTEN TO ME NOW, I'M GOING TO SCREAM!

Mum: Yes, sweetums, mummy is listening. What can I do for you?

LD1: I want to go to the Safari Park. NOW.

Mum: But that's not possible, darling. I can't drive, I'm in the middle of making dinner and, as you can see, I'm looking after next door's cat, making a phone call and writing next week's shopping list.

LD1: It's not fair. Everyone else in the street is allowed to go. I'm the only one in the entire street who's not allowed to. I don't think you love me.

Mum: Of course I do. Perhaps another time, eh?

LD1: That's not good enough. I want to go now. Right now. This instant.

Mum: I don't know…

LD1: Look, I'm not asking you because you pay my pocket money, I'm asking you because I need your permission.

Mum: Well…

LD1: Please please please please please please please please please please. Pretty please. With sugary bits on. If you let me go, I'll even be nice to my sister.

Mum: Oh go on then…

Forms of Persuasion

Skills Practice

Write a letter to your local **MP** persuading them to help reverse a decision to knock down the local sports centre, as it's the only facility available for young people in the area.

Step 1: Your letter is going to be formal, so look at techniques of formal persuasion and steer clear of techniques that might make you sound unreasonable.

How are you going to start your letter? Flattery is a good technique because it gets the reader on your side. However, in a formal letter you need to be careful that you don't exaggerate and sound false.

Step 2: List the arguments you're going to use, in order. Each idea should be in a separate paragraph, unless you wish to combine some ideas that may be similar.

Decide which persuasive techniques you're going to use for each idea. Finishing your letter using the rule of three technique is a good idea, because it acts as a natural catchy phrase.

Step 3: Read your draft. Do your ideas link together? Have you used connectives at the start of and within paragraphs to show how your ideas are linked?

Step 4: When you've drafted your letter and are happy with how it sounds, ask someone else to read it to see if the tone and style sound reasonable. What may sound fair to you, may not sound fair to someone else, so it's worth getting a second opinion.

Step 5: When you're happy with it, think about how you'll present it. If it's formal, you'll probably want to type it, using a sensible, clear font, or use a good quality pen and your best handwriting. The impression gained from the layout is also part of the persuasive technique.

Extension Activity

To improve your persuasion skills, have a go at writing to a friend to persuade them to go skydiving with you.

Remember you're talking to a friend – that will allow you to be informal.

Writing for an Audience

What is Covered in this Topic?

This topic covers...
- how to use features of non-fiction writing
- how to write for a real audience.

Writing Letters

If a new MP3 player was already broken when it was delivered from a shop miles away, you could write a letter asking for a refund or a replacement.

The temptation with faulty goods is to get angry and demand your money back. That's probably not a good idea at first, as it may upset or annoy the person who you bought it from. They may feel offended by the words you use. Then you might not get your money back, or a replacement, as quickly as you would like.

In the letter you would need to include...
- the date
- what you bought
- when you bought it – details of **receipts**, etc.
- what's wrong with it
- what you would like to happen
- your contact information.

Using a formal style will show that you're business-like and **efficient**, as will making sure there are no mistakes or crossings-out.

Customer Services

Writing for an Audience

Letters of Complaint

Here's a letter of complaint that was sent about a similar problem. It's not a good example of how to complain!

💡 *What do you think is wrong with this letter?*

Dear Mr. Manager,

I can't believe the ~~rabish~~ rubbish you sell in your shop. Only the other day, I bought this new MP3 player and it was smashed to bits when I took it out of the box at home! You want to watch what you sell, you do, or you could get in trouble.

Anyway, I want my money back or there's going to be big ~~trou~~ trouble. My uncle works for the police and he'll come round your shop and arrest you if you don't sort this out immediately. If I haven't heard from you within 4 days of you ~~getin~~ getting this letter, then I'll see you in court.

I'm also going to tell all my friends how bad your shop is. Fancy selling broken rubbish like this and charging good money for it! Unbelievable!

If you want this broken MP3 player back, you'll have to let me know, but you'll have to pay for the postage.

Yours truly,

Gerald Dowd

Adding Important Information

Try to learn from the mistakes made above when you draft your own letter:

- Use the name of a person when you're writing to them, if you know it. It will help to direct your complaint to the person who will deal with it more quickly. It also means that you're able to adopt a more personal, reasonable tone.
- Put a date on your letter. This helps you and the company you are writing to track the progress of the complaint.
- Put your contact details on the letter. If you don't, they won't be able to contact you.

Reviews

Reviews are a form of **non-fiction** writing.

Reading product reviews before buying something can warn you if the item is fragile or easily breakable.

Below is a review of the MP3 player that was complained about.

💡 *Which of the following features does the review share with the complaint letter? Which are different features?*
- *Formal style.*
- *Use of specialist vocabulary.*
- *Well-presented layout.*
- *Use of headings.*
- *Name of the writer included.*
- *Use of personal opinion.*

May 2008

GO G

200+ GIFT IDEAS INSIDE

NEW MP3 PLAYER FAILS TO DELIVER

RATINGS: ★☆☆☆☆

There were high expectations from this latest version of Zipple's ground-breaking MP3 player, but, unfortunately, those expectations have been dashed. On paper, the Zipple Classic offers incredible **specification** – a 320 gig hard drive, **compatibility** with 12 different music formats including *.flac and *.ogg files, the ability to play back and record video, connectors for 3 types of headphones and a composite and HDMI TV connection. Unfortunately, it's a case of a "quart in a pint pot". The playback on all formats is subject to incredible delays as the processor is simply too weak to cope with the demands placed on it.

The size and positioning of the audio and video connectors is also very confusing. Instead of placing video on one side and audio on the other, the two are mixed and as a result it's all too easy to plug the wrong lead into the wrong socket, with **potentially** expensive damage resulting.

Assuming that you've got good eyesight to find the right connections and you're happy to wait 30 seconds for each media file to play, the sound quality is exceptional – until the machine starts to stutter and the playback is interrupted.

No doubt there will be a number of early **adopters** of technology who will rush out and buy this, but a more sensible option would be to wait for the design and software bugs to be sorted out and buy version 2, which must surely follow later this year.

Disappointing.

Review by Scott Ligon

Writing for an Audience

Instructions

Instructional writing is very important. If instructions are written well, they make an item easier to operate and make sure that the item is used correctly. If they're poorly written, then things could go wrong.

Below is a set of basic instructions for the Zipple Classic MP3 player:

- The instructions are written as a numbered list to allow the reader to follow them in the correct order.
- Diagrams are used to help clear up things that aren't obvious just from the words.

- Short, simple sentences help the reader take things one step at a time. The word 'you' is used frequently to talk directly to the reader, who is following the instructions.
- Formal vocabulary is used so that instructions can be understood by as wide a range of people as possible.
- Brackets are used to add extra detail to the main advice and instructions.
- Imperative verbs are used to tell someone directly – often near to or at the start of an instruction – what they should do.

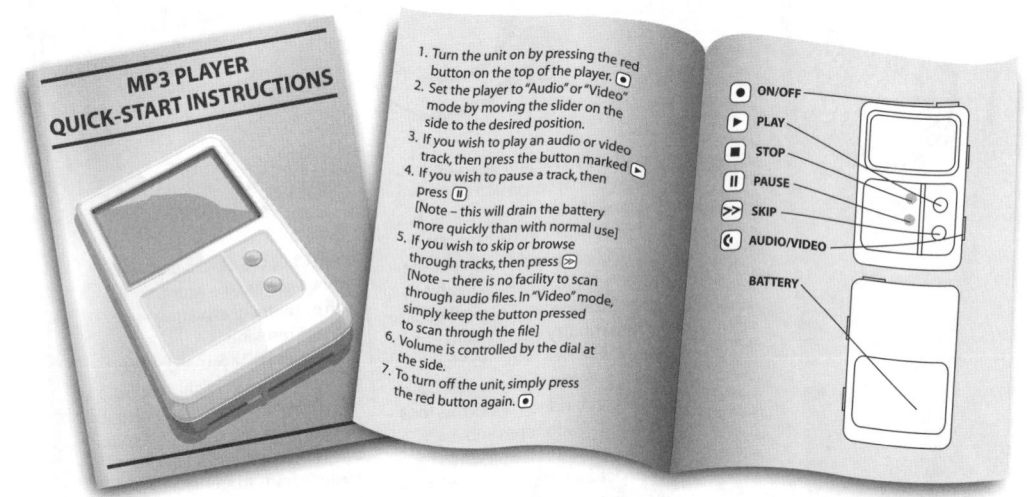

Quick Test

1. Is a letter of complaint an example of fiction or non-fiction?
2. Should a review always have a formal style?
3. Why are numbered lists good for instructions?
4. Why are short sentences good in instructions?
5. Brackets are used to add extra information to instructions – true or false?

Key Words Exercise

What is the correct definition of each key word?

1 Non-fiction
- **a)** Stories
- **b)** Scientific documents
- **c)** Prose writing that is not made up

2 Receipt
- **a)** A written acknowledgment of having received a specified amount of money, goods, etc.
- **b)** A piece of paper
- **c)** Something you throw away

3 Efficient
- **a)** Useful and helpful
- **b)** Performing in the best way possible, combining maximum output with the least effort
- **c)** Well-behaved

4 Specifications
- **a)** A list
- **b)** A detailed set of requirements or features
- **c)** The order in which things work

5 Compatibility
- **a)** Capable of being used with something else
- **b)** Able to be like something else
- **c)** A useful list

6 Potentially
- **a)** Definitely
- **b)** Certainly
- **c)** Possibly

7 Adopters
- **a)** People who do things wrong
- **b)** People who won't try new things
- **c)** People who take on new things

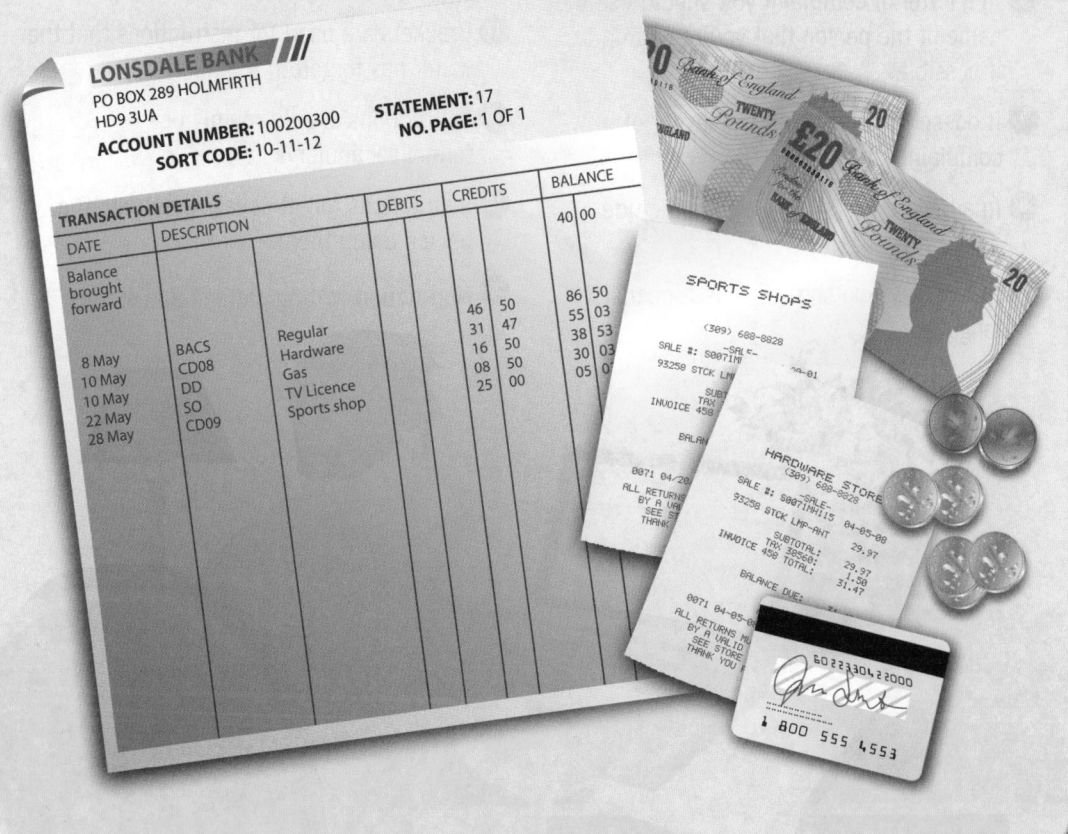

Writing for an Audience

Are the following statements about non-fiction writing true or false?

1. In a letter of complaint you should include the date you sent the letter.

2. In a letter of complaint you should use a formal tone.

3. In a letter of complaint it's good to be sarcastic.

4. In a letter of complaint you should say to the person you are complaining to what you want them to do.

5. You don't need to include your contact information in a complaint letter, as the person you're writing to should have it.

6. In a letter of complaint you should use the name of the person that you're writing to, if possible.

7. It doesn't matter about the layout of a complaint letter.

8. In a review, you should always include a picture.

9. In a review, you shouldn't use specialist language.

10. In a review it's normal to include the name of the person writing the review.

11. In a review you shouldn't include opinions.

12. In a review you shouldn't include facts.

13. Headings are helpful when writing a review.

14. Instructions don't need to be in any particular order.

15. Instructions should mainly use complex, lengthy sentences.

16. Diagrams help people to understand instructions.

17. Brackets are used for instructions that the writer has forgotten to include.

18. Instructions should mainly use formal vocabulary.

19. Instructions might speak directly to the person using them.

20. Non-fiction writing can include stories.

Skills Practice

Write a review of a brand new wrist watch, the Tick-Tock 1200Z, giving your opinions on it.

The review must be between 200 and 250 words and mention the following features of the watch:

- It has a stopwatch and lap-counter.
- It's solar powered so will never need a new battery.
- It's voice-controlled.
- It has a large, clear display.
- It's available in men's and women's designs.
- It's made from shock- and water-proof materials.
- It's very expensive compared to similar watches.

Step 1: Think of a heading for your review that quickly tells the reader your overall opinion of the watch. Decide what order you're going to put your ideas in – make a paragraph-by-paragraph list.

Step 2: Draft your ideas and count how many words you've written. Keep within the word limit, because you're writing for a magazine that only has a certain amount of space. To save space, take out repeated phrases, combine sentences and ideas and decide which information is essential.

Step 3: Choose a rating for your review that matches the overall opinion you've given. Find a review of a similar product in a magazine and look at how much space you will have to write it up. Write your final draft to fit that same space.

Step 4: Find and add an appropriate picture to go with the review. Use ideas from the layout and vocabulary of actual articles to make your writing seem authentic and realistic.

Extension Activity

Imagine that you've bought the watch, but after a few weeks it stops working. Write a letter of complaint asking for a refund or a replacement.

Audience and Purpose

This topic looks at...
- different kinds of purpose
- different kinds of audience
- writing to inform and instruct
- writing for an audience.

Purpose

It's important to recognise that every piece of writing that's produced has a **purpose** and is aimed at a particular **audience**.

The purpose of a piece of writing can vary tremendously – it can range from describing complex ideas on a topic to a scribbled note asking for a parcel to be left next door.

No matter how important or how trivial the writing is or seems, it's likely to have a purpose.

Here are some broad purposes that writing can have (sometimes a piece of writing might have more than one of these purposes):

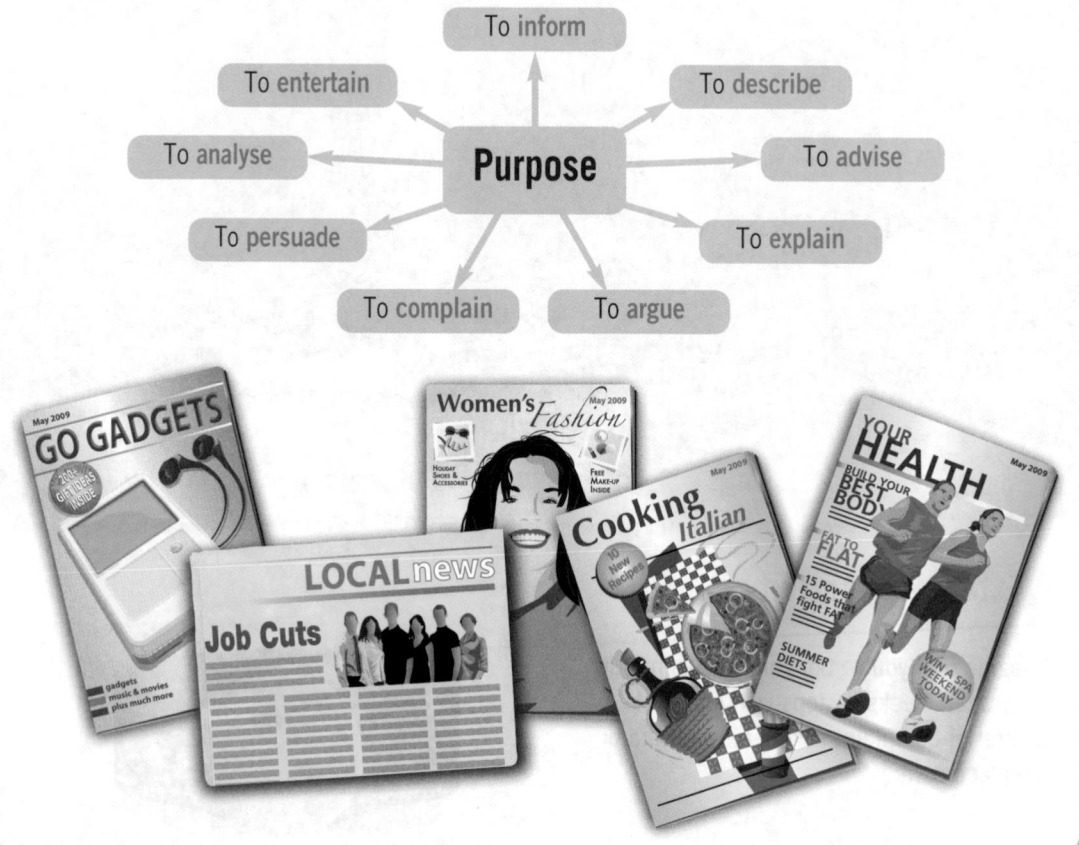

To inform

To entertain

To describe

To analyse

Purpose

To advise

To persuade

To explain

To complain

To argue

Audience

The audience that a piece of writing is aimed at can be as varied as its purpose. The audience could be...

- very broad (e.g. everyone), *or*
- very narrow (one person).

Your writing could be aimed at a particular audience, for example...

- people of a particular age group or gender
- people who do a particular job
- people who share an interest
- an individual person.

How many more types of audience can you think of?

Deciding on Your Audience and Purpose

Although purpose and audience are different things, the two are very closely linked. To decide on the audience and purpose of a piece of writing, you should...

- ask yourself why the piece was written – the answer to that question will tell you the purpose
- ask yourself who the piece is aimed at – the answer to that question will tell you the audience.

Writing to Inform an Individual

Here is a note you might write for your milkman.

The note was written to inform that you only want two pints of milk. It was written for the milkman.

2 pints today please

So, a note to your milkman will have an audience of one person – the milkman – and its purpose will be to inform him of how much milk you want.

Audience and Purpose

Writing to Inform Many People

A national newspaper report might have the same purpose as a milkman's note – to inform – but its audience could be millions of people.

BLIZZARDS BLAST BRITAIN

Yesterday most parts of the country were blasted by gale force winds and blinding blizzards as temperatures plummeted to well below freezing.

Writing to Instruct

A recipe could have the purpose to **instruct** you how to make a particular dish. Its audience might be anyone who's interested in making that dish.

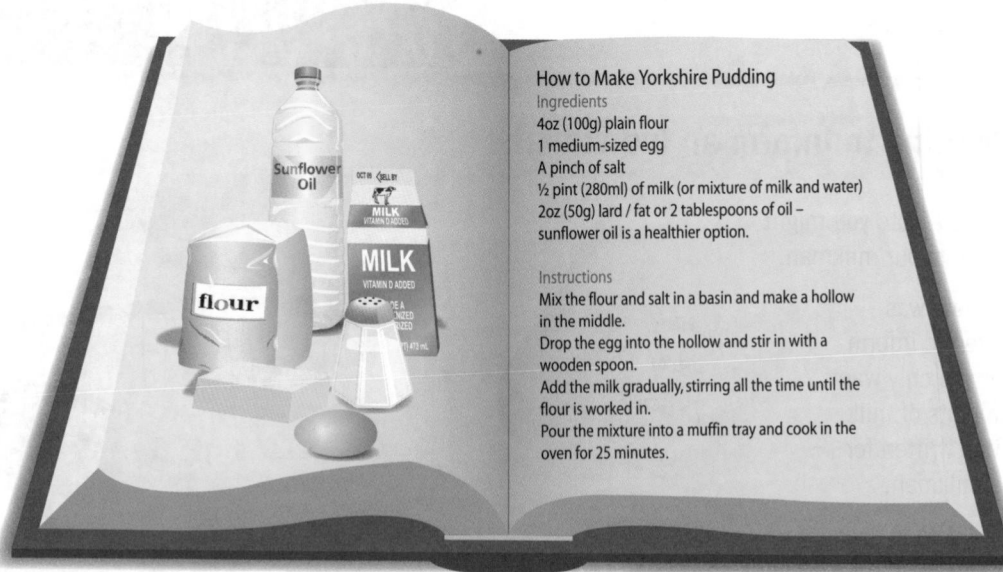

How to Make Yorkshire Pudding

Ingredients
4oz (100g) plain flour
1 medium-sized egg
A pinch of salt
½ pint (280ml) of milk (or mixture of milk and water)
2oz (50g) lard / fat or 2 tablespoons of oil – sunflower oil is a healthier option.

Instructions
Mix the flour and salt in a basin and make a hollow in the middle.
Drop the egg into the hollow and stir in with a wooden spoon.
Add the milk gradually, stirring all the time until the flour is worked in.
Pour the mixture into a muffin tray and cook in the oven for 25 minutes.

Writing for a Particular Audience

A child's nursery rhyme is written for a particular audience. It could have the purpose to entertain and the audience would be young children, such as the following example:

> Hickory, dickory, dock,
> The mouse ran up the clock.
> The clock struck one,
> The mouse ran down,
> Hickory, dickory, dock.

Particular Audiences

The table shows some examples of purposes for writing and the audiences they're aimed at.

💡 *Think about other types of writing and their audiences and purposes.*

Type of Writing	Audience	Purpose
Website giving information on 'cheats' or 'walkthroughs' on a computer game.	Anyone interested in learning more about that computer game.	To inform the audience about ways to get through different levels of the game.
A story from a bedtime story book.	A young child.	To entertain and help them go to sleep.

Quick Test

1. Complete the following sentences:
   a) The _____ is the reason why a piece of writing is written.
   b) If you're not satisfied with something, you might write to _____ .
   c) The purpose of a newspaper is to _____ .
   d) The audience of an identification book on British birds would be _____ .
2. What would be the purpose of a leaflet on how to mend a puncture?

Audience and Purpose

Key Words Exercise

Work out the key words from the clues below, then find them in the word search.

U	J	R	D	E	S	C	R	I	B	E	S	E	W
E	N	T	E	R	T	A	I	N	Y	W	S	E	H
C	C	O	M	P	L	A	I	N	D	O	W	D	Y
E	E	C	B	V	F	W	E	X	P	U	Q	A	H
Y	S	P	E	C	M	M	Q	R	O	D	Y	U	Y
C	Y	N	S	O	E	S	U	C	F	J	C	S	G
I	L	Y	I	E	O	P	K	I	Q	Z	B	R	Z
N	A	D	V	V	C	V	D	C	N	S	H	E	T
S	N	K	D	R	N	N	Z	Y	A	F	C	P	O
T	A	Q	A	M	T	Y	E	O	R	K	O	B	A
R	R	V	M	O	O	X	U	I	C	G	K	R	M
U	A	R	G	U	E	L	I	S	D	Y	L	T	M
C	A	O	H	C	M	L	N	M	F	U	H	E	T
T	S	G	B	R	X	C	E	X	P	L	A	I	N

1 To examine ideas or language carefully.

2 You might do this if you're not happy.

3 Novels and short stories might do this.

4 All writing aims at one of these.

5 Newspapers _____ readers.

6 Writing that gives you a clear picture of a scene could _____ it.

7 Asking yourself why a piece of writing has been written will tell you its _____ .

8 You might do this if you don't agree with someone else's view.

9 You might do this if you want to change someone's mind.

10 A set of instructions for setting up a new computer does this.

11 A leaflet telling you about smoke detectors in the home will _____ you about them.

12 Instructions can help to _____ how to do something.

Give your ideas on the audience and purpose of the following types of writing.

The audience and purpose of each type of writing might not always be clear-cut, but write down your ideas, giving various possibilities.

1. A ghost story.
2. A magazine article on skateboarding.
3. A recipe for onion bhajis.
4. A fairy tale.
5. A '*Kidscape*' web page on school bullying.
6. A newspaper report about a freak snowstorm.
7. A chapter in a text book on Science for lower secondary pupils.
8. A letter of complaint about a faulty camera you bought from eBay.
9. A bedtime story.
10. A homework essay on a Shakespeare play.
11. A '*Doctor Who*' story.
12. The leaflet in a packet of headache tablets.
13. A romantic novel.
14. A guide book on Paris.

Audience and Purpose

Find three different kinds of writing that you come across in everyday life.

You could choose some of the following types:

- A leaflet
- A newspaper report
- Instructions
- A letter
- An advertisement
- An extract from a text book
- An encyclopaedia entry
- The opening of a novel
- A poem
- A review.

Look carefully at the three pieces of writing that you've chosen. For each one...

- identify the audience
- identify the purpose
- analyse how each one uses language – pick out individual words and phrases and say what effects you think they give
- say what effects the layout or presentation has.

Work with a partner and compare the pieces you selected and what you found.

Talk about your findings. Make a chart of your results on a large sheet of paper. You could lay it out like this:

Type of Writing	Purpose	Audience	Language Used	Presentation or Layout

Developing a Point of View

What is Covered in this Topic?

This topic looks at…
* the ways that views can be presented
* writing persuasively.

Presenting a Point of View

Some kinds of writing involve presenting a point of view on a particular topic or issue. Often the point of this writing is to argue a case or **persuade** the reader to take a particular **viewpoint**.

The following piece of writing gives an argument in favour of wind farms. Look carefully at how the writer puts forward her point of view.

Don't Let the Lights Go Out

Do you want to stop climate change? Do you want to use clean, renewable energy that will not harm the environment? If the answer to these questions is YES then you must support the development of wind energy. These farms could provide us and future generations with an energy source that will not run out.

Once the wind farms have been built they provide a clean, renewable source of energy with no pollution or waste products to deal with.

Another point in their favour is that they occupy such a small amount of land. They can be placed on farmland and the farmers can still farm the land around them. If they are no longer required in a certain area they can be dismantled and removed and the environment will not have been harmed.

Some people say they are an eyesore and ruin the landscape, but if they are carefully sited their visual impact can be lessened. On the other hand, some people feel that wind farms are not ugly and don't spoil the views. In contrast they think they look impressive and do not detract from the beauty of the countryside at all. Wind farms can also be built offshore where there is plenty of wind and where they are not even visible from the shore.

If we are to save our environment and keep the lights on, we must act now, otherwise it will be too late. Support wind farms!

Developing a Point of View

Techniques to Add Effect

The use of **rhetorical questions** and **repetition** can add effect to a sentence.

Rhetorical questions...

- are questions that aren't meant to be answered
- are meant to give the impression that the answer is obvious
- are used to add effect and emphasise a viewpoint to writing or speech.

Repetition is used in the wind farm extract to add emphasis to the point, for example, 'Do you want...?', 'Do you want...?'

This repetition makes it clear that the sensible answer must be yes. It's meant to encourage the reader to agree with the writer's views.

By using these techniques, the writer's viewpoint is developed, with points made in favour of wind farms.

Counter Arguments

A **counter argument** is when you take the opposite view of an argument and give points to counter those views.

Here are some useful words and phrases when countering a view that doesn't agree with your own:

- But
- Nevertheless
- Alternatively
- On the other hand
- Some people feel / think
- The most important thing is.

Emphasis

A **warning** of effects or consequences can add emphasis to a piece of writing. For example, the sentence, 'If we are to save our environment and keep the lights on, we must act now otherwise it will be too late' is saying that if you don't do something soon, something will happen that can't be stopped.

The use of **exclamations** adds emphasis to the points made, such as 'Support wind farms!', and creates the impression that the writer is passionate about their views.

Fact and Opinion

When views are expressed on a topic you will probably find that those views contain both **fact** and **opinion**.

Have another look at the piece on wind farms. Can you see both fact and opinion in it?

The table shows some of the facts and opinions that you might have noticed in the wind farm article.

Facts	• Wind farms don't pollute the atmosphere or produce waste products. • Wind farms occupy a relatively small land area. • Wind farms can be taken down. • Wind farms can be built out at sea.
Opinions	• Wind farms are an eyesore. • Wind farms ruin the landscape. • Wind farms look impressive. • Wind farms don't spoil the beauty of the countryside.

Expressing Your Own Views

When writing a piece in which you express your own views on a topic, it's important that you plan carefully.

You could use the following approach when **planning** your piece:

1. Think carefully about the topic you're going to write about and make sure that you're clear in your mind about it.
2. Decide on your point of view.
3. Write down all the ideas you can think of both *for* and *against* the view you've taken.
4. Decide on the points you're going to make.
5. Arrange your points in a logical order that develops your ideas clearly.
6. Think about the evidence you'll use to support your views.
7. Decide how you're going to end your piece of writing.

Developing a Point of View

Structuring Your Writing

You can now plan the **structure** of your writing:

1. Introduction – an opening paragraph in which you catch your reader's attention and make the topic clear. It should also explain your basic point of view.
2. Main section – presents the points in favour of the view you're taking, giving reasons and evidence to support it. You could also include points that don't agree with your view and counter them.
3. Conclusion – briefly sums up your ideas and emphasises your point of view. You need to think of a way to create some kind of impact at the end that leaves your reader thinking.

Use different **techniques** to make your points, for example…

- rhetorical questions
- repetition
- counter arguments
- warnings
- exclamations.

Don't over-use any of these techniques, especially exclamations, rhetorical questions and repetition – they'll lose their impact if you use them too much.

Remember that you need to…

- create an impact in your opening
- express your views clearly
- structure your ideas logically
- support your points with evidence
- use other viewpoints and counter them
- have a strong conclusion.

Wind farms

Eyesore?
Impressive?

FACTS – Don't pollute
– No waste

Quick Test

1. True or false – an opinion is definitely true.
2. True or false – a rhetorical question requires an answer.
3. True or false – writing needs careful planning.
4. True or false – an exclamation can add emphasis.
5. True or false – if you use any one technique too much it can lose its effect.

KEY WORDS
Make sure you understand these words before moving on!

- Persuade
- Viewpoint
- Rhetorical question
- Repetition
- Counter argument
- Warning
- Exclamation
- Fact
- Opinion
- Planning
- Structure
- Techniques

Work out the key words from the clues below, then complete the crossword.

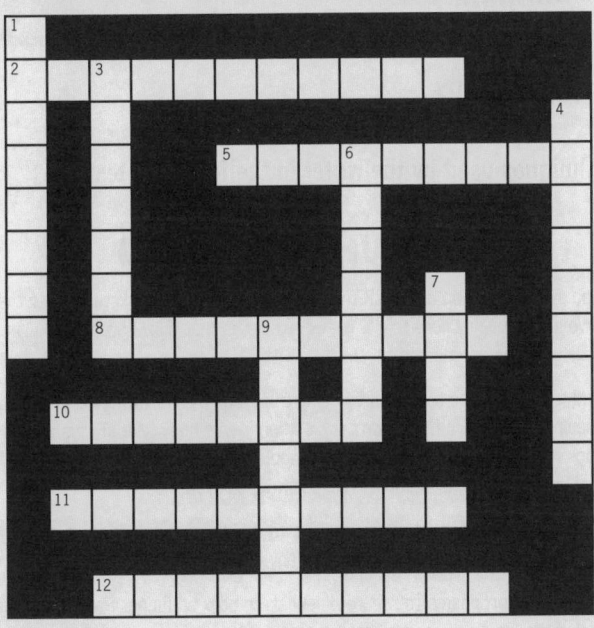

Across

2. You shouldn't use these too much! (11)
5. A way of looking at things. (9)
8. Don't bother answering this question. (10)
10. A good piece of writing requires thinking ahead. (8)
11. A technique that can be used to emphasise a point. (10)
12. You might use a variety of these to make your writing more effective. (10)

Down

1. Give a point of view to influence the reader. (8)
3. You might give this kind of argument when you don't agree with someone's point of view. (7)
4. To present your views effectively you need to arrange them in an order. (9)
6. Take notice of this if you know what's good for you. (7)
7. No question about this. (4)
9. This might be true – or maybe not. (7)

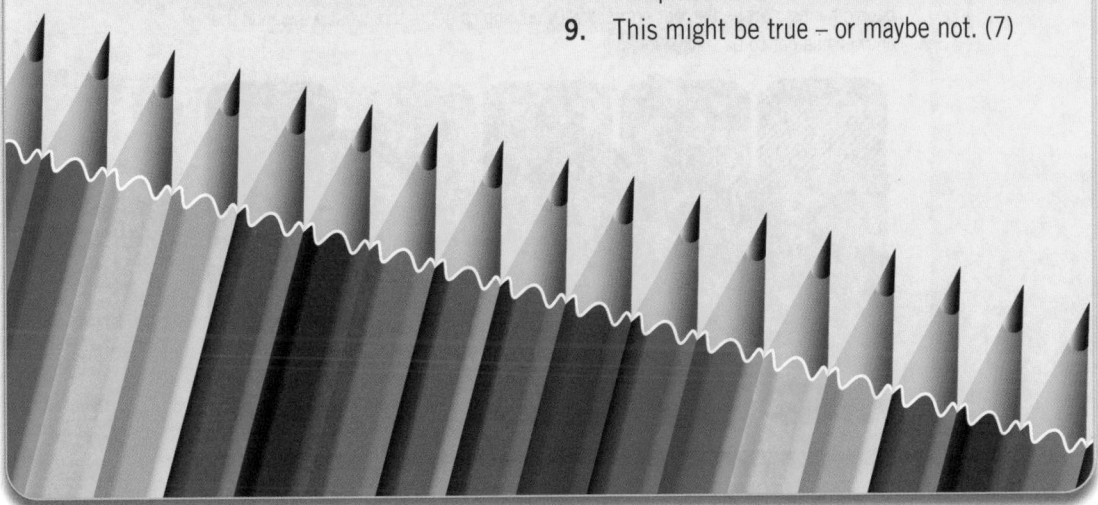

Developing a Point of View

Testing Understanding

Identify the seven techniques used by the writer in the following text.

NOWHERE TO GO

1

Have you ever felt like an outcast? That's what it's like to be a skateboarder these days. We just have nowhere to go. It's as simple as that. Nowhere to go. Why is that? Well your guess is as good as mine.

2

We used to skate in the town centre using the steps by the Town Hall and the ramps in the car park. Of course, we didn't try it when it was busy. We always waited until the shops had closed and it was quiet. If people were around, we moved on. We don't go out of our way to annoy people. We just want to skate.

3

The trouble is, we have nowhere to go. The council has banned us from skating in the town centre but have not provided us with any facilities.

There have been proposals to create a new skate park at Tunnet Park but it has been reported in the local newspaper that these proposals have been turned down and this has been confirmed by Councillor Lamber. This was because of the number of objections from people. Some people seem to feel that skateboarders are hooligans out to cause trouble. On the other hand, all the evidence from areas where skate parks have been built shows that young people who use the skate parks don't cause any trouble and no longer try to skate in the town.

5

6

Another argument that some people use is that the skate park would take up a huge part of the park. In fact, the plans show that the skating ramps would occupy an area of 60m long by 40m wide, with the highest ramp being 5m high. This is a very small part of the park, which is a mile long and nearly a mile wide.

4

The nearest skate park is almost 30 miles away and that is too far to use on a regular basis. Other facilities are poor too. The nearest swimming pool is twenty miles away. There is one playing field and very few clubs for young people to go to. If young people in our town are not provided with better facilities then we are likely to see more young people hanging around street corners with nothing to do. Is this what we want? The answer has got to be – No! No! No!

7

Choose a topic that you feel strongly about and prepare your ideas, ready to write a persuasive essay on it.

Step 1: Choose your topic. Make sure you choose a topic that you have views about.

Step 2: Make sure you're clear what your views on the topic are.

Step 3: Write down all your ideas on the topic. It's useful to make a list of all the points both *for* and *against* the view you've taken. You might want to use some of the arguments against your view to counter them.

Step 4: Decide on the key points that you're going to make and what evidence you're going to use to support them.

Step 5: Structure your ideas in a logical order.

Step 6: Think about how you're going to finish your piece of writing. Remember that you should try to leave your reader thinking about the points you've raised.

Step 7: Write a rough draft of your essay and then check through it carefully.

Step 8: Make any changes you think necessary to improve it further and do a final draft.

Using the ideas from the essay you wrote, prepare a talk on the topic. Your talk shouldn't last more than five minutes.

When preparing your talk...
- **decide how much information you're going to include**
- **write a list of the points that you're going to make.**

You might find it helpful to prepare some small cards with short words or phrases on to prompt your memory and make sure that you don't miss anything out.

Don't...
- write out your speech in full
- try to learn your speech as it'll sound unnatural when you give it
- try to read out your speech because then it's more like reading out an essay – using only prompt cards will help you to resist the temptation to rely on notes.

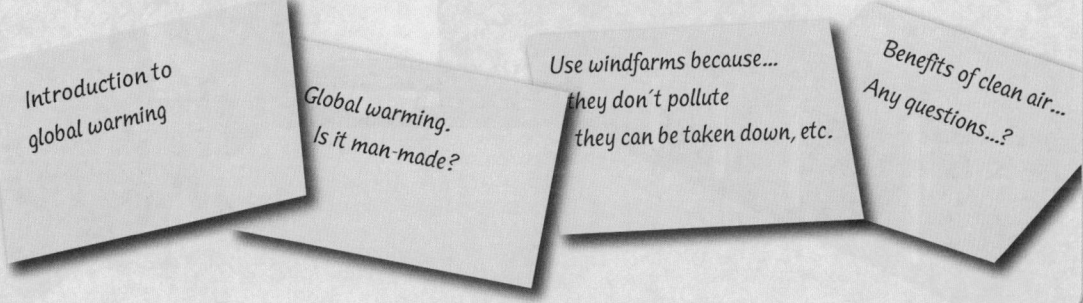

Introduction to global warming

Global warming. Is it man-made?

Use windfarms because... they don't pollute they can be taken down, etc.

Benefits of clean air... Any questions...?

Presenting Information 1

What is Covered in This Topic?

This topic looks at...
- different forms of information
- different techniques for presenting information.

Information

Information comes in many different forms and can be **presented** in lots of different ways.

The diagram shows some forms of information that you might have noticed before.

Although these are very different kinds of writing, they have one thing in common – their **purpose**.

Their purpose is to inform the reader in one way or another. They may have other purposes too, but to inform the reader is a key one.

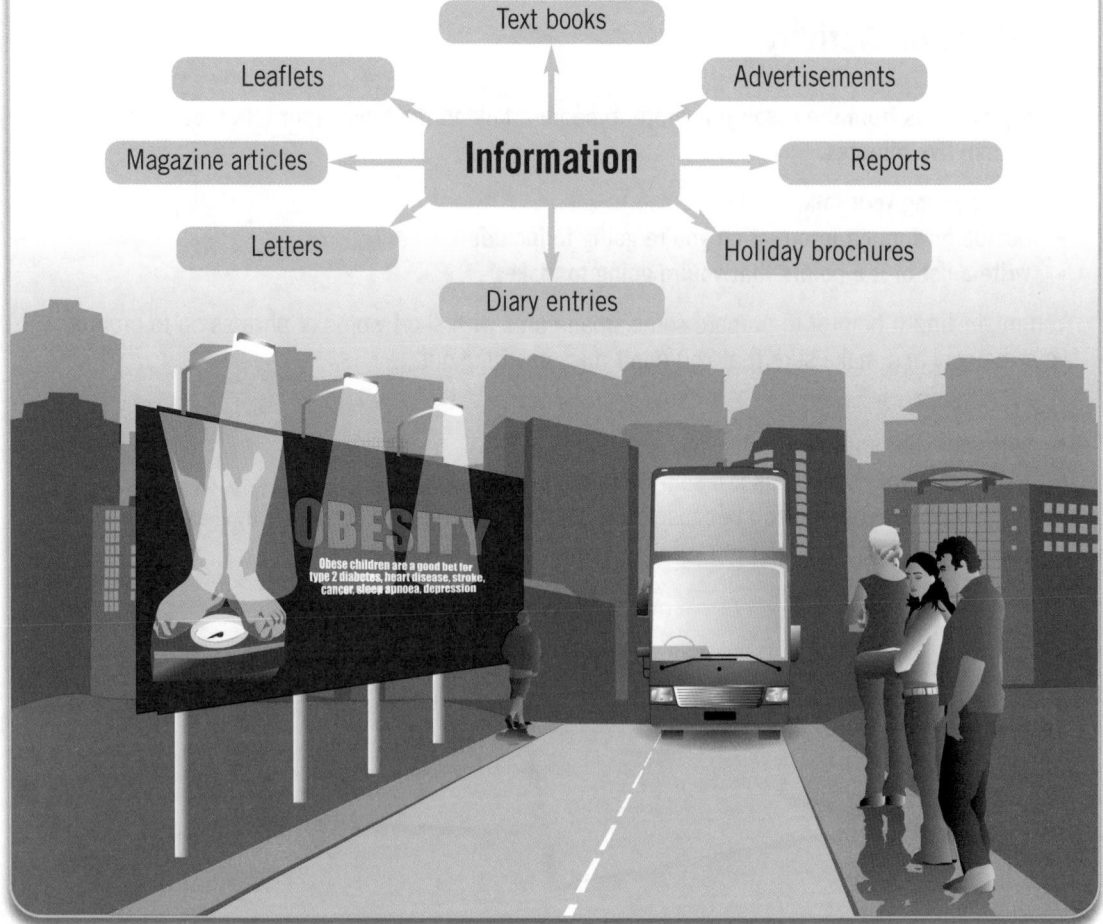

Text books

Leaflets

Advertisements

Magazine articles → **Information** ← Reports

Letters

Holiday brochures

Diary entries

OBESITY

Obese children are a good bet for type 2 diabetes, heart disease, stroke, cancer, sleep apnoea, depression

Information presented in texts should be clear and easy to understand.

Various **techniques** can be used to present information in an **interesting** and **effective** way.

There are many typical features that you might find used when presenting information.

Headings

Sub-headings

Bullet points

Different **fonts**

Different sizes of letters

Use of colour

Bold print

Underlining

Diagrams

Photographs

Graphs and **charts**

Tables

THIS IS A HEADING
This is the sub-heading of this poster

It includes:
- bullet points
- bullet points
- bullet points

Also **different** fonts USED in text

Different sizes of **letters used**

Use of colour within text

Words stand out using **BOLD** text or by <u>underlining</u>

Also use tables, charts and graphs

Facts	• Wind farms don't pollute the atmosphere or produce waste products. • Wind farms occupy a relatively small land area.
Opinions	• Wind farms are an eyesore. • Wind farms ruin the landscape. • Wind farms look impressive. • Wind farms don't spoil the beauty of the countryside.

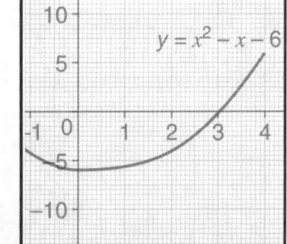

$y = x^2 - x - 6$

Presenting Information 1

Identifying Techniques

Look at the following leaflet to see how information is presented.

How many features of presenting information can you spot in this leaflet? Think about the effects they create.

A range of techniques are used to make the holiday leaflet interesting, easy to read and full of detailed information.

The leaflet uses some of the following techniques:

- Large letters draw attention to key messages, for example, 'Loads to do' and 'Exciting indoor and outdoor fun pools'.
- Use of sub-headings.
- Use of bullet points to list special attractions.
- Language to attract the reader, for example, 'relax', large', 'superb'.
- The idea that the weather conditions don't matter.
- Details of prices.
- Eye-catching illustrations.
- Use of colour.
- Opening times are given.
- Map to show location.
- Further details, for example, telephone number, e-mail address, web address.

Quick Test

1. What does all writing that presents information have in common?
2. Complete the following sentence: When you're presenting information in writing, it should be _____ and _____.
3. Why would you use bullet points in a piece of writing?
4. What are fonts?
5. What techniques other than writing could you use to present information?

KEY WORDS

Make sure you understand these words before moving on!

- Information
- Presented
- Purpose
- Technique
- Interesting
- Effective
- Heading
- Bullet point
- Font
- Diagram
- Photograph
- Graph
- Chart
- Table

Presenting Information 1

Unscramble the anagrams to find the key words, then copy and complete the crossword.

Across

1. Quenchite
3. Ahendig
8. Fevetfice
10. Tublel toinp (2 words)
13. Raidgam
14. Spendtree

Down

2. Thrac
4. Monitorfain
5. Tennistiger
6. Taleb
7. Ghothoprap
9. Sorepup
11. Pargh
12. Tonf

Carefully read the following holiday brochure and look at the kind of information that it contains.

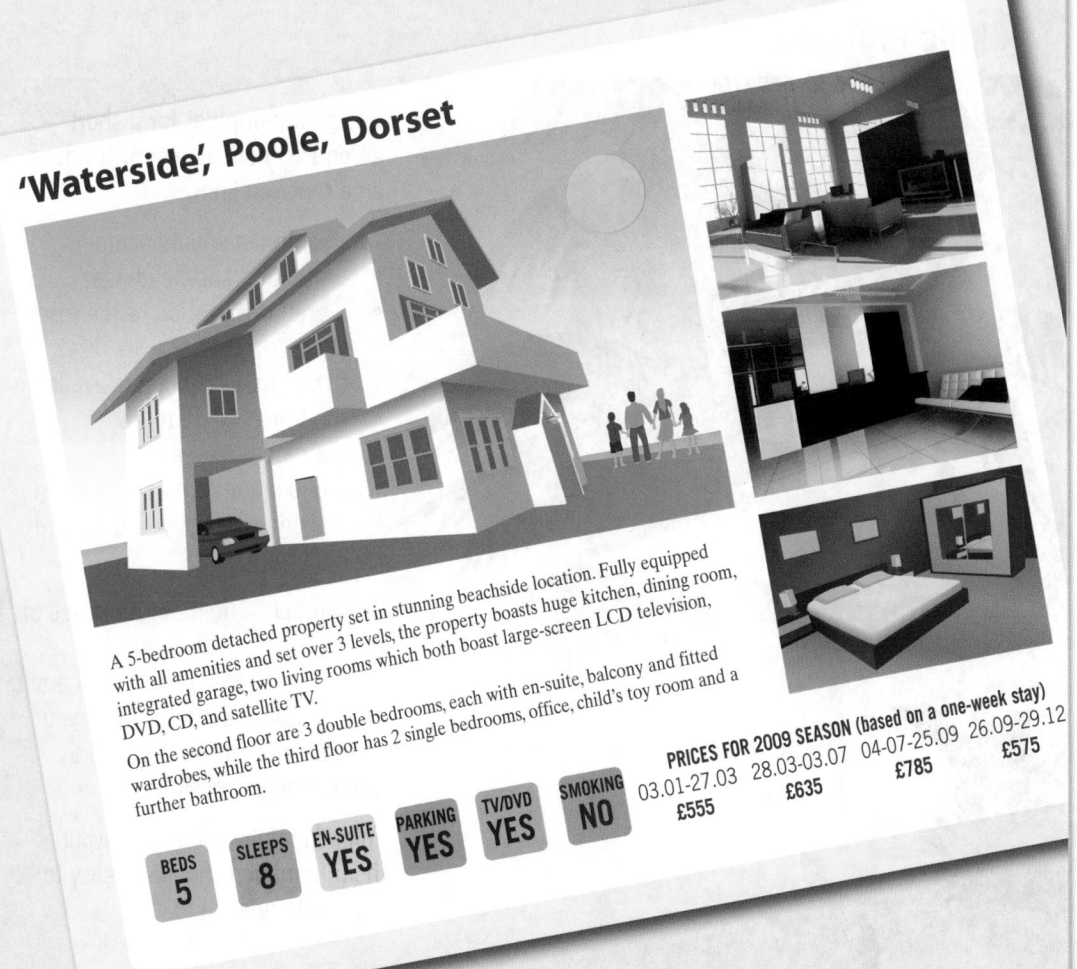

'Waterside', Poole, Dorset

A 5-bedroom detached property set in stunning beachside location. Fully equipped with all amenities and set over 3 levels, the property boasts huge kitchen, dining room, integrated garage, two living rooms which both boast large-screen LCD television, DVD, CD, and satellite TV.

On the second floor are 3 double bedrooms, each with en-suite, balcony and fitted wardrobes, while the third floor has 2 single bedrooms, office, child's toy room and a further bathroom.

BEDS 5 | **SLEEPS** 8 | **EN-SUITE** YES | **PARKING** YES | **TV/DVD** YES | **SMOKING** NO

PRICES FOR 2009 SEASON (based on a one-week stay)

03.01-27.03	28.03-03.07	04-07-25.09	26.09-29.12
£555	£635	£785	£575

1. What do you notice about how the information is presented here?
   Make a list of your ideas.

2. See if you can easily find out the following information from how it's presented in the brochure above.
   a) How many does the property sleep?
   b) Does it have a TV and DVD player?
   c) Does it have a parking space?
   d) Is smoking allowed?
   e) Is it close to the beach?
   f) How much would it cost to rent the cottage for a week in February?
   g) What's the most expensive time to rent it for a week and how much does it cost?

Presenting Information 1

Design a pamphlet for a short guide to a holiday resort, town, or area that you know well.

Your pamphlet should contain...
- a title and sub-headings
- a brief description of the resort, town or area
- the various attractions available
- the things to do there
- the places to see
- the location or map
- any other things you think are important.

Remember – the main purposes of your writing are to inform the reader about your chosen place and to persuade them to visit, so you need to try to make it sound as interesting as possible.

Think carefully about the layout – the information should be easy to read and understand.

Extension Activity

Exchange your pamphlet with a partner and see what you think of each other's ideas.

Make a list of comments and make any changes that you think would improve it. Then try producing a version of it on a computer, using different fonts and colours to make it more persuasive.

Presenting Information 2

This topic looks at...
- how advice and information can be presented
- different techniques to present advice and information
- analysing advice leaflets.

The Purpose of Advice and Information Texts

Advice and **information** texts can take many forms, but the most common forms that you're likely to come across are **leaflets**, **pamphlets**, advice sheets and **posters**.

The main **purpose** of these kinds of texts is to give clear information or advice in a brief, quick and interesting way.

As their main purpose is to advise and inform, most texts of this kind contain lots of **facts**. The way that **language** is used is very important.

Features of Advice and Information Texts

A variety of **techniques** can be used to **present** information clearly and effectively. Here are some of the techniques that are often used:
- headings
- sub-headings
- bullet points
- different fonts
- bold print
- underlining
- colour
- illustrations.

A **slogan** – an eye-catching phrase that captures the reader's attention – is sometimes used in this kind of writing.

Sport

A Game of Two Halves

Analysing Advice Leaflets

Now look at this advice card.

💡 *What features are used and what effect do they create?*

The heading is a kind of slogan – it also makes use of a pun – it plays with the well-known expression 'lighten up' and uses it here to mean 'lighten up' your house by keeping lights on to deter burglars.

Bullet point list to advises on ways to reduce the risk of burglary. Note that this list is quite short and the points give the essential information briefly so that the reader can take in the main points quickly and easily.

A series of 'Top Tips' gives advice on how to use lighting to deter burglars. These contain more information about various things that you can do with some specific details, e.g. types of switch, photo-electric cells, as well as the kind of lighting that isn't recommended.

Illustrations to show the difference in appearance between the house lit up and the one in darkness linked to the question 'Which home is more attractive to a burglar?'

The use of bold capital letters to emphasise how using lighting can deter burglars.

Advice on how you can find out more information.

Telephone number given in bold, which makes it clear and easy to read.

LIGHTEN UP

Which home is more attractive to a burglar?

You can reduce the risk of becoming the victim of a burglary by
- leaving a light on inside the house
- using a timer switch to turn inside lights on
- using outside lighting

USING LIGHTING IN THIS WAY CAN ACT AS A DETERRENT TO BURGLARS

For further Crime Prevention Information please contact the Crime Reduction Officer at your local Police Station.

Tel: 0845 606 0 606

Or refer to the West Yorkshire Police website:

www.westyorkshire.police.uk

Yorkshire & Humber
CRIMESTOPPERS
0800 555 111
working in partnership with the police

WEST YORKSHIRE POLICE

Strikeback
stinging the criminals!

Card number 7

LIGHTEN UP
TOP TIPS

- Leave a light on in more than one well-used room such as the lounge and bedroom, and vary the room you illuminate to avoid predictability

- Use a timer switch to operate the lights as it starts to get dark, especially during autumn and winter, when the days are shorter - frequently change the times that the light comes on so that times do not become predictable

- Outdoor security lighting should operate either on a timer switch or permanently from dusk to dawn - low energy lighting that is controlled by a photo-electric cell (a light sensitive, dusk to dawn switch) is recommended as it is very energy efficient and inexpensive to run - West Yorkshire Police do not recommend the use of movement activated (PIR) lighting

- Outdoor lights, including all wiring should be sited out of reach.

- Privacy for you is also privacy for the burglar to work unseen - keep plants and hedges trimmed and illuminate the dark corners of your premises

Produced by HQ Community Safety

Some advice and information texts only use a few words to put across their message. The words that are used, though, are very carefully chosen to create the effects required.

Look at this example:

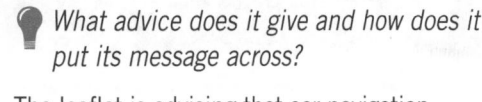

The only thing it can't find is itself!

Please remove all belongings from your vehicle when leaving it unoccupied

💡 *What advice does it give and how does it put its message across?*

The leaflet is advising that car navigation systems (and other valuables) should be removed from cars when the car is left unoccupied.

The large image of the 'sat nav' dominates the leaflet and draws attention to the idea that they are probably the main targets for thieves these days.

The heading 'The only thing it can't find is itself' has a humorous tone to it while at the same time putting across a serious message.

It has a strong visual impact and the clever combination of carefully chosen words and image creates this effect.

Presenting Information 2

When analysing an advice or information leaflet you need to adopt a structured approach to your analysis. Here is a checklist of things that you could look for and comment on.

Overall impact	Before you start to look at the leaflet in detail, think about your initial impression of it and the effect it has on you.
Heading	What kind of effect does the heading create? Think about the language they use, e.g. puns, a slogan and the presentation (e.g. size and colour). Are sub-headings used?
Content	What kind of information is given? How is language used? You should comment on examples of specific words and phrases and the effects they create when analysing leaflets. Are facts or opinions used? Are questions used?
Presentation	How is the information presented? Look for features such as the use of bullet points, illustrations, tables, boxes, different fonts and colours.

Quick Test

Complete the sentences below.

1. Secondary headings are called

   _____.

2. Different styles of lettering are called

   _____.

3. A pun is a play on _____.

4. A good slogan will capture the reader's

   _____.

Complete the following sentences by finding the missing key words.

1. Things that are true are called _____.

2. Advice and information leaflets use a variety of _____ to present ideas.

3. A list of ideas can be presented as a series of _____

   _____.

4. Diagrams and _____ can be used to help make the information clear.

5. The first thing you read on an advice leaflet is usually the _____.

6. Information and advice is often presented in the form of a pamphlet, _____

   or _____.

7. The main _____ of these kinds of texts is to give clear advice

   and information.

8. The recommending of a certain kind of action or behaviour is called _____.

9. Plays on words are called _____.

10. Advice leaflets tell you things and give you lots of _____.

11. The purpose of leaflets is to _____ information clearly and straightforwardly

    and to do this _____ needs to be used effectively.

12. A catchy phrase is called a _____.

Healthy
Eating

You are what you eat!

A good diet is central to overall good health, but which are the best foods to include in your meals, and which ones are best avoided? This section looks at the facts, to help you make realistic, informed choices.

Presenting Information 2

Testing Understanding

Write an analysis of the following advice leaflet, commenting on the following:
- The effects of the heading.
- The content and language.
- The presentation and techniques used.
- The overall effectiveness of the leaflet.

TOP TIPS – for warm weather

- Your dog should always be able to move into a cooler, ventilated environment if he/she is feeling hot.
- Never leave your dog alone in a car. If you want to take your dog with you on a car journey, make sure that your destination is dog-friendly – you won't be able to leave your dog in the car and you don't want your day out to be ruined!
- If you have to leave your dog outside, you must provide a cool, shady spot where he/she can escape from the sun at all times of the day.
- Make sure your dog always has a good supply of drinking water, in a weighted bowl that can't be knocked over. Carry water with you on hot days and give your dog frequent small amounts.
- Never leave your dog in a glass conservatory or a caravan. Even if it is cloudy when you leave, the sun may come out later in the day and make it unbearably hot.
- Groom your dog regularly to get rid of excess hair. Give long-coated breeds a hair-cut at the start of summer, and later in the season, if necessary.
- Dogs need exercise, even when it is hot, but walk your dog early in the morning or later in the evening. Never allow your dog to exercise excessively in hot weather.
- Dogs can get sunburned too – particularly those with light coloured noses or light coloured fur on their ears – ask your vet for advice on pet-safe sunscreen.

RSPCA

STAY COOL

On a warm day cars heat up like ovens so don't take your dog along for the ride.

RSPCA, Wilberforce Way, Southwater, Horsham, West Sussex RH13 9RS   Tel: 0300 1234 555
A charity registered in England and Wales. Charity no 219099
PB3 4.09

Printed on 55% recycled paper/ 45% virgin fibre sourced from sustainable forests

Skills Practice

Design your own advice / information poster on a topic of your choice.

Think carefully about the following when designing your poster:
- Your use of headings / sub-headings.
- Your use of language.
- Your use of techniques to make your presentation more effective.

When you have finished your poster write an analysis of it explaining what overall effects you wanted to achieve and what decisions you made when designing it.

You should explain...
- why you chose the heading
- how you decided on the advice / information to include
- the effects you wanted to achieve through language
- the effects you wanted to achieve through presentation.

Extension Activity

Design a short questionnaire asking for views on how well your poster put across the advice / information. Ask three or four other people to look at your poster and fill in your questionnaire, and then examine the results carefully to see if you think there is any way you could improve your poster.

QUESTIONNAIRE

How effective are the two headings?

How effective are the sub-headings?

Do you think the language has impact?

Do you think this poster could be improved? If so, give some suggestions.

Writing Formal Letters

What is Covered in this Topic?

This topic looks at...
- the purposes of writing formal letters
- setting out a letter
- using language.

Formal Letters

Although communication by e-mail is very common nowadays, letters of all kinds are still written and received everyday. Some are handwritten (in fact some job advertisements still ask for a handwritten letter of **application**), but the vast majority are word processed and some letters are mass produced.

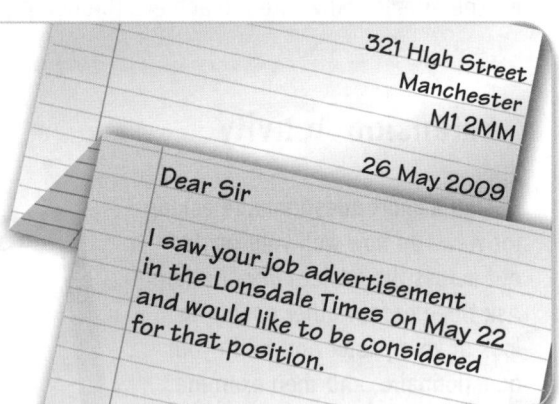

321 High Street
Manchester
M1 2MM

26 May 2009

Dear Sir

I saw your job advertisement in the Lonsdale Times on May 22 and would like to be considered for that position.

The Purposes of Formal Letters

Formal (or 'business') letters are written for a wide variety of purposes.

Here are some of the purposes:

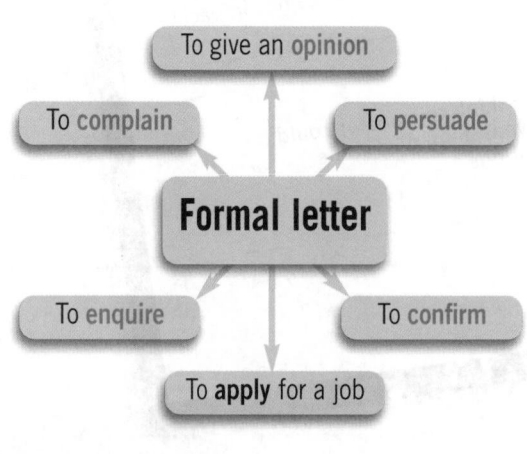

To give an opinion

To complain

To persuade

Formal letter

To enquire

To confirm

To **apply** for a job

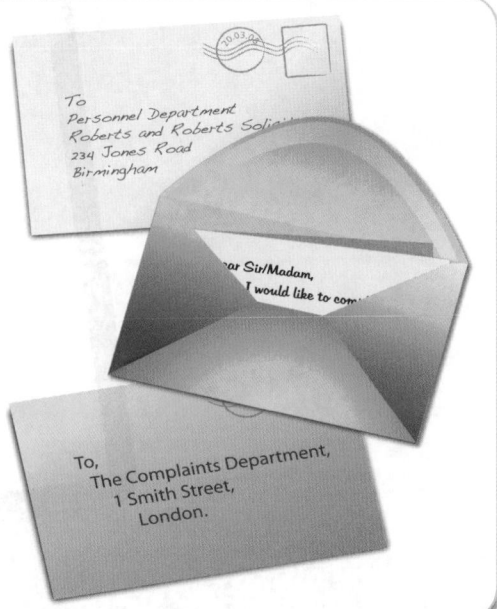

To
Personnel Department
Roberts and Roberts Solic...
234 Jones Road
Birmingham

ear Sir/Madam,
I would like to com...

To,
The Complaints Department,
1 Smith Street,
London.

How to Lay Out a Formal Letter

Here is an example of a formal letter.

💡 *What elements do you notice?*

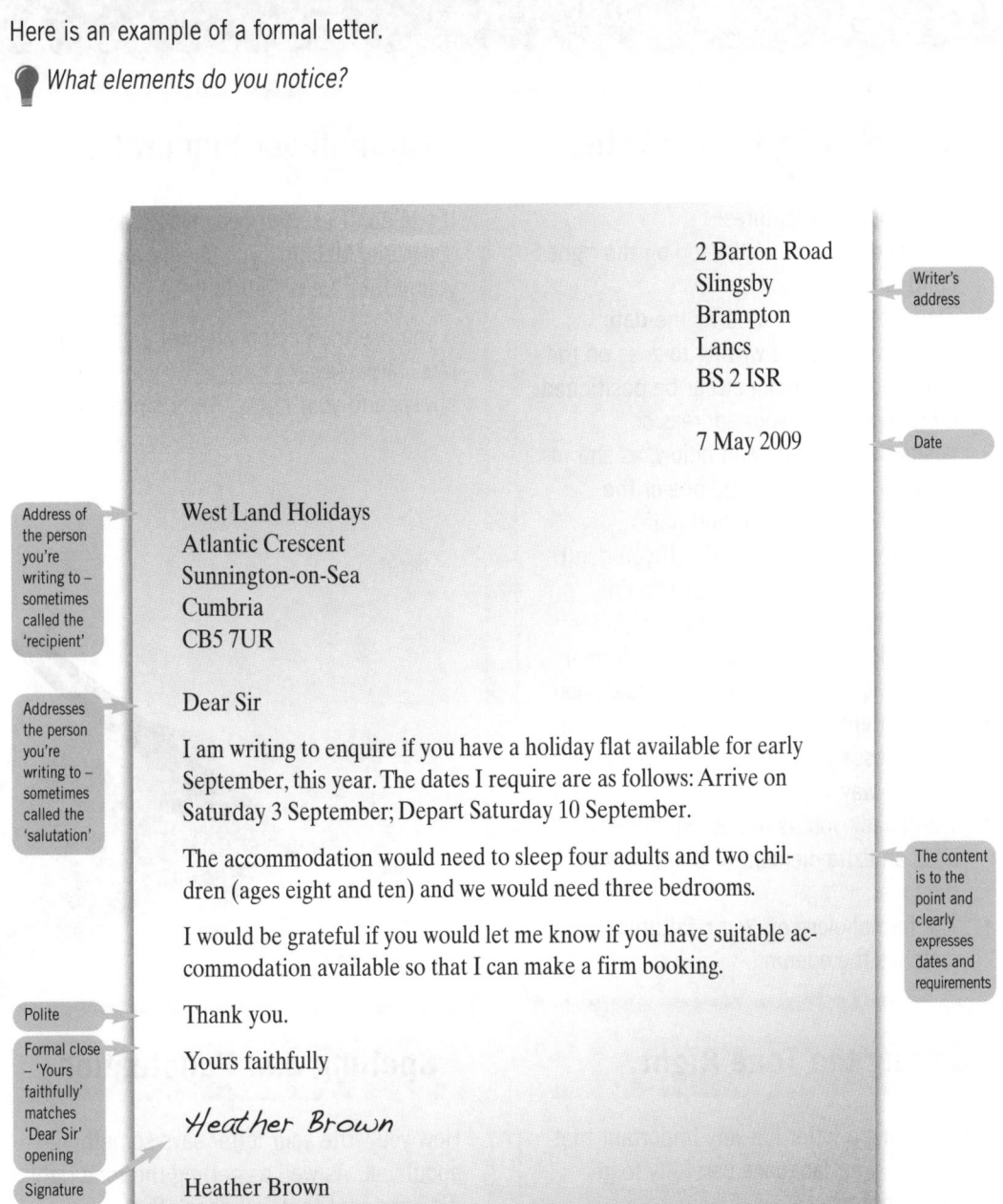

Writer's address

2 Barton Road
Slingsby
Brampton
Lancs
BS 2 ISR

Date

7 May 2009

Address of the person you're writing to – sometimes called the 'recipient'

West Land Holidays
Atlantic Crescent
Sunnington-on-Sea
Cumbria
CB5 7UR

Addresses the person you're writing to – sometimes called the 'salutation'

Dear Sir

I am writing to enquire if you have a holiday flat available for early September, this year. The dates I require are as follows: Arrive on Saturday 3 September; Depart Saturday 10 September.

The accommodation would need to sleep four adults and two children (ages eight and ten) and we would need three bedrooms.

I would be grateful if you would let me know if you have suitable accommodation available so that I can make a firm booking.

The content is to the point and clearly expresses dates and requirements

Polite

Thank you.

Formal close – 'Yours faithfully' matches 'Dear Sir' opening

Yours faithfully

Heather Brown

Signature

Heather Brown

N.B. When writing formal letters you can also punctuate with commas, e.g. after the address, salutation and formal close. Either way is acceptable.

Writing Formal Letters

Features of a Formal Letter

Note the following features:

- Your **address** goes at the top on the right hand side.
- The address is followed by the **date**.
- The address you're writing to goes on the left hand side (it can either be positioned directly opposite your address or positioned opposite and below, as shown on page 26. It should be one or the other, though, not half and half.)
- The letter begins 'Dear Sir'. If you don't know the name of the person you're writing to then you should use either 'Dear Sir' or 'Dear Madam'. This formal opening is sometimes called the '**salutation**'.
- The **content** of the letter is clear and all the necessary information is given in a concise way.
- The 'Thank you' is not essential but it adds an extra element of politeness to the tone.
- The formal close of 'Yours **faithfully**' matches the opening.

Faithfully or Sincerely?

If you don't use the person's name, e.g. 'Dear Sir / Madam', you should always end your letter 'Yours faithfully'.

If you use the person's name, e.g. 'Dear Mr / Mrs / Miss / Ms _____', you should always end your letter 'Yours **sincerely**'.

Getting the Tone Right

When writing a letter it's very important that you choose your **language** carefully to get the **tone** right.

Whatever your purpose in writing the letter, you're likely to get a much better response if you use a **polite** tone.

Even if you're complaining you still need to be polite. If you're unpleasant or abusive, the person reading your letter isn't likely to want to help you.

Spelling and Punctuation

How you write your letter says something about you. As well as getting the tone right it's important that you check that your spelling and punctuation are correct.

Letters of Complaint

Look at the following example:

Heather Brown succeeded in booking her holiday, but unfortunately things didn't go as smoothly as she had hoped and so she had to write to complain to the company.

Here are two possible approaches she might have taken. Which do you think is the most effective?

Dear Mr James

I am writing to complain about the holiday flat booked through your company that we used for our family holiday two weeks ago. I can honestly say that I have never stayed in such a dump in all my life. It was like a slum and hardly anything worked. Your brochure said it was well equipped but that was rubbish because it wasn't.

I would like you to give me my money back or I will never book with you again.

Yours sincerely

Heather Brown

Dear Mr James

I would like to complain about the holiday flat that we stayed in recently and booked through your company. Unfortunately the flat did not live up to the description in your brochure. It was clear that the flat had not been properly cleaned as the carpet and some of the crockery was dirty. The light in one of the bedrooms did not work and the grill on the oven was broken. There were only three glasses and two teaspoons even though the flat was meant to sleep six people.

I'm sure that you will agree that this is not satisfactory and would be grateful if you would look into the matter for me. Under the circumstances I feel that a refund of at least part of the rental fee would be justified.

Yours sincerely

Heather Brown

Quick Test

1. What goes under your address on a letter?
2. If you began a letter 'Dear Mrs Nugent' how would you end it?
3. When would you use 'Yours faithfully'?
4. Where does your address go on a letter?

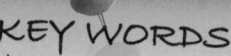

KEY WORDS

Make sure you understand these words before moving on!

- Application
- Formal
- Business
- Complain
- Opinion
- Persuade
- Confirm
- Enquire
- Address
- Date
- Salutation
- Content
- Faithfully
- Sincerely
- Language
- Tone
- Polite

Writing Formal Letters

Unscramble these anagrams and link them to the correct definition.

When applying for a job your letter of application should be a _____ letter.

NICELYRES

If you use the person's name you should end your letter 'Yours _____'.

ATED

Another term for a formal letter is a _____ letter.

SADREDS

You should put the _____ under the address.

PIELOT

If you're not happy with something you might write a letter to _____ .

ENTO

In the top right hand side you put your _____ .

AHFITLYFLU

When you apply for a job you usually write a letter of _____ .

NOTCENT

In a letter you should always be _____ .

ASNAILTOUT

If you want someone to agree with your view you try to _____ them.

MONCRIF

Choosing the right words is important to get the right _____ .

QUIREEN

In a letter you might express your own _____ .

ADRUPEES

If you begin a letter 'Dear Sir' or 'Dear Madam' you should end it 'Yours _____'.

INPOINO

If you want to find something out you might _____ about it.

CAPTAINPOIL

MANICLOP

What you write in your letter is called the _____ .

SUBSINES

If you want to make sure you're booked on a holiday you would write to _____ the dates and other details.

RALFOM

The formal opening part of the letter is known as the _____ .

Read the following letter carefully and identify any mistakes or problems that you find in it.

7 Dymock Road
Haweschester
Buckdenshire
HW4 2RT

Zippo Computers
18 Cockerbury Trading Park
Wetherbury
Northshire
WE3 6TU

Dear Sir

I recently bought a new series 1000 XPZ laptop computer from you by mail order. Unfortunaly something seems to have gone wrong with it. When I switch it on their is a loud buzzing sound, the screen goes blue and then the computer shuts down. I rung youre customer services depatment and thay said I needed to write to you explaining the problem.

I think this is rubbish service and you had better do something about it.

Yours sincerely

I. M. Moody

I. M. Moody

Writing Formal Letters

1 Write a letter complaining about something that you have bought recently that has proved to be faulty.

In your letter make sure that you...
- explain the problem clearly and straightforwardly
- state when and where you bought the item
- say what you would expect them to do
- use a polite and reasonable tone throughout.

2 Write a letter to a travel company confirming your holiday booking.

You should make sure that you cover the following points in your letter:
- The exact dates of your holiday – making sure that your arrival and departure dates are clearly stated.
- The accommodation that you have booked, e.g. the number of bedrooms, facilities, etc.
- The number of adults and children that will be arriving.
- Any other information that you think is important.

Extension Activity

Create a poster for your classroom wall showing how to write a formal letter.

Your poster should give an example of a formal letter (choose your own topic for the letter) and all features should be clearly labelled. The features should cover the following:
- Correct positioning and layout of addresses
- Date
- Salutation
- Content to suit purpose and audience
- The formal ending (giving alternatives according to salutation).

Your poster should also include between four and six bullet points giving the key points to remember when writing a formal letter.

Reading Prose and Poetry

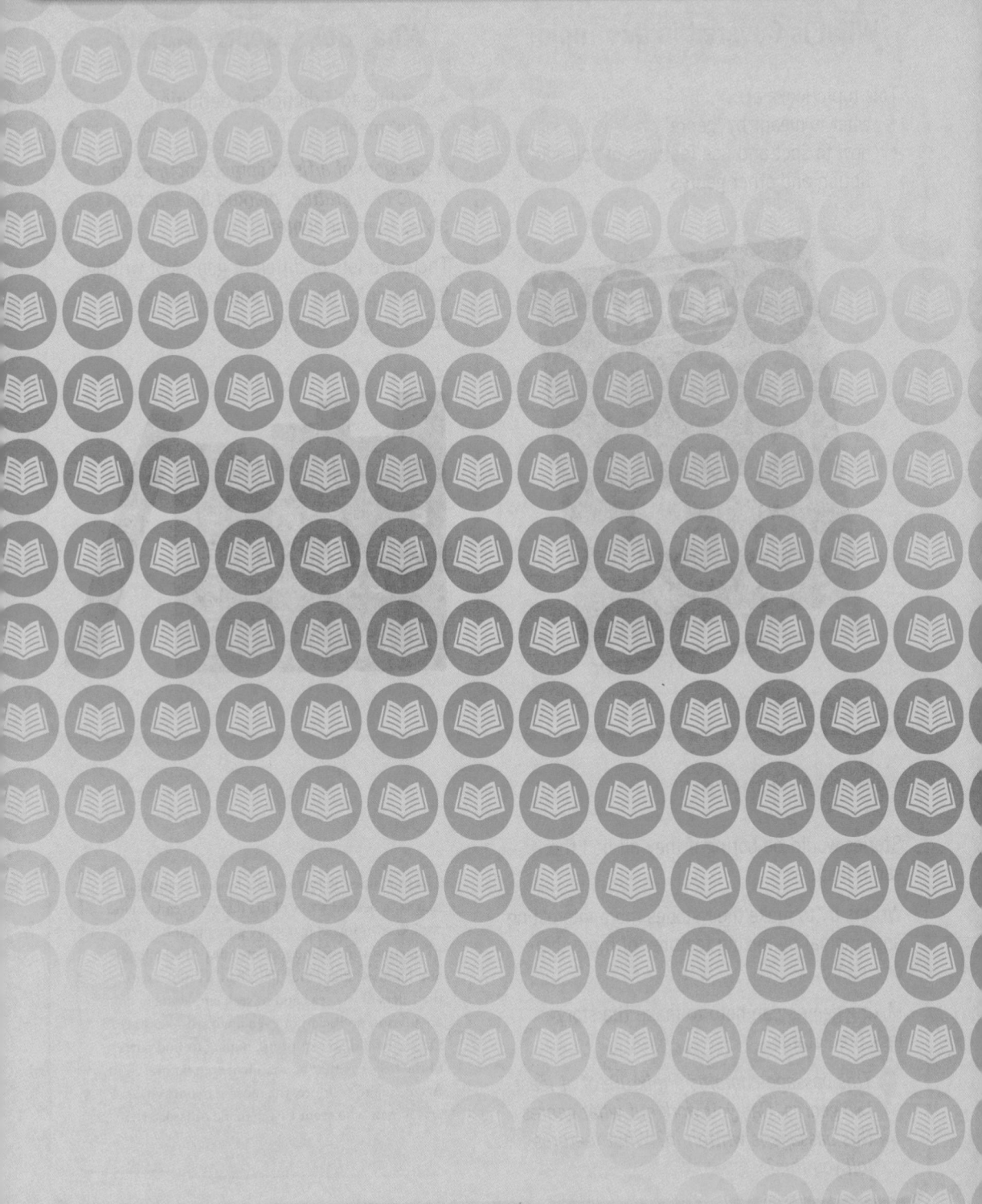

Genre & Science Fiction

What is Covered in this Topic?

This topic looks at...
- what is meant by 'genre'
- how to spot and use features of science fiction and other genres.

What does Genre Mean?

According to a dictionary definition, 'genre' means:

A category of artistic composition, as in music or literature, marked by a distinctive style, form, or content.

There are lots of different genres of writing, for example, horror, crime, romance, comedy, epic, and historical.

Mixing Genres

Stories would be boring if they all had the same features.

Writers try to make their stories more interesting and original by mixing features of more than one genre.

Mixing genres can help to make the story less predictable.

💡 *This passage contains a mixture of at least two genres. Can you work out what genres this passage is written in? What features tell you this?*

The fair isle of Berwyn was a lonely, single peak that rose defiantly out of the distant ocean, a land well-known for its magically gifted people. From its narrow valleys and gloomy, mist-filled villages and hamlets, many Acadians had set off to seek the rulers of the seas and to seek employment as an advisor, politician or even a wizard-like mage. Others would go exploring, hoping to find parts of the lost seas that no man had seen before. According to folklore, the most fearsome voyager was a man who went by the name of Fulksar...

Different Genres

The following extracts are examples of different genres.

💡 *What features help you to identify the genre of each extract?*

Dirk Clayton looked down the long, dusty street and watched the tumbleweed roll across, occasionally hitting the cacti that clung between the saloons and dime stores. From the distant end of the street came the thudding sound of a horse's hooves. A dark figure gradually rode into view, the rider wearing mud-encrusted chaps, leather boots and a Stetson hat pulled down over the eyes.

'Howdy,' came the deep, dull voice. 'Have you seen the Sheriff? I got a score to settle...'

Colorado Smith adjusted his hat and flicked off the sweat – the jungle heat was getting to him now, but he couldn't give up. In the faint distance came the sound of the chanting tribesmen, tracking his every move. Every twig that he stepped on was a clue to where he was. Would they reach the Golden Statue of Sullaria before he did? If they did, then the fate of the world was in doubt. He had to get there first. He moved on, slipping, sliding and gliding through the dense undergrowth, racing and panting towards the distant mountain where the golden prize awaited him.

The dark door hid a deadly secret. Slowly it creaked open and a small draught found its way towards Barry's face. Strange thoughts raced through his mind about the legends that had grown about that room, about people who had disappeared when entering there and who'd never been seen again. Would he be joining that group, or would the precautions he'd taken be enough? He gripped the gun at his waist tightly, took a nervous step forward and headed into the misty gloom.

'Mission control to Dallas Wayne. Do you receive me?' The hum of the ship's engines was the only sound in the darkness of space. Where before there was the chatter of the crew, now there was nothing. A few lights blinked and spluttered automatically. A hollow grinding interrupted the calm.

The mothership had docked. Stars twinkled peacefully, forming a strangely calm background to what they were about to find within. The docking bay snapped open and the sound of human movement disturbed the emptiness. But it wasn't empty. Something was waiting.

Holly looked across the room and gazed longingly at the dark, handsome figure opposite. He stood tall and strong, confidently talking to one of his colleagues. She wished that she could dare to go and talk to him, but she didn't have a reason or an excuse and felt that she would make a fool of herself if she did. He slowly turned, as if he knew she was watching. His face broke into a grin and he winked knowingly in her direction. Holly's heart skipped as she realised that the grin was aimed at her – she blushed a deep crimson and coughed nervously. How did he know that she existed? She was only the girl who made the tea and he was the big man in the boardroom...

Genre & Science Fiction

Science Fiction

Writing in a certain genre will contain features that are common across a variety of similar types of story.

In science fiction, you might find that...

- stories are set in the future
- stories ask the question, 'What if...?'
- some stories consider an **alternative** view of history
- unusual **technology** is involved
- aliens, space travel or other worlds are involved.

Can you see any of these features in the passage from The War of the Worlds?

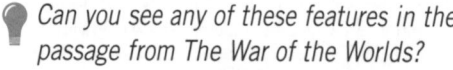

THE WAR OF THE WORLDS

The end of the cylinder was being screwed out from within. Nearly two feet of shining screw projected. Somebody blundered against me, and I narrowly missed being pitched onto the top of the screw. I turned, and as I did so the screw must have come out, for the lid of the cylinder fell upon the gravel with a ringing concussion.

I stuck my elbow into the person behind me, and turned my head towards the Thing again. For a moment that circular cavity seemed perfectly black. I had the sunset in my eyes.

I think everyone expected to see a man emerge – possibly something a little unlike us terrestrial men, but in all essentials a man. I know I did. But, looking, I presently saw something stirring within the shadow: greyish billowy movements, one above another, and then two luminous disks – like eyes. Then something

resembling a little grey snake, about the thickness of a walking stick, coiled up out of the writhing middle, and wriggled in the air towards me – and then another. I heard inarticulate exclamations on all sides.

There was a general movement backwards. I saw the shopman struggling still on the edge of the pit. I found myself alone, and saw the people on the other side of the pit running off, Stent among them. I looked again at the cylinder, and ungovernable terror gripped me. I stood petrified and staring.

A big greyish rounded bulk, the size, perhaps, of a bear, was rising slowly and painfully out of the cylinder. As it bulged up and caught the light, it glistened like wet leather. Two large dark-coloured eyes were regarding me steadfastly. The mass that framed them, the head of the thing, was rounded, and had, one might say, a face. There was a mouth under the eyes, the lipless brim of which quivered and panted, and dropped saliva. The whole creature heaved and pulsated convulsively. A lank tentacular appendage gripped the edge of the cylinder, another swayed in the air.

An example of Science Fiction writing, from *The War of the Worlds* by H.G. Wells.

the news

ALIENS SUCKED OUT HIS BRAINS!

To make the story more interesting, science fiction uses...

- well-chosen detail
- similes and metaphors
- adjectives
- short sentences to shock
- lexis (choice of words) of fear.

💡 *Can you find at least one example of each in the extract from The War of the Worlds on page 158?*

A genre will typically contain words to do with its style, in order to create the mood of that genre.

💡 *Which of the words in the table below might you find in science fiction writing? They might all appear in a story, but which are most typical of the genre?*

rocket	cyber	heat
universe	planet	sky
flower	space	expression
galactic	ground	UFO
metallic	calm	legs
robot	heat	alien
darkness	male	horse

Quick Test

1. Are there only different genres in literature?
2. Which genre deals with the question 'What if...?'
3. Can you have a mixture of genres in one piece of writing?
4. Does writing in a genre guarantee that it is interesting?
5. What problem is there if a writer sticks too closely to the features of a genre?

KEY WORDS

Make sure you understand these words before moving on!

- Composition
- Distinctive
- Form
- Mage
- Dense
- Cylinder
- Concussion
- Cavity
- Inarticulate
- Ungovernable
- Steadfastly
- Pulsated
- Appendage
- Alternative
- Technology

 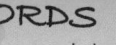

Genre & Science Fiction

Key Words Exercise

The lists below contain 15 words and 20 meanings, so 5 of the meanings don't match any of the words. Match each word with its meaning.

Word	Meaning
Composition	Thick
Distinctive	Thin
Form	Not very clearly spoken
Cylinder	A round, tube-shaped container
Concussion	A kind of wizard
Cavity	Shape or structure
Inarticulate	A robot
Ungovernable	Clear and having definite characteristics
Steadfastly	Something that has been composed or created
Pulsated	The state of being stunned
Appendage	A hole
Alternative	Rubber boots
Technology	Throbbed
Mage	Jumped
Dense	Something added on
	A different way of doing something
	Not possible to control
	With determination
	Equipment or machinery designed to do a job
	A bat

Choose the correct options in the following sentences.

1. Genre is a word that describes the particular *style / author / cover* of a piece of writing or other *film / music / composition*. All genres have their own *authors / comments / features,* which help the *author / reader / writer* to identify them. In science fiction, for example, the text will include references to such things as *castles / adventure / future technology*.

2. Different genres contain different features. Romance stories will contain *dreamy / scary / mysterious* descriptive words, whereas cowboy stories might contain references to *ships and the sea / jungles and gold / horses and guns.*

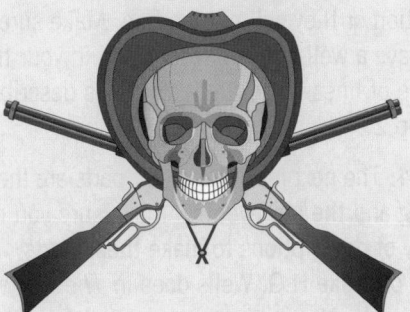

3. It can get *boring / interesting* if writers stick too closely to the features of one genre in their story. To get round this, writers often *lose / use* features of more than one genre to make their story more *clever / original / dull*.

4. Using the features of a genre will give your story a top *grade / style / boost* but it won't make it interesting unless you describe those features well. You will need to also include *appropriate / big* words to develop your style.

5. Using descriptive techniques, which includes *punctuation / adjectives* and *similes / paragraphs,* is very important.

Here are some statements about features of different genres. Which of the statements are true and which are false?

1. You can't mix features of different genres.

2. The science fiction genre doesn't have to contain references to aliens.

3. Historical romance is a genre.

4. In examples of the mystery genre you will always find detectives and policemen.

5. In the romance genre, you will always have a happy ending.

6. You can mix historical features and science fiction in the same story.

7. A romance story might have a cowboy in it.

8. Using features of a genre doesn't guarantee better writing.

9. In adventure stories, the heroes are never women.

10. Using well-chosen adjectives will improve your writing, no matter what the genre.

TRUE OR FALSE?

356

Genre & Science Fiction

Write a science fiction story that includes the ideas listed below:

OUTER SPACE

ALIENS

A Distant Planet

NEW TECHNOLOGY

Futuristic-Sounding Names

People from Earth

A Battle between Aliens and Earth people

a cliffhanger OR twist at the end

IT MUST BE SET IN THE FUTURE

Step 1: Decide the order of events in your story. Work out how and where you're going to include the ideas given here. This will be your outline plan.

Step 2: To make your story more interesting, you will need to find ways of describing the features. Use a thesaurus to come up with lists of adjectives and adverbs to describe the main features and events in your plan. If you know how to create similes and metaphors, these would be good to use too.

Step 3: The most important part of your story is the opening; you need to grab the reader's attention or they will not read on. Make sure you have a well-chosen description in your first couple of lines – use the techniques described in step 2.

Step 4: The next most important parts are the ending and the key events – make sure you use plenty of descriptions to make these parts stand out, like H.G. Wells does in *The War of the Worlds*. After you have done that, start to draft the whole story.

Step 5: When you have completed your draft, let someone else read it. Listen to their suggestions for improvements – can they spot the features of the genre? Which parts work well? Which parts could do with more work? Redraft it before finally completing your science fiction masterpiece!

Drama Texts

This topic looks at...
- features of drama texts
- differences between types of drama texts.

What is Drama?

Drama is a work of prose or verse, usually telling a story. It's written for actors who play the characters and perform the dialogue and action.

Drama scripts are not just for plays. Films and radio performances use drama scripts too. Each type of script has slightly different features.

The following is an example of a stage script from *The Happy Man*, by H. Adams.

SCENE 1:	*[At the Palace. A Court Room adjoining the King's Bedchamber. Dawn is just about to break. Lights gradually increase as the scene progresses.]*
	Two Sentinels on guard, up C.
	Chair L. Chair R.
	[Enter the LORD CHAMBERLAIN (L) on tip-toes, carrying a huge book. He is a harassed, fussy little man. He is obviously very tired and flops down on chair (L) dropping the heavy book on the floor, with a loud bang. He jumps up and hisses, Sh----- Sh-------, looking anxiously towards the Royal bedchamber (L). The silent Sentinels remain motionless. The LORD CHAMBERLAIN sits again, gives a terrific yawn and speaks, half to himself and half to the guards, purely for the benefit of the audience.]
LORD CHAMBERLAIN:	Oh-h-h-h dear! I'm worn out! Night after night reading Court Documents to the King – to send him to sleep! Then the minute I think His Majesty is well away, he calls me back as I am tip-toeing out of the room, and bids me read more, till I have to keep my eyelids open with my fingers – I'm sure His Majesty sleeps peacefully enough till I begin to nod. *[Stretches arms and legs.]* Ooh! How stiff I am with sitting. *[Turning more towards Sentinels.]* How you fellows manage to stand there all night without falling asleep beats me. Or perhaps you really are asleep, standing up with your eyes open, eh?
	[No response]

Drama Texts

Features of a Stage Play

A play is set out very differently from a story or poetry and contains different features.

Stage directions are instructions to the actor / actress, which tell them...
- how to move
- where to move
- how to say their lines
- where characters or objects need to be on a stage.

Stage movements are always the same, even if a play is performed in a different theatre. There are standard stage name areas, as seen in the diagram opposite.

💡 *Stage directions are set out differently to speech. Why do you think this is?*
- *In The Happy Man script, where do the two chairs go?*
- *Which side is the Royal bedchamber on?*
- *Where are the two Sentinels standing?*

Properties – props – are the items the actors need for the performance. Sometimes they're printed as a list, or described in the stage directions. It's the Props Manager's job to go through the script and make a list of what's needed.

💡 *Which props are described in The Happy Man and will definitely be needed?*

💡 *Which props are not described, but you think might be needed, because of clues you can work out from the characters and setting?*

Use of **brackets** and **italics** – these are used to separate speech lines from stage directions, so the cast can see the difference between words and actions when learning their lines.

The names of the speakers are at the side of the script to show who is speaking.

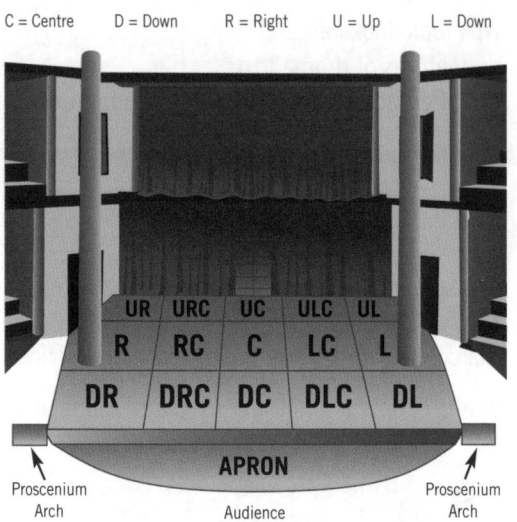

C = Centre   D = Down   R = Right   U = Up   L = Down

UR	URC	UC	ULC	UL
R	RC	C	LC	L
DR	DRC	DC	DLC	DL

APRON

Proscenium Arch   Audience   Proscenium Arch

STAGE PROPS

Film and Television Scripts

Film and television scripts have similarities with stage play scripts, but there are important differences too.

This example of a television script shows some of the differences in stage directions.

SCENE:	*The inside of a hotel ballroom.*
	[The band have just finished playing and a member of the audience approaches the lead singer]
AUDIENCE MEMBER:	Hi. Would you mind having a word with that girl over there? She doesn't know the difference between Cajun and Zydeco music.
LEAD SINGER:	She doesn't?
AUDIENCE MEMBER:	I'm sure she'd appreciate it if you could go over and explain. She's a bit shy, you see, and doesn't want to ask in person. Her name's Emma.
	[Cut to: Long shot of other band members gazing jealously at the lead singer, who is approaching the girl. They turn to look at each other and nod in agreement]
BAND MEMBER:	Right. That's the final straw. He's got to leave the band now.
	[Cut to close-up of the lead singer and the girl talking]

The writer uses the word '**cut**' in the stage directions. This is for the actors, actresses and **technical crew**, such as the camera and sound operators.

A cut is when the picture quickly changes from one scene to another. Writing a television script is different from writing a stage script because it's for a different audience.

Effects and Shots

Sound effect instructions feature in television and film scripts, although not as much as in a radio script. It might be that the audience are watching a scene and there are different sounds or music on screen at the same time. A television, film or radio scriptwriter has to think of this more than a stage scriptwriter.

There are many types of camera shots:
- LS = **Long Shot** – the camera is looking from a long way away.
- MS = **Medium Shot** – the camera is focused on half of a person's body.
- CU = **Close-up** – the camera goes in close on something or someone.
- **Pan** – the camera moves sideways, or up and down.
- **Zoom** – the camera moves in or out from the subject.

Drama Texts

Adapting Texts for Stage and Television

Many successful books are made into films or television programmes. This means that the original novel has to be **adapted** for the screen. Sometimes, parts have to be left out, or new ideas brought in, so that the story works better on screen. This can be seen by comparing the opening of Jane Austen's novel, *Sense and Sensibility*, with its 1995 screenplay.

The novel's opening paragraph has a lot of explanation and little action, so the novel was adapted to make it more exciting for the film version.

> The family of Dashwood had long been settled in Sussex. Their estate was large, and their residence was at Norland Park, in the centre of their property, where, for many generations, they had lived in so respectable a manner as to engage the general good opinion of their surrounding acquaintance. The late owner of this estate was a single man, who lived to a very advanced age, and who for many years of his life, had a constant companion and housekeeper in his sister. But her death, which happened ten years before his own, produced a great alteration in his home; for to supply her loss, he invited and received into his house the family of his nephew Mr. Henry Dashwood, the legal inheritor of the Norland estate, and the person to whom he intended to bequeath it.

The film script goes straight to the important plot events, using stage directions to show what's happening. There are detailed instructions for the camera and technical crew.

💡 *Why might fans of a book not like a film or television version?*

> EXT. OPEN ROADS – NIGHT – TITLE SEQUENCE
>
> A series of traveling shots. A well-dressed, pompous-looking individual (JOHN DASHWOOD, 35) is making an urgent journey on horseback. He looks anxious.
>
> EXT. NORLAND PARK – ENGLAND – MARCH 1800 – NIGHT
>
> Silence. Norland Park, a large country house built in the early part of the eighteenth century, lies in the moonlit parkland.
>
> INT. NORLAND PARK – MR DASHWOOD'S BEDROOM – NIGHT
>
> In the dim light shed by candles we see a bed in which a MAN (MR DASHWOOD, 52) lies, his skin waxy, his breathing laboured.
>
> Around him two silhouettes move and murmur, their clothing susurrating in the deathly hush. DOCTORS. A WOMAN (MRS DASHWOOD, 50) sits by his side, holding his hand, her eyes never leaving his face.
>
> MR DASHWOOD (urgent) Is John not yet arrived?

Quick Test

1. On a stage plan, what does 'DL' stand for?
2. In a film script, what does 'LS' stand for?
3. What are 'properties' better known as?
4. What might brackets or italics be used for in a script?
5. In a film script, what does 'pan' mean?

Key Words Exercise

Work out the key words from the clues below, then find them in the word search.

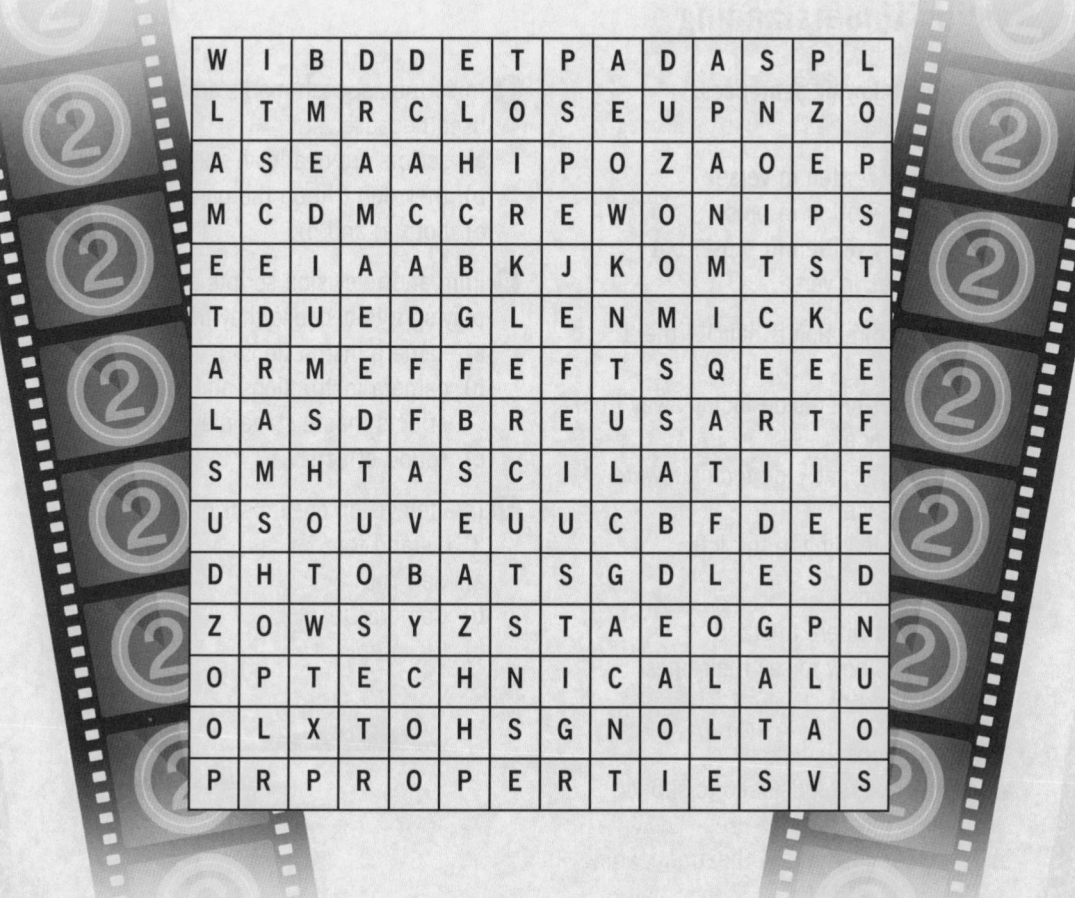

W	I	B	D	D	E	T	P	A	D	A	S	P	L
L	T	M	R	C	L	O	S	E	U	P	N	Z	O
A	S	E	A	A	H	I	P	O	Z	A	O	E	P
M	C	D	M	C	C	R	E	W	O	N	I	P	S
E	E	I	A	A	B	K	J	K	O	M	T	S	T
T	D	U	E	D	G	L	E	N	M	I	C	K	C
A	R	M	E	F	F	E	F	T	S	Q	E	E	E
L	A	S	D	F	B	R	E	U	S	A	R	T	F
S	M	H	T	A	S	C	I	L	A	T	I	I	F
U	S	O	U	V	E	U	U	C	B	F	D	E	E
D	H	T	O	B	A	T	S	G	D	L	E	S	D
Z	O	W	S	Y	Z	S	T	A	E	O	G	P	N
O	P	T	E	C	H	N	I	C	A	L	A	L	U
O	L	X	T	O	H	S	G	N	O	L	T	A	O
P	R	P	R	O	P	E	R	T	I	E	S	V	S

1. A work of prose or verse that tells a story.
2. They tell actors what to do.
3. Full name for props.
4. They often surround written stage directions.
5. The font style often used for stage directions.
6. When the camera is far away.
7. When the camera is between close and far.
8. When the camera is near.
9. Camera moves sideways or up and down.
10. Camera moves in or out.
11. Noises.
12. The crew who work with cameras and sound.
13. A quick change from one film scene to another.
14. A script that is based on a novel.

Drama Texts

Complete the following sentences.

1. Drama texts...
   a) are never written in verse
   b) are never written in prose
   c) are mainly written in prose, but sometimes in verse.

2. In the stage direction [Chair L.] the 'L' stands for...
   a) on the left-hand side facing away from the audience
   b) on the left-hand side facing towards the audience
   c) the chair leaning to the left.

3. Stage directions...
   a) tell actors where to stand
   b) tell actors how to say their lines
   c) both a) and b).

4. The word 'Props'...
   a) comes from stands used to support scenery on stage
   b) is a word used in the theatre meaning 'Everything's OK'
   c) is a shortened form of the word 'Properties'.

5. In scripts, speech marks aren't used because...
   a) scripts are nearly all speech anyway
   b) they don't fit on the page
   c) both a) and b).

6. Film and television scripts are different to play scripts because they include...
   a) camera instructions
   b) camera instructions and more sound effects than a stage play
   c) sound effects.

7. In a television or film script, the initials 'CU' stand for...
   a) See You
   b) Camera Up
   c) Close-up.

Write a drama script for the first scene of a stage play. You can choose the topic, setting and plot.

Step 1: Decide where your play is set, what's going to happen and how many characters will be involved. Don't forget to include characters that appear on stage but don't speak. Make a list so that you remember who to include.

Step 2: Start by writing a stage direction describing the opening scene on the stage. Use the correct way of describing positions of furniture, props and actors/actresses.

Step 3: Begin writing your lines. If you want characters to say things in a certain way, remember to include stage directions for the actors, which give help and advice about this.

When writing speech, remember to think about how speech differs from normal prose. You might include pauses, repetition, stuttering and slang if the characters require it.

Step 4: Complete the draft of your script and read it through with a friend – does it sound the way it should? Are your stage directions clear? Can other people work out from your script how they should stand and move? If anything needs to be changed, redraft it before you complete the final version.

If you want to perform your play, make a copy of the script for every person who needs one, including each actor or actress, and the director if there is one.

Adapt your play script into a television script.

Alternatively, write a television script from scratch on a new subject. You could also try adapting a favourite story into a television or film script.

Novels and Short Stories

What is Covered in this Topic?

This topic looks at...
- the features of novels and short stories
- approaches to studying your text
- analysing characters.

Features of Novels and Short Stories

Novels and short stories have many things in common – the main difference is, as you might guess, that short stories are a lot shorter than novels. Other than that, though, both...
- tell stories created out of the writer's imagination
- want to interest and entertain the reader
- usually contain characters
- usually use dialogue
- often explore various ideas or themes.

Approaching your Text

When you're studying a novel or a short story, (often called a text) the first thing you need to do is to read it so that you get a clear idea of what it's about and the storyline or plot.

Here are some things that you can do while you're reading your text, which will help later when you come to study it in more detail:

- Keep a 'log' of your ideas on the text as you read it – jotting a few brief points in a notebook.
- Jot down your ideas or anything interesting that you've noticed about the characters.
- Note down anything that strikes you about the setting or atmosphere.
- Note down anything that catches your attention about the language that's used – maybe a particular piece of description or a phrase or image that you found striking.

Here's one approach you could use to help you develop your understanding of the text.

Read through the novel or short story to get an overall picture of the story.

> Look at how the writer opens the story.

> As you're reading it, make a brief summary of each chapter – just pick out the key points.

> To get an overview you need to have a clear idea of the plot, characters and ideas that the writer explores.

> Think about the narrative viewpoint (or perspective) – is the story told in the first person (I) or the third person (he, she)?

> Have ideas about the characters – who they are, how they act, what they do, how they relate to other characters and look at the way the writer describes them.

> Look at how the writer creates an impression of the setting of the story – look at the language used to describe it.

> Look at how the writer ends the story.

Novels and Short Stories

Analysing Characters

Characters in novels and short stories aren't real people, but the writer wants them to be believable and convincing to you.

When you're asked to **analyse** characters in a story, you're really being asked to look at the ways writers use language to give you an impression of them.

In order to do this, you need to understand some of the methods and **techniques** that writers can use to create characters and present them to you through the story.

How Writers Create Characters

Look at the following two passages in which Charles Dickens presents different characters.

 What impression do you form of each character? What techniques does the writer use?

Hard Times by Charles Dickens

He was a rich man: banker, merchant, manufacturer, and what not. A big, loud man, with a stare and a metallic laugh. A man made out of a coarse material, which seemed to have been stretched to make so much of him. A man with a great puffed head and forehead, swelled veins in his temples, and such a strained skin to his face that it seemed to hold his eyes open and lift his eyebrows up. A man with a pervading appearance on him of being inflated like a balloon, and ready to start. A man who could never sufficiently vaunt himself a self-made man. A man who was always proclaiming, through that brassy speaking-trumpet of a voice of his, his old ignorance and his old poverty. A man who was the Bull of humility.

A year or two younger than his eminently practical friend, Mr Bounderby looked older; his seven or eight and forty might have had the seven or eight added to it again, without surprising anybody. He had not much hair. One might have fancied he had talked it off; and that what was left, all standing up in disorder, was in that condition from being constantly blown about by his windy boastfulness.

Great Expectations by Charles Dickens

She was dressed in rich materials – satins, and lace, and silks – all of white. Her shoes were white. And she had a long white veil dependent from her hair, and she had bridal flowers in her hair, but her hair was white. Some bright jewels sparkled on her neck and on her hands, and some other jewels lay sparkling on the table.

Dresses, less splendid than the dress she wore, and half-packed trunks, were scattered about. She had not quite finished dressing, for she had but one shoe on – the other was on the table near her hand – her veil was but half arranged, her watch and chain were not put on, and some lace for her bosom lay with those trinkets, and with her handkerchief, and gloves, and some flowers, and a Prayer-book, all confusedly heaped about the looking-glass.

It was not in the first few moments that I saw all these things, though I saw more of them in the first moments than might be supposed. But, I saw that everything within my view which ought to be white, had been white long ago, and had lost its lustre, and was faded and yellow. I saw that the bride within the bridal dress had withered like the dress, and like the flowers, and had no brightness left but the brightness of her sunken eyes. I saw that the dress had been put upon the rounded figure of a young woman, and that the figure upon which it now hung loose, had shrunk to skin and bone.

How Writers Create Characters (cont.)

Here are some ideas you might have noted about *Hard Times*:

- Details are given about Bounderby's status and profession.
- His physical appearance and size are stressed, e.g. 'big', 'a stare', 'great puffed head', 'swelled veins' and a simile is used to emphasise this further with the description of him 'being inflated like a balloon'.
- The sounds he makes are also emphasised, e.g. 'metallic laugh', a 'loud man', 'brassy speaking-trumpet voice'.
- We get the impression of a loud, brash, boastful and bullying kind of man.

Here are some ideas you might have noted about *Great Expectations*:

- Dickens contrasts the narrator's initial impression with what he sees as he looks more closely at the woman.
- At first he sees rich satins, laces and silks and bright jewels on the woman's neck and hands.
- He then sees that everything that should be white has become yellowed with age, the flowers withered and the woman old and shrunken.
- The woman is described through her clothing and jewellery. The vividness is achieved through the use of a variety of adjectives, e.g. 'rich materials', 'bright jewels', 'sunken eyes'.

In summary, writers use the following techniques:

- Description – often writers describe what their characters look like, how they dress, how they walk, etc.
- Actions – you also learn about characters through what they do, how they act and how they behave in the story.
- Dialogue – what the characters say and how they say it can add to your impression of a character.
- Feelings – the writer can tell us what a character feels or thinks.

Quick Test

1. Novels and short stories should capture the reader's _____.
2. What is one of the main purposes of novels and short stories?
3. The ideas that novels explore are called _____.
4. Another word that means the same as storyline is _____.

KEY WORDS

Make sure you understand these words before moving on!

- Novel
- Short stories
- Imagination
- Interest
- Entertain
- Characters
- Dialogue
- Themes
- Texts
- Plot
- Setting
- Atmosphere
- Viewpoint
- First person
- Third person
- Analyse
- Techniques

Novels and Short Stories

Key Words Exercise

Work out the key words from the clues below, then copy and complete the crossword.

ACROSS

2. Narrative _____. (9)

4. Books that you read are these. (5)

6. Ideas in a story. (6)

7. Spoken words. (8)

10. A long story. (5)

11. A story but not a novel. (5)

14. Good stories _____ the reader. (8)

15. The purpose of a novel is to

_____. (9)

16. 'I like this work.' is written in the first

_____. (6)

DOWN

1. You could 'cut it with a knife'. (10)

3. Writers use this when writing stories. (11)

5. It wasn't first, it wasn't second but it was

_____ person. (5)

6. Writers use a variety of these. (10)

8. Storyline. (4)

9. These need to be convincing. (10)

12. When you look at a story closely you

_____ it. (7)

13. Where it all happens. (7)

Look at the following extract from *Of Mice and Men* by John Steinbeck in which he describes two characters. Read the extract carefully and answer the questions that follow.

1. What aspect of the characters does Steinbeck focus on to begin with?

2. What is your impression of the first man and how is language used to create this impression? Gives specific examples of language used and the effects created.

3. How does the second man contrast with the first? What is your impression of him and how is language used to create this impression?

4. Which of these characters do you think is the dominant one and why?

5. What does the dialogue tell you about the characters?

For a moment the place was lifeless, and then two men emerged from the path and came into the opening by the green pool. They had walked in single file down the path, and even in the open one stayed behind the other. Both were dressed in denim trousers and in denim coats with brass buttons. Both wore black, shapeless hats and both carried tight blanket rolls slung over their shoulders. The first man was small and quick, dark of face, with restless eyes and sharp, strong features. Every part of him was defined: small, strong hands, slender arms, a thin and bony nose. Behind him walked his opposite, a huge man, shapeless of face, with large, pale eyes, with wide, sloping shoulders; and he walked heavily, dragging his feet a little, the way a bear drags his paws. His arms did not swing at his sides, but hung loosely and only moved because the heavy hands were pendula.

The first man stopped short in the clearing, and the follower nearly ran over him. He took off his hat and wiped the sweat-band with his forefinger and snapped the moisture off. His huge companion dropped his blankets and flung himself down and drank from the surface of the green pool; drank with long gulps, snorting into the water like a horse. The small man stepped nervously beside him.

'Lennie!' he said sharply. 'Lennie, for God's sakes don't drink so much.' Lennie continued to snort into the pool. The small man leaned over and shook him by the shoulder. 'Lennie. You gonna be sick like you was last night.'

Lennie dipped his whole head under, hat and all, and then he sat up on the bank and his hat dripped down on his blue coat and ran down his back. 'Tha's good,' he said. 'You drink some, George. You take a good big drink.' He smiled happily.

Novels and Short Stories

Pick a novel or short story that you have read, either as part of your English lessons or as part of your own private reading. (You can choose more than one story if you want to.)

Pick out three characters from your chosen novel or short story.

For each character select a passage from the novel or story where the writer describes your selected character.

Write an analysis of each passage showing how the writer presents the character.

You should write about the following:
* The impression you form of the character.
* The techniques the writer uses to create a sense of character.
* How language is used to create effects.

Remember to give examples of language used and the effects created to support the points you make.

Extension Activity

Pick one of your characters and draw a picture of him or her based on the description given in the novel or story. You might find it useful to use a large sheet of paper for your drawing – it doesn't have to be a brilliant artistic work – you could even use a 'cartoon' approach.

Around your picture of the character you could put quotations that you have picked out from the text that describe the character and have helped you to visualise him or her.

Staring eyes

Large, silk top hat

Wild red hair

Bright polka-dot bow tie

What is Covered in this Topic?

This topic looks at...
- the parts that make up a poem
- how imagery can help make a poem effective
- sound effects in poetry
- rhyme and rhythm.

Parts of a Poem

Poems communicate ideas. Language can be used in many ways to express different ideas. In a poem, the language and ideas combine to make the poem effective.

Here are some of the parts that make up a poem:

Content – what the poem is about, its idea

Rhythm – the 'beat' of a poem

Poem

Imagery – the way the poet creates a 'picture' in your mind to give a vivid description

Sound effects – sometimes called aural imagery

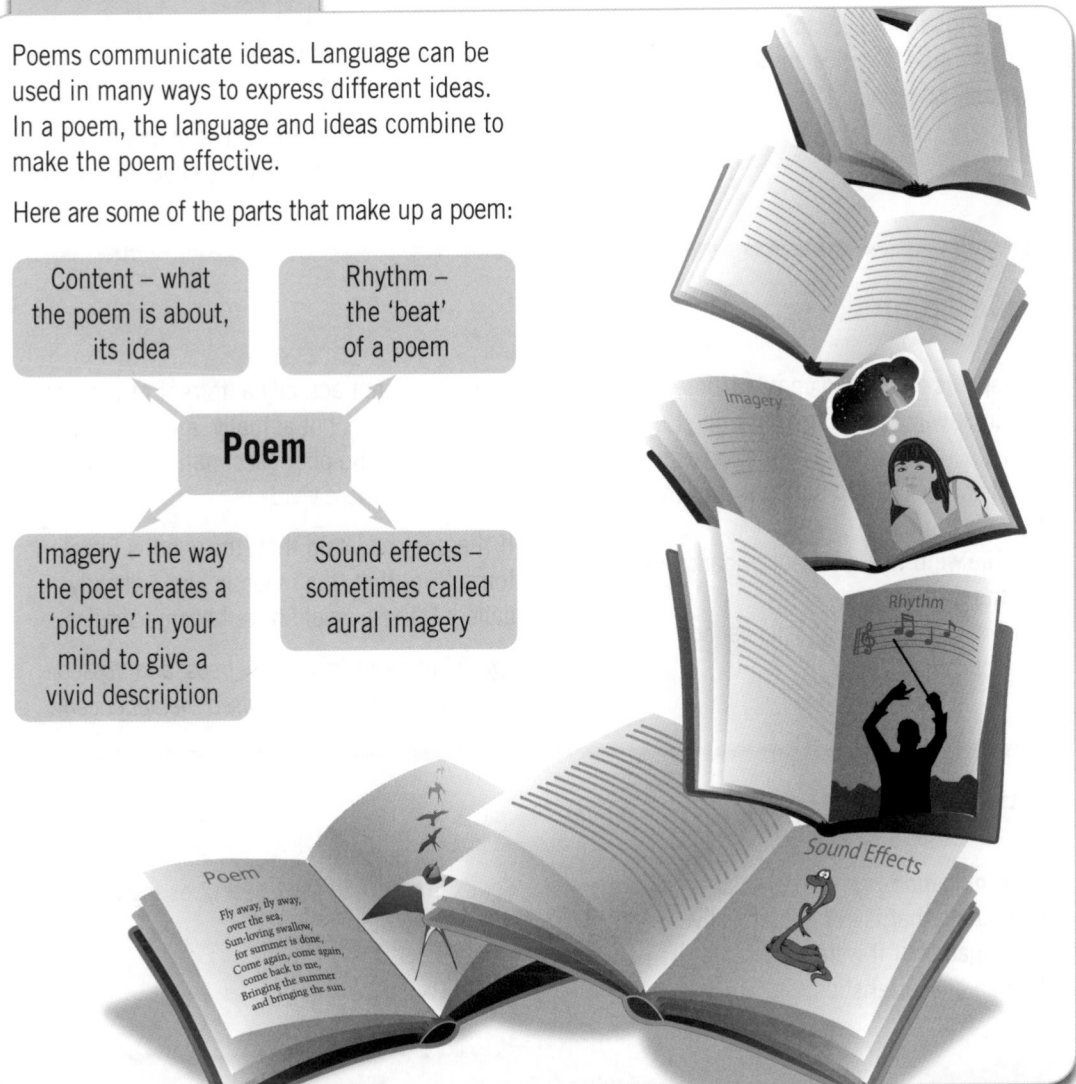

Imagery

Rhythm

Sound Effects

Poem

Fly away, fly away,
over the sea,
Sun-loving swallow,
for summer is done;
Come again, come again,
come back to me,
Bringing the summer
and bringing the sun.

Reading Poetry

Imagery

When poets use language to create a 'picture' of what they're describing, it is called **imagery**. It is also sometimes called figurative language.

Similes

Similes are when one thing is compared to another to make a description more vivid.

This helps the reader to imagine and picture it in their mind. Similes are used all the time in everyday speech.

For example...
- daft as a brush
- white as a sheet
- dropped like a stone
- slept like a log.

Poetic similes are a more interesting and original simile. Similes always use 'like' or 'as' to make the comparison.

Metaphors

Metaphors also make comparisons, but in a different way to similes. They don't use 'like' or 'as' – instead they say that one thing *is* another. Look at the metaphors in the following lines:
- The wind was a torrent of darkness among the dusty trees.
- The moon was a ghostly galleon tossed upon cloudy seas.

The wind is not actually a 'torrent of darkness' and the moon is not actually 'a ghostly galleon', but the poet uses metaphors to make their writing more vivid.

If the poet had said that 'the wind is like a torrent', or that 'the moon is like a ghostly galleon', these would have become similes.

 Think about how 'gusty trees' and 'tossed upon cloudy seas' are used metaphorically.

Personification

Personification is a kind of imagery where something that is not actually alive is described as if it were a person or had human characteristics.

For example, T.S. Eliot describes fog as though it were a person:

> The yellow fog that rubs its back upon the window panes

Sound Effects

Rather than creating a picture in the mind with words, the use of sound effects can create imagery and make a description more vivid.

This is called **aural** imagery. The **techniques** a writer can use to create sound effects are...

- alliteration
- assonance
- onomatopoeia.

Alliteration

Alliteration is created by the repetition of words with the same **consonant**.

A consonant is any letter other than the **vowels** 'a', 'e', 'i', 'o', and 'u'. The following example uses alliteration by repeating the letter 'w':

> He wandered alone in the wet, wild, wilderness.

 What effect do you think this repetition has?

Assonance

Assonance is similar to alliteration but it uses the repetition of vowel sounds. For example:

> The curfew tolls the knell of parting day,
> The lowing herd winds slowly o'er the lea

The repeated long 'o' sound gives a feeling of the weariness at the end of the day.

Onomatopoeia

Onomatopoeia is when a word sounds like the sound it is describing, for example...

- bang
- crash
- hiss
- plop.

Reading Poetry

Rhyme

Rhyme can have an important effect on the sound of a poem. Words at the ends of lines usually rhyme, although sometimes lines can rhyme within a line – this is called internal rhyme.

The pattern of rhyme within a poem is called the **rhyme scheme**. You can work out this pattern by looking at which lines rhyme together.

Fly away, fly away, over the sea,	A
Sun-loving swallow, for summer is done,	B
Come again, come again, come back to me,	A
Bringing the summer and bringing the sun.	B

In this Christina Rossetti poem, *The Swallow*, the first and third lines, and the second and fourth lines, rhyme, so it has an ABAB rhyme scheme.

💡 *Think about the effect this rhyme scheme has on the poem.*

Rhythm

Rhythm is the beat or tempo of a poem.

The rhythm can create a sense of movement in a poem to suit the setting, tone or mood of the poem. It might be slow or plodding, or it might give a strong impression of movement, as in this example:

> I sprang to the stirrup, and Joris, and he;
> I galloped, Dirk galloped, we galloped all three;
> 'Good speed!' cried the watch, as the gate bolts undrew,
> 'Speed!' echoed the wall to us galloping through.

It is not only important that you can spot these features, but being able to say something about the effects they create.

💡 *Read a poem aloud, tapping out the beat of the words as you read them.*

Quick Test

1. Name three different kinds of imagery.
2. What is the name of the kind of imagery that uses sound effects?
3. What is 'slipping and sliding down the slope' an example of?
4. What sounds is assonance the repetition of?
5. What is 'Bang!' an example of?

KEY WORDS

Make sure you understand these words before moving on!

- Imagery
- Simile
- Metaphor
- Personification
- Aural
- Technique
- Alliteration
- Consonant
- Vowel
- Assonance
- Onomatopoeia
- Rhyme scheme
- Rhythm

Work out the key words from the clues below, then copy and complete the crossword.

Across

2. The 'beat' of a poem. (6)
7. 'The wind cut through me' is an example of this. (8)
9. 'E' is an example of one of these. (5)
11. Similes and metaphors are examples of this. (7)
12. Describing something that's not alive as if it's a person. (15)
13. Poets use a variety of these to create effects. (10)
14. 'Tremendous tumbling torrent' is an example of this. (12)

Down

1. The rhyme pattern of a poem. (6)
3. 'Like' or 'as' is usually used in these. (6)
4. Not a vowel. (9)
5. 'Bang!', 'Crash!' and 'Thud!' are examples of this. (12)
6. Some poems do this, some poems don't. (5)
8. The repetition of vowel sounds. (9)
10. This kind of imagery uses sounds. (5)

Fly away, fly away, over the sea,
Sun-loving swallow, for summer is done;
Come again, come again, come back to me,
Bringing the summer and bringing the sun.

Reading Poetry

Testing Understanding

1 Carefully read the following poem by Andrew Young.

Identify an example of each of the following techniques in the poem:

a) A metaphor
b) A simile
c) Onomatopoeia
d) Personification
e) A rhyme scheme.

Hard Frost

Frost called to water 'Halt!'
And crusted the moist snow with sparkling salt;
Brooks, their own bridges, stop,
And icicles in long stalactites drop,
And tench in water-holes
Lurk under gluey glass like fish in bowls.

In the hard-rutted lane
At every footstep breaks a brittle pane,
And tinkling trees ice-bound
Changed into weeping willows, sweep the ground;
Dead boughs take root in ponds
And ferns on windows shoot their ghostly fronds.

But vainly the fierce frost
Inters poor fish, ranks trees in an armed host,
Hangs daggers from house-eaves
And on the windows ferny ambush weaves;
In the long war grown warmer
The sun will strike him dead and strip his armour.

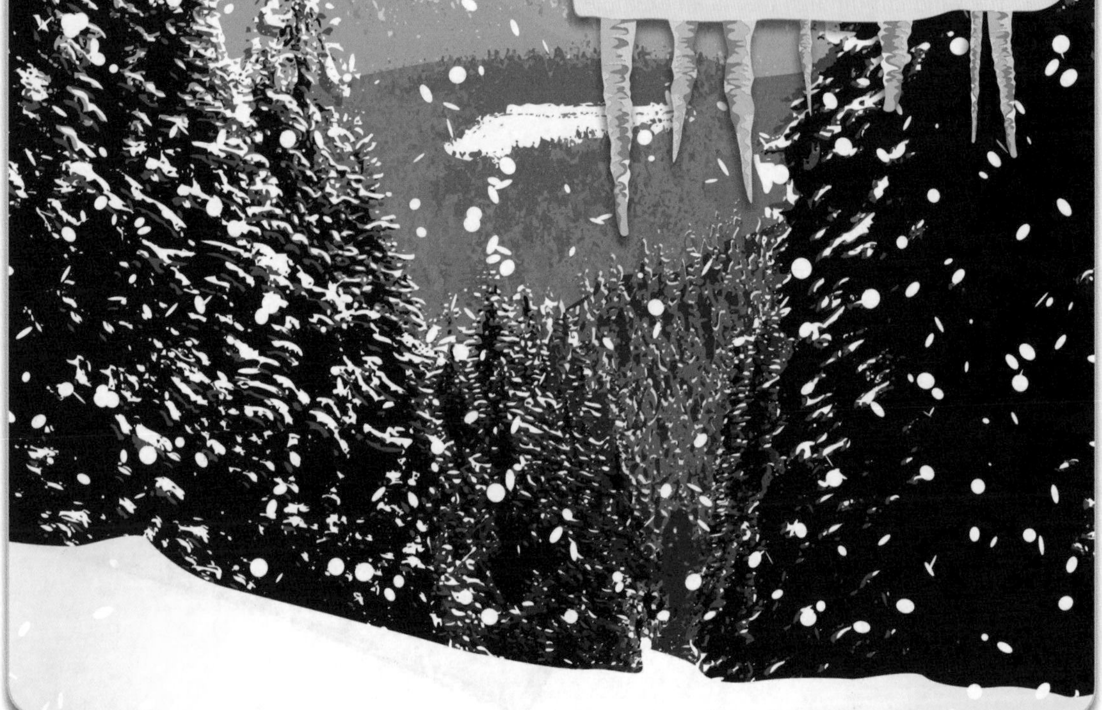

Carefully read the following Ted Hughes poem,
Football at Slack.

Football at Slack

Between plunging valleys, on a bareback of hill
Men in bunting colours
Bounced, and their blown ball bounced.

The blown ball jumped, and the merry-coloured men
Spouted like water to head it.
The ball blew away downward -

The rubbery men bounced after it.
The ball blew jumped up and out and hung on the wind
Over a gulf of treetops.
Then they all shouted together, and the ball blew back.

Winds from fiery holes in heaven
Piled the hills darkening around them
To awe them. The glare light
Mixed its mad oils and threw glooms.
Then the rain lowered a steel press.

Hair plastered, they all just trod water
To puddle glitter. And their shouts bobbed up
Coming fine and thin, washed and happy

While the humped world sank foundering
And the valleys blued unthinkable
Under depth of Atlantic depression -

But the wingers leapt, they bicycled in air
And the goalie flew horizontal

And once again a golden holocaust
Lifted the cloud's edge, to watch them.

Now write about your thoughts and ideas on
the poem. Focus on the following ideas:
- What the poem's about.
- The use of metaphors.
- The use of similes.
- The use of aural imagery.
- The use of particular word and phrases.

Remember that when writing about a poem it's
important to not only identify words, phrases,
metaphors, similes, etc., but also to write
about the effects they create in your mind.

**Working with a partner, each choose a poem of your own and study it carefully. Then swap poems
and read your partner's poem.**

Write down at least four questions about the poem to ask your partner. Try to ask questions about
the language and techniques used rather than just what the poem's about.

Ask your partner your questions and discuss the poem between you. Then answer your partner's
questions on your poem and discuss your ideas together.

Analysing Poetry

What is Covered in this Topic?

This topic looks at...
- how to approach a poem
- features to look for
- studying a twentieth Century poem
- studying a pre-twentieth Century poem.

Approaching a Poem

When studying a poem the first thing you should do is read it carefully several times and form a general understanding of what it's about (the poem's meaning).

Then ask yourself three questions:
1. What is the poem about? (The content and meaning of the poem.)
2. How does the poet use language? (The style the poem is written in.)
3. Why does the poet use language in that way? (The effects created by the poem.)

Features to Look For

In analysing how a poem is written and the effects created, you need to look at the way in which the poet has used language.

Here are some things that you might look at:
- The vocabulary (specific words and phrases).
- The use of imagery i.e. figurative language (e.g. metaphors, similes, personification).
- Sound effects (e.g. onomatopoeia, alliteration).
- The tone and mood (created through the language).
- Rhythm and / or rhyme.
- Structure.

Remember, you need to be able to spot these features, but you also need to be able to explain the effects that they create in the poem and on you – the reader.

Analysing a Twentieth Century Poem

Poetry deals with all kinds of themes and ideas but they are often linked to the times in which they were written and the kind of world in which the poet lives.

In this poem, the poet, Carol Ann Duffy, imagines a war photographer developing his photographs, remembering all the horrors he has seen.

As he develops one of his photographs the face of the victim begins to form and the memory of the suffering of this moment comes flooding back to him.

Read the poems carefully.

 What effects are created by the highlighted images in the poem below? What are your overall feelings about the poem?

The film is on spools but contains the undeveloped photographs of the suffering of the many people he photographed.

The developing is a solemn process as it will reveal images of suffering.

Back to the safety of England – a contrast to the land he has returned from where children running in the fields can be blown up by land mines.

A man's image begins to form as the photo is developed – twisted with pain and suffering, a half-formed ghost because the image hasn't fully formed yet but also a ghost because the man is probably dead now.

The hundreds of photos he has taken showing the suffering caused by war.

When the pictures appear in the Sunday paper the reader is momentarily moved but then forgets it as they go for a bath and a pre-lunch beer.

War Photographer by Carol Ann Duffy

In his darkroom he is finally alone
with spools of suffering set out in ordered rows.
The only light is red and softly glows,
as though this were a church and he
a priest preparing to intone a Mass.
Belfast. Beirut. Phnom Penh. All flesh is grass.

He has a job to do. Solutions slop in trays
beneath his hands which did not tremble then
though seem to now. Rural England. Home again
to ordinary pain which simple weather can dispel,
to fields which don't explode beneath the feet
of running children in a nightmare heat.

Something is happening. A stranger's features
faintly start to twist before his eyes,
a half-formed ghost. He remembers the cries
of this man's wife, how he sought approval
without words to do what someone must
and how the blood stained into foreign dust.

A hundred agonies in black-and-white
from which his editor will pick out five or six
for Sunday's supplement. The reader's eyeballs prick
with tears between the bath and pre-lunch beers.
From the aeroplane he stares impassively at where
he earns his living and they do not care.

Analysing Poetry

Analysing a Pre-Twentieth Century Poem

Thomas Hardy's poem is also about war but from an earlier time. Drummer Hodge is a young British army drummer boy who died in South Africa during the Boer War (1899–1903). Drummer boys were often about 11 or 12 years old.

Read the poem carefully and think about these ideas:

- How Drummer Hodge is buried.
- How Hardy gives a sense that he is far from home.
- The tone of the poem.
- What effect you think Hardy might have wanted it to have on the reader.

You might have noted the following:

- There is no dignity or ceremony about his burial. He is simply thrown into the grave 'Uncoffined', just as he was found.
- Hardy uses South African words such as 'kopje-crest', (a small hill), veldt (open grassland plains), and mentions the 'foreign constellations' (the star constellations are different in the southern hemisphere).
- The tone of the poem is sad and regretful and emphasises the futility and waste of life that is one of the consequences of war.

Drummer Hodge by Thomas Hardy

They throw in Drummer Hodge, to rest
   Uncoffined – just as found:
His landmark is a kopje-crest
   That breaks the veldt around;
And foreign constellations west
   Each night above his mound.

Young Hodge the drummer never knew –
   Fresh from his Wessex home –
The meaning of the broad Karoo,
   The Bush, the dusty loam,
And why uprose to nightly view
   Strange stars amid the gloam.

Yet portion of that unknown plain
   Will Hodge for ever be;
His homely Northern breast and brain
   Grow to some Southern tree,
And strange-eyed constellations reign
   His stars eternally.

An Earlier Pre-Twentieth Century Poem

When reading *Drummer Hodge* you probably didn't notice many differences in terms of vocabulary between that poem and a poem that might have been written more recently. In some pre-twentieth century poems, though, the differences are more noticeable.

Look at this poem written by Ben Jonson, a poet and dramatist, after the death of his first son, Benjamin, who died at the age of seven.

💡 *What do you notice about the language?*

On my first Sonne by Ben Jonson

Farewell, thou child of my right hand, and joy;
My sinne was too much hope of thee, lov'd boy,
Seven yeeres tho'wert lent to me, and I thee pay,
Exacted by thy fate, on the just day.
O, could I loose all father, now. For why
Will man lament the state he should envie?
To have so soone scap'd worlds, and fleshes rage,
And, if no other miserie, yet age?
Rest in soft peace, and, ask'd, say here doth lye
Ben. Jonson his best piece of poetrie.
For whose sake, hence-forth, all his vowes be such,
As what he loves may never like too much.

You will have noticed the following:
- The spelling is quite different from modern spelling (although we can still understand the words).
- Some words have apostrophes in them where we wouldn't normally use an apostrophe today.
- Some words are ones that we don't use nowadays, e.g. 'wert' meaning 'was' and 'tho' which is an abbreviation of 'thou', meaning 'you'.

When reading pre-twentieth Century poetry you might find...
- old fashioned words that we don't use nowadays
- the word order is different from the modern word order we would use
- ideas that relate to the particular historical time it was written in
- references that you might need to look up to fully understand what they mean
- spellings that differ from modern English.

Quick Test

1. The words in a poem are called the _____.
2. Onomatopoeia and alliteration create _____ effects in a poem.
3. Name three kinds of imagery (figurative language).
4. When analysing a poem you need to explain the _____ created by the language.

KEY WORDS
Make sure you understand these words before moving on!
- Content
- Language
- Style
- Effects
- Analysing
- Vocabulary
- Imagery
- Sound
- Tone
- Mood
- Rhythm
- Rhyme

Analysing Poetry

Solve the clues to complete the quiz word and spell out the key words across the middle.

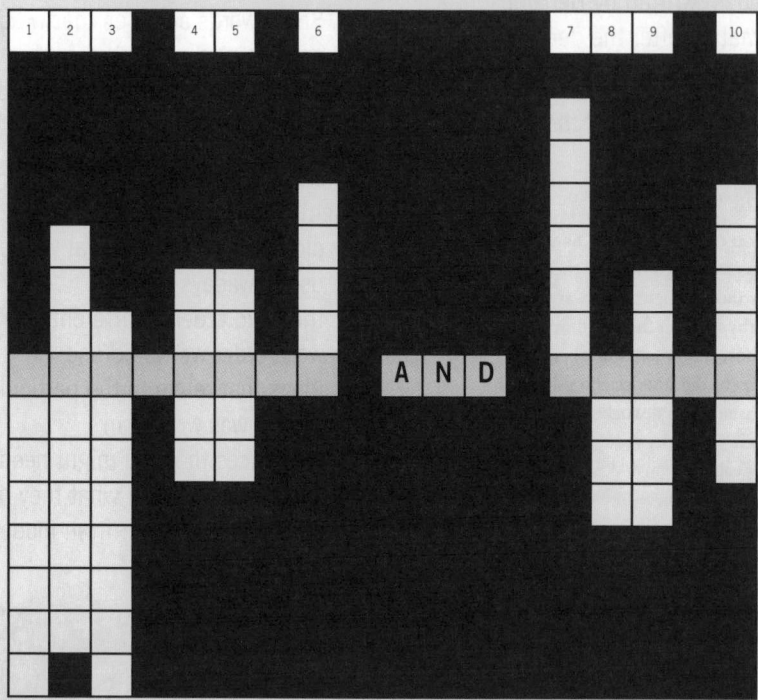

1. Poets choose the _____ they use very carefully when writing a poem.

2. The words they use.

3. You do this when you examine a poem carefully looking at the effects the language creates.

4. Onomatopoeia can be used to create a _____ effect.

5. A simile is an example of an _____.

6. Lines that end in a similar sound do this.

7. You need to explain the _____ created by the features you identify.

8. A voice might have a particular _____.

9. The 'beat' of a poem.

10. The idea in a poem.

Read this poem carefully and write an analysis of it.

Remember to ask yourself the following:

- What the poem is about (meaning).
- How the poet uses language.
- Why the poet uses language in that way.

Comment on these features, explaining the effects that are created:

- vocabulary
- use of imagery
- tone.

Blackberry-Picking by Seamus Heaney

Late August, given heavy rain and sun
For a full week, the blackberries would ripen.
At first, just one, a glossy purple clot
Among others, red, green, hard as a knot.
You ate that first one and its flesh was sweet
Like thickened wine: summer's blood was in it
Leaving stains upon the tongue and lust for
Picking. Then red ones inked up and that hunger
Sent us out with milk-cans, pea-tins, jam-pots
Where briars scratched and wet grass bleached our boots.
Round hayfields, cornfields and potato-drills
We trekked and picked until the cans were full,
Until the tinkling bottom had been covered
With green ones, and on top big dark blobs burned
Like a plate of eyes. Our hands were peppered
With thorn pricks, our palms sticky as Bluebeard's.

We hoarded the fresh berries in the byre.
But when the bath was filled we found a fur,
A rat-grey fungus, glutting on our cache.
The juice was stinking too. Once off the bush
The fruit fermented, the sweet flesh would turn sour.
I always felt like crying. It wasn't fair
That all the lovely canfuls smelt of rot.
Each year I hoped they'd keep, knew they would not.

Analysing Poetry

Choose a poem of your own and write an analysis of it.

Use the following approach:
- Read the poem through carefully several times.
- Make a note of the ideas that come into your head to begin with.
- Write down what you think the poem is about.
- Make notes on how the poet uses language (e.g. vocabulary, metaphors, similes) and the effects that they create.
- Describe the kind of tone and / or atmosphere created.
- Make a note of other effects created in the poem (e.g. rhyme, rhythm, alliteration, onomatopoeia).
- Note your overall thoughts and feelings about the poem.
- Use your notes to write up your analysis remembering to quote specific examples to illustrate your ideas.

Extension Activity

Use your completed analysis to prepare a talk to give to your class about your poem.

Plan what you're going to say carefully – don't just read out your analysis.

Structure your talk so that you give your audience a clear idea about what your chosen poem is about.

End your talk by saying why you chose this poem and what you find interesting or enjoyable about it. Allow time for your audience to ask you questions about it at the end.

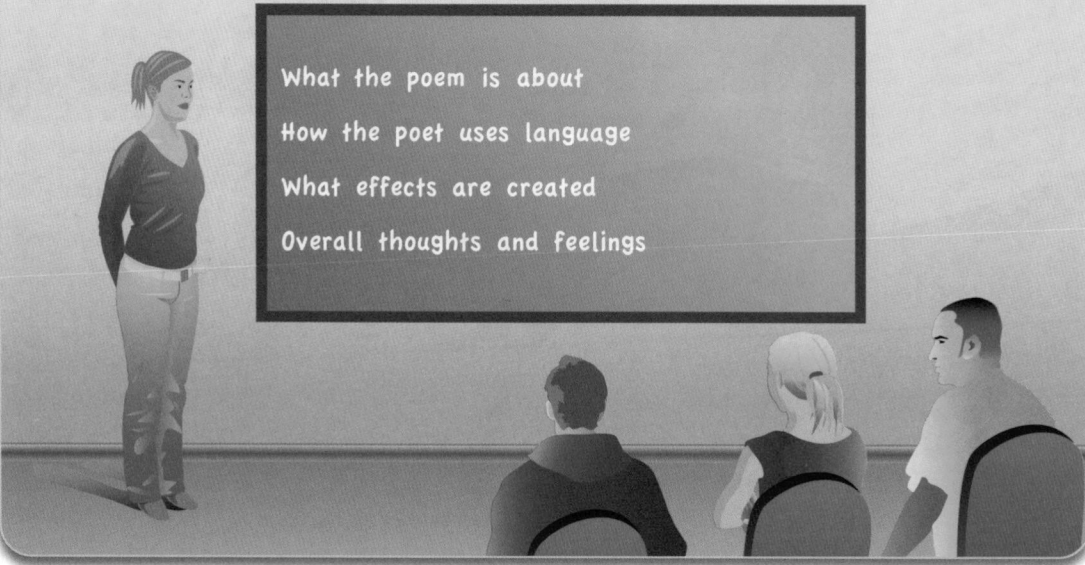

What the poem is about

How the poet uses language

What effects are created

Overall thoughts and feelings

Writing From Different Cultures

What is Covered in this Topic?

This topic looks at...
- poetry from different cultures
- prose from different cultures
- how language is used.

Different Cultures and Traditions

Writing can come from a wide range of different cultures, each with their own distinctive traditions and ways of life.

💡 *How many examples of literature from different places in the world have you read?*

Here are some broad areas:

Even within each of these broad areas there are many different kinds of cultures and traditions, each with their own distinctive ways of life. This is reflected in their writings.

Europe

USA

Asia

Different Cultures and Traditions

South America

Africa

Australia

How Writings Differ

From what you've read from writings from other cultures, you might have noticed the following:
- Different traditions, customs, beliefs, rituals and ways of life are described.
- Unfamiliar words are used to describe particular things.
- Non-standard or dialect forms are sometimes used to reflect the voice of the speaker or writer.

Writing From Different Cultures

Poetry From Different Cultures

Read the following poem carefully and think about...
- what the poet describes
- what kind of atmosphere she creates
- how she uses language.

Blessing by Imtiaz Dharker

The skin cracks like a pod.
There never is enough water.

Imagine the drip of it,
the small splash, echo
in a tin mug,
the voice of a kindly god.

Sometimes, the sudden rush
of fortune. The municipal pipe bursts,
silver crashes to the ground
and the flow has found
a roar of tongues. From the huts,
a congregation: every man woman
child for streets around
butts in, with pots,
brass, copper, aluminium,
plastic buckets,
frantic hands,

and naked children
screaming in the liquid sun,
their highlights polished to perfection,
flashing light,
as the blessing sings
over their small bones.

Here are some ideas you might have noted about the poem:
- The poem describes the bursting of a water pipe in a village where water is very scarce and how the people respond to this event.
- The atmosphere the poet creates is one of great excitement as everyone rushes to catch as much water as they can in any kind of container they can find.
- The dry, drought conditions are captured vividly through the use of a **simile** – 'The skin cracks like a pod'.
- **Metaphors** are used to create a vivid impression of the scene, e.g. 'the sudden rush of fortune', 'silver crashes to the ground', 'liquid sun'.
- **Vocabulary** is used to create the sense of excitement, e.g. 'roar of tongues', 'frantic hands', 'children screaming'.

Prose From Different Cultures

The following extract from *Green Days By The River*, by Michael Anthony, is set in Trinidad. Read through it carefully.

💡 *What do you notice about the vocabulary that the writer uses?*

The description contains several words that you're probably not familiar with but which are commonly used terms in Trinidadian culture. You might have noted these terms:

- Sapodillas, shaddocks, star-apples and pomerac, which are all kinds of fruit that are found in Trinidad.
- Roti – a kind of bread commonly baked in the West Indies.
- Creole – from a mixture of European and another culture.
- 'Ortoire' – the name of the river.

You will have also noticed how the writer describes activities, which are typical of life in that part of the world and that culture, e.g. fruit picking and rice cutting.

MR GIDHAREE let me climb some other fruit trees and we collected some fruit in an old sack he had. I picked sapodillas, shaddocks, and star-apples, and he showed me where the banana trees were. These had huge bunches of ripe bananas and here was where the birds feasted. Most of the bunches were rotting and fly-infested and the bananas themselves were half-eaten by birds.

'You want?' he said.

'No. Don't really feel like it so much. But I smelling pomerac.'

He smiled and looked up. 'You nose good, boy.'

In the tangle of branches above the banana trees were clusters of the red, pear-shaped fruit we called pomerac, and finding the tree now, I climbed and picked a good deal. When I came down again, he said, 'Okay. What you pick is for you – for when you going home'

'You don't want none?' I wished he would take some, at least.

'Just a couple for Rosie, that's all.'

I took out some nice ones and put them aside then I pulled up one of the vines on the ground and tied the sack-mouth. Then I took the sack into our little hut and I came back and took Rosalie's fruit into the hut. Tiger, the spotted dog, woke up when I went in the second time, and at once he pricked up his ears and was on the alert.

'Tiger:' I said, 'lazy!' I approached him cautiously. Somehow I was still afraid of this one.

He looked up at me with soft eyes. Then he wagged his tail a little. I went out again, and Mr Gidharee said, 'Listen, we going down by the rice now.'

'All right.'

'When you feel peckish, say. We have plenty roti in the bag.' I said nothing.

He looked at me as if doubtful. 'You ain't one of those *creole* who shame to eat roti!'

'Me? No, Mr Gidharee. Not me.'

'Oho,' he said.

We cut rice paddies for about two hours steadily, working in the part of the field near the river. The sun was hot now, and Ortoire, like a long, slithering snake, eased beside us. We were using grass-knives, and after Mr Gidharee had shown me what to do, I did not need any more showing and we cut rice man for man.

Writing From Different Cultures

Approaching Writing From Different Cultures

In addition to the language used and the effects created, there are other features you can look for in writing.

Here are some ideas:

Attitudes

Vocabulary of the culture / tradition

Environment / living conditions

Cultural features

Cultural differences / similarities

Beliefs / religion

Descriptions of places

Quick Test

Complete the sentences below.

1. Another word for dialect form is

   _____ _____ .

2. Literature from different cultures can come from anywhere in the _____ .

3. Another word for a ceremony is a

   _____ .

4. A writer sometimes uses non-standard forms of English to reflect the speaker's

   _____ .

Unscramble the anagrams to find the key words, then draw a line to match them to the right definition.

A person's or group's religious ideas.

A kind of imagery where one thing is said to be another.

CAROVALBUY

RUTCLUE

The words or language used.

SAILRUT

The customs, way of life, traditions, etc., of a particular group of people.

CUTMOSS

RANDSANDNOT

The form of speech of a particular region or part of the world.

COVIE

Literature from different cultures can come from all over the _____.

RADIOTINT

These are often carried out at religious ceremonies.

FIBEELS

Dialect is a _____ form of English.

DOLWR

A comparison where one thing is said to be like another.

CITADEL

A custom, belief or way of doing things, handed down from generation to generation.

EARTHMOP

MILEIS

Non-standard English can be used in writing to create a sense of _____.

The usual ways of behaving or doing things.

Writing From Different Cultures

Testing Understanding

Be a Butterfly by Grace Nichols

Don't be a kyatta-pilla
Be a butterfly
old preacher screamed
to illustrate his sermon
of Jesus and the higher life

rivulets of well-earned
sweat sliding down
his muscly mahogany face
in the half-empty school church
we sat shaking with muffling
laughter
watching our mother trying to save
herself from joining the wave

only our father remaining poker face
and afterwards we always went home to
split peas Sunday soup
with dumplings, fufu* and pigtail*

Don't be a kyatta-pilla
Be a butterfly
Be a butterfly

That was de life preacher
and you was right.

* fufu – dough made with corn meal
* pigtail – salted, cured pig's tail

Read this poem carefully and answer these questions.

1. What does the Butterfly represent to the preacher in the first stanza?
2. How does the speaker and most of the congregation respond to the preacher's sermon? How does the speaker feel at the end of the poem?
3. How does the father react?
4. What does the description of the Sunday lunch tell you?
5. Can you find any examples of non-standard English?

Look at some other poems from different cultures and pick one for more detailed study.

You will find your school's resource learning centre or library useful in finding examples of poetry from other cultures. Or you may have anthologies in the classroom that you can use.

When you have chosen your poem make notes on it using these questions as a checklist:
- What does the title of the poem suggest to you?
- What is the poem about?
- Does the poet use dialect or non-standard English?
- Does the poet use imagery (e.g. metaphors, similes, etc.)?
- What effects are created by the language used?
- Does the poet create an impression of the culture / traditions / beliefs, etc? If so, how are they presented and what effects do you think they have on the poem?
- What do you feel about the poem overall?

When you have completed all your notes, write them up as a full analysis of the poem.

Work with a partner to take turns to read your poems aloud to each other (you could try recording your readings and listening to them several times).

Talk about your responses to each other's readings. Does reading the poems aloud change your ideas about them in any way?

Shakespeare

Shakespeare 1

What is Covered in this Topic?

This topic looks at...
- the background to Shakespeare's theatre and drama
- how Shakespearean language is linked to modern-day language
- features of historical writing.

The Original Globe Theatre

Shakespeare was a shareholder in the original Globe Theatre and many of his plays were presented there. The original Globe Theatre...
- was opened in 1599 in London
- was a wood-framed building, roughly circular in shape
- could hold between 2000 and 3000 people
- burned down in 1613 when a cannon used as an effect in *Henry VIII* set fire to it. **Excavations** in the 20th Century revealed the site. Part of the Globe lies under protected buildings, so further **archaeology** isn't allowed.

The Audience

- It cost one old penny to watch the plays. For two pennies, you could sit under cover in a **gallery** with a good view where other people could see you.
- Up to 1000 penny-paying **groundlings** would stand in the 'pit' in front of the stage, squashed and exposed to the weather.
- Shakespeare wrote about groundlings unkindly, saying, in *Hamlet*, that they could only understand simple performances.
- It was possible to buy food and drink in the theatre and if the play or the actors weren't liked, it could be thrown at them!

Performance

- Plays didn't begin as they do now – there were no lights or curtains to tell the audience that the play was starting.
- Shakespeare used several ways to get the audience's attention. For example, *Romeo and Juliet* starts with a spoken **prologue**, followed by **bawdy** jokes and a large fight.

Actors and Props

- There were very few props. They were often left on stage as there was no easy way of removing them.
- There were some stage and sound effects, such as fireworks and musical instruments.
- Actors entered the stage from the rear, where they would get ready first. They might appear from trapdoors or from above on a rope if the play demanded it.
- All parts were played by men as it was a sign of shame for a woman to act on stage.
- Teenage boys would play younger girls, but would fall out of favour or move onto other parts when their voices broke.

Shakespeare 1

Inside the Globe

This diagram shows what it was like inside the Globe Theatre.

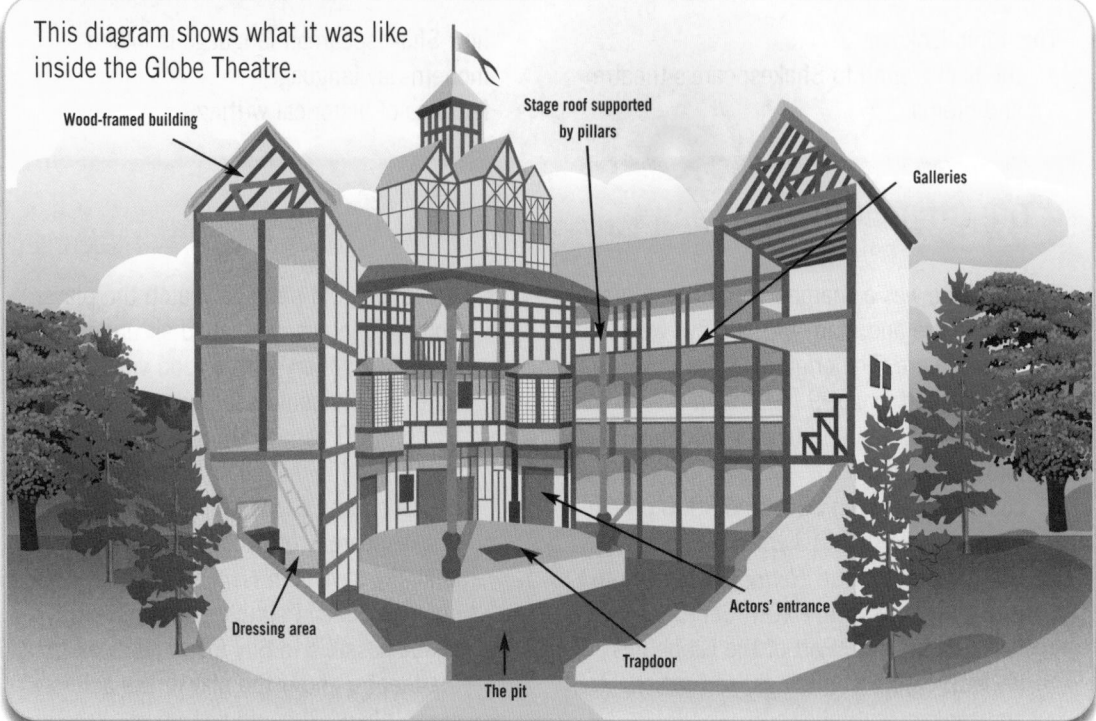

Wood-framed building

Stage roof supported by pillars

Galleries

Dressing area

The pit

Trapdoor

Actors' entrance

Eyewitness Account

Read this account by Sir Henry Wooton, written in July 1613, of the burning down of the Globe Theatre.

💡 From this account, what can you work out about the costumes of the actors in this play?

💡 What do you think 'certain chambers being shot off at his entry' is describing? (Clue – think of the chambers of a gun)

💡 Why didn't the audience notice the fire at first?

Now, to let matters of state sleep, I will entertain you at the present with what happened this week at the Bankside. The King's players had a new play, called All is True, representing some principal pieces of the reign of Henry VIII, which was set forth with many extraordinary circumstances of pomp and majesty, even to the matting of the stage; the Knights of the Order with their Georges and garters, the Guards with their embroidered coats, and the like: sufficient in truth within a while to make greatness very familiar, if not ridiculous. Now, King Henry making a masque at the Cardinal Wolsey's house, and certain chambers being shot off at his entry, some of the paper, or other stuff, wherewith one of them was stopped, did light on the thatch, where being thought at first but an idle smoke, and their eyes more attentive to the show, it kindled inwardly, and ran round like a train, consuming within less than an hour the whole house to the very grounds.

Macbeth

Macbeth was written and first performed, it is believed, in 1606.

Plays were performed in the open and, as there were no stage lights, they had to be performed in the daytime.

Shakespeare had to give the audience an idea of the setting from the characters' words in the play, rather than from lighting effects.

💡 *Can you see how he does this in the extract from the opening scene of Macbeth below?*

Macbeth – Act 1 Scene 1

The passage below contains words that aren't used much nowadays. For example...

- hurlyburly = confusion
- exeunt = exit
- ere = before
- anon = see you later.

> *Thunder and lightning.*
> *Enter three Witches*
>
> First Witch   When shall we three
>   meet again?
>   In thunder, lightning,
>   or in rain?
> Second Witch   When the hurlyburly's done,
>   When the battle's lost and won.
> Third Witch   That will be ere the set of sun.
> First Witch   Where the place?
> Second Witch   Upon the heath.
> Third Witch   There to meet with Macbeth.
> First Witch   I come, Graymalkin!
> Second Witch   Paddock calls.
> Third Witch   Anon.
> ALL   Fair is foul, and foul is fair:
>   Hover through the fog
>   and filthy air.
>
> *Exeunt*

💡 *Do any words in the passage have similarities with modern words, phrases or ideas?*

Shakespeare 1

Modern Meaning

Some Elizabethan words Shakespeare uses are similar to modern words. The following extract shows Lady Macbeth talking about what the witches have promised her husband Macbeth, and what she feels about him.

> Glamis thou art, and Cawdor, and shalt be
> What thou art promised. Yet do I fear thy nature.
> It is too full o' the milk of human kindness
> To catch the nearest way. Thou wouldst be great;
> Art not without ambition, but without
> The illness should attend it.

Here are some more Shakespearean words and their modern meanings:

- Nature = Character.
- Milk of human kindness = Goodness.
- Catch the nearest way = Take a short cut.
- Attend = Go with.

Deciphering Shakespeare

Shakespeare often uses words that we don't use anymore. This witch's speech could be hard to understand so a copy of the play that includes a glossary or notes will be useful.

> Weary se'nnights nine times nine
> Shall he dwindle, peak, and pine;
> Though his bark cannot be lost,
> Yet it shall be tempest-toss'd.
>
> ---
> *Notes
> se'nnights = seven nights
> dwindle, peak, and pine = waste away in agony
> bark = ship or boat
> tempest-toss'd = thrown about by storms

 Try to translate this short speech, using the notes above.

Understanding Shakespeare

It's not too hard to understand Shakespeare if you learn about the way he writes.

Sometimes he changes word order to...
- fit a rhyme
- fit a certain number of beats / syllables
- add emphasis.

Word order is called **syntax**, so Shakespeare is changing the normal syntax.

Can you find an example of this in the Macbeth extract on page 201?

Quick Test

1. In which city was the Globe Theatre found?
2. Who played all the parts in plays in Shakespeare's time?
3. What was the area called at the front of the stage where the groundlings stood?
4. What was the main way that Shakespeare helped to set the scene without lighting?

KEY WORDS
Make sure you understand these words before moving on!
- Gallery
- Groundlings
- Prologue
- Bawdy
- Excavations
- Archaeology
- Pomp
- Masque
- Thatch
- Kindled
- Syntax
- Syllables

Key Words Exercise

Match each key word with its meaning.

Gallery		Rude and loud
Groundlings		The study of history through digging up the past
Prologue		Showing-off linked to well-off people
Bawdy		Changing word order
Excavations		Set fire
Archaeology		Digs done by archaeologists
Pomp		A kind of play
Masque		People who paid a penny to stand and watch a play
Thatch		Beats in a word or a line of text
Kindled		An introduction to a play before the main story begins
Syllables		Roof material made from straw
Syntax		Raised seats in the theatre

Anagrams

Use the following clues to unscramble each word:

1. Shakespeare's famous tragedy about the Prince of Denmark.

   LEAMTH

2. Shakespeare's play about doomed lovers.

   ORMOE DNA JULTIE

3. Shakespeare's play about an evil Scottish king.

   HCAEBMT

4. Shakespeare's main theatre.

   HTE BOLGE

5. In a Shakespearean theatre, this was where the covered seats were.

   RLAGLEY

Shakespeare 1

Are the following statements true or false?

1. The original Globe Theatre was built in 1601.

2. The original Globe Theatre could hold between 2000 and 3000 people.

3. The cheapest place to stand in the Globe Theatre was the pit.

4. It cost one pound to stand in the pit.

5. Plays took place at night at the original Globe.

6. *Romeo and Juliet* starts off with a love scene.

7. The Globe Theatre used scenery that was moved on and off stage during the play.

8. Actors at the Globe might pop up through a trapdoor if it was needed.

9. Women played some of the best parts in Shakespeare's time.

10. Fireworks might be used in an original Globe play.

11. The original Globe burned down.

12. The last play performed at the original Globe was *Henry VIII*.

13. There are four witches in the opening scene of *Macbeth*.

14. Lady Macbeth is Macbeth's mother.

15. Shakespeare wrote in a completely different type of language to that used today.

16. A prologue would come at the end of a play.

17. Musical instruments would be used to create sound effects for the performance of Shakespeare's plays.

18. A groundling was an actor.

19. The original Globe put on performances for hundreds of years.

20. Fruit and vegetables might be thrown at the performers.

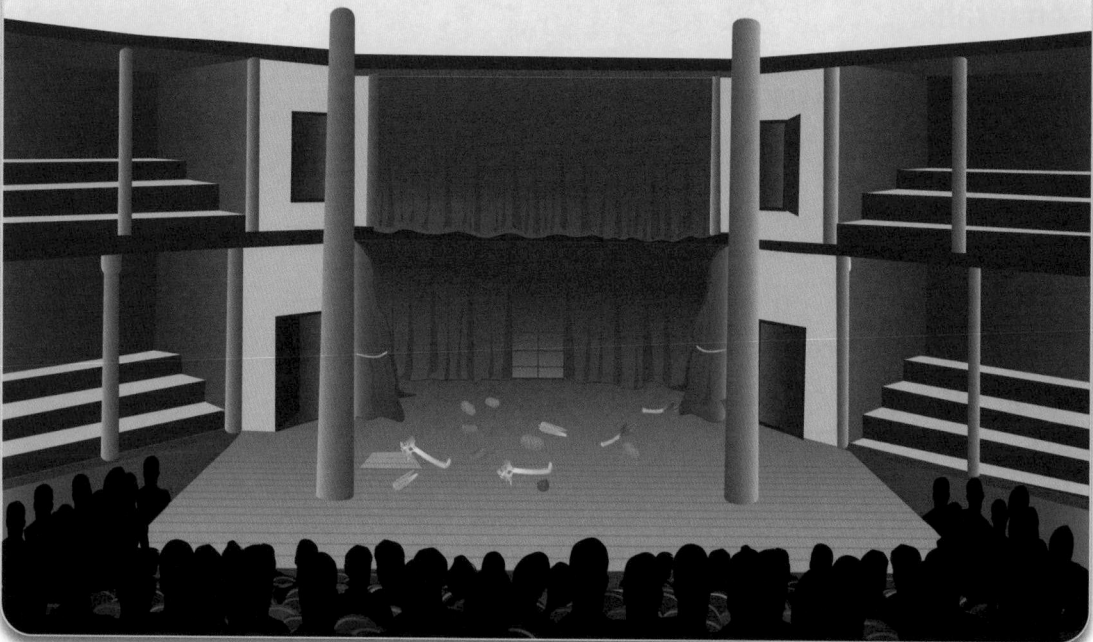

Skills Practice

Use the information in this topic to produce a guide to Shakespeare's original Globe theatre. Your guide must be aimed at tourists who don't know much about the theatre. It should be 250–300 words long and might include pictures.

Step 1: Your audience consists of tourists. How will this affect the information that you include?

How much detail will they need? Are all tourists the same, or should you consider the different kinds of tourists who might be interested in the original Globe?

How will the fact that you're writing for some people who don't know much about the original Globe affect...
- your choice of vocabulary?
- your style – formal or informal, or a mixture of both?
- the amount of detail you include?

Step 2: Look through the topic and make a list of information you think would be interesting to tourists. Make a list in order of importance and number it so that 1 = the most important.

Step 3: Do a word count of what you've included in your list. Do you think you have the right amount of information? If you have too much information, use the order of importance you have made to remove some things at the bottom of your list. If you haven't got enough, look at what else you could add.

Step 4: How are you going to organise your information? Sort it into paragraphs or sections based on topics. For example, if you have three points about what the theatre looked like, put them all in the same section or paragraph.

Step 5: Decide what pictures you might use and where you will put them so that they fit with the text. What pictures would grab the reader's attention? Draft your layout and text to see if it works. Drafting it on a computer will help you to play around with the order to see what works best.

Extension Activity

Rewrite the guide for a different audience – for example, Year 4 pupils. What would you do differently and why?

Shakespeare 2

What is Covered in This Topic?

This topic looks at...
- the various types of plays Shakespeare wrote
- Shakespeare's characters
- how Shakespeare used soliloquies and asides
- Shakespeare's language.

Types of Shakespeare Plays

Shakespeare wrote his 38 plays between 1590 and 1613. He wrote many different kinds of plays about different situations and characters. His plays can be divided into these main types:

Tragedies   Comedies

Histories   Romances

Tragedies

In Shakespeare's **tragedies** the main character always dies at the end. Often, several other characters die or are killed too. Some of his best known tragedies are:
- *Romeo and Juliet*
- *Macbeth*
- *Othello*.

Comedies

A comedy is something that makes us laugh. Shakespeare's **comedies** contain very funny events and characters, but some contain very serious situations too. To Shakespeare's audience, a comedy ended happily, for example...
- *Twelfth Night*
- *A Midsummer Night's Dream*
- *The Merchant of Venice*.

Histories

The **histories** are plays about events and characters from history, usually kings or important leaders. Some well-known history plays are:
- *Richard III*
- *Henry V*
- *Julius Caesar*.

Romances

Romances are sometimes called Shakespeare's '**Last Plays**' because they were the last ones he wrote. These make use of fantasy or magic in their plots. Some well-known romance plays:
- *The Tempest*
- *The Winter's Tale*.

Twelfth Night

Twelfth Night is one of Shakespeare's comedies. The play is about identical twins Viola and her brother Sebastian. They are shipwrecked and become separated on the coast of Illyria.

The **plot** or storyline of the play is about the adventures that happen to the pair before they're reunited and involves disguise, mistaken identity and love.

The Structure of the Comedy

'**Structure**' is the word used to describe how the events of the play's storyline are arranged in a certain order. Shakespeare's comedies had a typical structure, which the play *Twelfth Night* follows:

1. Characters meet and fall in love.
2. Various things go wrong, such as mistaken identity.
3. The problems are all sorted out.
4. The play ends happily with the lovers together.

Learning About Characters

Characters are a key part of plays and we learn about them in various ways. In a play you can learn about characters by looking at...
- how a character behaves
- what the character says
- what other characters say about them.

Sir Toby Belch is one of the comic characters in Twelfth Night. *What can you find out about him from these extracts from the play?*

1. *Maria: By my troth, Sir Toby, you must come in earlier o' nights.*
2. *Maria: That quaffing and drinking will undo you.*
3. *Sir Toby: With drinking health to my niece. I'll drink to her as long as there is a passage in my throat and drink in Illyria.*

Shakespeare 2

Soliloquies

One of the techniques Shakespeare uses to give us more information about a character is the **soliloquy**. This is a speech made by a character when they're alone on stage or when they seem to be talking directly to the audience.

A soliloquy can...
- let the audience know the character's thoughts and feelings
- let the audience know what the characters intend to do
- give information that other characters don't know.

Romeo and Juliet

In the tragedy *Romeo and Juliet*, Romeo falls in love at first sight with Juliet. This is an extract from Romeo's soliloquy as he walks alone in the orchard, beneath her window:

> But soft, what light through yonder window breaks?
>   It is the east, and Juliet is the sun.
> Arise fair sun and kill the envious moon,
>   Who is already sick and pale with grief
> That thou her maid art far more fair than she.
>   Be not her maid since she is envious.
> Her vestal livery is sick and green,
>   And none but fools wear it; cast it off.

Romeo compares Juliet to the sun – she is so much brighter than the moon, which is cold and pale in comparison.

In mythology, Diana was goddess of the moon and was served by maids dressed in 'vestal livery'.

💡 *Write your own modern version of what Romeo is saying in this soliloquy.*

Imagery

Shakespeare uses **imagery** to make Romeo's words more effective and dramatic. Imagery is a particular way of using language to make it more descriptive and powerful.

Metaphors and Similes

Shakespeare uses a particular type of imagery called a **metaphor** when he says that 'Juliet is the sun'.

A metaphor compares one thing to another. Unlike a **simile**, which would say Juliet is 'like' the sun, a metaphor actually says Juliet 'is' the sun.

Shakespeare also uses **personification**, which is when something that's not human is given human feelings or characteristics. For example, Shakespeare says that the moon is 'envious'.

💡 *What other examples of imagery can you see in this next part of Romeo's speech? You might find an example of...*
- *a simile*
- *a metaphor.*

> The brightness of her cheek would shame those stars,
> As daylight doth a lamp; her eyes in heaven
> Would through the airy region stream so bright
> That birds would sing, and think it were not night.

Quick Test

1. True or false – 'Arise fair sun and kill the envious moon' is a simile.
2. True or false – *The Tempest* is a history play.
3. True or false – Viola is a character in *Twelfth Night*.
4. True or false – *Romeo and Juliet* is a tragedy.
5. True or false – a soliloquy is meant to be heard only by the audience.

KEY WORDS
Make sure you understand these words before moving on!
- Tragedy
- Comedy
- History
- Romance
- Last plays
- Plot
- Structure
- Soliloquy
- Imagery
- Metaphor
- Simile
- Personification

Shakespeare 2

Match each key word with its meaning.

Simile	A kind of metaphor where something that's not human is described as if it has human feelings or qualities.
Plot	A comparison, using the words 'like' or 'as'.
Histories	Another term for Romances.
Metaphors	The way the action of a play is put together.
Romances	Plays with a happy ending.
Imagery	A comparison, saying that one thing actually is the other.
Soliloquy	The storyline of a play.
Comedies	Plays based on historical figures.
Structure	Plays that have a fantasy or magical element and were the last plays Shakespeare wrote.
Personification	What a character speaks while alone on stage.
Tragedies	The use of words to create a picture or 'image'.
Last plays	Plays that end with the death of the main character(s).

Anagrams

Use the following clues to unscramble each word.

1. The way a play is put together.   TRUCRUTES
2. A comparison using 'like' or 'as'.   ESMILI
3. A play about a Roman Emperor.   LUISJU RECSAA
4. 'The sun smiled down on us' is an example of this.   FEARININOTIPOCS
5. These plays often include magic.   SAROMENC

Testing Understanding

1 Are the following statements true or false?

a) Shakespeare wrote 38 plays in all.

b) *Othello* is an example of a comedy.

c) Shakespeare's tragedies usually end with the death of the main character.

d) *The Merchant of Venice* is a comedy.

e) *Richard III* is a history play.

f) *The Tempest* is a tragedy.

g) Romeo is the hero of *Twelfth Night*.

h) Sir Toby Belch is a character in *A Midsummer Night's Dream*.

i) Viola in *Twelfth Night* has a twin brother.

j) In a soliloquy, a character speaks to the other characters in the play.

2 Which of the following extracts are similes and which are metaphors?

a) '...she hangs upon the cheek of night
   Like a rich jewel in an Ethiop's ear.'   (*Romeo and Juliet*)

b) '...thou echoest me,
   As if there were some monster in thy thought
   Too hideous to be shown.'   (*Othello*)

c) 'If I catch him once upon the hip,
   I will feed fat the ancient grudge I bear him.'   (*The Merchant of Venice*)

d) 'Death is my son-in-law, death is my heir,
   My daughter he hath wedded.'   (*Romeo and Juliet*)

e) '...Although I joy in thee,
   I have no joy of this contract tonight.
   It is too rash, too unadvised, too sudden;
   Too like the summer lightning, which doth cease to be
   Ere one can say, "It lightens".'   (*Romeo and Juliet*)

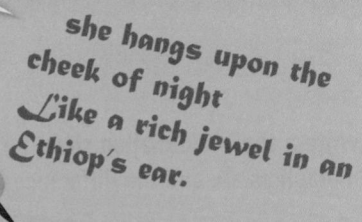

she hangs upon the cheek of night
Like a rich jewel in an Ethiop's ear.

Shakespeare 2

Choose a Shakespeare play. You could pick a play you know and have studied before, or choose another one if you want to.

Step 1: Say what kind of play it is and write a brief summary of the plot. Find two soliloquies from the play and explain...
   a) where each soliloquy comes in the play
   b) who the speakers are
   c) what information, ideas, feelings, etc. they reveal to the audience
   d) what each soliloquy tells you about the character.

Step 2: Now find three examples of similes and three examples of metaphors from your play. Explain each example, writing about...
   a) what things are being compared
   b) the language Shakespeare uses
   c) the effects created by the simile or metaphor
   d) what you think about each one.

Extension Activity

Write a short information sheet for other students in your group, explaining what similes and metaphors are and the differences between them.

Illustrate your information sheet with examples from Shakespeare plays.

Present the information sheet to your class, explaining why you chose the examples that you used.

Shakespeare's Language

This topic looks at…
- Shakespeare's use of antithesis and oxymoron
- the use of personification
- the effects of hyperbole
- the use of puns.

Language Techniques

Although plays combine both words and action, **language** is at the heart of all Shakespeare's plays. It is through the language that the whole effect of the **drama** is created.

In order to create his effects, Shakespeare uses different kinds of language **techniques** that work together to create the overall experience of the play for the audience.

Here are some of the techniques that he uses in his plays:

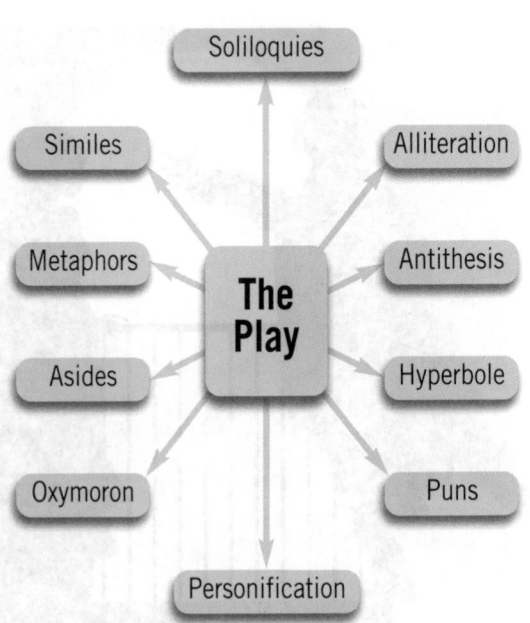

Soliloquies · Similes · Metaphors · Asides · Oxymoron · **The Play** · Alliteration · Antithesis · Hyperbole · Puns · Personification

SCENE 1

ROMEO:

But soft, what light through yonder window breaks?
It is the east, and Juliet is the sun.
Arise fair sun and kill the envious moon,
Who is already sick and pale with grief
That thou her maid art far more fair than she.
Be not her maid since she is envious.
Her vestal livery is sick and green,
And none but fools wear it; cast it off.

Shakespeare's Language

Antithesis

Antithesis puts two opposing thoughts or ideas together. It's a technique used a lot by Shakespeare, but one that we also use in our own everyday speech.

For example, if you say 'I love the subject, but I hate doing the work', you're using antithesis.

One of the best-known examples of antithesis from a Shakespearean play is the opening line of Hamlet's famous **soliloquy**: 'To be, or not to be: that is the question.' (A soliloquy is a speech given by a character when they're alone on the stage.)

In this soliloquy, Shakespeare juxtaposes the opposite ideas of existing or not existing. (**Juxtaposition** is when one idea is put next to another, i.e. a contrasting idea.)

The quotes below show some more examples from Shakespeare's plays.

The following example is the witches' chant from *Macbeth*:

> Fair is foul, and foul is fair;
> Hover through the fog and filthy air.

In *Othello*, Othello accuses his wife Desdemona of being false to him:

> Heaven truly knows that thou art as false as hell.

Here Othello uses antithesis (heaven / hell and true / false) in the simile to stress how false he believes Desdemona to be.

Oxymoron

Oxymoron is a very similar technique to antithesis. It puts two opposing words or ideas together in order to make a striking phrase or expression. For example, in *Romeo and Juliet*, when Juliet says goodbye to Romeo she says:

> Good Night, Good night! Parting is such sweet sorrow,
> That I shall say good night till it be morrow.

Here Shakespeare creates an effective phrase to capture Juliet's joy in her love and the thought of seeing Romeo again, contrasted with the sorrow she feels at parting from him.

Personification

Another technique that Shakespeare often uses to add effect to his language is **personification**. This describes an object or idea as if it were a human with human thoughts and feelings.

For example in *Romeo and Juliet*, Romeo uses personification to describe the tomb that contains Juliet:

> Thou detestable maw, thou womb of death,
> Gorg'd with the dearest morsel of the earth,
> Thus I enforce thy rotten jaws to open,

💡 *How do you think the tomb is described here?*

'Maw' is an old word that means 'stomach' – so in this example Romeo is describing the tomb as if it's a living thing that has eaten Juliet ('the dearest morsel of the earth'). He also describes it as a 'womb' – again something that a living being has. He intends to force the being's jaws open to get to his love.

In the following example from *Macbeth*, Shakespeare describes the country of Scotland, which is suffering under Macbeth's rule, as if it were a living thing that could be physically injured and feel pain and weep.

> I think our country sinks beneath the yoke;
> It weeps, it bleeds, and each new day a gash
> Is added to her wounds.

💡 *Think about the effects created by the use of personification in these examples. How has it made the image of the tomb or the country more vivid in your mind?*

Hyperbole

Hyperbole is the **exaggerated** and **extravagant** use of language to create a special impact or effect.

In the following example Othello, having passed through a violent storm at sea, is reunited with his beloved Desdemona. Look at the extravagant language that he uses to describe the storm and express his joy at being with Desdemona again.

💡 *Do you notice any other technique used here too?*

> It gives me wonder great as my content
> To see you here before me. O my soul's joy!
> If after every tempest come such calms,
> May the winds blow till they have waken'd death!
> And let the labouring bark climb hills of seas
> Olympus-high and duck again as low
> As hell's from heaven! If it were now to die,
> 'Twere now to be most happy; for, I fear,
> My soul hath her content so absolute
> That not another comfort like to this
> Succeeds in unknown fate

As well as hyperbole you might also have noticed the use of antithesis (tempest / calm, hell / heaven).

Shakespeare's Language

Puns

Shakespeare's plays are full of **puns** because the Elizabethan audiences of the times loved them. A pun is a play on words in order to create a funny effect. Puns work by playing around with words that have a double meaning or that sound similar to another word that means something quite different to the first word.

Lots of Shakespeare's puns are still obvious (and funny) today. However, sometimes it's not always easy to spot the puns or appreciate how funny they must have been to an Elizabethan audience. There are two reasons for this:

- The language has changed and so the meaning of the pun isn't immediately obvious.
- The modern sense of humour isn't quite the same as it was in the sixteenth century.

So, sometimes you might need to work at a pun to see what it might have meant to Shakespeare's audience.

The following two examples are from *Romeo and Juliet*:

Here Romeo is love-sick and gloomy, and his friend Mercutio is trying to cheer him up.

💡 *Can you spot the words that are played with?*

> Mercutio: You are a lover; borrow cupid's wings,
> And soar with them above a common bound.
> Romeo: I am too sore empierced with his shaft
> To soar with his light feathers.

This example plays on the idea of soar (to fly) and sore (something painful).

Even when fatally wounded in a sword fight, Mercutio makes a pun.

> Romeo: Courage, man. The hurt cannot be much.
> Mercutio: No, 'tis not so deep as a well, nor so wide as a church door; but 'tis enough, 'twill serve. Ask for me to-morrow, and you shall find me a grave man.

Notice here how the play is on the word 'grave', which means 'serious' and is also the place where a dead person is buried.

Quick Test

1. A play on words is called a

   _____.

2. Exaggerated language is called

   _____.

3. A soliloquy is a speech given when the speaker is _____ on the stage.

4. When one idea or word is placed beside a contrasting idea, it's called

   _____.

KEY WORDS
Make sure you understand these words before moving on!

- Language
- Drama
- Techniques
- Antithesis
- Soliloquy
- Juxtaposition
- Oxymoron
- Personification
- Hyperbole
- Exaggerated
- Extravagant
- Puns

Key Words Exercise

Work out the key words from the clues below, then find them in the word search.

1. Hyperbole is the _____ and _____ use of language.

2. A play is a form of this.

3. When contrasting words or ideas are placed next to each other it is called _____.

4. Shakespeare uses different _____ to create effects in his plays.

5. Describing a thing or an idea as if it were a living person.

6. A speech given by a character when he / she is alone on the stage.

7. Exaggerated language.

8. A striking phrase that uses opposing ideas.

9. Shakespeare uses many different kinds of _____ techniques in his plays.

10. Plays on words.

11. Two opposite thoughts or ideas that are put together.

E	S	T	A	A	F	C	A	Y	V	K	S	J	J	P
X	O	L	E	N	N	B	T	A	S	J	H	U	T	E
T	L	A	P	C	D	T	R	A	H	G	D	X	S	R
R	I	N	H	P	H	L	I	T	E	N	R	T	E	S
A	L	G	Y	F	C	N	H	T	G	C	A	A	V	O
V	O	U	P	T	D	Q	I	K	H	V	M	P	L	N
A	Q	A	E	R	F	E	J	Q	H	E	A	O	M	I
G	U	G	R	I	G	W	F	P	U	L	S	S	O	F
A	Y	E	B	H	B	R	A	P	U	E	A	I	C	I
N	W	E	O	Q	J	Y	E	L	S	N	S	T	S	C
T	Y	S	L	X	K	J	T	E	T	L	S	I	K	A
Q	N	R	E	T	E	I	O	D	A	Y	D	O	L	T
D	I	E	U	O	X	Y	M	O	R	O	N	N	G	I
J	E	X	A	G	G	E	R	A	T	E	D	S	T	O
P	E	R	S	O	P	E	X	A	G	E	R	A	D	N

Shakespeare's Language

1 In *Romeo and Juliet*, Juliet (from the Capulet family) finds that Romeo is from the family of her family's enemies (the Montagues). Shakespeare uses antithesis to express Juliet's feelings.

Explain how antithesis is used here and the effect it creates.

> My only love, sprung from my only hate!
> Too early seen unknown, and known too late!
> Prodigious birth of love it is to me
> That I must love a loathed enemy.

2 At the beginning of the play Romeo is in love with a girl called Rosaline, but she doesn't feel the same about him. Oxymoron is used to express his feelings.

Explain how oxymoron is used here and the effect it creates.

> O brawling love! O loving hate! . . .
> O heavy lightness! serious vanity!
> Misshapen chaos of well-seeming forms!
> Feather of lead, bright smoke, cold fire, sick health!
> Still-waking sleep, that is not what it is!
> This love feel I, that feel no love in this.

3 Explain the following puns from various Shakespearean plays.

a) From *Henry IV Part 1*:

> Pistol: To England will I steal, and there I'll steal.

b) From *Hamlet*. Hamlet's father is dead and Hamlet's uncle, who he really dislikes, has taken over as King and has married Hamlet's mother.

> Claudius: But now, my cousin Hamlet, and my son,-
> Hamlet: [Aside] A little more than kin, and less than kind.
> Claudius: How is it that the clouds still hang on you?
> Hamlet: Not so, my lord; I am too much i' the sun.

c) From *Othello*. Othello approaches the sleeping Desdemona holding a burning torch or candle. He intends to kill her.

> Othello: Put out the light, and then put out the light.

Choose a Shakespearean play that you have studied or that you know.

1. Find one or more examples of Shakespeare's use of either antithesis or oxymoron in your chosen play. Explain how these example(s) work and what effects are created.

2. Find one or more example(s) of the use of personification in your chosen play. Explain how these example(s) work and what effects are created.

3. Find one or more puns in the play and explain how they work.

4. Write a short essay on how Shakespeare uses language in the play and the effects it creates. You could focus on just one section or act of the play.

Extension Activity

We use oxymorons or antithesis in everyday speech. For example…
- ill health
- small crowd
- probably definite.

Work with a partner to make up some of your own examples of oxymorons or antithesis. For each one write a short explanation of the phrase.

Reading Non-Fiction Texts

Reading for Meaning 1

What is Covered in this Topic?

This topic looks at...
- different reading styles
- how to create a factual account
- spotting the differences between facts and opinions.

Reading Techniques

There are different ways to read texts. It depends on...
- what kind of text it is
- why we need to read it.

These are the main reading techniques:
- **Skim reading** – running your eyes over the text. You don't take everything in – you just get a general idea of what it's about.
- **Scanning** – reading quickly in order to find specific pieces of information.
- **Extensive reading** – reading to obtain a general understanding of a subject and reading longer texts for pleasure.
- **Intensive reading** – reading shorter texts to find specific information.

For example, you would use different reading techniques for the following situations:
- Skim reading to get an idea of the main news of the day from a newspaper.
- Intensive reading of a section of a contract.
- Scanning the TV section of a newspaper to see what time a programme is on.
- Extensive reading of a novel before you go to bed each night.
- Intensive reading of a travel brochure to find information on a particular hotel.
- Scanning a magazine to see which articles you'd like to read in more detail later.

Reading for Meaning 1

Using Reading Techniques

When you're scanning for information, you need to keep in mind the key words that apply to what you're looking for. You should look for other versions of those key words, or words with similar meaning.

The following passage contains a lot of detail about the weather in the Lake District, some of which may be relevant to a walker. To find out certain facts or information, a walker may quickly scan it to pick out the details and the key words that are important to their journey.

💡 *Scan the passage to find out when the driest and warmest times to visit the Lake District would be. Keep in mind relevant key words like 'dry' and 'warm'.*

The Lake District is on the northwest coast of England. Its location and its mountains make it the dampest, wettest part of England. The UK Met Office reports average annual precipitation of more than 2,000 millimetres (80in), but with quite large local variations. The entire area has above average rainfall, but there's a wide disparity between the amount of rainfall in the eastern and western lakes. The rainfall is caused by the mountains.

Seathwaite in Borrowdale is the wettest inhabited place in the British Isles, with average rainfall of 3,300 millimetres (130in) a year. Nearby, Sprinkling Tarn is even wetter than this, recording over 5,000 millimetres (200in) per year. In contrast, Keswick, at the end of Borrowdale, receives 1,470 millimetres (60in) per year, and Penrith (just outside the Lake District) only 870 millimetres (30in). The driest months are usually March to June, with October to January the wettest. However, at lower ground levels there is little difference between months.

The Lake District is a windy place, although sheltered valleys experience gales on average only five days a year. The coastal areas have 20 days of gales and the mountain tops can have 100 days of gales per year.

The sea climate means that the Lake District has relatively moderate temperature variations through the year. Mean temperature in the valleys ranges from about 3°C (37°F) in January to 15°C (59°F) in July. (Moscow, in comparison, at the same latitude, ranges from -10°C to 19°C / 14°F to 66°F)

Snow is expected during winter but the low height of many hills means that they can be snow-free at any time of the year. Normally, significant snowfall only occurs between November and April. On average, snow falls on the mountain, Helvellyn, 67 days per year. During the year, valleys typically experience 20 days of snow falling, a further 200 wet days, and 145 dry days.

When reading intensively, you need to go backwards and forwards over the text to sort out the information that you need.

💡 *Read the passage more closely to find...*
- *the best parts of the Lake District to visit for weather and the best times to go*
- *the worst parts of the Lake District to visit for weather and the worst times to go.*

Facts and Opinions

It's important to be able to tell the difference between **fact** and **opinion**. For example, if you wanted to find a good hotel, you'd want to know what facilities it offered but also what other people thought of it.

The brochure for the hotel might contain a mixture of facts and opinions. While you would probably accept the facts as true, you would want to check the opinions carefully.

The following passage is an example of the difference between fact and opinion. The facts are highlighted in red and the opinions are highlighted in blue.

Robin Hood, it is believed, was a famous outlaw, who apparently lived in Sherwood Forest. His main rival was alleged to be the Sheriff of Nottingham and his wife was supposed to be Maid Marian. These details are what we think we know from famous legend, but the truth may be somewhat different.

The Court records for York mention a 'Robert Hude' who was seen before the court in 1226. In 1227, the same man was referred to as 'Robinhud'. In 1226, it is also recorded that the Sheriff of Nottingham, a man named William De Grey, was in conflict with a group of outlaws in Sherwood Forest, according to contemporary documents – 1266, 40 years later. It could be that a number of people built upon the legend of the outlaw and over time, the legend grew.

In the grounds of Kirklees Priory, there is a grave marker with the name 'Robard Hude'. Is this proof that the story was true? It would be nice to think so.

The facts in the passage above are identified by the following:
- They contain numbers, e.g. dates and figures.
- The verbs in the sentences are strong and express clear, definite ideas.
- They contain names that can be checked.
- They refer to the **origin** of their information.

Can you see how the facts in the passage above can be identified in these ways?

Opinions are identified by the following:
- They contain **conditional** words or phrases, e.g. 'supposedly'.
- They use **modals**, e.g. 'would', 'could', 'might'.
- **Personal voice** is used and / or opinions are given, e.g. 'I think.'

Can you see how the opinions in the passage above can be identified in these ways?

Reading for Meaning 1

Opinions as Facts

Skilful writers can give opinions that sound like facts, which you have to be careful of when reading. Look at the following statements:

- Fact – The Battle of Hastings took place in 1066.
- Opinion presented as fact – The gruesome Battle of Hastings took place in 1066.

Adding one word to the sentence has changed the fact into opinion. Who is to say that the Battle of Hastings was 'gruesome'? By adding an adjective which suggests a judgement is being made, the fact has been changed into an opinion.

If you add a **comparative** adjective to a sentence, it can still stay as a fact. For example…

- the Empire State building is *taller* than the Eiffel Tower
- Luke is the *smallest* boy in the class.

In both examples the adjectives are used to compare two or more things.

If you use a **null comparative**, however, the sentence becomes an opinion, because you're not comparing it properly to another thing.

For example…

- our burgers are better
- Robert is taller.

Here are some examples of facts:

- World War Two lasted from 1939 to 1945.
- 36 people caught the Hanley bus today.

Here are some examples of opinions presented as facts:

- 2 unlucky people were involved in an accident.
- In 1066, King Harold was unluckily defeated at the Battle of Hastings.

Quick Test

1. What kind of reading is used when you quickly run your eyes over a text?
2. What kind of reading is used when you quickly find specific information?
3. What is reading for pleasure classed as?
4. What is reading shorter texts in order to extract specific information called?
5. Is this statement a fact or an opinion presented as fact? 'The girls were smaller than their brothers.'

KEY WORDS
Make sure you understand these words before moving on!
- Facts
- Mean
- Origin
- Opinions
- Scanning
- Disparity
- Modal
- Variations
- Extensive reading
- Intensive reading
- Skim reading
- Precipitation
- Conditional
- Comparative
- Personal voice
- Null comparative

Key Words Exercise

Match each key word with its definition.

Key Word	Definition
Comparative	A comparison where you aren't really comparing to anything else.
Modal	Word meaning 'rainfall'.
Conditional	Reading technique designed to identify key facts quickly.
Null comparative	Word that means 'the place where something began'.
Disparity	One person's view.
Opinions	Some things that can be proved.
Extensive reading	Word that contains or expresses some doubt.
Origin	Reading technique where you would study a passage in detail to extract information.
Personal voice	Word which, in this topic, means 'average'.
Intensive reading	Things that can't be proved, but which someone believes.
Precipitation	A word like 'could'.
Mean	Reading technique you would use to get a general idea of what something is about.
Scanning	Word meaning 'differences'.
Variations	The difference between one thing and another.
Skim reading	Reading longer texts.
Facts	Having put one thing next to another for the process of comparison.

Reading for Meaning 1

Skim read the following passage to get a general idea of what it's about.
Then scan it to identify...

a) all the facts
b) all the opinions
c) all the opinions pretending to be facts.

Finally, read it intensively to make sure that what you've found is correct.

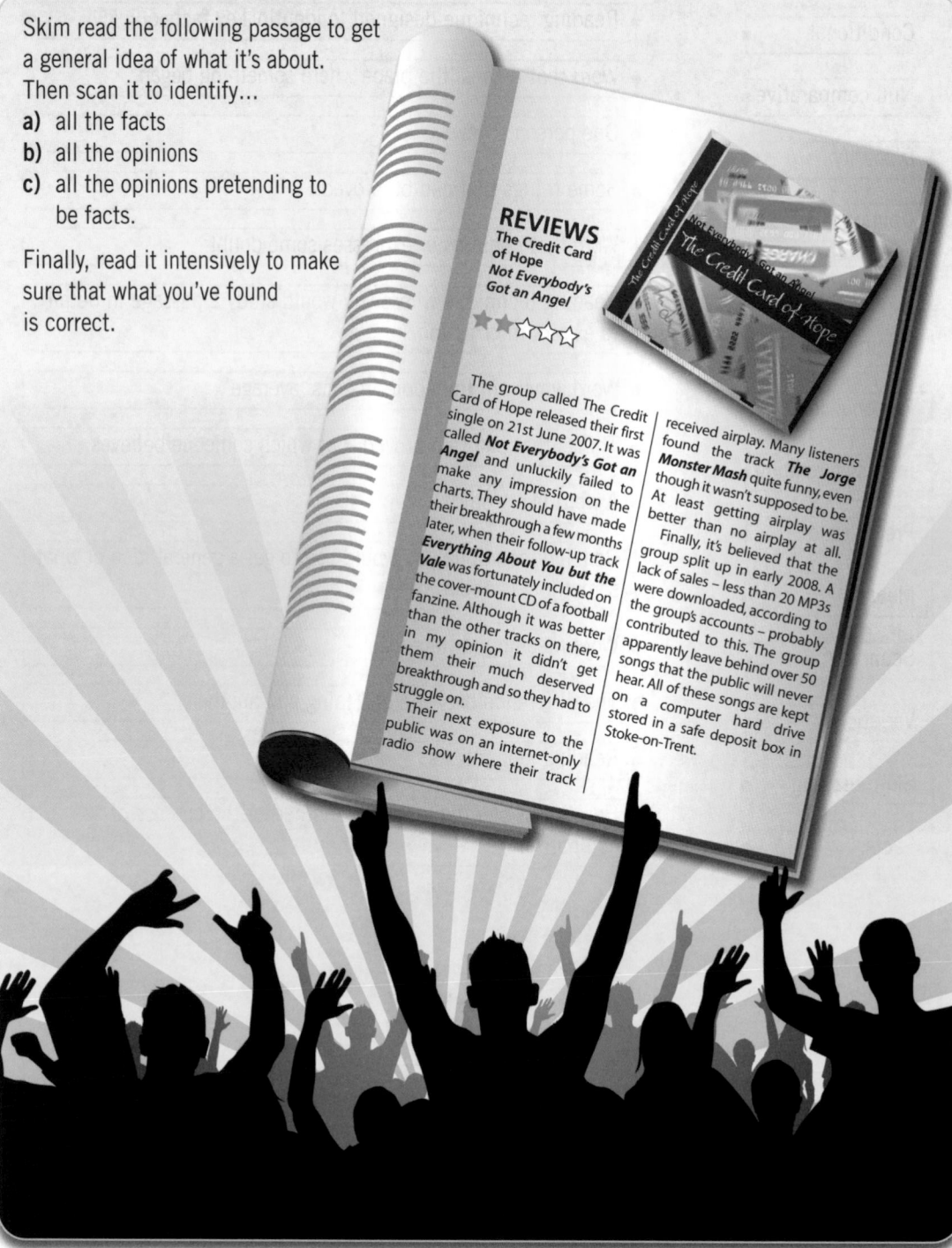

REVIEWS
The Credit Card of Hope
Not Everybody's Got an Angel

The group called The Credit Card of Hope released their first single on 21st June 2007. It was called **Not Everybody's Got an Angel** and unluckily failed to make any impression on the charts. They should have made their breakthrough a few months later, when their follow-up track **Everything About You but the Vale** was fortunately included on the cover-mount CD of a football fanzine. Although it was better than the other tracks on there, in my opinion it didn't get them their much deserved breakthrough and so they had to struggle on.

Their next exposure to the public was on an internet-only radio show where their track received airplay. Many listeners found the track **The Jorge Monster Mash** quite funny, even though it wasn't supposed to be. At least getting airplay was better than no airplay at all.

Finally, it's believed that the group split up in early 2008. A lack of sales – less than 20 MP3s were downloaded, according to the group's accounts – probably contributed to this. The group apparently leave behind over 50 songs that the public will never hear. All of these songs are kept on a computer hard drive stored in a safe deposit box in Stoke-on-Trent.

Write a passage about a hotel for a travel brochure. Make the hotel sound a reasonable place to stay, without telling lies. Include a mixture of...

- facts
- opinions
- opinions presented as facts.

Step 1: Here are the available facts about the place you're going to write about. Decide which of the following facts to group together as paragraphs:

Hotel Sunny Vista	75 rooms – all doubles
5 minutes from the beach – by car	38 rooms have a sea view
Hotel is next door to the sewage works	All rooms have ensuite facilities
25 rooms have a balcony, facing the sewage works	The hotel was voted 'Best Hotel in Town' in 2002 – before the sewage works were built
The average temperature in August, recorded outside the hotel, was 35°C	The hotel is facing a 24-hour supermarket

Step 2: Some of the facts about the hotel make it sound good. How might you change them, using opinions presented as facts, to make the hotel sound better?

Example – People believed, in 2002, that the hotel was the best in town and this might still be the case now.

How might you phrase the 'bad' things to make them sound better? Try using personal opinions for this.

Step 3: When you've drafted your description, give it to someone else to read and ask them if it would be the kind of hotel they would stay at. Ask them if they have any doubts about the way the hotel is described. If they have doubts, look at those parts of your description and see if you can make them sound more factual and convincing.

In a brochure, photos would accompany the descriptions. Have a look at some travel brochure photographs.

Why do you think that brochures tend to have lots of close-up shots of hotels and not many photos that show the hotel's surroundings?

How does this clever framing of photographs act like the photographer's opinion?

Reading for Meaning 2

What is Covered in This Topic?

This topic looks at...
- different kinds of non-fiction texts
- analysing the content of non-fiction texts
- analysing how non-fiction texts use language
- approaching your own analysis.

Non-fiction texts

The term **non-fiction** covers a wide range of different kinds of writing and usually contains **factual information**. Non-fiction texts can include the following:
- Non-fiction
- Newspapers
- Guidebooks
- Reports
- Information from websites
- Magazine articles
- Text books
- Travel writing
- Autobiographies
- Biographies.

How many other kinds of non-fiction texts can you think of?

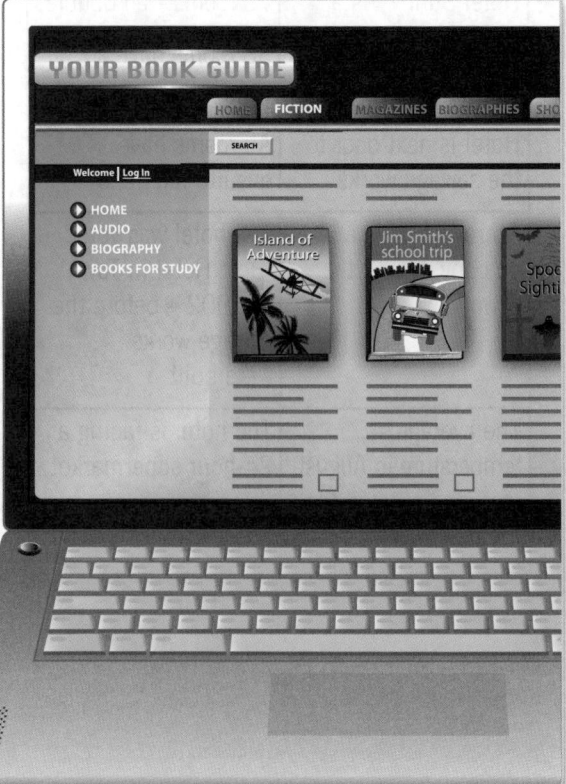

Reading Texts

When reading a text you should think about...
- the **content**, ideas and issues
- the way that language is used (sometimes called **style**)
- the way the information is **presented** – sometimes **texts** use diagrams, pictures or **illustrations** to add effect to the writing
- your own thoughts and responses to it.

Below is a non-fiction text about global warming. Read it carefully and jot down your ideas about…

- the **ideas** expressed (the **topic** or content)
- the ways that language is used, with examples
- the way in which the information's presented
- your views on the content and the way it's presented.

How effective do you think this piece is? Does it get its message across effectively?

Climate Change for Kids

Global Warming

Lots of people have studied the climate all around the world. They agreed several years ago that climate change really was happening. As a result, all countries in the world came together in a big conference at Kyoto in Japan.

Here they began to try and agree what to do about climate change. Lots of promises were made but countries haven't been very good at carrying them out.

Since then, the evidence of change has become stronger and stronger. The special computer 'models' which scientists had used have become more and more accurate. The ice sheets in both the Arctic and the Antarctic are melting, in some cases very fast. Sea levels are rising.

Temperatures are rising, especially in the Arctic and Antarctic. Glaciers on other mountains of the world are melting very fast – especially in the Himalayas. Animals and plants which like warmer conditions are moving further north and south. Yes, it's happening all right.

The world is hotting up. And I'm sorry to say it's all people's fault.

Reading for Meaning 2

Examining Non-Fiction (cont.)

In the passage from the *Climate Change for Kids* website, you might have noticed some of the following ideas and techniques used.

Title	The title, *Climate Change for Kids*, is aimed at a younger audience and makes the topic of the piece immediately clear.
Quotation	The quotation about how the ice will affect the polar bear has a 'shock' effect – it makes you think about the seriousness of climate change using a very specific example.
Background information	Some background to climate change is given with mention of Kyoto. The emphasis is on the idea that little has been done and that temperatures continue to rise.
Examples	Examples of the effects of global warming are given, e.g. 'Glaciers... are melting very fast', 'Sea levels are rising'.
Informal style	The language and style is quite informal. The use of words like 'lots' and contractions such as 'haven't' makes it appeal more to its target audience, which in this case is young people.
Illustrations	The use of pictures and cartoons to illustrate the text add to its impact. The cartoons illustrate some key points in the text but in a way that emphasises the serious message.

Writing Your Own Analysis of a Text

The following steps show one approach you can use when writing your own **analysis** of a text:

1. Look at the title of the piece of writing. This gives an immediate indication of what the writing's about. Read the text to get a general idea of the topic.

2. Read through the text to get ideas of what it's about, what points it makes, opinions expressed, etc. Think about the audience it's aimed at and the **purpose**.

3. Re-read the text carefully and make a note of the key points the writer makes.

4. Think about how language is used to suit the audience and purpose. Give specific details of the use of language and **comment** on the **effects** created.

5. Think about the effects of any headings, pictures, photographs, captions, illustrations, etc.

Make sure you use the PEE approach when writing an analysis:

- **Point** – make a point.
- **Evidence** – give an example.
- **Explanation** – comment on its effects, explain the significance, etc.

Quick Test

1. What kind of information does non-fiction usually contain?

2. Complete the following sentence:
   The way that language is used is called _____.

3. What is it called when you look carefully at how language is used?

4. What does the term PEE approach stand for?

Reading for Meaning 2

Key Words Exercise

Work out the key words from the clues below, then find them in the word search.

E	C	N	E	D	I	V	E	Z	S	F	L	A	U	N
Q	B	I	G	T	E	X	T	S	N	R	V	G	I	O
V	A	D	N	A	G	A	N	P	O	U	R	E	N	I
K	J	E	W	M	P	E	I	V	I	B	Q	S	N	T
P	B	A	E	P	J	F	A	C	T	U	A	L	O	A
C	D	S	S	T	Y	L	E	L	A	A	V	E	I	N
C	O	I	Z	U	L	F	Z	D	R	I	A	Z	T	A
L	T	N	V	S	F	B	R	E	T	H	N	L	C	L
C	B	N	T	E	K	P	Q	T	S	L	A	M	I	P
I	V	R	C	E	R	J	E	N	U	Q	L	T	F	X
P	H	T	I	A	N	W	S	E	L	I	Y	N	N	E
O	P	S	N	R	G	T	N	S	L	F	S	I	O	H
T	D	X	L	Y	Z	O	I	E	I	A	I	O	N	Y
A	U	D	I	E	N	C	E	R	E	R	S	P	R	T
A	S	R	M	D	O	E	A	P	T	O	P	C	S	N

1. The opposite kind of writing to that in a novel or short story.
2. When analysing writing, what approach should you use? (3 words)
3. When looking at a piece of writing you need to identify its _____ and its _____ .
4. When you write about how language is used and the effects that it creates, you're writing an _____ .
5. In writing a piece a writer often uses a particular _____ of writing.
6. Things like headings and pictures can add to the way a piece of writing is _____ .
7. The theme or subject of a piece of writing.
8. Non-fiction writing is often _____ information.
9. What does non-fiction writing contain?
10. What are pieces of writing often called?
11. Writers often express their _____ in their writing.
12. What is another word for pictures or diagrams?
13. The material in a piece of writing is called its _____ .

Read the following extract carefully. It's taken from the Bullying UK website giving advice to young people about bullying.

http//:www.bullying.co.uk

introductiontobullying

We all know that bullying goes on in every school but it's the way it's dealt with which makes the difference between life being tolerable or a misery. Bullies are very cunning and are expert at getting away with it.

Bullying includes:
- People calling you names
- Making things up to get you into trouble
- Hitting, pinching, biting, pushing and shoving
- Taking things away from you
- Spreading rumours
- Threats and intimidation
- Damaging your belongings
- Stealing your money
- Taking your friends away from you
- Posting insulting messages on the internet or by IM (cyberbullying)

How to solve the problem

If you are being bullied, tell a friend, tell a teacher and tell your parents. It won't stop unless you do. It can be hard to do this so if you don't feel you can do it in person it might be easier to write a note to your parents explaining how you feel, or perhaps confide in someone outside the immediate family, like a grandparent, aunt, uncle or cousin and ask them to help you tell your parents what's going on.

Your form tutor needs to know what is going on so try to find a time to tell him / her when it won't be noticeable. You could stay behind on the pretext of needing help with some work. If you don't feel you can do that, then go to the medical room and speak to the school nurse.

The best idea is if a teacher can catch the bullies red-handed. That way, you won't get into bother from anyone for telling tales. It will be clear to everyone what has been going on. Don't be tempted to hit back because you could get hurt or get into trouble. Hitting someone is an assault.

Try to stay in safe areas of the school at break and lunchtime where there are plenty of other people. Bullies don't like witnesses. If you are hurt at school, tell a teacher immediately and ask for it to be written down. Make sure you tell your parents.

a) Identify the audience and purpose for this piece of writing.
b) What key thing does the writer say someone being bullied should do?
c) Name three kinds of bullying that might take place.
d) How does the writer try to encourage anyone being bullied to tell someone about it?
e) What kind of language does the writer use?
f) Does the way the information is presented help you to follow it?

Reading for Meaning 2

Write your own analysis of a text.

Choose a piece of non-fiction writing to use as the basis of a written analysis. Don't choose too long a piece (250 to 300 words will be fine). You could pick a piece from a text book, magazine or the internet or anywhere else you choose.

Write about...
- the audience and purpose of the writing
- the key point or points that the writer is making
- how the writer presents the information
- the way language is used and give examples of this.

Remember to use this method:
- Point
- Evidence
- Explanation.

Extension Activity

Talk to a friend about a film or TV programme that you've recently seen. See if your views and ideas are the same or if they differ in any way.

Write down the main points your friend makes and your own ideas too.

Use the ideas from this as the basis of a review on the film or TV programme.

Write your review and then let your friend read it; discuss his or her responses to it.

Reading for Meaning 3

What is Covered in this Topic?

This topic looks at...
- reading texts
- making notes
- finding information.

Reading your Text

How you approach reading a text can depend on what your **purpose** is in reading it. For example, the way in which you read a novel that you're really enjoying is likely to be different to the way in which you read an encyclopaedia to look for a particular entry.

 *How do you think that they would differ?*

You would probably read an enjoyable novel quite carefully at a reasonable, steady pace to take in all the details and enjoy the development of the characters and action, but in searching for a particular entry in an encyclopaedia you would probably cover a lot of text very quickly until you found the bit you wanted.

Remember, there are four different types of reading. The methods you will use depend on your purpose:

- **Skimming** – reading the text quickly and just 'skimming' it to get the main ideas. This can give you a quick overview of the text and also give you an idea of where certain points or pieces of **information** can be found.
- **Scanning** – a technique that you often use when you're looking for a particular piece of information. You will usually know what you're looking for to begin with and your initial scanning of the text might help to locate it quickly. It's also the kind of technique that you would use if looking for an entry in a telephone directory or a word in a dictionary.
- **Extensive reading** – this is the kind of reading you would probably use when reading a novel for pleasure, or a letter from a friend. It's the kind of reading you use when wanting to get a clear idea of what the text is saying.
- **Intensive reading** – this is a detailed reading to get an accurate idea of what the text says. You might use this to get a detailed understanding of a specific topic or to look closely at the way the language is used. For example, you might use this technique when analysing a poem or other piece of writing.

Reading for Meaning 3

Making Notes

Making **notes** from books, magazines, the Internet and other sources can be very useful and even essential when preparing for activities such as writing an essay, sitting a test or producing a project of some kind.

Notes can remind you of things you've read, remind you of the key points, or help you to organise your revision.

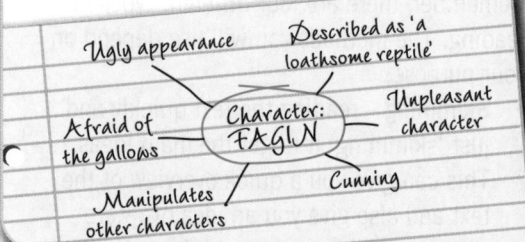

Here are some points to think about when making your notes:

- Know why you're making your notes – what information are you looking for?
- Leave out anything that you don't need or which isn't relevant – sometimes notes are less useful because the note-maker hasn't been selective in the information they have included.
- Make sure that you note down the information accurately – inaccurate information will lead to mistakes in your work later.
- Use different note-making techniques to suit your purpose, e.g. bullet points, pattern notes or mind-maps.

Highlighting and Annotation

Depending on the kind of information you're making notes on, it can sometimes be useful (and quicker) to use **highlighting** and **annotation** on a copy of your text.

In this example, the student has highlighted the key ideas and jotted down brief notes to act as memory joggers when they look at the text again.

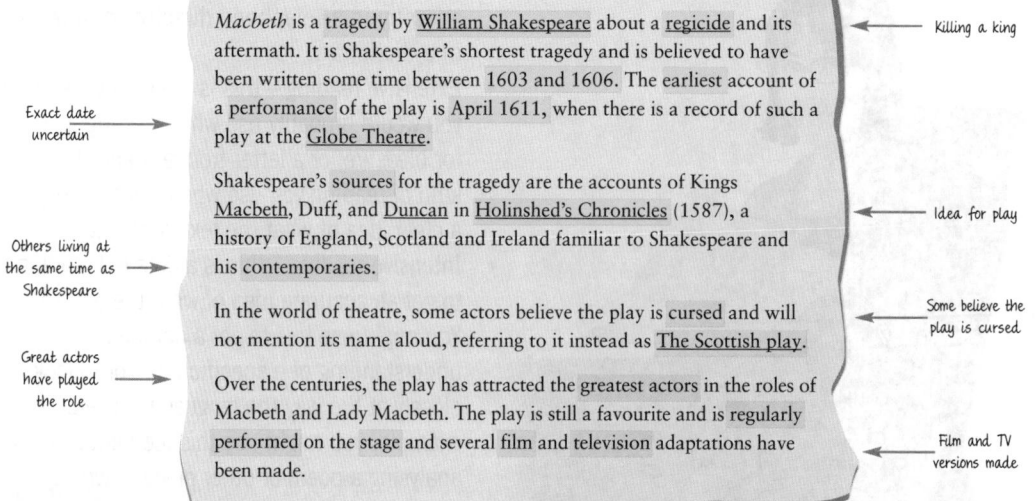

Comprehension

When you're asked to find specific information from a text you need to use your **comprehension** skills. This involves you understanding the text well. Before trying to answer any questions you should...

- read the text through at least once
- read the questions through carefully and make sure that you're clear what they're asking.

Remember to use skimming and scanning techniques to find the information you want and focus on certain points.

The Daily News

BANK OF ENGLAND CUTS BASE RATE BY HALF A PERCENT

In October 2008, when the global financial markets were in freefall, the Bank of England and other European banks cut their base rates by 0.5 percent in order to kick start the economy and avoid an economic downturn.

Writing a Summary

You might need to summarise the information in a text, either as part of your note-making or as part of a task that you've been set.

In order to write a **summary** you need to identify the **key points** in the text.

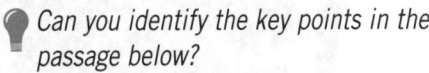 *Can you identify the key points in the passage below?*

John Logie Baird and the invention of the television are part of History. But the idea of the television did not start with Logie Baird in the 1920s.

In the late nineteenth century, a number of scientists had made important discoveries that Baird would use in his first version of a television. Henri Becquerel found that light could be changed into electricity and, importantly, Ferdinand Braun had invented the cathode ray tube. By the 1920s there were 50 serious attempts to invent the television from Russia, America, Germany, Britain and Japan. Many researchers had well resourced and staffed laboratories but the man who invented the television did not.

John Logie Baird was born in 1888 near Glasgow. He had made money selling socks and soap. He sold off this business to follow his dream of inventing a television. It became an obsession and to survive he had to borrow money from friends and use whatever materials he could, including scraps.

By 1925, he was ready to give the first public display of a working television. The chosen place was Selfridges in Oxford Street, London. Shoppers saw slightly blurred but recognisable images of letters. In 1927, Baird demonstrated colour television and a video-recording system he called a 'Phonovision'. In 1928, Baird made the first transatlantic television transmission and one year later he started regular 30-line mechanical broadcasts.

In 1936, the BBC started the world's first regular high-definition service from Alexandra Palace using the Baird system, though it was abandoned one year later in favour of a system developed by Marconi-EMI. By 1939, 20,000 television sets were in use in Great Britain, just 14 years after Baird's first public demonstration of his system at work. In 1940, Baird gave a demonstration of a high-definition full colour stereo television.

Writing a Summary (cont.)

Here are some key points you might have noted:

- Television was invented by John Logie Baird.
- The actual idea of television began in the late nineteenth century.
- Many others attempted to invent television, often with well-equipped laboratories.
- Baird was born in 1888 near Glasgow and had little money or resources and had to borrow money to try to achieve his dream of inventing the television.

- In 1925, he gave the first public display of a working television in London.
- In 1927, Baird demonstrated colour television and a video-recording system.
- In 1928, he made the first transatlantic television transmission.
- In 1936, the BBC started the world's first television service using Baird's system.
- By 1939, 20,000 television sets were in use in Great Britain.

Quick Test

1. What's the first thing you need to be clear about when making notes?
2. What does annotation mean?
3. Comprehension means _____ your text.
4. When writing a summary you need to identify the _____ _____ in a text.

KEY WORDS

Make sure you understand these words before moving on!

- Purpose
- Skimming
- Information
- Scanning
- Extensive reading
- Intensive reading
- Notes
- Highlighting
- Annotation
- Comprehension
- Summary
- Key points

Complete each sentence by finding the missing key word.

1. Understanding a text involves using your _____ skills.

2. When reading a novel you probably use _____ _____ techniques.

3. A quick read just to get the main point of a text is called _____.

4. Different reading techniques can help you find the _____ you're looking for in a text.

5. Making notes on a copy of your text is called _____.

6. A _____ involves you identifying the key points from a text and writing a shortened version of it.

7. You can use _____ to mark the key words on a page and make them stand out.

8. _____ are an important way of recording ideas on what you read and can be an important tool for revision.

9. Detailed reading that you might use when analysing a text is called _____ _____.

10. How you read a text depends on your _____ for reading it.

11. In writing a summary, you first need to identify the _____ _____.

12. When looking for a number in a telephone directory you would use _____ techniques.

Testing Understanding

Read this extract, which is taken from *The Perfect Storm* by Sebastian Junger, and answer the questions that follow.

Early fishing in Gloucester was the roughest sort of business, and one of the deadliest. As early as the 1650s, three-man crews were venturing up the coast for a week at a time in small open boats that had stones for ballast and unstayed masts. In a big wind the masts sometimes blew down. The men wore canvas hats coated with tar, leather aprons, and cowhide boots known as 'red jacks'. The eating was spare: for a week-long trip one Gloucester skipper recorded that he shipped four pounds of flour, five pounds of pork fat, seven pounds of sea biscuit, and 'a little New England rum'. The meals, such as they were, were eaten in the weather because there was no below-deck where the crews could take shelter. They had to take whatever God threw at them.

The first Gloucester fishing vessels worthy of the name were the thirty-foot chebaccos. They boasted two masts stepped well forward, a sharp stern, and cabins fore and aft. The bow rode the seas well, and the high stern kept out a following sea. Into the fo'c'sle were squeezed a couple of bunks and a brick fireplace where they smoked trashfish. That was for the crew to eat while at sea, cod being too valuable to waste on them. Each spring the chebaccos were scraped and caulked and tarred and sent out to the fishing grounds. Once there, the boats were anchored, and the men hand-lined over the side from the low midship rail. Each man had his spot called a 'berth', which was chosen by lottery and held throughout the trip. They fished two lines at twenty-five to sixty fathoms (150-360 feet) with a ten-pound lead weight, which they hauled up dozens of times a day. The shoulder muscles that resulted from a lifetime of such work made fishermen easily recognisable on the street. They were called 'hand-liners' and people got out of their way.

The captain fished his own lines, like everyone else, and pay was reckoned by how much fish each man caught. The tongues were cut out of the fish and kept in separate buckets; at the end of the day the skipper entered the numbers in a log book and dumped the tongues overboard. It took a couple of months for the ships to fill their holds – the fish was either dried or, later, kept on ice – and then they'd head back to port.

1 **a)** How many crew did the early boats have?
   b) What did they use for ballast?
   c) What sometimes happened to their masts?

2 Describe what the fishermen wore.

3 What do you think Junger means when he says 'The eating was spare'?

4 What were the first proper fishing boats called and how long were they?

5 Why do you think the fish the crew ate was called 'trashfish'?

6 What method of fishing do you think hand-lining is?

7 How were these fishermen easily recognisable on the street?

8 How were the fishermen paid?

9 Why were the tongues cut out of the fish they caught?

10 How were the fish preserved until the boat got back to port?

Select your own piece of writing. It can be a piece of fiction or non-fiction writing on any topic that you choose and should be about 350–400 words in length.

Write 8–10 questions on your piece of writing that you think would test someone's understanding of it.

Think carefully about the questions that you create and try to vary the style, e.g. some answers might be easily found in the passage but others might need working out from the things that have been said.

For each question that you create, ask yourself 'Could I answer this question if I had never seen the passage before?'

Questions

1.

2.

3.

4.

5.

6.

7.

8.

9.

10.

Work with a partner and exchange your passages and questions.

Read each other's passages and try to answer each other's questions.

When you have finished, discuss these points:
- How easy or hard you found each other's questions.
- Any specific problems that you found in answering them.
- What kind of reading techniques you used in approaching the passage and the questions.

Make notes on the discussion and the key points made on both passages and sets of questions.

Media Texts

What is Covered in this Topic?

This topic looks at...
- types of media texts
- features of media texts
- the main types of media you may encounter in day-to-day life.

What are Media Texts?

'Media' refers to the ways that ideas are communicated. Media texts can take many forms, for example...
- newspapers, magazines and leaflets
- radio and television programmes
- emails, telephones and text messages
- film posters, **websites** and maps
- everyday media, such as notes left in the kitchen.

Each of these text types is still affected by the audience you're writing for and the purpose of your writing.

Everyday Printed Media

Each media text can be studied in depth on its own, but there are several main media types you may encounter in everyday life.

Newspapers – Not all newspapers target the same audience:
- **Broadsheets** tend to be more serious and formal.
- **Tabloids** tend to be less serious, and deal with celebrity and entertainment stories more.

A newspaper's purpose is to inform and entertain. Broadsheets tend to inform more, while tabloids tend to entertain.

💡 *Can you name any broadsheet and tabloid newspapers?*

Magazines – Who a magazine is written for varies as there are many **specialist** magazines, all targeting their own specific audience. For example...
- film magazines are written for film-goers
- home improvement magazines are written for people who like DIY.

Like newspapers, a magazine's purpose is to inform and entertain.

Brochures and leaflets – Like magazines, brochures and leaflets cover thousands of subjects and are written to suit specific audiences.

Their purpose is to…
- sell a product and provide information about it
- to provide advice, e.g. a health leaflet.

Adverts – Adverts are written to attract the people the companies hope to sell their products to. Each advert is designed and styled to attract and appeal to its target audience.

The aim is to sell a product. Occasionally they might provide more information, but their main aim is to sell things.

Everyday Electronic Media

Websites – There are as many different types of websites as there are subjects and genres, so it's difficult to say who they're written for and aimed at. Each one needs to be looked at separately, based on its content.

Email – An email is an electronic letter, so there are as many types of email as there are types of letter. There are personal emails, emails of complaint, junk emails – spam, etc.

Text messages – A large proportion of text messages are written for friends or people we know well, so this affects how they're written. For example, shortened slang may be used in a text sent to a friend. Some text messages are sent to advertise or sell products.

Printed Media Example

This is an example of how a newspaper reports a UFO sighting.

It refers to 'readers' and 'phone calls' and uses 'our', which are characteristic of the way newspapers write about, and to, their audience.

> BRITAIN is turning into an alien nation, according to readers who have flooded us with reports of UFO sightings.
>
> Following our story of a UFO seen in Stoke-on-Trent, we were inundated with phone calls from people who had seen similar things all over the country.
>
> Some claimed they had seen alien spacecraft over Sneyd Green where our original UFO was snapped.
>
> A man, who asked to be known just as Grant, took a photo of a strangely-shaped object which appeared to be 'buzzing' the local Co-op.

Media Texts

Electronic Media Example

This is an example of how electronic media, such as websites, report news. It refers to a specialist subject and suggests a link to click on.

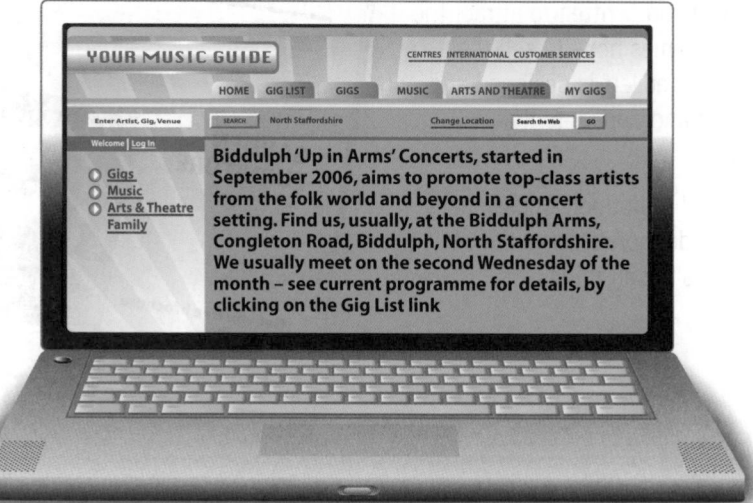

Features of Newspapers

Here is a typical local tabloid newspaper's front page:

It contains the following features:
1. Newspaper name – the masthead.
2. The regional edition.
3. A guide to what's in the paper.
4. Main news headline.
5. Teaser to inside story.
6. Advert.

Features of a Website

A website can contain the following features:
1. Website **banner**.
2. Menu.
3. Teaser for features contained elsewhere on the site.
4. Member access.
5. Introductory **blurb**.
6. Search **facility**.

It has some features similar to the front page of a newspaper – both have a heading to identify the paper or site and both include teasers to get the reader to explore inside.

They might also both have headlines if there's a main story to broadcast.

Quick Test

1. A newspaper is a media text – true or false?
2. A tabloid newspaper is usually less serious than a broadsheet – true or false?
3. Media texts can't be used to entertain – true or false?
4. What is the masthead on a newspaper?
5. What is a teaser on a newspaper?

Media Texts

1 Are the following key word definitions correct or incorrect?

a) Broadsheet – A type of newspaper that was originally quite large and is generally more serious in style and content.

b) Tabloid – A type of newspaper that was originally quite large and is generally more serious in style and content.

c) Specialist – A word describing general magazines.

d) Brochure – A type of text often used to display goods or things for sale.

e) Advert – A type of text that persuades people to buy something.

f) Local – Based all over the country.

g) Teaser – A contents list.

h) Masthead – The bottom of a newspaper, where the advert is.

i) Facility – A place where you can find what's on a website.

j) Menu – A list of options or features.

k) Blurb – The back of a newspaper.

l) Banner – Part of a website that often includes information on the purpose of the site.

2 When you have identified which definitions are incorrect, work out the correct definitions.

Testing Understanding

Are the following statements true or false?

1. 'Media' refers to the ways that ideas are communicated.

2. Sticky notes left in the kitchen are a form of media text.

3. Text messages aren't media texts.

4. Broadsheet newspapers usually contain a lot of celebrity and entertainment gossip.

5. Tabloid newspapers usually contain a lot of celebrity and entertainment gossip.

6. Magazines are often written for specialist audiences.

7. Brochures are only used to sell holidays.

8. Adverts are never used to give information, only to sell.

9. Websites have nothing in common with newspapers.

10. Email stands for 'electronic mail' and is a type of letter.

11. Spam email is a form of media text.

12. Text messages aren't proper media texts because they use slang.

13. Text messages contain slang because we mainly use them to communicate with people we know and who generally understand us.

14. A leaflet is an example of a printed media text.

15. A text message is an example of a printed media text.

16. A text message is an example of an electronic media text.

17. Newspapers often contain small glimpses on the front page of what's inside, in order to get people to buy them.

18. A newspaper masthead is so-called because it's at the top of the front page, like a masthead used to be the top part of a sailing ship.

19. Electronic media texts don't have any features that are different from printed media texts.

20. Printed media texts and electronic media texts can both be interactive with their readers.

Media Texts

Design a tabloid newspaper's front page. The stories and features to include on the front page are:

- Main story – Famous celebrity goes missing.
- Teaser story – Prime Minister increases teachers' wages by 200%. Picture on front page and few details, full story inside.
- Name of paper, edition and date (for you to invent).
- Advert for a holiday company.
- Other features, which might include teasers for entertainment and celebrity features inside the paper. Look at tabloid newspapers to get ideas.

Step 1: Decide what your paper is going to be called and which edition and date it will be. Think of a headline for your main story. Use no more than six words so that it's catchy. You might also use a pun or alliteration.

Step 2: Make a sketch plan of the page. Use tabloid-sized paper if it's available. Work out how much space you need for the main story. Estimate how many words or paragraphs you'll be able to fit in.

Step 3: Write the main story. Keep paragraphs short and vocabulary straightforward in order to appeal to the kind of reader you want to attract. Draft your other text on your plan, including the headline.

Step 4: When everything fits, start the final version. If you don't have tabloid-sized paper, you could piece together your newspaper from a number of smaller sheets, like a jigsaw. This is how early newspapers were put together, before computers simplified the process. Computer desktop publishing software would be a good way to piece together and rearrange the page.

Step 5: Compare your newspaper to an actual tabloid – how close is it in style and layout? What might you have done differently to have made it even more realistic?

Design a website for an up-and-coming band. Include some of the features you have learned to make it attractive and informative.

Media Texts – Newspapers

What is Covered in this Topic?

This topic looks at...
- different types of newspapers
- the content of newspapers

- features of newspaper articles
- analysing a newspaper article.

Newspapers

All newspapers **report** news in some way but not all newspapers are the same. They can be very different in...
- the kind of **news** they cover
- the ways in which they cover the news
- the range of other material they contain
- their size
  - large format newspapers (e.g. *The Daily Telegraph*) are **broadsheets**
  - smaller format newspapers (e.g. *The Mirror*, *The Sun*) are **tabloids**.

Types of Newspapers

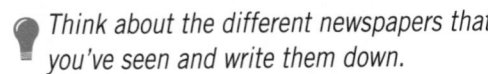 *Think about the different newspapers that you've seen and write them down.*

Type of Newspaper	What it Covers
National daily paper	Usually reports national and international news.
Regional daily paper	Covers the daily news of a particular town or area.
Weekend paper	Most national daily papers produce special editions on Saturdays and Sundays. These present news but often include items and free magazines covering various areas such as leisure, fashion, reviews, etc.
Weekly paper	Produced one day a week and usually covers a particular town or area.
Free paper	Normally based in one area; contains some news but has a lot of advertisements.

Media Texts – Newspapers

Contents of a Newspaper

Newspapers typically contain the following content:

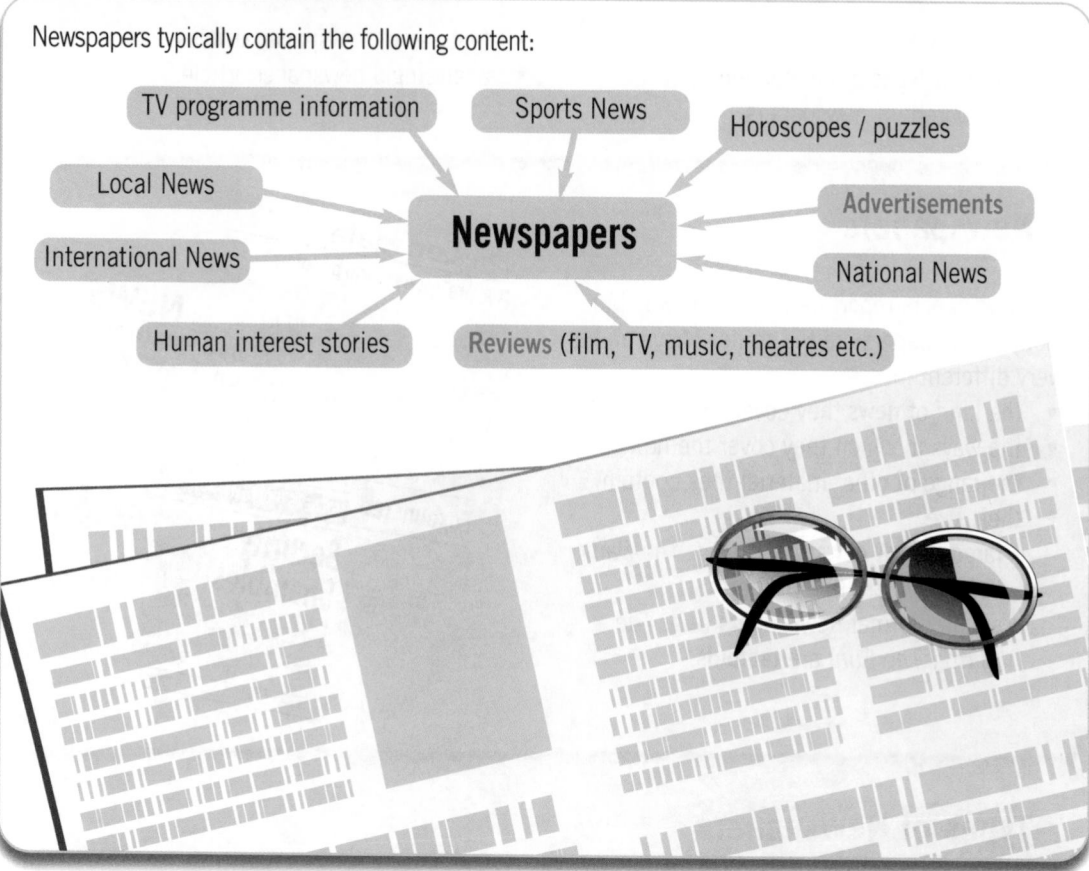

TV programme information

Sports News

Horoscopes / puzzles

Local News

Advertisements

International News

National News

Newspapers

Human interest stories

Reviews (film, TV, music, theatres etc.)

Features of a Newspaper

Newspapers are presented in a particular way:
- Stories and articles have headlines – the big headline on the front page is called a banner.
- The main story (also called the lead story) is on the front page and sometimes continues inside the newspaper.
- Newspapers often present a view on the main stories in a separate column called an editorial. The editor decides which stories and reports are to be included.
- Newspaper reports contain a lot of facts, although they sometimes contain opinion as well.
- Sometimes only one newspaper has the details of a particular story – this is called an exclusive.
- The text (or copy) is written in columns – the stories and reports are written by journalists.
- Pictures or photographs are often used, which usually have a title or explanation called a caption.

Weekly NEWS

Along Came a Spider!

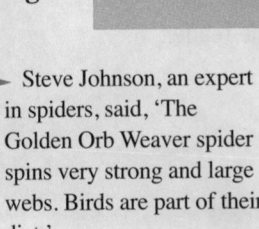

The Golden Orb Weaver spider: caught on camera attacking a bird.

A giant spider has been caught on camera eating a bird in Australia.

A Chestnut-breasted Mannikin was the unlucky victim, flying into the web of a Golden Orb Weaver spider and becoming trapped.

Although you might expect this kind of thing to happen every day in wild jungles and far-off places, this took place in somebody's back garden.

Steve Johnson, an expert in spiders, said, 'The Golden Orb Weaver spider spins very strong and large webs. Birds are part of their diet.'

After the bird flew into the web in Cairns, Australia, it became exhausted. When the bird became weak, the spider attacked. It then used its poison to break down the bird, ready to eat.

Golden Orb Weaver spiders are found in warm countries such as Australia, Africa and parts of the USA.

Luckily for us, a bite from one of these would feel like a sting and wouldn't kill you.

---

1. Striking headline taken from *Little Miss Muffet* nursery rhyme.
2. Opening paragraph introduces topic of spider and sets the scene – Australia.
3. Use of actual names of species involved.
4. Shock effect of this happening in a back garden.
5. Quotation on the strength of the spider's web from an expert with personal experience.
6. Further details of what happened and where.
7. Details of where these spiders are found.
8. Reassuring final line.
9. Caption on photograph helps explain what is happening.

Media Texts – Newspapers

Writing an Analysis

Try writing an analysis of the article about the spider.

To help you, here are some points to think about:

- How the headline catches the attention.
- How the opening paragraph is effective.
- How the use of the actual names of the bird and spider add effect.
- How the information that this happened in a back garden makes you feel.
- How the use of direct speech from the expert adds effect.
- How the details of how the spider dealt with the bird adds interest.
- How the final paragraph is effective.
- The effect of the article on the reader.
- The use of quotations.

Quick Test

1. How is the text of newspapers laid out?
2. What is the written material that reporters provide called?
3. What do photographs and pictures normally have alongside them?
4. What is the main story of a newspaper called?
5. Complete the following sentence:
The column in which a view is expressed about the main story is called an

_____ .

KEY WORDS

Make sure you understand these words before moving on!

- Report
- News
- Broadsheet
- Tabloid
- Review
- Advertisement
- Article
- Headline
- Banner
- Lead
- Editorial
- Editor
- Fact
- Opinion
- Exclusive
- Copy
- Column
- Journalist
- Photograph
- Caption

Work out the key words from the clues below, then find them in the word search.

H	I	T	E	E	H	S	D	A	O	R	B	V
E	D	N	E	T	W	E	R	I	L	E	D	W
A	A	E	F	S	O	V	O	E	A	V	N	O
D	E	S	A	S	A	I	T	Y	D	I	O	R
L	L	I	C	N	R	S	I	I	V	E	I	P
I	A	U	T	M	T	U	D	T	E	W	T	H
N	E	W	S	U	I	L	E	S	R	S	N	O
E	D	T	U	L	C	C	O	I	T	D	O	T
R	I	H	A	O	L	X	N	L	I	I	I	O
H	T	O	P	C	E	E	O	A	S	O	N	G
V	O	Y	H	E	A	L	I	N	E	L	I	R
I	R	E	P	O	R	T	T	R	M	B	P	A
W	I	D	J	O	U	R	P	U	E	A	O	P
B	A	N	N	E	R	I	A	O	N	T	E	H
T	L	O	N	Y	E	E	C	J	T	A	D	S

1. The main heading to a story or article.

2. Smaller format newspaper.

3. Large format newspaper.

4. Sometimes reports have these to illustrate them.

5. A reporter would submit one of these.

6. Things that are true.

7. Newspapers mainly report this.

8. A piece of writing on a particular topic is one of these.

9. Newspapers can include _____ on films and TV programmes.

10. A word that describes the newspaper's view on a key story or article.

11. The main purpose of these is to persuade people (maybe to buy something).

12. Another name for the material written by journalists.

13. The writing that explains a photograph.

14. Someone who writes for a newspaper.

15. A story that's only covered by one newspaper is called an _____ .

16. The main story of the newspaper.

17. Another name for the main, front page headline.

18. This person decides what to put in a newspaper.

19. Newspaper text is normally laid out in this format.

20. It's not a fact, but it may be true or false.

Media Texts – Newspapers

1 Identify whether the following statements are true or false.

a) Newspaper text is written in columns.

b) The writing that goes with a photograph is called a heading.

c) Some newspapers only cover local news.

d) The front page headline is called a poster.

e) Many newspapers contain sports news.

f) Journalists write material for newspapers.

g) The person who decides what news articles go into a newspaper is the editor.

h) Newspapers never contain advertisements.

i) Facts are things that are not true.

j) A news item published by only one paper is called an exclusive.

2 Read the following newspaper report and identify the effects created by the sections of text, A–H.

News Express

Only 30p

A JET SKIER TAKES OFF

B Rapid Response Rescue Plucks Jet Skier From Death

C A Sea Rescue helicopter plucked a jet skier from the sea in a dramatic rescue off the East Coast of Yorkshire yesterday afternoon. Two lifeboats were also involved in the rescue.

D Rob 'Rocket' Roberts was one of a group of jet skiers involved in a sponsored jet ski race down the East Coast. The race started at Scar Rock Harbour at 10.00 a.m. on Sunday morning. The sea was quite calm with a slight swell. An hour into the race, though, things changed drastically when a violent wind rose and sea conditions became horrendous. Most of the jet skiers managed to reach the shore, but Mr Roberts was hit by a huge, mountainous wave. His jet ski was smashed and he was thrown into the sea.

E 'I didn't know what hit me,' said Rob, 27, from Hartlepool. 'The wave was massive and came out of nowhere.

It lifted me and the jet ski high in the air and then smashed us down, throwing me into the water and completely submerging the jet ski. Thank goodness for the rescue services.'

F Al Curtis, coxswain of the Scar Rock lifeboat, said that winds were gusting up to 28 knots with waves of 5 to 6 metres and that 'once in the water Mr Roberts was caught in a strong tidal current and would have been swept away if we hadn't reached him quickly'.

G Jet skiing is a popular and rapidly growing sport and the numbers taking part in the East Coast Race have grown in recent years. The race has been held annually since 2003 and this is the first time there have been any problems.

H Happily, all ended well and Mr Roberts is recovering well in hospital.

Skills Practice

Write a newspaper report of your own.

Step 1: Choose a topic or subject for your report. For example, it could be based on...
- something that's happened to you
- an event that you've been involved in or heard about
- a report of a sports match, a school trip, etc.

Whatever subject you choose, make sure that you have enough information to write a report about it.

Step 2: Write down all the pieces of information that you're going to include in your report. If you have any direct comments from the people involved, include these here.

Step 3: Plan how you're going to structure your report:
- What you'll include in your introduction.
- The order that you're going to include the pieces of information.
- How you'll conclude your report.

Step 4: Write your report on a computer, creating a suitable and eye-catching headline. Lay your copy out in columns. Add pictures with captions to illustrate your report if you think these will make it more effective.

Extension Activity

1 **Interviews are an important way for journalists or reporters to gather information for the reports and articles they write.**

Step 1: Look at some interviews in newspapers and magazines or on the internet. You will find them on many different subjects, for example...
- celebrities
- sportsmen and women
- people who've done something unusual.

Step 2: Choose a friend or a member of your family and interview them about a particular topic or experience. For example, you could interview...
- an older relative about life in the past
- a friend who's taken part in a school production
- a friend or relative with an unusual hobby.

Step 3: Make a list of questions to ask. Be prepared to ask other questions when you're interviewing them if they say things you want to explore further.

Step 4: Record your interview with them.

2 **Use this interview as the basis of a report or article.**

Media Texts – Advertisements

What is Covered in this Topic?

This topic looks at...
- different types of advertisements
- the features of advertisements
- the language of advertisements
- analysing advertisements.

The Purpose of Advertising

Advertisements will be very familiar to you – you see them everyday. They're all around, for example, in magazines and newspapers, on advertising hoardings, on television, on the radio, pushed through letter boxes, etc.

Adverts come in many different forms and advertise all kinds of things.

But all adverts have the same broad **purpose**: to **persuade** people to think or behave in a particular way.

Types of Advertising

Here are some of the many things that are advertised. You'll probably have seen examples of them all at one time or another.

Products, e.g. computers, food and drink, holidays, clothes and furniture.

Services, e.g. finance and loans, plumbing and gardening.

Public Services, e.g. community projects, fire safety and health.

Careers, e.g. as a driving instructor, teacher or nurse

Advertising

Political, e.g. political parties and local councils.

Charities, e.g. the RSPCA, Help the Aged and Oxfam.

Features of Advertisements

Although all adverts are different, many of them use the same **techniques** and have certain features in common.

Here are some features/techniques you might have noticed:

- Headings and **slogans** – these are the key words that catch people's attention and make them want to look at the advert and read it. The people who created the advert will have spent a lot of time making sure the advert is both eye-catching and persuasive.

- **Appeal** – all adverts are designed to appeal to something that you want or need, for example, comfort, excitement, fashion, money, or a sense of conscience.
- **Language** – some adverts contain very few words and rely on **photographs** or **images** to create their **effects**. Some just use a catchy slogan. But many use various language techniques, such as alliteration or rhyme, to make their point.

An Example of an Advert

The advert shown here for Eternity rings has the following features:

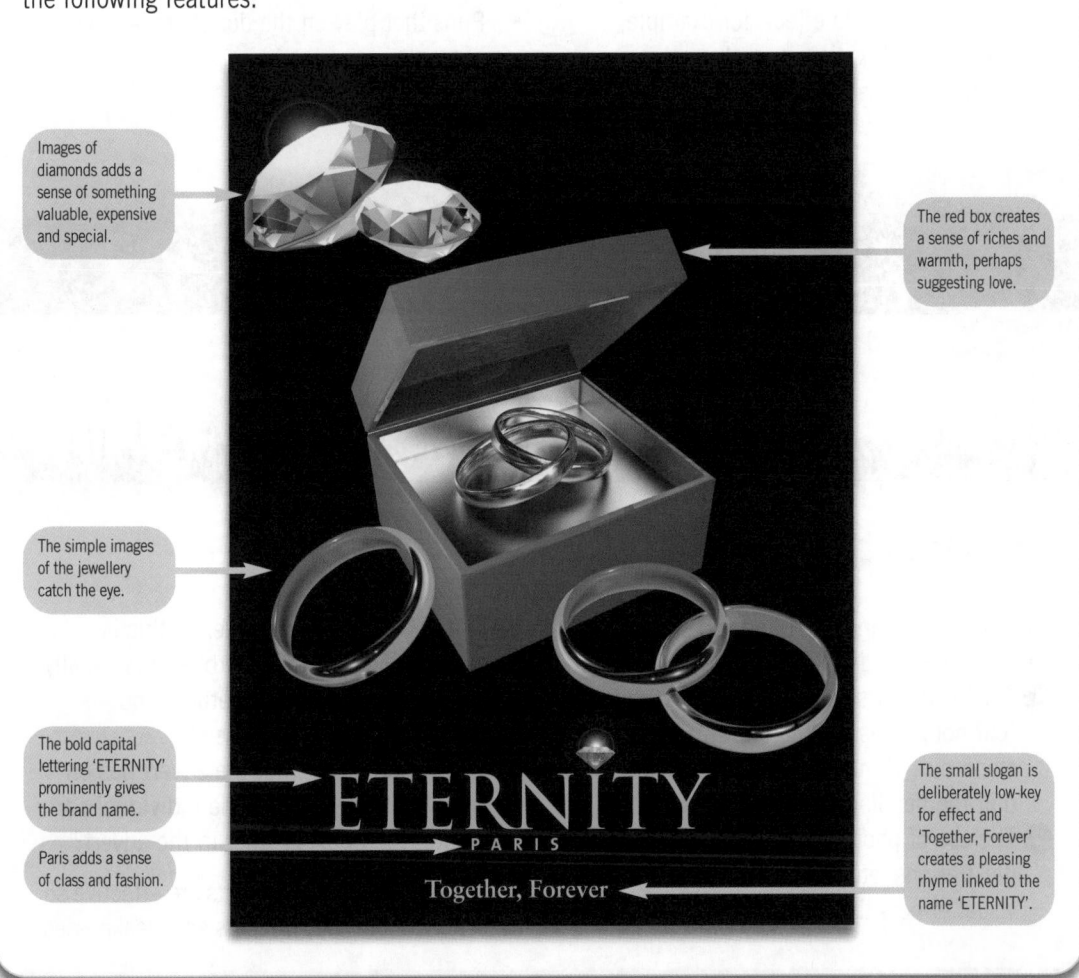

Images of diamonds adds a sense of something valuable, expensive and special.

The red box creates a sense of riches and warmth, perhaps suggesting love.

The simple images of the jewellery catch the eye.

The bold capital lettering 'ETERNITY' prominently gives the brand name.

Paris adds a sense of class and fashion.

The small slogan is deliberately low-key for effect and 'Together, Forever' creates a pleasing rhyme linked to the name 'ETERNITY'.

ETERNITY
PARIS

Together, Forever

Media Texts – Advertisements

Language in Advertisements

Here are some of the language techniques that are often used in adverts:

- **Exaggeration** – words are used that give the best possible impression of the **product**; exaggeration is often used to achieve this, for example, 'The most fantastic offer!'.
- Use of **imperatives** – verbs that command you to do something, for example, 'Buy now!'.
- Claims that can't be proved – for example, 'You can't afford to miss this offer!'.
- Appealing words, often **adjectives** – descriptive words that draw in the reader and create a vivid effect, for example, 'beautiful', 'luxurious', 'exclusive', 'delicious', 'tasty', 'stylish'.

- **Repetition** – important or striking words are repeated for emphasis.
- Sound appeal – the use of alliteration, assonance or rhyme to create effects, for example, e.g. 'soft, smooth and sophisticated'.
- The use of similes to make descriptions more vivid and appealing, for example, 'as smooth as silk', 'as cool as a mountain stream'.
- The use of seemingly technical or scientific language, for example, 'a unique scientifically tested turbo-suction power motor'.
- **Puns** that play on the double meanings of words.

as cool as a mountain stream

How to Analyse an Advert

When analysing an advert and the effect that it creates you should look at four key points:

1. The heading / slogan – these are usually (but not always) in bigger print, so they stand out. Think about the effects and tone that the heading / slogan creates.
2. The use of photos / pictures / designs / illustrations, etc. Think carefully about the visual effects that are created.
3. The details given in the text – this is sometime called the 'blurb' and is usually in smaller print. What features and techniques have been used?
4. The overall effect that the advert has on you. What effect do all the individual parts create when put together in the advert?

Don't forget that not all adverts are effective so think about both the strengths and weaknesses.

Analysing an Advert

Look at this Magnum ice cream advertisement and study the techniques used in it.

💡 *Think about your overall response to the advert. Does it make you want to buy the ice cream?*

Note the catchy slogan: 'Enjoy the Royal Treatment'.

The gold pattern and 'M' crest set against a burgundy background give a feeling of richness and royalty.

Striking images of the ice cream surrounded by gold scrolls and topped with crowns give an instant sense of richness and luxury.

'Temptation' appears in large print, which draws attention to the ice cream's name. It also gives the impression of something that's a little bit naughty and indulgent.

'New' gives an impression of something new and exciting.

Adjectives are used to create effect – 'smooth', 'rich', 'indulgent', 'delicious'.

Repetition of 'chocolate' and 'chocolatey' emphasises the nature of the product.

ENJOY THE ROYAL TREATMENT

THE NEW MAGNUM
TEMPTATION

Temptation Caramel and Almonds and Temptation Chocolate. Smooth ice cream, rich sauce and indulgent chocolatey pieces all encased in delicious Belgian chocolate.

MAGNUM
WORLD'S PLEASURE AUTHORITY
www.mymagnum.co.uk

Quick Test

1 What is the purpose of advertisements?
2 What is an imperative?
3 Why might repetition be used in an advertisement?
4 Why might adjectives be used in an advert?

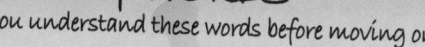

KEY WORDS
Make sure you understand these words before moving on!

- Advertisements
- Purpose
- Persuade
- Techniques
- Slogan
- Appeal
- Language
- Photographs
- Images
- Effects
- Exaggeration
- Product
- Imperatives
- Adjectives
- Repetition
- Pun

Media Texts – Advertisements

Solve the clues to find the key words and complete the crossword.

Across

1. You take these with a camera. (11)
4. A term for describing words. (8)
10. What it's for. (7)
11. Various techniques create different

_____. (7)
12. Adverts often use visual

_____. (6)
13. Different _____ are used to create effects. (10)
14. A catchy heading. (6)
15. Adverts are often designed to sell these. (8)

Down

1. A technique that plays on double meanings of words. (4)
2. Words used to describe nouns. (10)
3. Commands. (11)
5. A bit over the top. (12)
6. You see these every day. (14)
7. The purpose of adverts. (8)
8. Again and again and again. (10)
9. In order to be effective, adverts must _____ to us. (6)

Look at the advertisement and answer the following questions.

1. What product is this advert for?
2. Who do you think the advert is aimed at?
3. Explain what effect is created by the main slogan and the sub-heading.
4. Why is the design with 'aah! Wednesday' used?
5. Where does the name of the company appear?
6. What is the purpose of the smaller print at the bottom of the advertisement?
7. How effective do you think the advert is?

FORGET THE TV NEWS.

Listen to your family's news, over chicken pie and gravy.

Make the pledge at bisto.co.uk & pick up family rewards

Media Texts – Advertisements

Look through magazines, newspapers, or any other sources where adverts are printed and choose two that you find interesting for some reason.

You don't have to find them both effective, although it would be useful if you thought at least one of them worked well.

Analyse each of your adverts carefully. You should look at the following features:
- The effect created by the heading(s) / slogan(s) and sub-heading(s).
- If other text is used, think about what information is given and how language is used.
- The visual effect created by photos / pictures / designs / illustrations, etc.
- The overall effect that the adverts have on you. Make sure you comment on both strengths and weaknesses and give reasons for your views.

Extension Activity

Now try designing an advertisement of your own.

Your advert can advertise anything you want. Think carefully about how you are going to create your effects. Here are some points to think about:
- What is your slogan or heading going to be?
- Are you going to use images of any kind?
- What kind of text will you use? What will it say? (Remember, you shouldn't add too much text otherwise people will not read it.)
- What techniques are you going to use to catch your reader's attention and make your advert persuasive?

When you have finished your advert, write an explanation of why you designed it as you did and what effects you wanted to create.

Then present your advert to a partner and discuss his / her response to it.

Speaking and Listening

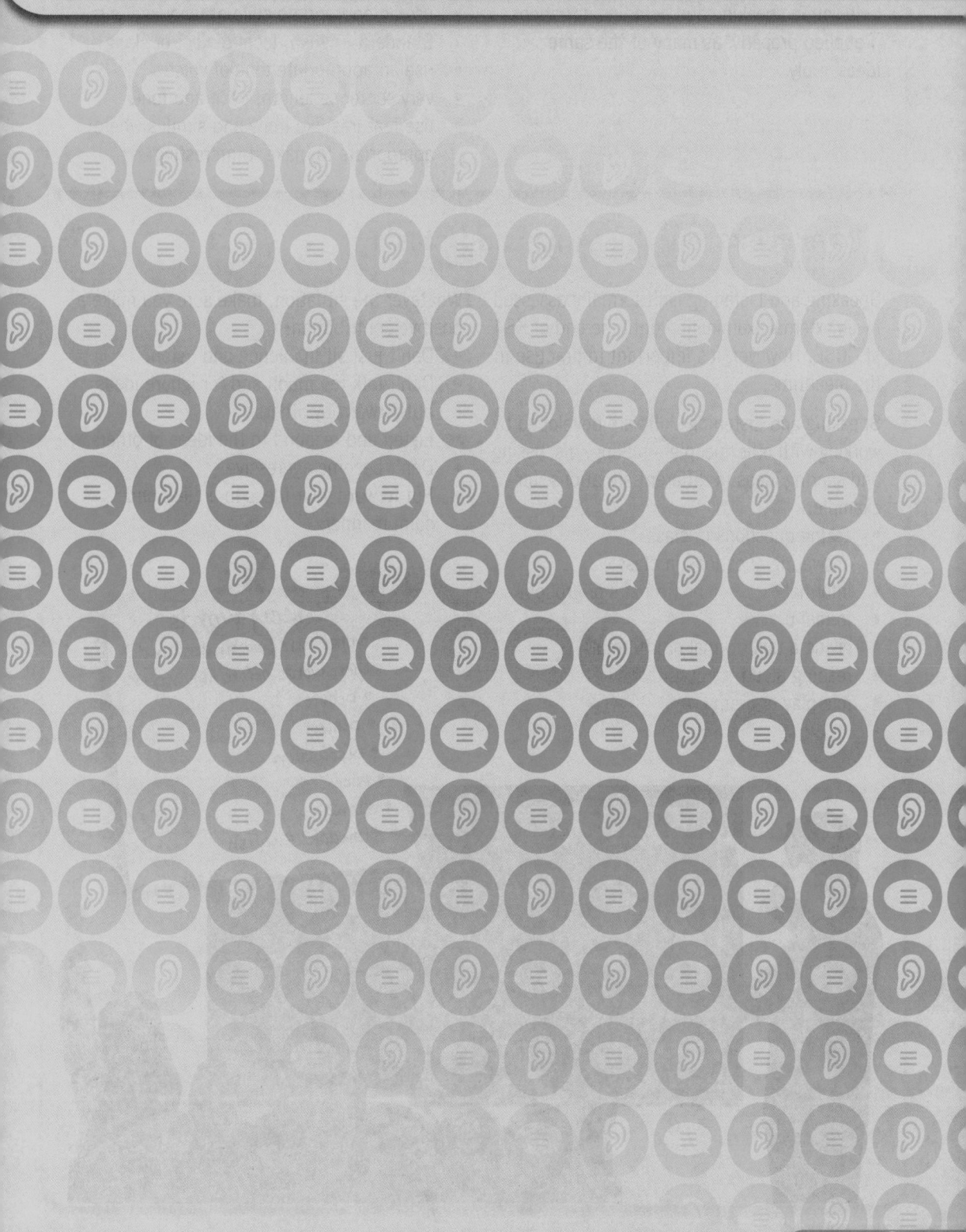

Transferable Skills

This coursebook focuses on reading and writing skills. However, lots of the skills covered will help you in speaking and listening situations if applied properly, as many of the same ideas apply.

For example, it is important to...
- consider your audience
- use an appropriate style of language, e.g. **Standard English**, local **dialect** or **slang**
- use an appropriate tone of voice
- vary sentence length, **pace** and tone
- use features like irony and similes where appropriate to make it interesting.

Developing Your Speaking and Listening

Speaking and Listening isn't formally assessed by an external examination until the end of KS4, at GCSE. However, it's important to practise in the meantime.

Speaking and Listening skills are developed by working with other people – talking, discussing and sharing ideas in different situations, for example...
- asking questions in class
- answering questions in class
- informal **discussions** (in pairs or groups)
- formal **debate**
- giving a talk (formal or informal)
- reading aloud
- role play or drama.

Whatever the situation, make sure you make a positive contribution:
- Don't just sit in silence and listen.
- Don't talk too much and / or ignore ideas put forward by others.
- Listen and respond to the ideas of others.
- Don't become aggressive.
- Put forward your ideas in a clear and calm manner.

Key words

Make sure you understand these words before moving on!
- Debate
- Dialect
- Discussion
- Pace
- Slang
- Standard English

ideas

ESSENTIALS

KS3
English Coursebook Answers
covers all three years

...wrong answers for the skills practice and ...es. They're designed to see how well you can ...in each topic.

...ritten tasks it's important to consider...
...dience
* sentence structure and punctuation
* spelling
* tone
* language
* layout / format.

When reading through your answer, refer back to the question and make sure you have fully covered each step / bullet point:
* Did you use **some of the features** you were supposed to?
* Did you use **all of the features** you were supposed to?
* Did you use **some of the features in original ways**?

In order to improve, you need to first try and use the features you have read about and gradually use them in more original, interesting and useful ways.

SPELLING

Page 10

Quick Test

1. Plurals **2.** Sibilants **3.** Homophones **4.** Deer **5.** Look it up in a dictionary

Page 11

Key Words Exercise

1.	accurate	8.	sound
2.	singular	9.	nouns
3.	consonants	10.	plurals
4.	collective	11.	meaning
5.	spelling	12.	dictionary
6.	homophones	13.	sibilance
7.	vowels		

Page 12

Testing Understanding

1. **a)** Classes **b)** Boxes **c)** Atlases **d)** Tables **e)** Windows **f)** Houses **g)** Inches **h)** Rays
2. **a)** boys **b)** qualities; opportunities **c)** mangoes; tomatoes **d)** heroes **e)** mosquitoes; weather **f)** trousers; waist; potatoes **g)** towed; buoys **h)** sopranos; haloes; lights
3. Todd and his **friends** followed the path into the valley. The **herds** of cattle roamed freely and there were lots of **sheep** too. All **manner** of **birds** flew in the sky and Todd and his **friends** felt the sun on **their** faces and the wind gently ruffle **their hair**. They had **heard** that bears roamed these hills but they didn't **see** any and so thought they must be in **their** lairs. In the streams they **saw** trout swimming and **salmon** jumping.

Page 13

Skills Practice

You should have identified the most common spelling mistakes

and why the mistakes occur. Your poster should be clear and visually effective.

Extension Activity

In creating your PowerPoint presentation, make sure that your slides are clear. Present examples of wrongly spelt words and the corrected versions. Don't try to put too much information on one slide.

GRAMMAR

Page 16

Quick Test

1. True **2.** False **3.** False **4.** False **5.** False **6.** True

Page 17

Key Words Exercise

Page 18

Testing Understanding

1. Proper nouns – Harry; Mrs Tompkins
   Collective noun – Class
   Common nouns – Desk; Teacher; Essay
   Abstract nouns – Satisfaction; Fact; Excellence
2. **a)** pride **b)** poverty **c)** confidence
3. **a)** Pride **b)** Flock **c)** Team **d)** Shoal **e)** Herd **f)** Crew **g)** Regiment (or battalion, platoon) **h)** Colony (or army) **i)** Fleet or convoy **j)** Clutch **k)** Bouquet (or bunch) **l)** Pack
4. **a)** Her; It **b)** Its; She **c)** Their; They; Their
5. **a)** Last; Beautiful **b)** Grey; Bitter; Icy; Barren
6. **a)** Hard (describes work) **b)** Grimly (describes hung) **c)** Happily (describes smiled)
7. **a)** On (preposition); And (conjunction); Out of (prepositions)
   b) About (preposition); But (conjunction); Of (preposition)
   c) Out to (prepositions); And (conjunction); In (preposition); Of (preposition)
8. **a)** The (definite) **b)** A (indefinite) **c)** The (definite); An (indefinite)

Page 19

Skills Practice

Make sure that ...
* your poster is attractive and eye-catching

- your poster is simple to understand (avoid too much written explanation on it)
- you think carefully about how you lay out the information.

In designing your information leaflets, make sure that…
- each leaflet gives information about each word class
- you include examples to illustrate key ideas
- you present the information in an interesting way.

Extension Activity

Don't try to cram too much on each of your PowerPoint slides. Remember that you need to focus on the key ideas and try to make it as visually interesting as possible. Make sure your sound commentary is clear and fits your PowerPoint presentation.

SENTENCES 1

Page 23
Quick Test
1. Four 2. Imperative 3. Phrase 4. Finite

Page 24
Key Words Exercise
1. simple 2. sentence 3. agree 4. finite 5. question 6. action
7. phrase 8. **In any order:** state; condition 9. exclamation
10. **In any order:** subject; verb 11. **In any order:** command; imperative
12. statement

Page 25
Testing Understanding
1. **a)** Command **b)** Statement **c)** Question **d)** Question
   e) Statement **f)** Exclamation **g)** Command **h)** Exclamation

2.

	Subject	Verb
a)	Joe	ran
b)	Rachael	passed
c)	an evil old witch	sat
d)	Harry and Mario	camped
e)	a large, silver candlestick	stood
f)	Annie	is
g)	Sam	threw
h)	Kim	crossed
i)	the boat	sank
j)	Sandra and Steph	are

3. **a)** We are going on a long walk tomorrow.
   b) You **are** a good student and work very hard.
   c) I am a keen cyclist.
   d) I thought you **were** going to help me tidy up.
   e) I **was** going to go out tonight but I haven't any money.
   f) My dogs **have** two meals a day.
   g) There **are** lots of people queuing for tickets.
   h) We **were** going to the seaside.

Page 26
Skills Practice
An effective poster should: be attractive and eye-catching; present the information clearly; be easily understood; give clear examples; be designed in a clear and logical way.

Extension Activity
In your presentation you should: explain clearly how you decided to design your poster; why you have used the layout you have; why you used the examples that you have; speak clearly; be prepared to answer questions.

SENTENCES 2

Page 30
Quick Test
1. A group of words that doesn't contain a finite verb and so doesn't make complete sense on its own. 2. To make your writing more varied and interesting. 3. Coordinating conjunction 4. One

Page 31
Key Words Exercise

Complex sentence –	A sentence with one main clause and any number of subordinate clauses.
Main clause –	A clause that has a finite verb and subject and makes complete sense on its own.
Phrase –	A group of words that doesn't contain a finite verb.
Simple sentence –	A sentence with just one finite verb.
Coordinating conjunction –	Joins two sentences together.
Compound sentence –	A sentence made up of two simple sentences.
Multiple sentence –	A sentence that contains more than one finite verb.
Subordinate clause –	A clause that doesn't make complete sense on its own.
Clause –	A group of words with a finite verb.

Page 32
Testing Understanding
1. **Any suitable answers, for example:**
   a) I didn't know about the problem so I can't explain it.
   b) She ran for the bus but she missed it.
   c) Shall we go to the cinema or shall we go bowling?
   d) We must leave now or we will miss the start.
   e) I will tidy up my bedroom but I don't want to.
   f) I will see you tonight and I will pick you up at 7.00pm.

2. **a)** Sam didn't revise much for his exam and he got a grade C. This simply tells you two facts – he didn't revise much and he got a grade C.
   Sam didn't revise much for his exam but he got a grade C. This suggests that it is a little surprising that although he didn't revise much he still got a grade C.
   b) We went to drama club and had some hot dogs and pop. This suggests that they had hot dogs and pop at the drama club.
   We went to drama club then had some hot dogs and pop. This suggests that after drama club they went somewhere to have hot dogs and pop.

3. **a)** swerving round the bend — phrase
   b) I love going on trips — clause
   c) you did well — clause
   d) coming out — phrase
   e) you drive me mad — clause

4. **a)** I put on my coat (main clause) because it was raining. (subordinate clause)
   b) As the door was locked (subordinate clause) he couldn't get in. (main clause)
   c) Before opening his notebook (subordinate clause) he sharpened his pencil. (main clause)
   d) He was slumped in the chair (main clause) staring vacantly at the television. (subordinate clause)
   e) I paid the bill (main clause) although the food was

disgusting. (subordinate clause)

Skills Practice

Make sure that your worksheets…

- explain things accurately
- are clear and easy to understand
- give an example of each kind of sentence
- use layout effectively to display information
- contain at least three questions to test understanding
- have an answer sheet.

Extension Activity

You should have discussed how successful you felt the worksheets were in explaining the ideas and how useful you found the questions that were designed to test your understanding.
Your discussions should have been constructive. If you had criticisms then you should have supported them with ideas on how the worksheets could be improved.

PUNCTUATION 1

Page 37

Quick Test

1. Full stop. 'Donna gets on with everyone. She is a very understanding person.'

2. Hyphen. 'The well-dressed man caught the train.'

3. Colon. 'Dan's favourite saying was often repeated: "Don't do anything that I'd do!"'

4. The Prime Minister's (**possession**) policies didn't (**omission**) please everyone.

5. a) There; Their
   b) Its; It's
   c) Too; To

Page 38–39

Key Words Exercise

a)	Correct	h)	Incorrect
b)	Incorrect	i)	Correct
c)	Incorrect	j)	Incorrect
d)	Correct	k)	Correct
e)	Correct	l)	Correct
f)	Incorrect	m)	Correct
g)	Incorrect	n)	Correct

Comprehension

1. Punctuation

2. Commas; Full stops

3. Omission; Possession

Page 39

Testing Understanding

The soil below London's streets holds many secrets. It's true to say that people have been living in London for thousands of years, but London has kept many of its secrets – until now. This is one of the secrets: 'An ancient Roman road beneath their garden' was what the headline in the London newspapers said. Mike Fredrickson – who'd lived in Southwark for many years – always wondered what the bits of tile were that he kept digging up and assembling in his shed. After many years of collecting these tiles, Mike and his wife took them to their council office where they heard that there was an archaeologist; an archaeologist who'd tell them what they'd found. Mike's decision to take the bits to the council proved to be inspired. They turned out to be part of a Roman mosaic from a self-contained villa beneath his back garden. Mike's hoping that his discovery will mean that he'll not have to buy a lottery ticket in future.

True or False?

1.	False	6.	True
2.	True	7.	False
3.	True	8.	False
4.	False	9.	False
5.	False	10.	True

Page 40

Skills Practice & Extension Activity

Please refer to the guide on page 266.

PUNCTUATION 2

Page 44

Quick Test

1. Speech marks
2. When there's a new speaker
3. Past
4. Colon
5. Describe the actions or scenes and give instructions

Page 45

Key Words Exercise

Direct speech (credit cheeps) –	Speech that uses the exact words that are spoken.
Punctuation (auctionpunt) –	These marks help to make written English readable.
Indirect speech (crinedt secpeh) –	Speech that reports what's been said.
Reported speech (deporter hecspe) –	Another term for indirect speech.
Pronouns (snoopurn) –	Words that stand in place of the noun.
Tense (enset) –	Past and present are examples of this.
Present (restpen) –	The tense that describes things that are happening now.
Past tense (taps neets) –	This describes things that happened yesterday, for example.
Adverbs (verbsad) –	Words that tell you more about the verb.

Play script (layp prisct) – A play is written in this.
Drama script (amard crispt) – Another term for 'play script'.
Speech marks (peshce krams) – These only go round the words that are spoken.
Quotation marks (tuqootain skarm) – Another term for 'speech marks'.
Stage directions (getsa creditsoin) – These tell you what's happening on stage.

Page 46

Testing Understanding

1. **a)** 'A Merry Christmas, Uncle! God save you!' cried a cheerful voice. It was the voice of Scrooge's nephew, who came upon him so quickly that this was the first intimation he had of his approach.
'Bah!' said Scrooge, 'Humbug!'
He had so heated himself with rapid walking in the fog and frost, this nephew of Scrooge's, that he was all in a glow; his face was ruddy and handsome; his eyes sparkled, and his breath smoked again.
'Christmas a humbug, uncle!' said Scrooge's nephew. 'You don't mean that, I am sure?'
'I do,' said Scrooge. 'Merry Christmas! What right have you to be merry? What reason have you to be merry? You're poor enough.'
'Come, then,' returned the nephew gaily. 'What right have you to be dismal? What reason have you to be morose? You're rich enough.'

   b) Here's one possible version. Yours may not be exactly like this because there is more than one way of putting it into indirect speech.
A cheerful voice had wished him a Merry Christmas and said that he wanted God to save him. It was Scrooge's nephew and he had come upon him so quickly that this had been the first intimation he had of his approach. Scrooge had dismissed this and said that he felt Christmas was humbug. Scrooge's nephew had heated himself with rapid walking in the fog and frost and was all in a glow, his face ruddy and handsome. His eye had sparkled and his breath was like smoke. He asked his uncle whether he really meant that Christmas was humbug and Scrooge had replied that he did. He went on to ask his nephew what right he had to be merry and what reason he had to be merry as he was poor. His nephew had answered gaily and had asked Scrooge what right he had to be dismal and morose as he was rich.

   c) Scrooge's nephew: (*cheerfully*) A Merry Christmas, Uncle!
   Scrooge: Bah! Humbug!

   (*Scrooge's nephew's face glowed and his eyes sparkled*)

   Scrooge's nephew: Christmas a humbug, uncle! You don't mean that, I am sure?

   Scrooge: I do. Merry Christmas! What right have you to be merry? What reason have you to be merry? You're poor enough.

   Scrooge's nephew: Come, then. What right have you to be dismal? What reason have you to be morose? You're rich enough.

Skills Practice

You should have made sure when writing out the conversation you've recorded, that you use all the conventions of speech punctuation. You should have paid particular attention to the use of...
- layout and the correct placing of speech marks
- the use of capital letters and of the use of other punctuation marks.

When converting this to indirect speech, you should have looked at...
- the use of tense, pronouns and adverbs
- the removal of speech marks.

Extension Activity

In creating your play script, you should have used...
- the correct layout of speech and the correct tense
- stage directions.

PUNCTUATION 3

Page 51
Quick Test
1. possessive 2. contractions 3. homophones

Page 52
Key Words Exercise

Page 53
Testing Understanding

1 **a)** I know _it's_ raining and the forecast says _it's_ going to get worse.

   b) The car has just had _its_ annual service so, with a bit of luck, _it's_ going to get us to Cornwall without a problem.

   c) The way that dog is baring _its_ teeth and snarling, I think _it's_ going to turn nasty.

   d) _It's_ always been an ambition of mine to become a film star but I don't think _it's_ going to happen.

   e) The eagle swooped down onto _its_ prey, grabbed it in _its_ talons and flew back to _its_ nest.

2. **a)** _They're_ coming to stay this weekend and _they're_ bringing _their_ nephew with them.

   b) I went _there_ last year and saw _their_ carnival procession but I've heard _they're_ not having one this year.

   c) _Who's_ coming with me to see _their_ performance and _whose_ car are we going in?

d) If **you're** short of money again **you're** going to have to use **your** savings.

e) If you've lost **your** book **you're** not going to borrow mine.

3. a) The car's headlights were not very bright and the road's twists and turns made driving difficult. (Cars' would also be accepted.)

b) The boys' changing room was very noisy and the teacher's voice could hardly be heard.

c) The young child's painting won the competition and was displayed in the town's art gallery.

d) The sun's rays shone through the window and the old lady's eyes were dazzled for a moment.

e) I'm going to the doctor's tomorrow so I'll get a prescription then.

Page 54

Skills Practice

Make sure that...

- one information sheet covers contraction apostrophes
- one information sheet covers commonly confused words
- one information sheet covers possessive apostrophes.

It's important that your information sheets present the information both effectively and accurately. Check your understanding of the material in the chapter very carefully.

Extension Activity

Your worksheets should give good practice of the ideas contained in your information sheets. An important part of the activity here is looking at your partner's information sheets and doing the worksheets, and discussing your thoughts about their material. Equally important is hearing what your partner has to say about your work.

THE WRITER'S CRAFT 1

Page 59

Quick Test

1. Ice; Pancake; Nails.

2. A simile.

3. A metaphor.

4. Alliteration.

5. Words that sound like the thing they are describing, e.g. Moo.

6. Tara was a nervous, trembling child at the dentists.

Page 60

Key Words Exercise

1. Adjective –	A word that describes a noun
Simile –	A comparison using 'as' or 'like'
Metaphor –	A comparison where one thing is said to be another
Clause –	A phrase that forms part or all of a sentence
Alliteration –	A group of words close together that begin with the same letter or sound
Onomatopoeia –	A word that sounds like the thing it's describing
Assonance –	Repeated use of similar or identical vowel

sounds, in words that are close together

Personification –	A kind of metaphor where abstract or non-human things are given human qualities
Pathetic fallacy –	A kind of metaphor where things from nature are given human qualities
Abstract –	Not real – an idea or concept

Comprehension

1. Adjective

2. Simile

3. Metaphor

Page 61

Testing Understanding

1. Sun smiled: Slowly struggled to succeed in reaching the summit.

2. Rays of the merciless sun.

3. My rucksack felt as heavy as molten lead.

4. The journey was a deadening weight on my mind; I gazed ahead at the towering challenge of the cliff above.

5. Fear and doubt tapped me on the shoulder.

6. The sun smiled; Rays of the merciless sun.

7. Struggled to succeed contains assonance in the repeated 'u'; Roasting, toasting.

Techniques

1. Pathetic fallacy

2. Simile

3. Assonance

4. Alliteration

5. Personification

6. Onomatopoeia

7. Alliteration, assonance and simile

8. Onomatopoeia, alliteration and assonance

Page 62

Skills Practice & Extension Activity

Please refer to the guide on page 266.

THE WRITER'S CRAFT 2

Page 66

Quick Test

1. 'ly'.

2. They can go before or after the verb.

3. They increase the speed or pace of the text.

4. It determines where the emphasis is placed in the sentence and affects meaning.

5. It can build up tension.

Key Words Exercise

E	P	H	S	O	H	E	G	U	H	C	L	X	T
N	E	V	L	A	T	M	O	A	Y	L	S	O	P
C	L	T	E	M	I	C	M	D	L	I	P	N	T
R	I	S	C	R	H	E	K	V	D	F	C	V	A
E	P	A	B	D	B	F	S	E	T	F	S	E	S
G	T	B	S	G	A	N	N	R	E	H	S	R	E
N	I	H	Q	I	L	R	G	B	F	A	T	C	P
A	N	I	S	E	T	A	C	I	D	N	I	T	I
H	D	Y	J	P	I	N	H	J	U	G	C	A	L
F	O	A	C	O	M	P	L	E	X	E	N	Z	O
F	N	S	I	S	P	I	L	L	E	R	I	B	N
I	A	O	N	U	O	P	M	O	C	V	N	I	Y
L	P	O	S	I	T	I	O	N	I	N	G	L	Z
C	E	R	E	P	E	T	I	T	I	O	N	K	O

1. Indicates

2. Ellipsis

3. Verb

4. Positioning

5. Complex

6. Adverb

7. Compound

8. Repetition

9. Cliffhanger

Testing Understanding

1. Verbs – Ran; Dashed; Glanced; See; Breathing; Hoped; Find; Picked; Want; Hurt.

   Adverbs – Quickly; Nervously; Cautiously; Deeply; Cruelly.

2. **a)–b)** There are many varieties of possible responses. There are no right answers to this.

3. **a)** Start **d)** End
   b) Split **e)** Start
   c) Start **f)** Split

Skills Practice & Extension Activity

Please refer to the guide on page 266.

WRITING FAIRY TALES

Quick Test

1. Features that are traditionally used.

2. True.

3. An idea that has been used too much and has lost most of its effect and become boring.

4. It's a problem that has to be solved by the characters.

5. It's a changed version of something, like a story.

Key Words Exercise

Convention –	Typical ways of writing that have developed.
Evolved –	Grown.
Cultures –	Different patterns of behaviour or life, resulting in overall ways of doing things.
Status –	Rank.
Carnivore –	A meat eater.
Third person –	The use of 'he' 'she' or 'it' in sentences.
Genre –	A format or style.
Plot-line –	Basic storyline.
Tradition –	The passing down of some elements of a culture from generation to generation.
Slavish – adherence	Believing something without questioning it.
Traditionalist –	A person who believes in the passed-down ways of doing things.
Adverb –	Words that describe how things are done.
Adaptation –	Different changed versions.
Feature –	Noticeable qualities.
Linear –	In a straight line.
Clichéd –	Repeated so often that it's become boring.
Crisis –	A problem.

Testing Understanding

a) Beautiful girl / Princess
Handsome Prince
Set in a wood / forest / castle
Ends 'Happily ever after' or similar
Written in the third person
Uses adverbs
Contains a crisis / problem
Characters make good choices
Characters make bad choices

b) Helpful animals
Helpful magic
Bad magic
Starts with 'Once upon a time'
Giants and / or monsters
Wicked stepmother / witch

Skills Practice & Extension Activity

Please refer to the guide on page 266.

IMAGINATIVE WRITING

Quick Test

1. The place or circumstance a story is set in.

2. Themes

3. Climax

4. First person; Third person

Page 82

Key Words Exercise

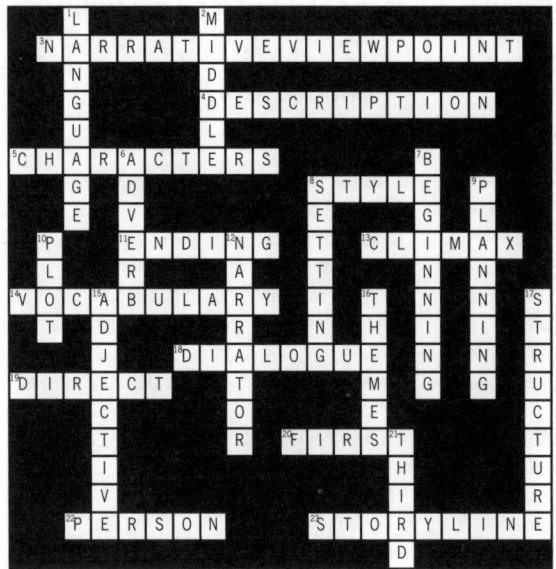

Page 83

Testing Understanding

1. The opening is important to capture the attention of the reader.
2. **Any three from:** An unexpected or unusual idea; By setting the scene; With dialogue that leads straight into the action; The description of a character; A dramatic event; By giving background information of the situation or characters
3. The way the story develops and the way the story is written.
4. So that the reader is left satisfied, perhaps with something to think about.
5. **Any two from:** A natural ending based on the development of the plot; A dramatic ending; An unexpected twist at the end; With information revealed that throws light on the characters or events; An ending that leaves things in the air and keeps you guessing
6. **a)** First **b)** First **c)** Third **d)** First **e)** Third
7. A word that describes a verb.
8. A word that describes a noun.
9. **a)** old (adjective); slowly (adverb); dusty (adjective)
   b) loudly (adverb); blue (adjective)
   c) slowly (adverb); golden (adjective); darkening (adjective)
   d) violently (adverb); trembling (adjective)
   e) quickly (adverb); smoking (adjective); suddenly (adverb)
10. There are too many adjectives used, which makes it sound flowery, exaggerated and artificial.

Page 84

Skills Practice

Make sure that you have carefully made notes on the stories and have covered the following points:
- How the writer sets the scene.
- If characters are introduced or described.
- If speech is used.
- What kind of opening each writer uses.

When writing your analysis, make sure that you use plenty of examples from your texts to support the points you make.

Extension Activity

Make sure that you include plenty of detail in your table. Use examples from the texts and explain how effective you think they are in engaging the reader.

CHARACTER AND ATMOSPHERE

Page 88

Quick Test

1. **a)** First person **b)** Third person
2. **a)** believable; convincing **b)** imagination

Page 89

Key Words Exercise

1. language 2. imagination 3. stereotypes 4. atmosphere / setting 5. mood / tone 6. adjectives 7. simile 8. metaphor 9. actions 10. feelings

Page 90

Testing Understanding

1. He was a **snub**-nosed flat-browed, common-faced boy enough; and as **dirty** a juvenile as one would wish to see; but he had about him all the airs and **manners** of a man. He was short of his age: with rather **bow**-legs, and little **sharp**, ugly eyes. His hat was stuck on the top of his head so **lightly** that it threatened to fall off every moment – and would have done so, very often, if the wearer had not had a knack of every now and then giving his head a sudden **twitch** which brought it back to its old place again. He wore a man's coat, which reached nearly to his heels. He had turned the **cuffs** back, half-way up his arm, to get his hands out of the sleeves: apparently with the ultimate view of **thrusting** them into the pockets of his corduroy **trousers**; for there he kept them.
2. An eerie or creepy atmosphere is created. Possible phrases that create the atmosphere include:
   - 'In the dusk.'
   - 'The rocket-hall was very dark.'
   - 'Footsteps sounded hollow.'
   - 'Bare boards.'
   - 'Intimate as a seaboot.'
   - 'Who could be listening?'

Page 91

Skills Practice

In creating your plan, think carefully about each stage. Include enough detail to create a useful framework but avoid putting so much detail in that you're almost writing the story instead of a plan.

Extension Activity

When giving your talk make sure that you clearly explain...
- the decisions you made when planning your story
- the effects you wanted to achieve.

Be prepared to answer any questions they might have. Avoid writing out your talk and just reading it. Remember, this should be a talk and not just simply reading out your notes.

DESCRIPTIVE WRITING

Page 95

Quick Test
1. verbs 2. sound 3. mood

Page 96
Key Words Exercise

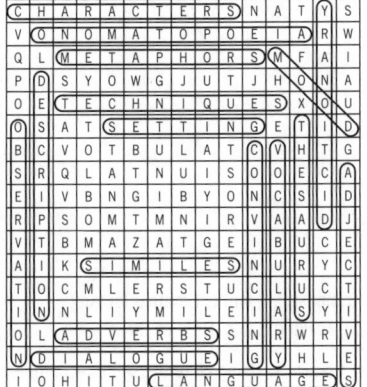

1. dialogue
2. setting; mood
3. characters
4. observation
5. convincing
6. description
7. language
8. thesaurus; dictionary
9. techniques
10. adverbs
11. similes; metaphors
12. adjectives
13. onomatopoeia
14. vocabulary

Page 97
Testing Understanding
1. • Description of Anne's physical appearance, e.g. 'Her eyes were honest and inquiring.'
   • Use of direct speech to capture her voice, e.g. 'I'll do that,' she combined dignity with sweetness.'
   • Description of her manner and way of behaving e.g. 'She was graceful'
   • Suggestions of what her character is like underneath, e.g. 'in this young woman there lurked a real firmness.'
   • The use of a simile to describe her hair, e.g. 'round, brown curls, like swallows' nests'
2. • Detailed visual description of the scene.
   • Use of personification ('The water was...stealing away.')
   • Use of adjectives, e.g. smooth, flowing.
   • A sense of peace and quietness created through natural description.

Page 98
Skills Practice
You should have focused closely on the key aspects of each subject for description.

In your writing you should have tried some or all of these techniques:
• Imagery such as similes and metaphors to help your readers re-create your description in their own minds.
• The use of the senses to create a vivid impression of the sights, sounds, tastes, smells and feelings.
• The use of adverbs and adjectives.
• The use of dialogue.
• A range of sentence lengths.

Extension Activity
You should have read your pieces of description clearly and with feeling to make your words come across as effectively as possible. Your partner should have commented on the following:

• Your use of language.
• The techniques you have used to describe your subject.
• Ways that you could improve your description.

You should have made constructive comments about how effective you found your partner's descriptions and given reasons for the points you made. It's likely that comments will focus on the use of language, the use of vocabulary and the effectiveness of imagery, e.g. metaphors and similes. Specific suggestions relating to these would be useful and interesting.

PERSONAL WRITING

Page 102

Quick Test

1. They help you to find information easily.
2. It could be used for bad reasons, e.g. by criminals.
3. It makes you seem more interesting.
4. It makes you sound more reasonable.
5. It saves the reader time in finding out information.

Page 103

Key Words Exercise

1. a
2. b
3. b
4. b
5. c
6. c

Page 105

Testing Understanding

1. a) My Top Ten facts; What I Did Today.
      They are explaining things to friends and give reasons why he might not be able to see them etc.
   b) About Me; My Likes; My Top Ten Facts.
      They offer interesting information that people might want to know more about.

2. a) 'Anyone who doesn't agree with me is a waste of space'; 'Cuz I'm gonna be famous'.
   b) Someone who uses slang gives the impression that they can't be bothered to use full standard English. They might want to sound cool, etc.

3. **Facts**: My name is Alex.

   If you want my autograph then e-mail me and send me a fiver and then I'll post it to you...

   I like playing the guitar.

   I can't be bothered with school.

   Today I learnt some new chords for the guitar.

   I'll have to sack him.

   Opinions: I'm gonna be famous.

...they're gonna stop me from getting to the top where I deserve to be.

I am the best guitar player for my age and anyone who doesn't agree with me is a waste of space.

...I'm great. I have loads of girls who fancy me and I'm not surprised because, well, who wouldn't?

I don't need to try hard because I'm gonna be famous.

The bass player in our band is just rubbish and couldn't play the amazing new song I wrote.

4. **a)** All the layout features and sections are the same, e.g. Name; Personal information; Sections and Headings; Both are written in an informal style and use photos.
    b) Alex's profile uses a background picture. The main photo of Alex is different in style to Robbie's, and the content is quite arrogant.
    c) They reveal Alex's arrogance and self-importance.
    d) Alex gives more opinions than Robbie.
    e) Robbie appears more reasonable. He uses more facts than Alex.

5. Any suitable answer which gives reasons based on your personal opinion and linked to the evidence in the profiles is acceptable. Answers based on the details of the language and content of the profile will be more convincing.

Page 105

Skills Practice & Extension Activity

Please refer to the guide on page 266.

FORMS OF PERSUASION

Page 109

Quick Test

1. It is being nice to someone in the hope that they will agree to your suggestions.

2. They are words designed to stir up feelings or emotions.

3. They give the impression that an argument is well-researched and, therefore, believable.

4. They are questions that imply a certain answer, without actually giving that answer.

5. It might offend the person it is being used on and have the opposite effect it is intended to.

Page 110

Key Words Exercise

1. Persuasion – The technique of getting someone to do what you want.
    Formal – Serious and following standards of politeness.
    Informal – Not serious – relaxed.
    Flattery – Using complimentary words to someone.
    Guilt – A word that describes the feeling you have when you make someone feel sorry.
    Rhetorical questions – Questions that only have one implied answer.

Statistics – Numbers.
Repetition – Saying something again and again.
Empathy – Putting yourself in the other person's place.
Shock tactics – What you use when you want to demand someone's attention straight away.
Emotive – Descriptive words that tug on the emotions.
Blackmail – Technique that involves threatening to reveal bad things about someone, or do bad things to them.
Compromise – Meeting someone halfway.

Page 111

Comprehension

1. Flattery; Guilty.

2. Emotive words.

3. Three part repetition.

Testing Understanding

1. Flattery; Threats and blackmail; Guilt; Emotive language; Demands; Repetition; Making deals; Rule of three.

2. Rhetorical questions; Statistics; Using all of the same techniques that were used, but more subtly, might have helped too.

Page 112

Skills Practice & Extension Activity

Please refer to the guide on page 266.

WRITING FOR AN AUDIENCE

Page 116

Quick Test

1. Non-fiction.

2. Generally it should, but opinions in the review might be a little less formal.

3. They give the reader the correct order to follow.

4. They stop the reader from having to take in too much information in one go. They're easier to understand and follow.

5. True.

Page 117

Key Words Exercise

1.	c	5.	a
2.	a	6.	c
3.	b	7.	c
4.	b		

Page 118

Testing Understanding

1.	True	8.	False	15.	False
2.	True	9.	False	16.	True
3.	False	10.	True	17.	False
4.	True	11.	False	18.	True

5. False	12. False	19. True
6. True	13. True	20. False
7. False	14. False	

Page 119

Skills Practice & Extension Activity

Please refer to the guide on page 266.

AUDIENCE AND PURPOSE

Page 123

Quick Test

1. a) purpose b) complain c) inform d) people interested in birds or birdwatching
2. To instruct

Page 124

Key Words Exercise

1. Analyse 2. Complain 3. Entertain 4. Audience 5. Inform 6. Describe 7. Purpose 8. Argue 9. Persuade 10. Instruct 11. Advise 12. Explain

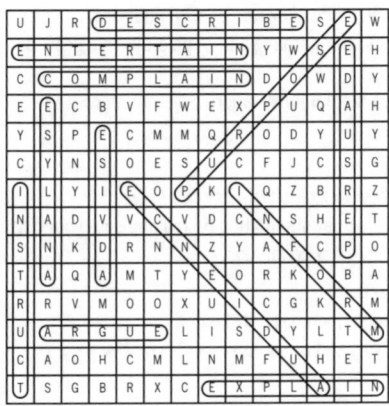

Page 125

Testing Understanding

1. **Audience**: Readers who enjoy scary stories; **Purpose**: To entertain / describe (maybe also to inform)
2. **Audience**: Anyone interested in skateboarding; **Purpose**: To entertain / inform / advise
3. **Audience**: Someone cooking an Indian meal; **Purpose**: To instruct / inform / advise
4. **Audience**: Young children; **Purpose**: To entertain
5. **Audience**: Children of school age; **Purpose**: Maybe to inform / advise / persuade someone being bullied
6. **Audience**: Anyone reading about news items; **Purpose**: To inform
7. **Audience**: Young person at school studying science; **Purpose**: To inform / instruct
8. **Audience**: Someone who has sold a faulty camera; **Purpose**: To inform / persuade / complain
9. **Audience**: A young child; **Purpose**: To entertain
10. **Audience**: A young person at school or a teacher; **Purpose**: To analyse / inform / describe
11. **Audience**: Fans of *Doctor Who*; **Purpose**: To entertain / inform / describe

12. **Audience**: Someone with a headache; **Purpose**: To advise / inform
13. **Audience**: Someone who likes romantic stories; **Purpose**: To entertain / describe
14. **Audience**: Anyone planning to visit Paris; **Purpose**: To inform / advise

Page 126

Skills Practice

Choose your three pieces of writing carefully and make sure that for each one you…
- identify the audience and the purpose
- analyse the language (remember to use examples and comment on the effect they create)
- think about the presentation and the effect it has.

Extension Activity

Make sure you include some details of language use and presentation.

DEVELOPING A POINT OF VIEW

Page 130

Quick Test

1. False
2. False
3. True
4. True
5. True

Key Words Exercise

Page 131

Page 132

Testing Understanding

1. Rhetorical question
2. Repetition
3. Outlining the problem / topic
4. Use of facts
5. Using views that don't agree with your own
6. Countering argument
7. Warning of consequences

Page 133

Skills Practice

Make sure that you choose your topic carefully and work through the steps, thinking clearly about each one. Check your rough draft carefully and make any changes that you think necessary.

Extension Activity

Make sure your talk does not last more than five minutes. Plan what you're going to say carefully. Don't just read out your notes.

PRESENTING INFORMATION 1

Page 137

Quick Test

1. Its purpose – to inform.
2. clear; easy to understand
3. To draw attention to certain points and present the ideas clearly.
4. Different styles of lettering.
5. Bullet points; Illustrations; Maps; Tables; Diagrams; Colour; Pictures; Photographs

Page 138

Key Words Exercise

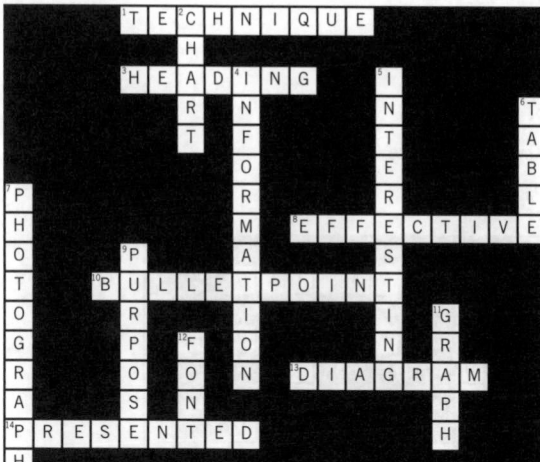

Page 139

Testing Understanding

1. Information is presented in a variety of ways:
   - Heading giving the name of the property and its location.
   - Written description.
   - Photographs.
   - A table giving dates and prices.
   - Symbols to summarise key features and other information.

2. a) Eight b) Yes c) Yes d) No e) Yes f) £555 g) 4th July to 25th September at £785

Page 140

Skills Practice

Remember that the main purpose of your writing is to inform the reader. Make sure that your leaflet contains plenty of information that makes your chosen resort or town sound interesting.

Also, think carefully about layout. Don't try to cram too much into the leaflet.

Extension Activity

Think carefully about how could improve your leaflet in light of your partner's comments.

Use different fonts and colours on a computer to make the leaflet more effective.

PRESENTING INFORMATION 2

Page 144
Quick Test
1. sub-headings 2. fonts 3. words 4. attention

Page 145
Key Words Exercise
1. facts 2. techniques 3. bullet points 4. illustrations
5. heading 6. In any order: leaflet; poster 7. purpose 8. advice
9. puns 10. information 11. present; language 12. slogan

Page 146
Testing Understanding
The heading:
- Large lettering captures attention.
- Use of pale blue highlights key words 'stay' and 'cool'.
- The use of letters shading from white to pale blue suggests a sense of coolness.
- Sub-heading gives factual information, which reinforces the key message.

Content and language:
- Advice given on how to look after a dog in hot weather.
- Bullet points give factual information on making sure your dog is well looked after in hot conditions.

Presentation and effects:
- The effect created by the image of the dog.
- Use of lettering styles and colour to suggest coolness.

Overall effectiveness:
- Assess your response to the leaflet.
- Did you find it effective? Give reasons for your views.

Page 147
Skills Practice
In your leaflet you should have used...
- headings / sub-headings
- colour and different fonts
- carefully chosen language, e.g. the use of slogans, puns, etc.
- techniques to make your presentation more effective, e.g. the use of bullet points, blocks of text, etc.

Your analysis should give a clear picture of what you wanted to achieve. You should have explained...
- why you chose the heading
- how you decided on the advice / information to include
- the effects you wanted to achieve through language
- the effects you wanted to achieve through presentation.

Extension Activity
You should look carefully at the comments on your poster and think about how far you agree with them, making a note of any ways you could improve your poster.

WRITING FORMAL LETTERS

Page 151

Quick Test

1. The date **2.** Yours sincerely **3.** When you begin 'Dear Sir' or 'Dear Madam' **4.** Top right hand side

Page 152

Key Words Exercise

FORMAL (RALFOM) –	When applying for a job your letter of application should be a _____ letter.
SINCERELY (NICELYRES) –	If you use the person's name you should end your letter 'Yours _____'.
BUSINESS (SUBSINES) –	Another term for a formal letter is a _____ letter.
DATE (ATED) –	You should put the _____ under the address.
COMPLAIN (MANICLOP) –	If you're not happy with something you might write a letter to _____.
ADDRESS (SADREDS) –	In the top right hand side you put your _____.
APPLICATION (CAPTAINPOIL) –	When you apply for a job you usually write a letter of _____.
POLITE (PIELOT) –	In a letter you should always be _____.
PERSUADE (ADRUPEES) –	If you want someone to agree with your view you try to _____ them.
TONE (ENTO) –	Choosing the right words is important to get the right _____.
OPINION (INPOINO) –	In a letter you might express your own _____.
FAITHFULLY (AHFITLYFLU) –	If you begin a letter 'Dear Sir' or 'Dear Madam' you should end it 'Yours _____'.
ENQUIRE (QUIREEN) –	If you want to find something out you might _____ about it.
CONTENT (NOTCENT) –	What you write in your letter is called the _____.
CONFIRM (MONCRIF) –	If you want to make sure you're booked on a holiday you would write to _____ the dates and other details.
SALUTATION (ASNAILTOUT)	The formal opening part of the letter is known as the _____.

Page 153

Testing Understanding

The date is missing. Wrong spellings – unfortunately; there, rang, your, department, they. Sincerely is used instead of faithfully. The tone of the final sentence is wrong – it's too aggressive and threatening.

Page 154

Skills Practice

1. Your letter should...
   * give a clear explanation of the problem

* give details of when and where you bought the item
* say what you would expect them to do
* use a polite and reasonable tone throughout.

2. Your letter should contain these features:
   * The exact dates of your holiday – making sure that your arrival and departure dates are clearly stated.
   * The accommodation that you have booked, e.g. the number of bedrooms, facilities, etc.
   * The number of adults and children that will be arriving.
   * Any other information that you think is important.

Extension Activity

Your poster should have covered the following:
* Correct positioning and layout of addresses
* Date
* Salutation
* Content to suit purpose and audience
* The formal ending (giving alternatives according to salutation).

Your poster should also include between four and six bullet points giving the key points to remember when writing a formal letter.

GENRE & SCIENCE FICTION

Page 159

Quick Test

1. No. There are different genres in art, music and film, among others.

2. Science fiction.

3. Yes.

4. No.

5. It gets boring and predictable.

Page 160

Key Words Exercise

Composition –	Something that has been composed or created
Distinctive –	Clear and having definite characteristics
Form –	Shape or structure
Cylinder –	A round, tube-shaped container
Concussion –	The state of being stunned
Cavity –	A hole
Inarticulate –	Not very clearly spoken
Ungovernable –	Not possible to control
Steadfastly –	With determination
Pulsated –	Throbbed
Appendage –	Something added on
Alternative –	A different way of doing something
Technology –	Equipment or machinery designed to do a job
Mage –	A kind of wizard
Dense –	Thick

Page 161

Testing Understanding

1. Style; Composition; Features; Reader; Future technology.

2. Dreamy; Horses and guns.

3. Boring; Use; Original.

4. Style; Appropriate.

5. Adjectives; Similes.

True or False?

1.	False	**6.**	True
2.	True	**7.**	True
3.	True	**8.**	True
4.	False	**9.**	False
5.	False	**10.**	True

Page 162

Skills Practice & Extension Activity

Please refer to the guide on page 266.

DRAMA TEXTS

Page 166

Quick Test

1. Down Left.

2. Long Shot.

3. Props.

4. For stage directions.

5. To move the camera left or right, up or down.

Page 167

1. Drama

2. Stage directions

3. Properties

4. Brackets

5. Italics

6. Long Shot

7. Medium Shot

8. Close-up

9. Pan

10. Zoom

11. Sound effects

12. Technical

13. Cut

14. Adapted

Page 168

Testing Understanding

1. c

2. b

3. c

4. c

5. a

6. b

7. c

Page 169

Skills Practice & Extension Activity

Please refer to the guide on page 266.

NOVELS AND SHORT STORIES

Page 173
Quick Test
1. interest **2.** to entertain **3.** themes **4.** plot

Page 174
Key Words Exercise

Page 175
Testing Understanding
1. He describes the way they are dressed – the denim trousers and jackets suggest they are workers. Their 'shapeless hats' reinforce this impression.
2. The first man gives the impression of a small but strong character ('strong features') with a sharp intelligent face alert to everything around him ('restless eyes'). We get the impression of a wiry and fit, strong man ('small, strong hands, slender arms, a thin and bony nose').
3. The second man is the opposite – 'a huge man', 'shapeless of face'. He seems big and slow – 'walked heavily', 'dragging his feet'. Note the animal imagery to describe him – 'the way a bear drags its paws'.
4. The first character is clearly the dominant one. The big man (Lennie) follows the smaller man (George). George tells Lennie not to drink so much – he seems to be looking after Lennie and tries to stop him doing something that might make him ill.
5. George gives Lennie orders and speaks to him like a child. Lennie's answers are very simple and child-like.

Page 176
Skills Practice
Your analysis of each passage should have focused closely on how the writer presents their characters. You should have covered the following:
• The impression you formed of the character.

- The techniques the writer used to create a sense of character.
- How language was used to create effects.

You should have given examples of the language used and the effects created to support the points you made.

Extension Activity

Make sure that you have used plenty of carefully chosen quotations to label your drawing.

READING POETRY

Page 180

Quick Test

1. **Any three from:** Simile; Metaphor; Personification; Aural (alliteration, assonance, onomatopoeia)
2. Aural
3. Alliteration
4. Vowels
5. Onomatopoeia

Page 181

Key Words Exercise

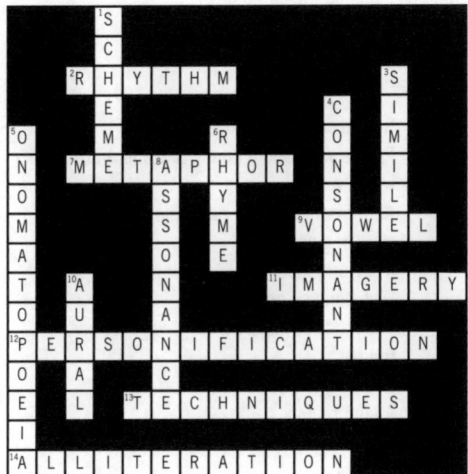

Page 182

Testing Understanding

1. **a)** Every footstep breaks a brittle pane; Dead boughs take roots in ponds; Ferns on windows shoot; Ranks trees in an armed host; Hangs daggers from house eaves **b)** Lurk under gluey glass like fish in bowls **c)** Tinkle **d)** Frost called to water; The sun will strike him dead **e)** AABBCC

Page 183

Skills Practice

Make sure that you have focused on the key areas suggested in the activity. Remember – don't just identify features such as metaphors and similes, but write about the effects that they create in the poem.

Extension Activity

You should have thought carefully about the questions for your partner. Make sure that the questions are to do with how the language is used rather than just what the poem's about.

ANALYSING POETRY

Page 187

Quick Test

1. vocabulary 2. sound 3. **In any order:** metaphor; simile; personification 4. effects

Page 188

Key Words Exercise

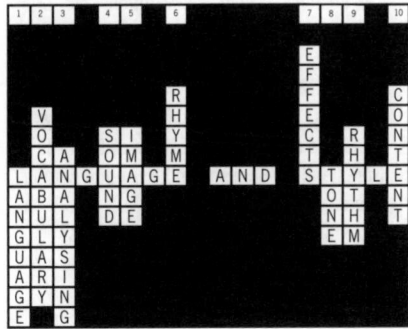

Page 189

Testing Understanding

There are lots of things you could comment on. Here are some suggestions:

Vocabulary

The vivid descriptions of the blackberries, e.g. 'red', 'green', 'glossy purple', 'stains upon the tongue', 'big, dark blobs', which give a very visual impression of the blackberries while at the same time suggesting taste with 'stains upon the tongue'.

Use of imagery

Similes; 'hard as a knot'; 'sweet like thickened wine'; 'big dark blobs burned / Like a plate of eyes'; 'our palms sticky as Bluebeard's'

Metaphors

'a glossy purple clot'; 'summer's blood'; 'inked up'

Tone

The tone in the first section is one of excitement and gives a strong impression of the eagerness to collect as many blackberries as possible. The tone changes in the second section of the poem to one of disappointment as the blackberries rot. This contrasts to the feeling in the first part of the poem.

Page 190

Skills Practice

Make sure that you choose your poem carefully. Choose one that you have plenty to say about. Use your notes as the basis of your analysis. Make sure that you have covered the following:

- What you think the poem is about.
- The use of vocabulary and imagery.
- The tone and atmosphere created (and how).
- The use of effects such as alliteration, onomatopoeia, etc.

Remember that you should have used individual words or short quotations from the poem to illustrate your ideas.

Extension Activity

You should plan your talk carefully so that you know what you're going to say. When giving your talk make sure that you don't read out from your notes though. If you need prompts you could write key ideas on cards to remind you of the order of your points and help you stick to your plan.

WRITING FROM DIFFERENT CULTURES

Page 194
Quick Test
1. non-standard English 2. world 3. ritual 4. voice

Page 195
Key Words Exercise

VOCABULARY –	The words or language used.
CULTURE –	The customs, way of life, traditions, etc. of a particular group of people.
RITUALS –	These are often carried out at religious ceremonies.
CUSTOMS –	The usual ways of behaving or doing things.
NON-STANDARD –	Dialect is a _____ form of English.
VOICE –	Non-standard English can be used in writing to create a sense of _____.
TRADITION –	A custom, belief or way of doing things, handed down from generation to generation.
BELIEFS –	A person's or group's religious ideas.
WORLD –	Literature from different cultures can come from all over the _____.
DIALECT –	The form of speech of a particular region or part of the world.
METAPHOR –	A kind of imagery where one thing is said to be another.
SIMILE –	A comparison where one thing is said to be like another.

Page 196
Testing Understanding
Here are some ideas that you might have noted:
1. The Butterfly represents the 'higher life' – living a good and sin-free life. Butterflies fly free in the heavens whilst caterpillars crawl on leaves or the ground.
2. They don't take him seriously and find it hard not to laugh. At the end, however, the speaker realises that the preacher was right and it is better to be a butterfly than a caterpillar.
3. He is the only one who can keep a straight face.
4. The food indicates a different culture with its references to things we are not familiar with, e.g. fufu and pigtail.
5. The spelling of caterpillar (kyatta-pilla); the lines 'That was de life preacher' / 'And you was right'.

Page 197
Skills Practice
You should have commented on the following:
- What the title of the poem suggests to you. The title of the poem can give you important clues about the poem itself (e.g. as in 'Be a Butterfly').
- What the poem is about. Try to be clear in your own mind what the poem is about – what is happening, what kind of message the poet wants to give you.
- Whether the poet uses dialect or non-standard English. If so, you should have thought about the effect that it has on the poem – its effect is going to be very important.
- Whether the poet uses imagery (e.g. metaphors, similes, etc.). If so, you should have given examples and commented on the effects created.
- What effects are created by the language used. You should have looked at individual words and phrases that strike you as

being important and explained why.
- Whether the poet creates an impression of the culture / traditions / beliefs, etc. If so, you should have commented on how they were presented and what effects you think they have on the poem.
- What you feel about the poem overall. You should have tried to give reasons for why you feel the way you do about the poem.

Extension Activity
Experiment with different ways of reading the poem and think about any differences or effects that you can create through your readings. Make sure that you talk to your partner and share your ideas.

SHAKESPEARE 1

Page 202
Quick Test
1. London.
2. Men and boys.
3. The pit.
4. Shakespeare used the characters' words to describe the scene, rather than by using lighting effects.

Page 203
Key Words Exercise

Gallery –	Raised seats in the theatre
Groundlings –	People who paid a penny to stand and watch a play
Prologue –	An introduction to a play before the main story begins
Bawdy –	Rude and loud
Excavations –	Digs done by archaeologists
Archaeology –	The study of history through digging up the past
Pomp –	Showing-off linked to well-off people
Masque –	A kind of play
Thatch –	Roof material made from straw
Kindled –	Set fire
Syllables –	Beats in a word or a line of text
Syntax –	Changing word order

Anagrams
1. Hamlet
2. Romeo and Juliet
3. Macbeth
4. The Globe
5. Gallery

Page 204
Testing Understanding

1.	False	11.	True
2.	True	12.	True
3.	True	13.	False
4.	False	14.	False

5. False   15. False

6. False   16. False

7. False   17. True

8. True   18. False

9. False   19. False

10. True   20. True

Page 205

Skills Practice & Extension Activity

Please refer to the guide on page 266.

SHAKESPEARE 2

Page 209

Quick Test

1. False 2. False 3. True 4. True 5. True

Page 210

Key Words Exercise

Simile –	A comparison, using the words 'like' or 'as'.
Plot –	The storyline of a play.
Histories –	Plays based on historical figures.
Metaphors –	A comparison, saying that one thing actually is the other.
Romances –	Plays that have a fantasy or magical element and were the last plays Shakespeare wrote.
Imagery –	The use of words to create a picture or 'image'.
Soliloquy –	What a character speaks while alone on stage.
Comedies –	Plays with a happy ending.
Structure –	The way the action of a play is put together.
Personification –	A kind of metaphor where something that's not human is described as if it has human feelings or qualities.
Tragedies –	Plays that end with the death of the main character(s).
Last plays –	Another term for Romances.

Anagrams

1. Structure 2. Simile 3. Julius Caesar 4. Personification
5. Romances

Page 211

Testing Understanding

1. a) True b) False c) True d) True e) True f) False g) False
   h) False i) True j) False
2. a) Simile b) Simile c) Metaphor d) Metaphor e) Simile

Page 212

Skills Practice

Choose your soliloquies carefully and make sure that you have explained…
* where each soliloquy comes in the action of the play
* who the speakers are
* what ideas are contained in the soliloquies

* what the soliloquies tell you about the characters
* how the language is used (make sure you have given examples to support your points).

Extension Activity

Make sure that your information sheet is clear and explains the differences between metaphors and similes effectively. It's a good idea to think about the visual effects of the information sheet.

SHAKESPEARE'S LANGUAGE

Page 216

Quick Test

1. pun 2. hyperbole 3. alone 4. juxtaposition

Page 217

Key Words Exercise

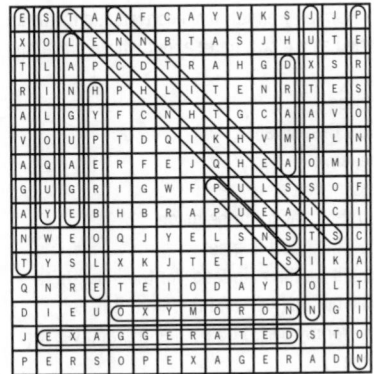

Page 218

Testing Understanding

1. Shakespeare uses antithesis in love / hate and love / loathe. The use of this antithesis emphasises the problem facing Juliet and the love she feels for Romeo even though, as a Montague, she should hate him.
2. An oxymoron is used in 'brawling love'. Love is making Romeo sad because he loves Rosaline, but she is indifferent to him.
3. a) The pun is on the word 'steal', which means 'to go secretly' and 'to rob', i.e. take things that are not his.
   b) Claudius calls Hamlet son (even though he isn't his son) and Hamlet uses the word 'sun' (meaning that Claudius is watching him too closely). There's also a play on 'kin' (relative) and 'kind' (being nice to him).

   c) The pun is on the word 'light', which is referring to the torch or candle that Othello carries and light also meaning Desdemona's life.

Page 219

Skills Practice

1. When you have identified your examples of antithesis or oxymoron make sure that you explain carefully what words are used to create the antithesis or oxymoron and explain the effects created.
   Example answer: in *Macbeth*, Shakespeare uses antithesis to create a vivid sense of the way things are slipping from good into evil:
   'Good things of day begin to droop and drowse,
   While night's black agents their preys do rouse.'
   (Act 3 Scene 2 lines 52–53)

   Here the idea of 'good things' and 'black agents' are set in opposition to each other with the link between 'black' and evil created. The idea of good things beginning to 'droop and drowse' gives the impression that good is in decline and the evil is gaining strength.

2. **You should have explained what is being personified and the effects created.**

   Example answer: In *Hamlet*, the dawn is described in this way:
   'But look the morn in russet mantle clad
   Walks o'er the dew of yon high eastward hill.'
   Here the dawn is described as if it were a person dressed in the golden brown that is the colour of dawn walking over a high hill to the east (where the sun rises). This creates a vivid picture in the mind of the dawn beginning to break and adds a sense of peace to the scene.

3. **You should have explained how the puns work and how the effects are created.**

   Example answer: In *Hamlet*, Hamlet has a conversation with a grave digger (described as a clown here) about whose grave he is digging.

Hamlet:	...Whose grave's this, sirrah?
First Clown:	Mine, sir. [sings] O, a pit of clay for to be made For such a guest is meet.
Hamlet:	I think it be thine, indeed; for thou liest in't.
First Clown:	You lie out on't, sir, and therefore it is not yours: for my part, I do not lie in't, and yet it is mine.
Hamlet:	Thou dost lie in't, to be in't and say it is thine: 'tis for the dead, not for the quick; therefore thou liest.

   The pun here is all based around the word 'lie' – meaning to lie down or lie in the grave but also meaning to tell an untruth. The word play here creates a moment of humour at a particularly tense moment in the play.

4. In your short essay you might have commented on some of these ideas:
   - The use of imagery, e.g. metaphors, similes, personification.
   - The use of vocabulary, e.g. commenting on the ideas that individual words or phrases have brought to your mind.
   - The use of antithesis.
   - The use of hyperbole.

Extension Activity

Think carefully about the effects that you want your examples to create. Discuss the effects with your partner before writing your explanations.

READING FOR MEANING 1

Page 224

Quick Test

1. Skim reading
2. Scanning
3. Extensive reading
4. Intensive reading
5. Fact

Page 225

Key Words Exercise

Comparative –	Having put one thing next to another for the process of comparison.
Modal –	A word like 'could'.
Conditional –	Word that contains or expresses some doubt.
Null comparative –	A comparison where you aren't really comparing to anything else.
Disparity –	The difference between one thing and another.
Opinions –	Things that can't be proved, but which someone believes.
Extensive reading –	Reading longer texts.
Origin –	Word that means the place where something began.
Personal Voice –	One person's view.
Intensive reading –	Reading technique where you would study a passage in detail to extract information.
Precipitation –	Word meaning 'rainfall'.
Mean –	Word which, in this unit, means 'average'.
Scanning –	Reading technique designed to identify key facts quickly.
Variations –	Word meaning 'differences'.
Skim reading –	Reading technique you would use to get a general idea of what something is about.
Fact –	Some things that can be proved.

Page 226

Testing Understanding

a) The group called The Credit Card of Hope released their first single on 21st June 2007. It was called *Not Everybody's Got an Angel*.

   Their next exposure to the public was on an internet-only radio show where their track received airplay.

   At least getting airplay was better than no airplay at all.

   All of these songs are kept on a computer hard drive stored in a safe deposit box in Stoke-on-Trent.

   Less than 20 MP3s were downloaded...

b) Although it was better than the other tracks on there, in my opinion it didn't get them their much deserved breakthrough and so they had to struggle on.

   Finally, it's believed that the group split up in early 2008. A lack of sales probably contributed to this. The group apparently leave behind over 50 songs that the public will never hear.

c) ...unluckily failed to make any impression on the charts. They should have made their breakthrough a few months later, when their follow-up track *Everything About You but the Vale* was fortunately included on the cover-mount CD of a football fanzine.

   Many listeners found the track *The Jorge Monster Mash* quite funny, even though it wasn't supposed to be.

Page 227

Skills Practice & Extension Activity

Please refer to the guide on page 266.

READING FOR MEANING 2

Page 231

Quick Test

1. Factual 2. Style 3. Analysing 4. Point, Evidence, Explanation

Page 232

Key Words Exercise

1. Non-fiction 2. Point, Evidence, Explanation 3. Audience; Effect
4. Analysis 5. Style 6. Presented 7. Topic 8. Factual
9. Information 10. Texts 11. Ideas 12. Illustrations 13. Content

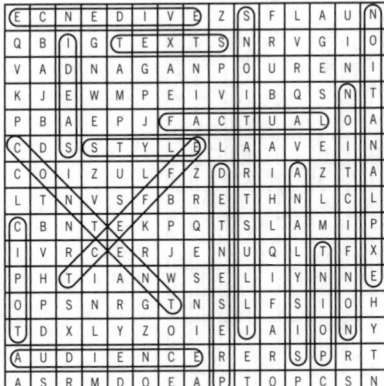

Page 233

1. **Testing Understanding**

    a) **Audience**: School children – the language suggests
    secondary age range. **Purpose**: To inform, advise and give
    help about being bullied. b) Tell someone. c) **Any three
    from:** Name calling; Making things up about someone so
    they get into trouble; Punching, hitting and physically
    hurting someone; Threatening someone; Taking someone's
    things off them; Spreading rumours about someone;
    Stealing from someone; Damaging someone's property;
    Sending threatening messages, e.g. e-mails, texts, etc.
    d) By suggesting they tell various people about it and
    different ways to tell them. e) The language is quite
    informal to make the reader feel at ease. It is
    straightforward vocabulary so it's easily understood. The
    tone is friendly and advising. f) Short paragraphs and
    bullet points help present the information clearly.

Page 234

Skills Practice

You should have chosen your piece of writing carefully and...
- identified the audience and purpose
- explained the key points the writer makes
- examined carefully how the writer presents information
- given examples of how language is used and the effects
  it creates
- used the Point, Evidence, Explanation approach.

Extension Activity

Your discussion with a friend is an important element in this
activity and you should have used the ideas from it as the basis for

your review. Remember to think about the purpose and audience
for your review when writing it.

READING FOR MEANING 3

Page 238

Quick Test

1. What information you need. 2. Making brief notes directly on a
copy of your text. 3. understanding 4. key points

Page 239

Key Words Exercise

1. comprehension 2. extensive reading 3. skimming 4. information
5. annotation 6. summary 7. highlighting 8. notes
9. intensive reading 10. purpose 11. key points 12. scanning

Page 240

Testing Understanding

1. a) Three b) Stones c) They sometimes blew down in strong winds
2. Canvas hats coated with tar, leather aprons and cowhide boots
3. Basic food and not a lot of it.
4. Chebaccos; thirty feet
5. Because it was poor-quality fish that wasn't worth selling. The
   best fish was brought back to port to sell.
6. Fishing with a line and hooks. When a fish is caught the line is
   pulled up by hand.
7. Because they were large muscular men.
8. By how many fish they caught.
9. To keep a check on how many fish each man had caught.
10. By drying it or later ice was used.

Page 241

Skills Practice

Make sure that you have...
- selected your passage carefully making sure that it has the
  right kind of material to ask a variety of questions on.
- thought about your questions carefully and made sure that they
  can be answered by reading the passage; remember, your
  questions are to test understanding of the passage and not
  general knowledge
- been careful about how you have phrased your questions –
  make sure that it is clear exactly what it is you're asking
- created a variety of question types.

Extension Activity

Remember to be constructive in your discussion and make
suggestions on how questions could be improved if you feel they
could be. Make notes on your discussion points as you go along
and write up the key points at the end.

MEDIA TEXTS

Page 245

Quick Test

1. True.

2. True.

3. False.

4. It's the newspaper name at the top of the front page.

5. It's a story partly written to get people to want to read inside
   the paper and, therefore, buy the paper.

Key Words Exercise

1. a) Correct   g) Incorrect
   b) Incorrect   h) Incorrect
   c) Incorrect   i) Incorrect
   d) Correct   j) Correct
   e) Correct   k) Incorrect
   f) Incorrect   l) Correct

2. Tabloid – A type of newspaper that is smaller in size and contains entertaining as well as serious articles.

   Specialist – A word describing magazines aimed at a specific audience.

   Local – Based in one region or area.

   Teaser – An article on the front of a newspaper which gets the reader to turn the page and read inside.

   Masthead – The top of the front page of a newspaper where the name of the paper is.

   Facility – A tool on a website which enables you to perform a task or operation.

   Blurb – A short piece of text that sums up a book, usually to promote it.

Page 247

Testing Understanding

1. True
2. True
3. False
4. False
5. True
6. True
7. False
8. False
9. False
10. True
11. True
12. False
13. True
14. True
15. False
16. True
17. True
18. True
19. False
20. True

Page 248

Skills Practice & Extension Activity

Please refer to the guide on page 266.

MEDIA TEXTS – NEWSPAPERS

Page 252

Quick Test

1. Columns
2. Copy
3. Captions
4. Lead
5. Editorial

Page 253

Key Words Exercise

1. Headline
2. Tabloid
3. Broadsheet
4. Photographs
5. Report
6. Facts
7. News
8. Article
9. Reviews
10. Editorial
11. Advertisements
12. Copy
13. Caption
14. Journalist
15. Exclusive
16. Lead
17. Banner
18. Editor
19. Columns
20. Opinion

Page 254

Testing Understanding

1. a) True b) False c) True d) False e) True f) True g) True h) False i) False j) True
2. a) Eye catching banner headline captures the attention.
   b) Sub-heading captures the drama of the event – note the alliteration of 'Rapid Response Rescue'.
   c) Opening paragraph sets the scene.
   d) Gives details of what happened – note the use of dramatic language. e.g. 'horrendous', 'huge', 'mountainous', and 'smashed'.
   e) Use of direct quotation.
   f) Use of expert opinion.
   g) Details about jet skiing adds background information.
   h) Reassuring conclusion ties up the details.

Page 255

Skills Practice

Make sure that you...
- choose the subject of your report carefully
- plan what you're going to put in it
- organise the structure
- word process it with a suitable eye-catching headline.

Extension Activity

1. Plan your questions carefully in advance but be prepared to take a different line or ask other questions if that seems a good idea.
2. Plan your report or article carefully, based on the information you've gathered.

MEDIA TEXTS – ADVERTISEMENTS

Page 259

Quick Test

1. To persuade people to do / feel something. **2.** A command.
3. To add emphasis to a word or idea.
4. To build a positive description.

Page 260

Key Words Exercise

Page 261

Testing Understanding

1. Bisto gravy.
2. Probably mothers (perhaps fathers) – whoever cooks the evening meal in the house.
3. The striking and unusual heading, 'Forget the TV news' captures the reader's attention. The sub-heading changes the focus – 'Your family's news' suggests it's good to eat together and talk to each other as a family. The 'chicken pie and gravy' creates a homely, comforting and tasty image.
4. The design is the Bisto logo, but it usually says 'Aah! Bisto'. The variation suggests Wednesday night, as mid-week, is a good time to sit down and eat together as a family.
5. The company name only appears in the web address given at the bottom of the advert.
6. The smaller print at the bottom draws attention to a scheme where you get some kind of reward. The lack of further details might encourage you to visit the website to see what it's about. Note the emphasis of 'family' here again.
7. The answer to this is your own personal response. Whatever your views are, make sure that you explain your comments and support them with specific references to the advert.

Page 262

Skills Practice

Make sure that you've commented on the following:

- The heading / slogan and sub-headings.
- The effects created by photos / pictures / designs, etc.
- The information given and how language is used.
- The overall effect that the adverts have on you.
- Think about the level of detail needed to answer the questions on the Bisto advert to help you approach your adverts.

Extension Activity

Make sure that you have thought about these points carefully:

- Your slogan or heading.
- The images you've used.

- The text you've used – why have you used certain words / phrases?
- What techniques you've used to catch your reader's attention and make your advert persuasive. Did you include techniques such as alliteration and repetition? How did you make your advert persuasive – did you use clever adjectives or imperatives, or was it more to do with the images?

Your written explanation of your advert should be quite detailed. You should have made a note of your partner's response to your advert.

Index

Index

Acknowledgements

The author and publisher are grateful to the copyright holders for permission to use quoted materials and images.

Page 41 © 1937 J R R Tolkien. Reprinted by permission of HarperCollins Publishers Ltd.
Page 64 Nigel Hinton: *Buddy*. Reprinted by permission of Orion Children's Books, a division of the Orion Publishing Group.
Page 65 John Steinbeck: *Of Mice and Men* (Penguin 2000) Copyright © John Steinbeck 1937, 1965. Reproduced by permission of Penguin Books Ltd.
Page 66 *The Lottery and Other Stories* by Shirley Jackson (Copyright © Shirley Jackson). Reprinted by permission of A.M. Heath & Co Ltd.
Page 73 Excerpt from *Little Red Riding Hood* from *Politically Correct Bedtime Stories: A Collection of Modern Tales for Our Life and Times* by James Finn Garner. Reprinted by permission of Souvenir Press Ltd.
Page 79: Extract from *Someone Like You* by Roald Dahl, published by Penguin Books Ltd. Reproduced by permission of Higham Associates
   Extract from *Stone Cold* by Robert Swindells (Hamish Hamilton, 1993) Copyright © Robert Swindells, 1993.
   Extract from *The Red Room* by H G Wells. A P Watt Ltd on behalf of The Literary Executors of the Estate of H G Wells.
P.86: Extract from *Nightmare Stairs* by Robert Swindells, published by Corgi. Reprinted by permission of The Random House Group Ltd
   Extract from *The Secret Passage* by Nina Bawden. Reprinted by permission of Curtis Brown Group Ltd
P.87: *Lord of the Flies* (1954) by William Golding. Extract reprinted by permission of the publisher, Faber and Faber Ltd., London
Page 95 *Coming up for Air* by George Orwell (Copyright©George Orwell) By permission of Bill Hamilton as the Literary Executor of the Estate of the Late Sonia Brownell Orwell and Secker & Warburg Ltd
Page 142 Leaflets supplied by West Yorkshire Police
Page 143 Leaflets supplied by West Yorkshire Police
Page 146 ©RSPCA Photolibrary
Page 158 H G Wells: *The War of the Worlds*. Reprinted by permission of A P Watt Ltd on behalf of The Literary Executors of the Estate of H G Wells.
Page 163 Excerpt from *The Happy Man* from Modern One Act Plays For Schools 1 by James L Charlton. Reprinted by permission of Pearson Education.
Page 166 Excerpt from *Sense and Sensibility: The Screenplay* (© Emma Thompson) is reproduced by permission of PFD (www.pfd.co.uk) on behalf of Emma Thompson.
Page 175 Extract from *Of Mice and Men* by John Steinbeck (Penguin, 2000). Copyright © John Steinbeck, 1937, 1965. Reproduced by permission of Penguin Books Ltd
P.182 *Hard Frost* by Andrew Young. Extract reprinted by permission of Carcanet Press Ltd.
P.183 *Football At Slack* by Ted Hughes. Extract reprinted by permission of the publisher, Faber and Faber Ltd., London
Page 185 'War Photographer' is taken from "Standing Female Nude" by Carol Ann Duffy published by Anvil Press Poetry in 1985
Page 189 'Blackberry-Picking' is taken from Death of a Naturalist © Seamus Heaney and reproduced by permission of Faber and Faber Ltd.
P.190: Extract from *The Watch House* by Robert Westall. Reprinted by permission of Macmillan Publishers Ltd.

P.233 from www.bullying.co.uk. Reprinted by permission of Bullying UK
Page 192 Imtiaz Dharker, *Postcards from god* (Bloodaxe Books, 1997)
Page 193 *Green Days* by the River by Michael Anthony, reproduced by permission of Carlton Publishing Group
Page 196 *Be a Butterfly* by Grace Nichols, reproduced by permission of Curtis Brown Group Ltd ©1984
P.229 Reproduced by permission of OneWorld (http://tiki.oneworld.net)
Page 237 ©Chris Trueman
Page 240 Copyright © 1997 by Sebastian Junger. Reprinted with permission of the Stuart Krichevsky Literary Agency, Inc.
Page 259 Magnum Temptations Advertisement reproduced with kind permission of Unilever
Page 261 ©Premier Foods

Page 20   ©iStockphoto.com/Kim Freitas
Page 26   ©iStockphoto.com/Joan Loitz
Page 30   ©iStockphoto.com/Rodrigo Eustachio
Page 36   ©iStockphoto.com/Helle Bro Clemmensen
Page 39   ©iStockphoto.com/Leon Bonaventura
Page 40   © iStockphoto.com/Rodrigo Eustachio
          ©iStockphoto.com/Jolande Gerritsen
          ©iStockphoto.com/Sergey Surkov
          ©iStockphoto.com
          ©iStockphoto.com/Kim Bryant
Page 45   ©iStockphoto.com/Nicholas Monu
Page 46   ©iStockphoto.com/Kim Freitas
          ©iStockphoto.com/Martynas Juchnevicius
Page 56   ©iStockphoto.com/Christos Georghiou
          ©iStockphoto.com/Helle Bro Clemmensen
          © iStockphoto.com/Stephen Dumayne
          © iStockphoto.com
Page 57   ©iStockphoto.com/Gennadij Kurilin
          ©iStockphoto.com/Helle Bro Clemmensen
          ©iStockphoto.com/Christos Georghiou
Page 58   ©iStockphoto.com
Page 60   ©iStockphoto.com/Charity Myers
Page 61   © iStockphoto.com/Raman Maisei
          © iStockphoto.com
Page 65   ©iStockphoto.com/Justin Welzien
Page 66   ©iStockphoto.com/Paul IJsendoorn
Page 67   ©iStockphoto.com/Rodrigo Eustachio
Page 69   ©iStockphoto.com/Kim Bryant
Page 71   ©iStockphoto.com/Kim Bryant
Page 73   ©iStockphoto.com/Steven Foley
Page 74   ©iStockphoto.com/Russell Tate
          ©iStockphoto.com/Chen Fu Soh
Page 76   ©iStockphoto.com/Jennifer Borton
Page 77   ©iStockphoto.com/Vanda Grigorovic
          ©iStockphoto.com/Rob Zeiler
Page 78   ©iStockphoto.com/Charity Myers
          ©iStockphoto.com/Rodrigo Eustachio
Page 79   ©iStockphoto.com
Page 80   © iStockphoto.com/Rodrigo Eustachio
Page 81   © iStockphoto.com/Joshua Blake
Page 83   ©iStockphoto.com
Page 85   ©iStockphoto.com/Charity Myers
Page 87   ©iStockphoto.com/Charity Myers
Page 102 ©iStockphoto.com/Viktor Gmyria
Page 103 ©iStockphoto.com
Page 107 ©iStockphoto.com/Vallentin Vassileff
Page 113 © iStockphoto.com/Russell Tate
          © iStockphoto.com
          ©iStockphoto.com/Kim Freitas
Page 115 © iStockphoto.com

Page 116 © iStockphoto.com
          © iStockphoto.com/Yulia Polishchuk
Page 120 ©iStockphoto.com/Joshua Blake
          © iStockphoto.com
          ©iStockphoto.com/Joshua Blake
Page 121 ©iStockphoto.com
Page 122 ©iStockphoto.com/Simon Oxley
Page 125 ©iStockphoto.com/Jolande Gerritsen
Page 126 © iStockphoto.com
          © iStockphoto.com/Yulia Polishchuk
Page 135 ©iStockphoto.com/Matt Tilghman
Page 137 ©iStockphoto.com/Tulay Over
Page 147 ©iStockphoto.com/Julien Grondin
Page 150 ©iStockphoto.com/Justin Welzien
Page 157 ©iStockphoto.com
          ©iStockphoto.com/Kim Bryant
          ©iStockphoto.com/Alejandro Raymond
          ©iStockphoto.com/Kim Freitas
          ©iStockphoto.com/Cruz Puga
Page 158 © iStockphoto.com/Tim Stapleton
          © iStockphoto.com
          ©iStockphoto.com/Dennis Cox
Page 159 ©iStockphoto.com/Pali Rao
Page 162 ©iStockphoto.com
Page 164 ©iStockphoto.com/Joe Lera
          ©iStockphoto.com/Sergey Surkov
Page 165 © iStockphoto.com
          ©iStockphoto.com/Kim Freitas
Page 167 ©iStockphoto.com/Luis Bellagamba
Page 168 ©iStockphoto.com
          ©iStockphoto.com/Kim Freitas
          ©iStockphoto.com/Nicholas Monu
Page 169 © iStockphoto.com/Kiyoshi Takahase
Page 170 ©iStockphoto.com/Kim Bryant
Page 177 ©iStockphoto.com/Charity Myers
          ©iStockphoto.com/James Thew
          ©iStockphoto.com/Peter Finnie
Page 190 ©iStockphoto.com/Kim Freitas
Page 199 ©iStockphoto.com/Evgeniy Ivanov
Page 200 ©iStockphoto.com/Justin Welzien
Page 201 ©iStockphoto.com/Kim Bryant
          ©iStockphoto.com/Steven Foley
Page 209 ©iStockphoto.com
Page 211 ©iStockphoto.com/Justin Welzien
Page 222 ©iStockphoto.com
Page 223 © iStockphoto.com/Boris Zaytsev
Page 226 ©iStockphoto.com/James Thew
Page 227 ©iStockphoto.com/Kim Bryant
Page 231 ©iStockphoto.com
          ©iStockphoto.com/Kim Bryant
          ©iStockphoto.com/Cruz Puga
Page 234 ©iStockphoto.com/Joshua Blake
Page 242 ©iStockphoto.com/Jolande Gerritsen
Page 244 ©iStockphoto.com/James Thew
Page 246 ©iStockphoto.com/Joshua Blake
Page 246 ©iStockphoto.com
Page 247 ©iStockphoto.com/Will Evans
Page 248 ©iStockphoto.com/Peter Finnie
Page 250 ©iStockphoto.com/Jolande Gerritsen
Page 256 ©iStockphoto.com/Kim Freitas

Page 158 © Nasa

All other images ©2009 Jupiterimages Corporation, and Lonsdale.

Nicholas Barber • Steven Croft

ESSENTIALS

KS3
English Coursebook
covers all three years

How to Use this Coursebook

This coursebook provides full coverage of the programme for study for Key Stage 3 English. It covers all the relevant content and skills, including the Level 1 Functional Skills for English, in a single book to provide a flexible resource that can be used to support any model for delivering the curriculum.

The questions and tasks in this coursebook provide skills practice relevant to the Assessing Pupils Progress (APP) assessment focuses, as well as helping to reinforce students' learning and improve their confidence.

The questions marked with a light bulb symbol (💡) also support APP, by providing opportunities for discussion so that you can probe the students' understanding.

The content is split into 36 topics, which are grouped into the following sections for easy reference:
- Grammar and Punctuation
- Writing Skills
- Creative Writing
- Non-Fiction Writing
- Reading Prose and Poetry
- Shakespeare
- Reading Non-Fiction Texts
- Speaking and Listening.

The first pages of each topic contain the content. They feature...
- **key words** picked out in colour in the text and listed in a box at the end of each topic
- a **Quick Test** to test understanding.

The final three pages in each topic contain questions and tasks to reinforce student's understanding and provide skills practice:
- **Key Words Exercise** – an exercise that ensures students understand the meaning of key words.
- **Testing Understanding** – a literacy exercise.
- **Skills Practice** – a relevant task to help develop the students' English skills.

The answers to all Quick Test and practice questions are included at the back of the coursebook.

This coursebook is supported by three workbooks for Years 7, 8 and 9, which feature increasingly challenging tasks and questions to support development and progression.

The workbooks provide further skills practice relevant to the APP assessment criteria and focuses, and help to consolidate students' learning.

To make cross-referencing between the coursebooks and workbooks easy, details of the relevant workbook pages are given on the last page of practice questions in each topic of this coursebook.

Together, the coursebook and workbooks can be used to...
- help identify relative strengths and weaknesses for curricular target setting
- generate evidence of attainment as part of day-to-day assessment
- build evidence of student achievement for periodic, level-related assessment.

We're sure you will enjoy using this coursebook, but following these helpful hints will help you make the most of it:

- Make sure you understand the key words for each topic before moving on.
- Use the tick boxes on the contents page to track your progress: put a tick in the box next to each topic when you're confident you know it.

- Try to write in Standard English, use correct pronunciation and good sentence construction. Read what you have written to ensure it makes sense.
- The questions marked with a light bulb symbol (💡) are intended to help you focus on different aspects of the text. No answers are included. Instead we suggest you write down your ideas and discuss them in a small group or with your teacher.